Constitution Making Under Occupation

COLUMBIA STUDIES IN POLITICAL THOUGHT / POLITICAL HISTORY

Columbia Studies in Political Thought / Political History
Dick Howard, General Editor

Columbia Studies in Political Thought / Political History is a series dedicated to exploring the possibilities for democratic initiative and the revitalization of politics in the wake of the exhaustion of twentieth-century ideological "isms." By taking a historical approach to the politics of ideas about power, governance, and the just society, this series seeks to foster and illuminate new political spaces for human action and choice.

Pierre Rosanvallon, *Democracy Past and Future*, edited by Samuel Moyn (2006)
Claude Lefort, *Complications: Communism and the Dilemmas of Democracy*, translated by Julian Bourg (2007)
Benjamin R. Barber, *The Truth of Power: Intellectual Affairs in the Clinton White House* (2008)

Constitution Making Under Occupation

The Politics of Imposed Revolution in Iraq

ANDREW ARATO

Columbia University Press *New York*

Columbia University Press
Publishers Since 1893
New York Chichester, West Sussex

Library of Congress Cataloging-in-Publication Data
Arato, Andrew.
The imposed revolution and its constitution : Iraqi constitutional politics during the American occupation / Andrew Arato.
p. cm. — (Columbia studies in political thought / political history)
Includes bibliographical references and index.
ISBN 978-0-231-14302-8 (cloth : alk. paper) —
ISBN 978-0-231-51243-5 (e-book)
1. Constitutional law—Iraq. 2. Constitutional history—Iraq.
3. Iraq—Politics and government.—2003– 4. Sistani, 'Ali al-Husayni.
5. Bremer, L. Paul 6. Postwar reconstruction—Iraq. I. Title.
KMJ2220.A97 2009
342.567—dc22
2008030562

Columbia University Press books are printed on permanent and durable acid-free paper.
This book is printed on paper with recycled content.
Printed in the United States of America

c 10 9 8 7 6 5 4 3 2 1

Contents

Preface vii

1. The Externally Imposed Revolution and Its Destruction of the Iraqi State 1
2. Postsovereign Constitution Making: The New Paradigm (and Iraq) 59
3. Sistani Versus Bremer: The Emergence of the Two-Stage Model in Iraq 99
4. Imposition and Bargaining in the Making of the Interim Constitution 135
5. The Making of the "Permanent" Constitution 205

Conclusion 251

Notes 265

Index 347

Preface

This book is part of a rescue operation: an attempt to redeem the still redeemable. The treasure it seeks to save lies not in the eighteenth century, or even in 1956, but in the recent history of democratic transformation. This treasure is about to be buried—who knows for how long—because of the perverse but revolutionary attempt of the Bush government to impose political democracy through military force and to use democratization as the ideological arm of a neoimperial project to establish a new type of control over the Islamic Middle East. That project is collapsing, but it threatens to bury worldwide projects for democracy and democratization under its rubble.

My concern here is for a dramatic new method of democratic constitution making, one that I call "postsovereign," in the sense that first, the constituent power is not embodied in a single organ or instance with the plenitude of power, and second, that all organs participating in constitutional politics are brought under legal rules. This method, whose roots go back to the American Revolution and some experiments in more recent French history (1945–1946), was revived in Spain in the 1970s, practiced in central Europe during the years of regime change (1989–1990), and perfected in the Republic of South Africa in the 1990s. It is still practiced in Nepal in the present decade, but with few outside that country noticing.[1] Its key characteristics are a two-stage process of constitution making (with free elections in between) and an interim constitution. The basic idea involves applying constitutionalism to both the *result* and the democratic *process* of constitution making. This method is the democratic alternative to revolutionary constitution making, which all too easily can step over the threshold to dictatorship. This method of constitution making was the one reluctantly adopted in Iraq by the country's American rulers, and unfortunately the idea could very well be entirely compromised by that adoption. Already in Latin America, in the Andean republics, the alternative of revolutionary-populist sovereign constitution making has reappeared, and after Iraq it will offer itself, despite its already authoritarian processes and predictably authoritarian outcomes, as the better, more radical, and indeed more democratic alternative. People may very well forget the South African example, instead remembering Iraq when interim constitutions and bound constitutional assemblies are raised as political and legal options.

Of course, perhaps the constitution-making process will be entirely disregarded in the case of Iraq, since matters such as state destruction, insurrection, and civil war currently and rightly occupy everyone's attention. Were Iraq an isolated, unique case that could never happen again, this might be possible. There is indeed little attention paid to Iraq in, for instance, Nepal, where the democratic transformation is indigenous (although some lessons could have been learned even here: for example, the desirability of avoiding co-opted transitional legislatures and the need to be extremely cautious with identity politics based on ethnicity). But the role of the United States in Iraq and the disasters it has caused make it unlikely that any aspect of this sad history will be forgotten. Remembered, it will likely be only as a series of cautionary tales, and the constitutional aspect will be one of these tales.

There have been recent "democratic" interventions and occupations along with an external role in constitution making before Iraq, in Bosnia, Cambodia, East Timor, and Afghanistan. None of the results have been very good, and the populist theories of participation that guided the international community that advised the constitution makers in these cases were also not very helpful. They opened the door almost without exception to executive dominance of the process. Yet most likely all of them will be remembered as preferable to what will be seen as the American approach typified by Iraq.

In my view, strangely enough, the method adopted in Iraq, born not of an American plan but of the conflict between the occupiers and the movement led by the Grand Ayatollah Sistani (if we forget the pathological aspects due to the persistence of imposition and exclusion throughout) was quite superior to what was implemented elsewhere during other occupations, including that of Japan (if not Germany). Yet because of what has happened in Iraq, future international efforts during military occupations are likely to avoid the specific instruments and policies used in that country. The story of Iraqi constitution making will not be forgotten, but it will be relegated to a dark chapter in the collective memory. At a time when there is a dramatic need to rethink the legal problems of when and how international interventions are permissible—and what to do during occupations after such interventions—forgetting or excluding some of the most important options available in constitution making is bound to have very negative consequences.

This book will focus primarily on constitution making in Iraq, in the context of both theoretical and comparative research. The theoretical focus of chapter 1 will be the problem of the state, distinguishing between revolution and liberation and between revolution and state destruction. Here I will compare Iraq to other efforts by the United States to impose constitutional revolutions from the outside, especially in Japan and Germany. The second chapter will focus on versions of what I see as the dominant contemporary paradigm of constitution making, and I consider from a theoretical point of view the special problems of the adoption of this method in Iraq. The third chapter, centered on Iraq entirely, discusses the political conditions of adopting this model. The penultimate and final chapters reconstruct in detail the making of the interim and "permanent" constitutions, respectively.

It is not my thesis that the right model of constitution making would have very likely saved the day. Instead, my argument presupposes (even if I only argue this formally in the last chapter) that the window of opportunity for democratization in Iraq was very small to begin with, and it was only slightly widened by the method of constitution making that was adopted. The illegal war itself, its thoroughgoing and only slightly disguised unilateralism, and the state destruction that followed all helped to keep the window narrow, but they did not shut it completely. Was it right to try to open this window in the first place? I have always been ambivalent about this question, but from the point of view of the Iraqis, it undoubtedly was right. Thus it was not wrong for people such as Noah Feldman and Larry Diamond to join such an effort, though they were incredibly naïve to think that it could be successful given this administration's ideology, motivations, and abysmal ignorance. It was even more right for various UN teams to try to intervene, and for a brief period I informally advised a high-level member of the most important of them, the team led by L. Brahimi. But here it was I who was naïve in thinking that the United Nations had sufficient instruments (or the right approach) to influence in the right direction an American policy already in considerable trouble.

From the American and international point of view, the question does arise whether all such efforts at forcing open a "window" of democratization are futile attempts to redeem the unredeemable. This question can even be asked about my book, which catalogues a variety of serious errors beyond the war and the invasion itself. Would it not have been better to write a single deterministic sentence about the whole sorry episode, simply stating that after an illegal and immoral war nothing can go right?

I don't think this particular book is open to this objection. Let me therefore say here in the preface that if a powerful country attempts something like what the United States has attempted in Iraq, the opportunity for successful regime change in general and constitution making in particular will be very small. The chances of failure will be much higher. The first lesson is: don't invade or occupy when you are the aggressor. (The United States did, and was.) If you have fully justifiable reasons to invade, get full international support. (The United States didn't, and didn't.) If, for some reason, through no fault of your own, you could not succeed at your goals of regime change or the imposition of a democratic government, hand over the occupied country to international authority and withdraw as soon as possible. (It was the fault of the United States, and it didn't.) If you did not hand the country over to international authority, then include all possible social forces in the country in political bargaining, defer to them, and then withdraw. (The United States didn't, and didn't.) And so on. This type of advice can be generalized as: abandon neoimperial policies in favor of internationalist ones, treat small countries and their political forces as partners, and change yourself from what you have been and been seen as for a long time (especially outside of Europe) into something quite different. With respect to Iraq, the advice is: if you adopt a method of constitution making linked to democratic and constitutionalist norms, follow the implications of those norms. Otherwise you are bound to fail. Again, the United States would have to seriously change in order to be able to follow that advice, and had it so changed, it would not have invaded a foreign country without just cause.

It is true that I focus on specific errors that could have been avoided: not having more troops, disbanding the Iraqi army, excluding nationalists from the bargaining process, holding bilateral negotiations with the Kurds only, and numerous others. But many of these errors were parts of the opportunity structure created by the invasion itself, and even if they were not predetermined, they were difficult to avoid. For an aggressive war mendaciously justified at home, one could not take too many troops and risk too many American lives. An aggressive war made the United States an enemy of Arab and even Iraqi nationalism, and thus the Iraqi army was a danger and the special relationship with Kurds preprogrammed. Moreover, even if these mistakes had not been made, their alternatives could also have been serious mistakes: too many American troops could have created even greater resentment, sooner; the Iraqi army could have become a serious part of conflicts with Shi'ites and Kurds; the bargaining process could have broken down if the Arabs and Kurds met face to face on the most contentious issues; and so on. We know what the errors were, but we don't know if the alternatives would have been errors or not. Within a neoimperial rather than internationalist policy, however, they probably would have been.

My contention is finally that the constitution-making method too would have greatly benefited from an overall framework of internationalization, and it was the neoimperial modality of imposition that produced its pathological transformation. Thus here too the issue is not to improve this or that aspect but to change the overall modality. Conversely, I believe that international legal regulation of constitution-making processes should not only learn from the Iraqi experience but positively use it to generate a better set of guidelines for the future, a set that would serve us better than either the rather obsolete Hague and Geneva regulations (regarding this area of legal and constitutional change) or other more recent precedents with better international frameworks but more problematic constitutional methodologies. All that went wrong in the Iraqi process indicates what should be done differently, and with keeping such possible improvements in mind, it may be worthwhile to assess the applicability of the postsovereign method in an occupied country where the goal is the recovery of democratic autonomy and the establishment of the rule of law as soon as is feasible.

There are several debts I would like to somehow make good. I thank the U.S. Institute of Peace for including me in a multiyear USIP/UNDP workshop in Washington D.C., in the area of constitution making, and especially its organizers Neil Kritz and Louis Aucoin. I learned a lot from our joint work, which will soon appear in book form. At this workshop I was especially fortunate to have met Jamal Benomar, who has done much to introduce me to the intricacies of Iraqi constitution making. With respect to advice on Iraq, I have learned an incredible amount (though never enough, of course) from Juan Cole's Web site *Informed Comment* (www.juancole.com), and he was gracious enough to open it to many of my guest editorials. Similarly generous with his comments and information was Nathan Brown, one of the best experts on this topic and on Middle Eastern constitutions in general.

As to general theoretical matters, the influence of three people stand out: János Kis in Hungary, Ulrich Preuss in Germany, and Bruce Ackerman in the United States. While none of them would accept responsibility for my views, I at least have learned a great deal (again, never enough) from their writings and from discussions with them. Both this book and my attempt to educate myself in constitutional theory would have been impossible without the stimulation and intellectual substance I have found in their works at various stages of my development.

I am grateful to all who have invited me to conferences and seminars dealing with this and related topics, especially Said Arjomand (who has since then been very generous with his advice) at Onati, Spain; Jeremy Waldron at Columbia; Ruti Teitel at New York Law School; Benedict Kingsbury at NYU's School of Law; Kim Scheppele at the University of Pennsylvania; Christian Barry and Paige Arthur at the Carnegie Council (twice); Alain Touraine and Pierre Rosanvallon at EHESS; Riva Kastoryanou and Renaud Dehousse at Sciences Po, both in Paris; Hubertus Buchstein, Tine Stein, and Ulrich Preuss in Berlin (twice); Carla Pasquinelli in Naples; Rainer Forst in Frankfurt; and Hartmut Rosa in Augsburg.

At the New School for Social Research, I am very grateful to my students in the various seminars and lecture courses on constitutional politics, Iraq, sovereignty, and constituent power, who have helped me with more problems than I can detail here, and the same goes for the North American and African students in the masters seminars I held in Cape Town in January 2006, who gave me such a hard time with the concept of "liberation." At the New School, my great discussion partner has been Andreas Kalyvas, with whom I rarely agree completely, but we have the most interesting exchanges in and out of class. Several discussions with Nehal Bhuta and Nida Alahmad (now at the University of Toronto) have been incredibly interesting and fruitful for my development, and of course the book documents Bhuta's influence at several points. Recently, a seminar discussion with S. Chaudhry, with whom I had many converging ideas, has been very helpful in clarifying what the ultimate juridical questions are in divided societies. Finally, I thank the two anonymous but highly sophisticated initial reviewers at Columbia University Press, whose suggestions, however radical, I followed in just about everything, not because I had to but because they were so obviously right.

Closer to home, my debates and discussions with two people, Jean Cohen and Julian Arato, have been amazing and very fruitful. There used to be two discussion partners here; now we are three, and the two of them have left their mark on this book and on so much else. The book is dedicated to them and to my daughter Rachel and grandson Sam, with love and admiration as always. I truly hope that Julian and Sam will be able to live in a world largely free of the consequences of what was done in Iraq in their name.

Constitution Making Under Occupation

[1]

The Externally Imposed Revolution and Its Destruction of the Iraqi State

> Our focus on democracy should not be presented to others as an imperial command . . . such a policy needs as its moral lodestone the traditional American value of prudence, not a neo-Trotskyite belief in a permanent revolution (even if it is a democratic rather than a proletarian one). The neoconservative insistence that the United States can be made safe only by making other nations accept American values is a recipe for provoking a clash of civilizations.
>
> —R. Ellsworth and D. K. Simes, "Realism's Shining Morality"

A Revolutionary Project

It is now commonly conceded that the United States, led on the ideological level by "neoconservative" intellectuals, tried to initiate and almost certainly failed to sustain a radical *revolutionary* project to remake the Islamic Middle East. Without reducing the cause of the war in Iraq to this one ideologically driven factor, few serious people would dare to deny that it was among its *causes* as well as part of its *meaning*. At the same time, the invasion of Iraq, the overthrow of its dictatorship, the occupation of the country for however long a period, and the initiation of a process of "regime change" have not generally been understood as a *revolution* or a revolutionary project.

We should not be surprised that it was a few conservatives opposed to all revolutions who were the first to properly decipher the *revolutionary* political character of what the United States has set in motion in Iraq.[1] Nevertheless, I myself have proposed the concept of "externally imposed revolution" from the very beginning[2] and would like to maintain it here against its main conceptual rivals, "nation building" and "regime change," despite one reservation.[3] Revolutions, as opposed to rebellions, have to involve a plausible process of establishing new regimes.[4] They fully establish their legitimacy with the construction of the new, not merely the old's destruction.[5] The imposed revolution in Iraq has postulated, authentically or not, such a terminal point of legitimacy, namely constitutional democracy. However, a civil war or permanent revolutionary instability are antitheses of a political regime. By this standard, the imposed revolution in Iraq has not only failed so far and almost certainly will end up as a failure, but, because civil war and instability were always much more likely than a stable new regime, failure seemingly was preprogrammed.[6] But failure was not a certainty. In my view, even the illegal war left open a small window of opportunity for a transition in Iraq toward some undetermined kind of constitutional democracy, and ultimately that is the possibility that validates the use of the term "revolutionary project." That this revolution was to be externally imposed is part of the reason why the window of opportunity for success was so narrow.

I find the use of the term "nation building" overambitious and highly misleading. It has been used most absurdly for the American occupation of Germany and Japan,[7] where, in the latter case, the identity of the nation as an "imagined community"[8] was not in serious doubt, and, in the former one, a West German nation was never actually intended or created, as the events of 1989 and soon afterward showed clearly enough.[9] In neither country was the meaning of "national community," thankfully enough, open and available for the occupying power to create or mold. This state of affairs is implicitly conceded by some authors who use the term. According to Noah Feldman in *What We Owe Iraq*,

> nation building in Germany and Japan aimed to transform former enemies into prosperous allies in the emerging new struggle . . . [knowing] *these nations* had the capacity for unity, organization, and productivity, we sought to make them over to move them into our column. . . . The objective was not to build democratic states for the benefit of their own citizens. . . . It was far less important that Germany and Japan be democratic than that they be capitalist and rich.
>
> (7, my emphasis)

Aside from the fact that these lines do not give enough credit to the actual stress on democratization and liberalization during the two occupations,[10] they concede by their very language that Germany and Japan were already *nations* before supposed nation building, with the latter term reserved for the development of capacities conducive to wealth, capitalism, and geopolitical adherence to the American side. Feldman then goes on to quickly concede that such are not our goals in Iraq. So why use the same and already misleading term "nation building"? Perhaps to create a "civic nation" with a viable identity out of the centrifugal main elements of Arab Shi'a, Arab Sunni, and Kurdish religious and secular populations hitherto held together (supposedly only) by a succession of authoritarian states? Feldman, in my view rightly, does not propose such an ambitious goal, which would justify his terminology: "with the Cold War behind us, the objective of nation building . . . must be to build stable, legitimate states whose own citizens will not seek to destroy us. . . . In short: the objective of nation building ought to be the creation of reasonably legitimate, reasonably liberal democracies" (8).

Terminology aside, what Feldman really seems to have in mind is either the "state building" of the social science literature[11] or "regime change" exactly as the neoconservatives have used this term.[12] The reasons become clearer upon examining Francis Fukuyama's essay "Nation-Building and the Failure of Institutional Memory." To be sure, while aggressively maintaining that "nations" can indeed be made by external powers, he does this on the basis of the single very questionable colonial case of India, and he entirely leaves out of his account the truly nation-building work of the movement led by the Indian National Congress. More importantly, he seems to concede (to unnamed European critics) the general inapplicability of the term, though he clings to it in the title of his essay.[13] "Outside powers can succeed at negotiating and enforcing ceasefires between, say, rival ethnic groups; it is seldom that they can make these groups understand that they are part of a larger, nonethnic identity." Indeed, according to him, what has occurred even in Germany and Japan was not "state building" ("state" apparently identified with "nation"!) but democratic relegitimation of government and the drafting of democratic constitutions. On the question of the state when distinguished from nation, Fukuyama is ambivalent. In another essay, he suggests nation building is a response to state failure, which leaves the American project in Iraq without a conceptual definition, because here, as he admits, state (suddenly clearly distinguished from nation) failure was caused, partly inadvertently and partly deliberately, by the invaders themselves.[14] James Dobbins in a recent essay has no such difficulties with respect to Iraq, because, as he sees it, nation building is the proper response to both failed and rogue states.[15] But his own bizarre definition of nation building ("the use of armed force in the aftermath of a conflict to underpin a transition to democracy")[16] is inconsistent with this stress on the state and is relevant only where state building is either not a problem or can be easily solved. Moreover, nation building is here almost synonymous with regime change, with the added and rather unnatural element of armed force built into the definition.[17]

The term "regime change" is formally less objectionable than "nation building" with respect to Iraq, despite its objectionable political uses. I will go further. Whoever the source of the theory may be, as it pertains to the desirability of democratic *regimes* from the point of view of the international order,[18] it is for me not difficult to agree with the claim that relatively liberal and relatively democratic political systems are in themselves desirable everywhere and would reduce in the longer term the risk of war among states and the chances of the citizens of such states joining the enterprise of international terrorism. How this goal is to be achieved, however, is an entirely different matter (as Kant already well knew, rejecting "republican imposition").[19] Despite its rather new current implication, the term "regime change" evidently does not in itself suggest external force or even political rupture. The problem with the term as opposed to "nation building" is that it is too general and permissive and not specific and demanding. Almost a synonym of political transition, "regime change" points more accurately to the locus of change (to *regime*, that is, the *form* of government, rather than *government* in terms of incumbency on one side and *state* structure on the other),[20] but it does not reveal much about the modality of change, which here is the crucial question. To be sure, this is an advantage in the Iraqi case, with respect to nation building. While the latter term is almost nonsensical, empirically, when an external power is in the driver's seat, the same is not true for regime change or political transition.

In a large and complex typology, Juan Linz and Alfred Stepan have isolated three ways in which defeat in war could play a major role in transitions from authoritarian to democratic forms of rule.[21] Interestingly, however, a careful study of their options, based on preexisting regime types (totalitarian, sultanist, post-totalitarian, and authoritarian, with the first two allowing the same externally dominated transition path only) reveals that they may be thinking ultimately of only two types of cases. The first is when a dictatorship, its state and society, suffer total defeat in war and an external power is free to occupy and impose for a considerable period without much resistance. Germany and Japan could be considered examples of this phenomenon,[22] even if, as I will later show, in neither case can we speak of absolute imposition. The second type is when a dictatorship suffers a military defeat that domestically discredits it and forces it to accept a process of internally steered and negotiated regime change with, or more usually without, some influence by the military victor. Here Greece in the 1970s and Argentina in the 1980s come to mind.[23] Neither type covers Iraq very well, because Iraqi society did not suffer total defeat, yet the military victor tried to assume total control over the transition process. Note that in all four examples, unlike Iraq, the dictatorship was the initiator of the hostilities it subsequently lost.[24] Perhaps too linked to examples of the past, Linz and Stepan do not take into account the possibility of an aggressive war against a dictatorship that may mobilize nationalist forces first on its behalf and later against the military victor. Even more importantly, the typology assumes that somehow the internal regime type and acts of the external power will be correlated in a harmonious way; in other words, it is strongly implied that a democratic external power (apparently, only they are relevant to democratic transitions!) that wins a war will choose the highly intrusive method only where there was totalitarianism or sultanism before, and not if the society has a sufficient level of organization, as under an authoritarian state, for example.[25] Two types of very possible "errors" are thereby disregarded: cognitively driven ones and normatively driven ones. In the first case, the victorious power and its experts may be simply wrong about the nature and politics of the society they defeat. In the second, they may not misunderstand the nature of the society but may wish to dominate it for whatever reasons, and they do not mind and may even wish to neutralize or suppress existing internal forces that were themselves not part of the dictatorship. We cannot exclude either or both of these possibilities, especially in the case of Iraq.[26]

If regime change or political transition is to be kept as the general class concept under which America's project in Iraq is to be understood, its specific modality has to be understood more clearly than it is possible in an analysis that draws its types from primarily historical cases. We need a more abstract scheme, and legal theory provides the answer. In the most persuasive comparative analysis, that of János Kis, *reform* is defined as continuity of both legitimate authority and legality, *revolution* as rupture in both dimensions, and *coordinated transition* or *negotiated (regime) transition* as rupture of legitimacy but generally with legal continuity (see table 1).[27] Legitimacy is understood here in the sociological sense of general or at least elite acceptance of the claims of the rulers to justify their rule, while legal continuity is understood, following Hans Kelsen,[28] as the limitation of change to a form that relies on a regime's own rule of change. It is assumed by the scheme that after ruptures of legality and legitimacy a transition path (one of the three varieties, since reform involves no rupture) will involve the construction of a new legality, a new legitimacy, or both, in the case of a revolution. Legality, of course, means a legal order in the sense of the positivists and not necessarily the rule of law.[29] Especially since both legality and legitimacy can be matters of interpretation and indeed contestation, we have to keep in mind the ideal-typical character of this scheme, as we must for all such schemes. In reality, we may very well encounter borderline cases and mixed and contested types. While the scheme is applicable in principle to transitions to authoritarian rule and to counterrevolutions as well as revolutions, here our concern is exclusively with transitions from dictatorships toward more democratic forms of rule, at least in the minimal sense of Dahl's polyarchy or near-polyarchy.[30] Finally, and most important here, the Kis's four-part scheme can be expanded to eight if we differentiate among externally induced and internally generated versions of each path.

Given the large variety of external interventions possible, it is easy to postulate that there have been historical examples of each of these forms with strong outside influence. Even the negotiated transitions of eastern central Europe in 1989 and 1990 depended on the withdrawal of Soviet guarantees to ruling parties. In the twentieth century, it is very probable that the United States alone has strongly promoted all four types of change in Latin America, though admittedly not usually in a democratic direction. In the Linz and Stepan scheme already referred to, military defeat played a role in the transformations of Greece and Argentina (transformations corresponding to "coordinated transition" in Kis's scheme), with comprehensive negotiations not playing the central role because of the various levels of collapse of the old regime forces. Thus the expansion of the scheme is both logically and historically justified.

Admittedly, while there are many situations where the idea of an externally influenced or imposed revolution may not seem very controversial, there are some problems with this notion when applied to an invasion and occupation of a defeated country. Charles Tilly rightly understands classical revolutions (following Trotsky) in terms of a doubling of governmental power and sovereignty between the old regime's forces and new contenders, with the latter occupying sovereign power alone in the case

TABLE 1
Regime transition paths (after János Kis)

		Legitimacy	
X 2		Continuous	Rupture
External Legality	Continuous	Reform	Negotiated or Coordinated Transition
Internal			
	Rupture	Autogolpe	Revolution

Note: In this chapter, I argue that the typology is complicated depending on what is transformed, since a type of change can occur on the level of *government*, *regime*, and/or *state*.

of revolutionary victory.[31] In the case of war, invasion, and occupation, an analogous process begins, but it occurs between a national government and a foreign power. However, except in the case of outright annexation, in the case of external invasion the doubling and subsequent resumption of unitary sovereignty over a territory seems to follow a different logic than in the case of internal revolution. Not every occupation following an invasion is revolutionary, but it does not require annexation to make something like a revolution. Some occupations can be seen as conservative. In fact, according to the Hague Convention of 1907, the occupying power was to be a placeholder for the absent governmental sovereign. Tilly's revolutionary scenario would then be abrogated when the absent sovereign was restored. Accordingly, in Nehal Bhuta's persuasive analysis, which uses Carl Schmitt's relevant concepts,[32] the occupation regime would have been a dictatorship, but a commissarial rather than a sovereign or a revolutionary one. A military occupation can be described as an externally imposed revolution only when it becomes transformative, instead of the classical *occupatio bellica*. Of course, annexation would be one form of transformative occupation that would do without new regime construction in the occupied country, since it would be incorporated into the already existing regime of the occupier. But the occupation government turning itself into the subject of new regime construction would be another no less revolutionary form and, as Bhuta rightly argues, it is the latter that was attempted in the case of Iraq.[33]

Does the externally imposed aspect vitiate or increase the authoritarian potential of revolutions? The most basic issue has to do with the internal logic of revolution itself, from the legal point of view, and this is why the category is often left out altogether from typologies of transitions *to* democracy even though such a transition is exactly the goal of many revolutions.[34] The authoritarian consequences of revolutions are almost indisputable empirically,[35] and Hannah Arendt's masterly analysis remains the best treatment of the elective affinity between revolution and dictatorship, even if in her book *On Revolution*[36] she produces an entirely exceptional and "successful" case that avoids this logic: the American Revolution. This thesis treats (following Carl Schmitt and *one version* of an old argument of the Abbe Sieyès) most revolutions as *revolutionary dictatorships*, with a part of the people (class, elite, party, or even one man) exercising constituent power *in the state of nature*, outside of all law and normative limitation, attempting to impose new rules on all others.[37] The argument is consistent with the typology used here, which keeps revolution in its framework for logical rather than empirical reasons, but it involves an asymmetry with other modalities of change: only here is a complete break in the forms of normative integration of political society. Revolution cannot be *de jure* anything but dictatorship, a point well understood by Lenin and Carl Schmitt.[38] Examining the nature of executive power during revolutionary breaks in legality reinforces the argument. Here the classical formula is that of a provisional or interim government that exercises either merely de facto powers or powers commissioned by the constituent assembly, powers that in either case tend to be unlimited by any separation of powers or checks and balances. Thus, extending Schmitt's still unusual language, the sovereign dictatorship is reinforced by a more classical emergency or commissarial one.[39] These dictatorial forms involve actual or anticipated resistance and thus authoritarian preventive measures or countermeasures in a society with any complexity and conflict potential, especially given the utopian aspirations released by most revolutions. However democratic the goals, the revolutionary means inevitably wielded by minorities almost always tend to vitiate them.

On first sight, *external* imposition of a revolutionary logic tends to double the imposition and thus potentially the authoritarian consequences. The historical record seems to support this supposition. Revolutions as defined here and called by that name by the actors themselves can certainly be externally influenced, promoted, and even imposed, as we know from numerous examples in the twentieth century. From the East European to the Asian cases, these have not been democratic revolutions in terms of their outcome and generally their ideology as well. Since the states doing the promotion have been dictatorships and have sought to export their social-political system, as Stalin explained to Milovan Djilas during World

War II,[40] the result surprised only some fellow travelers in the West. A large part of this record is thus irrelevant to our concern. Historically, however, the project to export democracy (republicanism) or at least constitutionalism by governments already organized according to these principles through violent external overthrow of authoritarian regimes is also not entirely new, if we can count the European old regimes among the latter. Yet the efforts of the French Revolution when still a republic to export its own political forms abroad more often than not culminated in military occupations, puppet regimes, or unstable revolutionary dictatorships.[41] The Latin American revolutions also involved external force vis-à-vis local old-regime forces, for example in the Andean possessions of Spain, and again the success was ambiguous.[42] In case of the United States, there have been many experiments in the violent overthrow of regimes, some of which at least were coupled with the export of democracy. Here too the success rate has been low, raised somewhat only by counting an outright colonial experiment such as the Philippines or a country with a long history of internal dictatorship, such as South Korea.[43]

In the end, Germany and Japan, two very special cases, as I have repeatedly argued,[44] remain the best historical evidence that democracy can be exported and imposed through the violent external overthrow of dictatorships. Linz and Stepan seem have these cases in mind when they imply that external imposition can accomplish a democratic transition where no other option has a chance. They do not, however, consider the contrast with internal revolutions, which is instructive. While empirical evidence based on two cases (whose differences with Iraq I systematically present below) proves little, it could nevertheless be abstractly argued that external imposition has the advantage, in that an external occupier and monitor not only can remove the forces of the old regime but can also block the efforts of newly mobilized actors to impose nondemocratic solutions. External occupation may force such new movements and parties to work together and accept solutions that would not have been their first choice but that they can come to accept as "the only game in town." For example, if a Shi'ite revolution had hypothetically overthrown Saddam, it would have been difficult to force victorious clerical leaders to accept any kind of power sharing and open competition with secular or Sunni elites. Even if the leaderships wished to compromise, they would generally not be able to restrain their victorious militants. In a revolution (legally a state of nature), to paraphrase Thucydides, the victor (inevitably a dictator, at least temporarily) takes what he can, and the defeated suffers what he must. With an American occupation, however, no indigenous force could be in a position to impose its own solutions unless the occupier so wished. (It is difficult to see this point now that both the interim constitution and the supposedly permanent one have been imposed on the Sunni part of the population, but this scenario would have been predetermined in an internal revolutionary scenario and was not in the externally imposed one.)

At the same time, in the case of external imposition there are fundamental problems with the *legitimacy* of a new transitional order even graver than in the case of an indigenous revolution.[45] The issue can be best explored and deepened if we consider another aspect of Arendt's treatment of revolution: her analysis of the term in two phases, liberation and "constitution."[46] According to her, a genuine revolution such as the American one would involve not only the destruction of an old regime, *liberation*, but also the project of the *constitution*, the construction of a relatively stable, new order that she identified (as did the founders of the United States) with the writing, enactment, and institutionalization of a written constitution. This stress, of course, is very welcome, since it highlights the importance of the topic of this book: constitution making. For the notion of revolution used here, I repeat, the bifurcation of the concept indicates not only breaks in legality and legitimacy, but also that the construction of new legality and legitimacy must be included. Given the at least minimally legitimating potential of legality (Weber's rational legal legitimacy, after all) in negotiated transitions and the continuity of legitimacy in the other types of change, revolutions thus face the most serious problems of legitimacy among the types of change mentioned here. The doubling of revolution between liberation and constitution opens up a huge gap between the work of liberation (the overthrow of the old regime) and the work of constitution (the creation of the new one), in which legality is almost transparently based on facts alone and legitimacy is based on future promises made by an agent.[47] Confidence and trust in such an agent becomes all important; distrust and lack of confidence can lead to disaster, by reducing the size of the group or groups that can identify with the new regime. And whatever the advantages of an external agency otherwise, this mode of producing a revolution only increases the need and the difficulty of legitimation.

In indigenous revolutions, that portion of the people that plays a heroic and self-sacrificing role in the work of liberation has at least a claim to represent the people and their interests before the latter can express themselves through democratic channels. The reason why new elites in control of provisional governments, inevitable components of revolutionary transformations, can be accepted as legitimate for a relatively short period is that they have worked to liberate the country from a (generally) hated old regime. In theory, they have suffered what the people have suffered, or even more, and their hopes in part at least also coincide with the hopes of the rest. In an age of nationalism, it is easier to identify moreover with members of one's own national groupings. In the case of an external imposition, however, it is almost impossible to distinguish liberation from occupation. Whatever the external liberator thinks of itself, it will have its own motives and interests, and these may not coincide with those of the country's population. After defeat in war, unless a country is freed from an external occupier or its obvious puppets, the liberators will be seen by some and probably to most as occupiers if they stay long enough to do any good, to really help stabilize and frame the political competition. Any interim government they sponsor, especially if it has no major political credit of its own in the work of liberation, will suffer from this legitimacy problem, and the inevitable role of such governments in shaping more permanent arrangements will be the object of hypercritical scrutiny and suspicion. The occupying power—the Americans—can claim that they will let the Iraqi people gain control over their interim process of democratization before elections can be held, but they must then a priori identify "the people" and its plausible representatives. If any important group is excluded, it can claim to represent all dissatisfied parts of the population against the occupiers and their appointees. Whatever their legal status, that excluded group may find it as easy to speak in the name of "the people" as those groups who represent the occupiers—and to many, much more plausibly.[48]

Liberation or Occupation?

To be more precise in our understanding of the kind of revolution the Americans wrought in Iraq, we must analyze the term "liberation." The concept has had an important place in Arendt's theory of revolution and in American self-understandings of their actions in Iraq. More recently, an increasing number of commentators[49] have pointed to the supposed transformation of a genuine liberation to something universally regarded as *occupation*, especially its legal codification as such by UN Security Council Resolution

1483,[50] as the beginning of the disaster in Iraq.[51] Are liberation and occupation incompatible? It depends, first of all, on the meaning of "liberation," and second, on the nature of the occupation in question. There are at least two meanings of the term "liberation," a less demanding and general one that narrowly focuses on the overthrow of an oppressor, and a more demanding one that in addition seems to imply and require that it should be an organized force (or forces) that is liberated and stands ready to take over the task of at least provisional governing.[52] In the case of internal revolution, which Arendt analyzed, the two concepts reduce to one, because a revolution carried out by indigenous forces implies that at the very least they will be free or *liberated* to govern provisionally and to play the constituent role of building a new regime. The difference, however, is very real in the case of an external "liberator." Here, for example, using the more demanding concept, liberation would have to entail the empowerment of a national government previously overthrown by a foreign occupier, drawn from elements including, for example, an underground army, resistance forces, or parties or movements capable of organizing political life. But what if none of these possibilities are available? According to the more general concept, it would still not be meaningless at all to consider a country liberated of a foreign oppressor or domestic dictatorship even if organized internal political force could not immediately take charge of the political process, because presumably its individuals could still be made free in their private capacity, and that could be the basis (*depending on the nature of political arrangements*) for the emergence of autonomous political forces. Thus it is obvious that neither concept would be compatible with the mere replacement of one oppressor by another. Neither a palace coup, nor the replacement of one colonial ruler by another, nor even the replacement of a dictator by a colonial ruler equally oppressive would count as liberation in either sense.[53] But what may be liberation to someone using the less demanding, more general concept would not be understood as such to another interpreter using the more demanding one. The latter may regard the very same state of affairs as a mere conquest of power followed by occupation, though not necessarily in a normatively negative sense.

The issue is further confused by the fact that when speaking of liberation in the general and less demanding sense the same events may represent, normatively speaking and in terms of fundamental interests and values, liberation to some and occupation to others. This issue does not come up in those liberations where a country is freed from the occupation of a hostile external power, but it was already an issue in a place such as my native Hungary, where the previous military occupation was by an allied power (Germany) and liberation was by an enemy power (the Soviet Union). In the actual case, Germany was a friendly power to some Hungarians and was hated by others, the Soviet Union was favored by very few and feared by many more, and probably most wanted to be occupied by neither at all. (I leave aside the question that in fact the Hungary of 1945 was more democratic until 1947 or 1948 at least than the Hungary before 1944, and thus the Soviet occupation could be represented as liberation in the more demanding sense from the point of view of many democratic, including non-Communist, forces.) The issue is even more complex—if at all possible—in the case of an indigenous but very oppressive dictatorship, say Iraq, overthrown by an aggressive external power seen by many groups as the enemy of the country's national and perhaps religious aspirations. One must probably imagine that from a normative point of view, for most Iraqis (the Kurds being exceptional) the same events represented initially *both* liberation and occupation, which had to be welcomed and feared at the very same time. And it may very well be that it was the subsequent nature of the actual liberation/occupation that came to decide for most of them—probably very quickly—which was the way they were going to see the American presence: either as Wittgenstein's rabbit (liberation) or hat (occupation).

How the Americans themselves answered a whole host of questions concerning the meaning of liberation was to play a very important role in Iraqi interpretations. There was no question that they regarded themselves as liberators and therefore legitimate. But their self-understanding concerning legitimacy (no more than regarding the legality of the invasion) did not automatically become the all-important view of others, without which legitimacy in the sociological sense would not be possible. Thus it very much mattered how the U.S. policymakers were going to answer one of the very first questions they faced: were they going to interpret liberation in the less or the more demanding sense? If it was to be in the more demanding sense, they needed to find the Iraqi version of the Afghan Northern Alliance[54] or, more absurdly, an Iraqi "de Gaulle" to whom they could hand *provisional* or *interim* power right away, so as not to become occupiers instead of liberators. There was, however, no Northern Alliance in Iraq in the sense of an armed force operating in the territory with some relative success against the government's own forces, except the Kurdish minority, whose rule over Iraq would have been resented even more by the majority

Arabs than would American rule. In 1991, when an Arab (or allied Arab-Kurdish) force on these lines could have emerged, internal uprisings in the bulk of the country were not supported by the United States because they would have brought power, supposedly, to the Shi'ite clerics allied with Iran. (The Northern Alliance was also friendly with Iran and Russia, but in the Gulf the stakes were much, much higher.) It seems that this argument was still alive in 2003, when the leader of SCIRI (the Supreme Council of the Islamic Revolution, then based in Tehran), the later tragically assassinated Muhammad Baqir al-Hakim, was publicly (for example, on PBS just before the invasion) asking for just such a role, and when this idea was still probably interpreted as handing Iraq to the allies of Iran. Power could also not be handed to Sunni generals, who also arguably possessed military forces within the country, because they were now understood to be incompetent, weak, and among the forces from which the country needed to be liberated. While handing power to the Shi'ite clergy was not possible, their second betrayal was also not possible. Thus earlier State Department ideas on this score were quashed.[55]

Thus the question became whether there could be a "de Gaulle," an exile leader such as Ahmed Chalabi or a set of leaders (Hakim; Jaffari, the leader of Da'wa; Talabani and Barzani, the two Kurdish leaders; and either or both Ayad Allawi and Chalabi; with one Sunni with no following, such as the aged A. Pachachi thrown in) to whom power could be handed in advance and who could form a provisional government immediately (or even before, in exile) upon overthrow of the Saddam regime. This would have been in fact the (externally facilitated version of the) classical revolutionary scenario, with the inevitable consequence that the provisional government would control the subsequent election of delegates to a constituent assembly.[56] Versions of this proposal were advanced before and during a conference of exiles in London in 2002 and before and after the actual invasion. But the analogy of Chalabi or even the gang of five, six, or seven exile leaders to Charles de Gaulle, who had a sizable army, control of some French colonies, an extensive internal underground network in France, and alliances with the powerful Communist underground, were always nothing short of ridiculous.[57] This time it was probably the State Department that torpedoed the plan to set up a provisional government in advance, with the president vetoing it in the end. The same drama, with the same six or seven claimants, repeated itself during the transition from Jay Garner's proconsulship to L. Paul Bremer's, with the same outcome.[58]

Some interpreters argue that the fact that Jay Garner was given no plan by the Pentagon was meant to put him in the position where he would have no alternative but to hand over the reins of power very quickly to a provisional government led by Chalabi.[59] Whether or not that was actually or deliberately the case, "the plan not to plan" did not work. It is more reasonable to assume that at all points contradictory things were decided under a president with a strong will but with poor analytical ability to see the difference among alternatives.[60] The end result was that there was a decision, by design or default, for liberation in its less demanding sense. This meant a more or less extended occupation, of course, but we must be careful to note here that the occupation was still to be aggressively represented as liberation.

The issue is put by many very cynically, and I have no way to dismiss or to prove the claims involved. The argument runs that the Americans removed the old dictatorship *in order* to establish their own power position in the region. This could be securely done only by occupation, not by way of a provisional regime to which power would be transferred. The point then would be not that they intended to establish an occupation regime outright, since there is a lot of evidence that they feared it and understood the associated practical and symbolic problems—but that they feared all other alternatives much more.

In any case, the appearance of having undertaken the invasion and occupation of Iraq on behalf of imperialist goals had to be most strongly avoided. An occupation regime is inevitably a foreign dictatorship, and, significantly, on the eve of his departure L. Paul Bremer asked for and received from President Bush the plenitude of all powers for himself at the top of the Coalition Provisional Authority. Lakhdar Brahimi was quite right technically to subsequently call him the dictator of Iraq.[61] But it should be noted that previously all attempts to establish a military occupation, with a U.S. general assuming the mantle of MacArthur, were strongly resisted.[62] Bremer's airs to openly play that role were greatly resented in Washington and by his own staff for, at the very least, public-relations reasons.[63] His was to be at all moments a dictatorship that had to be carefully disguised—a very difficult job indeed, given the arrogance and ignorance of the team that actually managed it on the American side.[64] A mere disguise, however, would not work in a country that had experienced both colonialism and neocolonialism unless measures were undertaken to indicate its good faith.

Continuing the train of this argument, the historical solution to the dilemma would have been to insist on that old staple of imperialist ideology, namely *tutelary* or *pedagogic* dictatorship, but fortunately that cannot work today. A foreign occupier would have to expropriate native authoritarian rulers, not on his own behalf but on behalf of future popular sovereignty and fundamental rights—the only two valid justifications in our liberal, democratic, postmetaphysical age. The claim would have been that the indigenous population (because of political culture, or because of having lived under an authoritarian regime for too long, or because of its economic conditions—take your pick) is not ready to exercise popular sovereignty and to respect the rights of individuals. Thus a long preparatory period under external referees and educators that will introduce gradually the new institutions would be necessary. This was still the idea under the famous League of Nations mandates (one of which created Iraq, more or less), but even then the timeframe for how long formal occupation was acceptable was already in the process of being greatly reduced.[65] Such a tutelary policy can combine various instruments of direct and indirect rule, as it in fact did under the British Mandate in Iraq, from which the Americans were to inherit, consciously or not, some administrative and even constitutional techniques.[66] For tutelary rule today, after the signing of the UN charter, decolonization, and the general taboo against colonialism, if the old arguments are to be used at all, one has to substitute international threats, as in the case of the cold war, or alternately restrict the functional area to which the claims are applied (for example, organizing elections) and, therefore, the acceptable duration of the formal occupation. All attempts to openly revive mandates and trusteeships under whatever name are clearly nonstarters[67] and fuel only the very plausible suspicion that the United States is involved in creating some kind of long-term protectorate in Iraq.[68] Thus Iraqis continually suspected a great number of occupation measures, some of which were obviously disastrous and others that could have been disastrous under different circumstances, as having to do with the secret desire of the United States and United Kingdom to extend the occupation in whatever legal form indefinitely.[69] Were they wrong? Feldman, a minor American participant, later (mid-2004) considered the dissolution of the Iraqi army to be a tremendous error. But afterward, according to him, there was no going back on the decision, and it became the "ethical" duty of U.S. forces to remain until a new Iraqi army under civilian control and capable of establishing public security could be created from the ground up. Facing this type of argument, it was easy to excuse the suspicion that (1) with militias taking over the task of local defense, the time period for forming a genuinely *national* army could be a very long one; and (2) the result with respect to the time factor could not have been merely an unintended consequence of well-intentioned but erroneous decisions.

The atmosphere of suspicion the Americans fostered further reduced their choices if they were going to in any sense keep alive the idea or the ideology, let us perhaps call it the latter, of *liberation*. The point was not only that they had to disguise dictatorship, but that they had to return this form to its classical essence: keep it short, and more technically, keep it commissarial: in other words, they had to avoid the usurpation of Iraqi sovereignty in its most fundamental, transformative dimension.[70]

Of the relevant issues, it was the question of time that came to be best understood. If Patrick Cockburn (supported by important Iraqi perceptions) is right in saying that under whatever guise the period of the CPA represented an experiment in imperial *direct* rule, from the outset the project was doomed to as rapid a failure as Arnold Wilson's attempt after World War I.[71] While there were indeed advocates in the U.S. government for a program of "robust occupation" in Iraq, as in postwar Europe, the stronger side in government, this time the Pentagon, militated for a short occupation when it failed to have its Iraqi clients installed in the first place.[72] This very much converged with Iraqi desires, and thus there was little chance that a program of long occupation could be formally adopted. While Bremer himself worked out a rather long period of CPA rule under a seven-point program that would have taken perhaps two years,[73] the time element was always the most vulnerable part of his mission, and in the end that element was radically curtailed. Of course, this did not mean that the United States was ready to leave Iraq altogether, after the end of a formal occupation regime. Iraqis were right to suspect that the status of some kind of protectorate was a serious possibility for them, perhaps on the model of arrangements with the British between 1932 and 1958.[74] It is almost certain that a future Iraqi government was projected that would negotiate extended troop presence and military bases, supposedly on its own initiative.[75] Also, a powerful U.S. embassy was going to take over many of the functions of the CPA. The models, to be sure, were supposedly Germany and Japan rather than neocolonial Iraq, but in any case they involved a very reduced period of formal occupation. Everything thus depended on how short a time a formal occupation regime really had to be restricted to and, even more, how it would be used.

Even as the duration of the occupation regime was in the process of being restricted under pressure, this regime had to solve very difficult tasks, taking into account two desiderata: effectiveness and legitimacy. The first had to do with generating outcomes acceptable from the point of view of (not always compatible) short- and long-term American interests, and this complicated task required that maximum powers would be exercised, given the shortness of the timeframe. If something had to be conceded, like the formation of a Governing Council or its Constitutional Committee, or surrendered, like the idea of making a permanent constitution, or devolved, like the role of picking the interim executive, or greatly accelerated, like the so-called transfer of sovereignty, the tendency always was to reduce the concessions to a façade behind which the CPA continued to exercise the real power—power that went beyond a commissarial dictatorship and toward a transformational or sovereign one.[76] All such moves, always transparent enough to the Iraqis, the external bloggers,[77] and eventually the international press, were utterly problematic from the point of view of legitimacy.

For legitimacy, the reduction of the time of the formal occupation mattered, but not enough. A process of legitimation built around the key words of "liberation" and "democracy" demanded other things than effectivity, namely the use of even the short time period for the gradual empowerment of Iraqi actors, understood as widely as possible. Either Iraqi actors had to be actually empowered or the actions of the American authorities had to be effectively represented as the basis of such future empowerment. To do this, one continually had to argue against democracy and participation (as that would have endangered effectivity) *in the name of* democracy. Authoritarian measures had to be given democratic window dressing or justified as the only possible road to democracy by pseudodemocratic public relations. Dealing with this contradiction is probably what generated the Bonapartist character of Bremer's rule in Iraq, whose subterfuges did not lose all power just because they were transparent. Indeed, the category of Bonapartist dictatorship is applicable here in two ways, as the depiction of a foreign-imposed transformational regime[78] and of a dictatorship that uses democratic public relations and a façade of participation, representation, and consultation to hide its authoritarian practices.[79]

Thus, behind the question of time and timing were three important substantive questions linked to legitimacy and effectivity and related to problems of government, constitution, and state. They all are functions of the ideology of liberation, which, like all genuine ideologies, had substantive dimensions that pointed beyond the ideological utilization itself. (1) If the problem initially was said to be one of finding a *broad enough* group of *capable* and *representative* leaders to form an Iraqi government, how could a relatively short formal occupation really and visibly stimulate the emergence of such a process, and to what extent could the duration of the occupation be legitimately extended in order to find such leaders? (2) If liberation (in the more demanding sense) could not rely on autonomous forces, could at least the process of making a constitution, of constituting a new regime, do so, and how long would one have to wait before that process could commence? (3) If finding a government and initiating a process of constitution making nevertheless extended the period of the occupation, could an occupation state be organized that would be able to guarantee security and essential services during this period without appearing unduly oppressive and visible to ordinary Iraqis? This third problem was vastly complicated by the American decision—a matter of choice rather than necessity—to dismantle the main pillars of the inherited Iraqi state: the army and the administration. Now the question became whether an occupation state could be used to rebuild the Iraqi state itself and whether such a task inevitably extended the period of the occupation, therefore possibly intensifying the resistance the occupation state was supposed to bring under control.

These three questions imply that the occupation regime could have been represented as liberation if it had been used in a timely and authentic manner to stimulate the emergence of autonomous forms of governmental participation, constitution making, and state building on the part of truly independent Iraqi actors. Significantly, these questions of legitimacy had to be answered both with respect to international law and UN Security Council resolutions, which had a bias against endless and unlimited occupational regimes, and to Iraqi opinion, which was even less permissive regarding foreign usurpation of sovereignty.

Below, I consider the problem of the duration of the occupation in relation to finding autonomous actors to form a government and write a constitution. Then I go on to discuss whether failures to promote autonomy could be ascribed to the absence of democratic intentions in the first place on the part of the imperial occupying power. After an excursus on historical comparisons and their lessons, mostly negative, I turn to an extended discussion of the occupation state and its failure. I end the chapter with a section on the relationship of state and constitution making.

Was the choice of formally turning the "liberation" of Iraq into an occupation, via UN SC Res. 1483 of May 22 (which formally referred to the CPA as "the Authority"), a serious error? Those who criticize the United States for not turning power over to a provisional government of exiles maintain this was the case.[80] Actually, a previous resolution (1472, of March 28) already referred to the "Occupying Power" and its duties, and 1483 went further only in explicitly placing the United States and the United Kingdom under the Hague and Geneva provisions for "belligerent occupation," which involved important restrictions as well as entitlements (par. 4–5).[81] Recognizing the CPA was merely the recognition of a fact, the fact of belligerent occupation, which before the CPA was administered by the U.S. military, according to international law. Especially given the particular generals involved, we now know that an explicitly military form of administration would probably have been smarter than Bremer's, but there was no reason for anyone at the United Nations to suspect this at the time. The same resolution went on to stress "the right of the Iraqi people freely to determine their own political future" and the "resolve that the day when Iraqis govern themselves must come quickly." It is a fair point that countries opposed to the war in Iraq should have held out for a statement that would have gotten a larger international role in establishing an inclusive process for building an Iraqi leadership, but in that case they may not have gotten the United States to verbally submit to the constraints of Hague and Geneva. In any case, they were much too weak and continually disorganized by the ambivalent but always pro-American position of the United Kingdom.

If, however, there is one UN Security Council resolution that should be strongly criticized, it is 1511, of October 16, 2003, which uncritically accepted the appointment of the Interim Governing Council as the organ (along with the ministries it supposedly controlled) that "embodies the sovereignty of Iraq" (par. 4) and its supposed control of the constitution-making process (par. 7).[82] UN representatives knew very well, as I know from personal conversations, that the IGC was both unrepresentative and mere window dressing for the dictatorial powers of the CPA. By the time the resolution was written and passed, the IGC was in fact already a nonfunctioning organ, with the exception of its constitutional committee, which exercised its independence through acts of resistance to CPA plans.[83] At the same time, the American advisors to the ministries treated themselves as if they were (and they were in fact) the people in charge, much as their British predecessors did in the 1920s.[84] No UN Security Council resolution drafted by the Americans and passed by rather uninterested other members could gloss over the fact that the United States in establishing the IGC missed two major opportunities: (1) finding a process by which new, inclusive, internal Iraqi leadership could be generated, and (2) gradually transferring real responsibilities to an Iraqi leadership.

It is very doubtful that most Iraqis would have seen as liberation the empowerment of a group of (four to seven) exile leaders, or what was sometimes called the Iraqi Leadership Council or ILC, as the new government of Iraq upon the overthrow of Saddam.[85] The only (indirect) evidence produced for this claim is by Galbraith, who repeatedly points out that parties headed by five of the most likely candidates, the leaders of the two Shi'ite parties, SCIRI and Da'wa, the two Kurdish parties, and Ayad Allawi, were to eventually receive from a high of 90 percent (with a Sunni boycott; actually, the figure is 88 percent) to a low of 75 percent (without a boycott; actually 71 percent) of the votes in the two subsequent parliamentary elections.[86] Thus, the argument goes that they had support to begin with and it would have been *politically* if not *electorally* legitimate for them to rule Iraq in the name of the people. The argument is fallacious on its face, even assuming all the numbers to be correct—which they are not—because incumbents with patronage are in the position to gain visibility and control electoral outcomes to significant extents. Equally important is that with respect to the problem of Sunni exclusion, the appointment of such a group could have promoted the outbreak of an even more extensive civil war even earlier. But in fact we cannot determine whether being put in the position of genuine governmental power by the Americans would have helped or hurt SCIRI and Da'wa, who in the actual case rallied behind the Ayatollah al-Sistani's subsequent challenge to the American occupiers and were certainly helped by that religious leader's popularity. In other words, the vote total Galbraith recounts, not entirely accurately (especially because he excludes the very significant vote for the followers of Moqtadah al-Sadr in the second figure: they received 22 percent of the Shi'ite seats, four or five more than Allawi's list), was in some important measure a function of a perceived oppositional status and not necessarily their support at the initial time nor what their support would have remained had they been appointed as the interim government. We certainly do not know how the Sadrist groupings, already strong in the second election, would have performed electorally had they been able to campaign against a government and Shi'ite rivals put into power by the Americans from the beginning. Finally, if Ahmad Chalabi had been the one leading such an interim government, as was first planned, it is worth noting that he was never successful in later political competition. Thus there is no reason to assume that he would have had any initial support (and there is a lot of evidence to the contrary), and we do not know how his lack of popularity would have affected his partners in an imposed government of exiles.[87]

Thus the Americans and Bremer were probably smart not to simply put in power an exile government of their supporters and in overruling Jay Garner's late effort (which may have been primarily a result of Pentagon manipulation and pressure) in that direction. But there were three other choices they should have made, but did not, that could have influenced the nature of their occupation regime. The first would have been to truly internationalize it. Evidently, the idea that an American occupation was self-interested was very strong in Iraq, and internationalization could have counteracted this.[88] The United Nations had a far better ability to negotiate with a wide variety of Iraqi actors. And there was a lot of local and cultural expertise available that the United States lacked but should have been able to draw on, and it could have been made available only with a genuine sharing of the control and responsibility. As it was, the Secretary-General's special representative could only make a small contribution to the political process before his tragic death. It is also true that the United Nations had a negative reputation in some Iraq quarters, and this may have led to early conflicts. But given that (1) the United Nations did not invade Iraq, (2) it had no long-range plans for its domination, and (3) it had the ability to bring to the scene an international group of representatives that would by its composition reassure all Iraqi sides made the international body or its agencies far more preferable than an American representative to manage the postconflict political process.

Second, local elections and provincial elections could have been extensively used from the beginning to generate autonomous leaders, as both Garner and some American military commanders wished. It was amazing that an occupation authority seeking new, internal leaders would not allow such a process to go forward and would quash the results where they already had taken place.[89] And third, when it came to the staffing of the Interim Governing Council advising the CPA, where, after all, the cost of including people with little political experience would have been small, amazingly enough the body ended up representing still an expanded version of the exile grouping that the Americans vetoed as an interim government. The same leaders they did not allow to govern were in effect given the patronage over the formation of future governing structures (and negatively, as well, as in their control over exclusion through de-Baathification). Thus instead of instituting a gradually more inclusive political process, the CPA did the reverse. And there was little embarrassment or even consciousness of the contradictions involved. When asked to include more radical Shi'ites or Sunni Arab nationalists, Bremer's favorite line became, preposterously enough, "it is a fundamental principle of democratic government that people do not shoot their way to power," forgetting that he himself had done exactly that, and so had all those he allowed to sit on the Interim Governing Council.[90]

Given the exclusionary nature of the IGC, would it nevertheless have been better to transfer real leadership functions to it instead of using it as window dressing? From the point of view of diminishing the neocolonial aspects of the occupation, it certainly would have been better. But in the few areas where members of the IGC took charge, disasters were not avoided—quite the contrary. For example, de-Baathification policy, in the hands of Ahmad Chalabi, turned out to be an even more destructive purge of Iraqi professional life than it would have been had Paul Bremer managed it. There is little question of the contribution made by this policy to the polarization of Iraqi society on ethnic grounds and almost certainly to fueling the Sunni-based insurrection. The fundamental problem thus was in putting together a protogovernmental organ, with or without powers, something that would have been avoided had either the United Nations been in charge or had the process proceeded from the ground up, on a power-sharing basis.

In one respect the IGC did have power, namely regarding appointments, and this power was preserved until the so-called transfer of sovereignty[91] and its own dissolution. In the end, the United States was not entirely able to avoid devolving some power to a legitimate instance, the United Nations, in generating Iraqi leaders to lead transitional governments. Sergio de Mello had a minor role in helping to make the powerless IGC more representative. But he failed to secure any representation for secular Sunni or Arab nationalist politicians. When it came to picking an interim government to which sovereignty would be transferred, in the face of the Grand Ayatollah

Sistani's objections, the United States was forced to formally defer to UN Special Representative L. Brahimi, who initially wanted to bypass the IGC altogether. We can now say that Brahimi failed to control this process, and while the United States (Ron Blackwill as much as Bremer) got the very candidates it wanted to run the interim government, the IGC got most of its important members in key positions as well. With the Chalabi-led de-Baathification process playing a major role, very few new leaders were generated in a process[92] that preserved at most a paper-thin international legitimacy in the light of Brahimi's own comments.[93] In any case, the choice of A. Allawi as prime minister suggested perhaps a *future* strategy of greater reconciliation among Iraqi groups than the one pursued by Bremer, and initially many Iraqis may have taken the restoration of sovereignty at face value, as did the legalistic UN Security Council. In any case, the interim government was to stay in power for only six months, and everything depended on the rules according to which elections and the process of the constitutional assembly were going to operate.

Politically, establishing a process of legitimate constitution making was less visibly important than gradually empowering an internally based, inclusive Iraqi governing structure. Theoretically, the reverse relationship holds, because a constitution was supposed to regulate the whole postoccupation period. International law seems to reflect this theoretical emphasis. While it contains few rules, largely indirect, for an occupying power's organization of (generally military) executive powers, the Hague and Geneva Conventions are indeed concerned with legislation under occupation that can have long-term effects on the destiny of a population. Article 43 of the 1907 Hague Convention puts the matter thus: "the authority of the legitimate power having actually passed into the hands of the occupant, the latter shall take all steps in his power to re-establish and insure, as far as possible, public order and safety [i.e., civil life], while respecting, unless absolutely prevented, the laws in force in the country."[94] This rule, subsequently confirmed by the Fourth Geneva Convention (art. 54–56, 64) of 1949, has been interpreted both in terms of an almost absolute prohibition[95] and as highly, indeed absurdly, permissively,[96] but it is almost impossible to reconcile it with a project of regime change[97] or transformative occupation[98] carried on by the occupying power, when the very purpose of *occupatio bellica* was that the occupation should be temporary and should allow the return of a territory to its own sovereign authority.

It is another matter that subsequent occupations violated these rules more often than they obeyed them, and that given contemporary standards of human rights and in relationship to some authoritarian regimes whose territory is occupied we are dealing with a hopeless case of underregulation.[99] In the case of Nazi Germany, the problem was solved by the revival by Kelsen and others of the old category of *debellatio* (subjugation), which made belligerent occupation irrelevant when a state was completely destroyed and when a territory could not be returned to its original sovereignty.[100] In such a case, the occupying power has full sovereignty, including all legislative and constituent powers, Kelsen argued, though the makers of the *Grundgesetz* disagreed.[101] On first appearance, Iraq seems to fit Kelsen's case of *debellatio*, since its government and subsequently its state organs were completely destroyed, and in any case it would have been a better argument for the U.S. assumption of constituent powers than the one made by John Yoo, except for two factors. First, as Jean Cohen has recently showed, since Geneva IV, in conjunction with the UN Charter and its right of self-determination and reinforced by the 1970 Declaration of Friendly Relations, has transferred its concept of protected sovereignty under occupations from government to people, *debellatio* has become an irrelevant concept as long as a population within a territory is still capable of self-determination.[102] And second, as already mentioned, the United States and United Kingdom have willingly placed themselves under the law of belligerent occupation, with its restrictions (UN SC Res. 1483, par. 4–5).

The voluntary submission to Hague and Geneva can be interpreted in two ways, one intended and one logically inevitable, even if not intentional. Clearly by March 2003, U.S. policymakers realized that they were not going to immediately transfer power to an Iraqi provisional government—that there was not going to be liberation in the more demanding sense, in other words—and that they needed international legitimacy for their occupation. This was especially important because the 1970 Declaration of Friendly Relations by the UN General Assembly implied that occupations resulting from illegal wars, that is, wars neither of self-defense nor ordered by the UN Security Council according to chapter VII, were themselves illegal.[103] Of course, the United States and United Kingdom held that their war was legal according to a rather contorted argument,[104] but this view was a distinctly minority one in the international political and legal communities. Legalizing the occupation thus was necessary in its own right and could even be considered as a *post facto* confirmation of the legality of the war itself,[105] unless the Security Council's action was to be construed as violating the Declaration of Friendly Relations.

At the same time, the unintended consequence of the action was to put the United States under the new post–Geneva IV interpretation of the law of occupation stressing popular rather than state or governmental sovereignty. After all, in Kelsen's terms, with respect to governmental sovereignty, Iraq according to the Hague Convention would have been a case of *debellatio*, as there was no absent governmental sovereign whose rights could be protected.[106] The law of occupation is meaningful in Iraq only if we understand the sovereign whose rights survive even though suspended as the popular rather than the governmental sovereign. This means that the United States now legally committed itself to a form of occupation that would be compatible with liberation in the less demanding sense at least, and specifically to a process in which, regardless of who controls executive powers in the beginning, "the constituent power" (and in general most legislative powers with long-term effects) would be exercised by the Iraqi people themselves. Or, alternately, the United States allowed a resolution to pass that would legalize its occupation (and perhaps put to rest the question of the war's illegality as well), but at the cost of pointing to usurpation if American authorities themselves established a sovereign rather than commissarial dictatorship or a transformative rather than belligerent occupation.[107]

Paragraph 4 of 1483 "calls upon the Authority [the occupying powers] . . . to promote the welfare of the Iraqi people through . . . the creation of conditions in which the Iraqi people can freely determine their own political future," and this was immediately interpreted by some as implying the creation of a constitution that would be a framework for elections.[108] The same lines, however, could also be interpreted as referring to the creation of conditions under which the Iraqi people could "freely determine" their future constitution, and the phrase "consistent with the Charter of the UN and other relevant international law" in the same paragraph and the requirement to "comply fully" with Geneva 1949 and Hague 1907 imply this latter reading.[109] Indeed, a way of making the two regulations consistent with problems of occupation of countries with previous regimes whose legality cannot be left untouched is again to focus on the stress on popular sovereignty in Geneva.[110] In that case, the normatively valid core of the law of occupation remains the idea that if there is to be the creation of a new legal and constitutional system in a country under foreign occupation, the decisions concerning how such a system is to be created belong to agents that can legitimately speak in the name of the country's own population and not to the occupying power or its agents. This idea converges with the common sense of democratic theory. We assume that democracy is a system that emerges from the autonomous activity of its (potential) citizens and is never, or rarely, the gift of political elites, who would seek to preserve undemocratic advantages hidden in new institutions.[111] The theory of democratic legitimacy can further clarify the matter. Any set of modern democratic institutions have distributional consequences and imply the rule of political elites through mechanisms of representation. We therefore assume that strong legitimation requirements have to be satisfied during the beginning stages of a new democracy, requirements that do not require the mythological attribution of purely democratic constituent power as the source of the new regime but that must go well beyond the idea that elites (especially foreign ones) have imposed it because they had the power to do so.[112]

Properly interpreted, then, UN SC Res. 1483 throws light on the two conditions under which an occupation regime can remain "liberation" in the less demanding sense: speed and autonomy. UN SC Res. 1483 insists on a speedy termination of the occupation and on the planting of the seeds of an autonomous Iraqi administration during it (par. 9). The separation between liberation and constitution in the concept of revolution allows the posing of the same two conditions: the temporal space between liberation and constitution making should be reduced, with the latter process organized autonomously and with the occupying power withdrawing, to the benefit of an indigenous process of self-determination. However, the issue is related to the previous one of forming an interim government. Arguably, unless a relatively inclusive Iraq government were formed, independent of the occupation authority and before the beginning of the constitution-making process, the latter could not be represented as a fundamental break with the logic of the occupation. Such a government, it was increasingly felt, could only come from elections, but elections were not possible without a new constitution.[113] Thus the American authorities had to choose between two evils, even if they regarded them as such only on the public relations level: (1) the option that a constitution, despite international law, would be imposed by them, and (2) that they would empower what they regarded as a weak and unrepresentative interim governmental organ, the IGC, to be in charge of the process. As usual, they chose both options, but the second was meant to be only the Iraqi veil for the first: American imposition. That veil was greeted by UN SC Res. 1511 as "welcoming the decision of the Interim Governing Council of Iraq to form a preparatory constitutional committee to prepare for a constitutional conference that will draft a constitution . . . and *urging* it to complete the process quickly." I believe it was 1511 rather than 1483 that helped to legitimate the process of imposed constitution making in Iraq—but not, as we will see, in the Iraqi eyes, which really counted. It is a great paradox of the recent constitutional history of Iraq that it was autonomous political and social action on behalf of popular (or populist) democratic constitution making that was to put an end to the open constitutional usurpation of the CPA, putting the process in a channel where it was arguably compatible with creatively interpreted international regulations.[114] Yet once again it was to become a question whether the formal process was not meant as window dressing for a deeper, exclusionary, and imposed one after all.[115] This question was superseded by a probably more important one: whether constitution making could work at all in the context of state failure.

Democracy, Empire, and Empire's Democracy

Arguably, the attempt to make occupation and liberation compatible at all was not succeeding on the level of having a sufficiently short occupation regime that would allow the emergence of related autonomous and legitimate processes of government formation and constitution making. There was a strong suspicion among Iraqis, even after the formal transfer of sovereignty, that neither process would be autonomous. In short, the American invasion was suspected of being an imperialist enterprise rather than, as it is treated here, an attempt to externally impose democracy. Cockburn for example, as already mentioned, not only repeatedly notes Iraqi perceptions that the American occupation was an imperialist one, but he himself is inclined to treat the enterprise and its choice of governing structures as classically colonialist. Which interpretation is right? Are they incompatible? Is their possible relationship a clue to why occupation could not be successfully represented as liberation, even in its less demanding sense?

Even if imperialist motivations were made part of the overall explanation of why Iraq happened the way it did, they can explain neither that an outright American military intervention occurred under such unpromising circumstances nor the actual course of the invasion, occupation, and especially the disastrous choices the occupiers were to make.[116] Imperialism would have been compatible with a realistic attempt to contain Iraq and control the Persian Gulf (as Scowcroft argued in effect)[117] or, after an invasion, with the establishment of indirect forms of rule based on the existing Iraqi state, a trajectory the U.S. State Department experts had long prepared for. Only within the larger framework of an externally imposed revolution, imagined, as I will argue below in a particularly radical manner, would imperialism take the form that it did, even if nonimperialists (Cockburn) or nonrevolutionaries (Scowcroft) could quickly foresee where it would necessarily lead. Revolutions, however, need ideologies or ideological motivations. Since, especially in our age, this ideology could not be an imperialist one, "democracy" (flying high in the period of the 1990s), authentically or not, entered the breach.[118]

During my many classes and lectures on this and related topics, students and others ask whether the idea of democratizing Iraq was ever seriously intended by the United States or the Bush administration and whether or not the real motives had to do with long-term imperial control of the Persian Gulf region and its resources. On one level, such a question involves pure metaphysics, postulating a collective actor, the United States, its administration, or, worse, U.S. Imperialism or U.S. Capital, actors that do not exist.[119] Such actors are the vector sums of complex decisions made by many individual and group actors, and we rarely have access to all of their internal disagreements, conflicts, and decision-making processes, despite the growing literature on the subject. What can tentatively be said is that the decision to invade Iraq was the sum of several conflicting perspectives, of which the economic interest expressed in the imperialism thesis[120] was certainly one, and of which a democratization lobby that imagined a transformation of the Middle East in our image was probably another. We tend to personalize the first with the names of Cheney and Rumsfeld, the second with the neoconservative ideologists. It is now known that hard realists such as Henry Kissinger were ready to join them using a version of the deterrence argument, because the United States after being attacked by "radical Islam" had to reply on a significantly large scale, and Afghanistan was not enough.[121] There is also the considerable likelihood that people concerned with the president's electoral fortunes and internal powers were ready to use an external political adventure to enhance these. Certainly all subsequent moves in Iraq through the 2004 election track very well (as Iraqi actors continually noted) with the electoral needs of the president.

Finally, we should not neglect the desire for absolute security, which was so well articulated in the "one percent" doctrine David Suskind has reconstructed for us, though given the absurdity of this idea[122] it is hard to say whether for a Cheney or a Rumsfeld this argument was motive or merely rationalization.[123]

Initially then, the role of democratic regime change was probably just one—and probably not the most important—of the motivations that brought a diverse group of actors together to support the war. Two factors have changed that. One was the failure of the older realism in its "two-pillars" policy to manage American influence in the Persian Gulf. Paradoxically, this became clearer as the older realists around the first President Bush, who were certainly concerned with our power position in the oil-rich region, and their academic supporters came to strongly oppose the plans for the war.[124] Their opponents could now charge that it was the earlier realism, based on the Nixon doctrine and its proxies, that established Saddam as the second pillar of American policy, which led to the invasion of Kuwait, gravely threatening the much more important first pillar, Saudi Arabia, the center of the region.[125] Dictators were unstable, unreliable, and dangerous.[126] But while we could opt for direct intervention instead of using surrogates, we could not adopt a policy of long-term direct or at least obtrusive presence rejected by the Nixon doctrine, as it would be openly imperialist, would not be supported by the American electorate, and would have required a standing military force the United States no longer possessed. It was within this intellectual context that the neoconservative argument for democratic regime change was adopted by other factions in the administration, not necessarily because they were fully convinced but because they had no other alternative if direct presence and dictatorial proxies were both rejected. It could be that the idea always was to leave sufficient force behind to make sure that the new democracies behaved. Or, on the basis of bad historical analogies born of the cold war, it was perhaps assumed that countries owing their democratization to the United States would remain out of gratefulness on the American side. Democratic governments overthrown by the United States itself were conveniently forgotten, or it was assumed that a process of democratization controlled from the outset and monitored later on could avoid such unfavorable outcomes as Mossadegh's or Allende's governments. It was also certainly assumed that managing the democratic transition and making financial contributions to the right parties could significantly contribute to the outcome of producing democracies that turned out right. The historical problems with actual democracies could have been explained away by reference to undesirable worlds where the United States was not the sole superpower and where small countries could gain significant support elsewhere.

The second factor was the total, dramatic, and utterly embarrassing failure of the WMD justification for the war—the primary justification.[127] For a considerable period afterward, democratic regime change was the only justification that remained standing, and thus it had to be pursued much more seriously than some of the architects of the war may have initially intended. It took the state failure (described below) as the justification to shift to defining Iraq as being the primary front in the War on Terror, the location where Al Qaeda had to be defeated. That justification was also present from the beginning, but it was based on even more elaborate disinformation and perversion of intelligence than the WMD hysteria. For a time, this justification could not be articulated without calling attention to the fact that it was the war itself that brought foreign terrorists to Iraq, and that it was the destruction of the state that established such a powerful base for them—if indeed their position is as strong as the propaganda would have it. For a considerable period, then, democratization and democratic regime change, with all its paraphernalia of elections, constitution making, referenda, governments of national unity, and so on, had to be taken utterly seriously.

At the same time, the defeated realists[128] were quick to remind the winners of the debate, the warmakers in the name of democracy, that not just any democracy would do in Iraq. The United States could not have expended all the "blood and treasure" it had in Iraq to merely deliver the country *horribile dictu* to the friends of Iran, the Shi'ites, who just happened to be the country's demographic majority. You have to have a democracy that turns out right, one that puts and keeps in power friends of the United States. It is a mistake to rush into elections before that result can be ascertained. On the most sophisticated level, this argument logically meant that the United States should not have invaded Iraq at all in the name of regime change, just as Bush, Scowcroft, and Baker did not go to Baghdad in 1991. This issue, however, was now irrelevant. Slightly more practically, Scowcroft implied that the U.S. government would be still better off with some kind of authoritarian regime where one would have to manage only a small group and not whole electorates or political parties. This advice was impractical, ran counter to the spirit of the times, and was not in fact openly offered. What Scowcroft did suggest was to delay the process and to extend the occupation, advice that was still probably very impractical, because it could produce a nationalist backlash against the Americans, who would appear as successors to the British imperialists, perhaps resembling the events of 1920. There was indeed not only a Sunni insurrection to worry about but the possibility of one based in Shi'ite strata as well. At all costs, fighting such a two-front war had to be avoided. Thus the interpretation of the advice ultimately reduced to what the CPA was actually trying to do, namely to work toward a relatively quick transition to "democracy" while retaining sufficient control to ensure that this new regime turned out right from the American point of view.[129] Such a democracy, with its implied postulate of certainty, is not really democracy;[130] it is merely an empire's democracy[131] or a new Bonapartism.[132] It is quite another question whether such a system can be stabilized after an aggressive war, in a country with multiple lines of political cleavage. In Iraq, an empire's democracy continually hovered between open imposition and outright failure of the whole governing process. In retrospect, it is tough to believe that anyone could have believed that such a democracy was possible under the given conditions. Misunderstood historical analogies certainly helped to spread the misconception.

Excursus: Historical Comparisons and Their Warnings

From the very beginning, those in charge of the American invasion and occupation of Iraq were willing to take seriously only the German and Japanese historical examples, which were, however, very poorly understood. James Dobbins notes four reasons for this highly anachronistic interest: the success of these efforts, their very large scale, the absence of salient controversies regarding them, and the fact that the Department of Defense rather than the State Department or USAID was in charge, as opposed to more recent and controversial efforts.[133] From a more theoretical perspective, the historical precedents of Germany and Japan also offered the promise that the legitimation problems of an externally imposed revolution were in principle soluble. What was most certainly not noticed was that these very problems were handled in significantly different ways in the two countries considered as models. External imposition can indeed be seen as two very different things: (1) imposing a fully democratic solution from the outside, or (2) merely removing the impediments to genuinely internal solutions. According to Carl J. Friedrich, the process of the democratization of Germany should be understood as the second of these types: the restoration of democracy.[134] In the words of the best American historian of this process: "German political life reached 'point zero' in May 1945. But there were still latent political traditions of pre-Hitler Germany on which a reconstruction of the body politic could fall back. There were also scores of political and intellectual leaders and thousands of faithful followers who had somehow weathered the totalitarian storm and were rallying now to rebuild society and state."[135]

Both parts of this statement are important. Unlike the Japanese state, the German state collapsed both as a territorial and as an organizational entity. As we have seen, Hans Kelsen, followed by other international lawyers, applied the term *debellatio* to Germany, implying the total absence of sovereignty and therefore the inapplicability of the Hague rules for belligerent occupation. It is also true that the reconstruction of democracy was on the whole an autonomous German process. For both reasons, therefore, it may be more fitting to choose the Japanese example as a lesson for Iraq, because here the work of imposition was much more drastic and democracy more obviously created than merely restored.[136] Note, however, that in Japan radical rupture was also avoided to a far greater extent than in Germany. The Americans made a determined attempt not to smash the internal capacity of the Japanese state. The Japanese cabinet and Diet were not removed but instead had to follow the directives of the American military rather than the directives of the dominant Japanese military groups, as they did in the years 1930 through 1945.[137] Most importantly, General MacArthur was strongly sympathetic to the Japanese government's desire to allow the emperor, representing the unity of the state, to remain in place. The retention of the emperor was key to maintaining the coherence and loyalty of the police and the bureaucracy. Finally, even in the midst of imposition, the important *fiction* of legal continuity was maintained: the new constitution of 1947 was formally passed as a mere amendment to the 1889 Meiji constitution.[138]

The problem of legitimation in Germany, where the state was completely destroyed, was handled through the restoration of democracy through largely indigenous processes; in Japan, where democratization was imposed, the solution relied on the preservation of the inherited state along with a species of traditional legitimacy. This difference should not hide the fact that the initial conditions of political transformation in Japan and Germany in 1945 were far more similar to each other than either was to contemporary Iraq.[139]

(1) Germany and Japan were under the externally overthrown dictatorship for twelve and fifteen years, respectively; Iraq had been a dictatorship for forty years or more.

(2) Both Germany and Japan were completely defeated in the greatest war in history, with societies capable of little organized resistance; in Iraq, only the government was defeated.

(3) Germany and Japan were constitutional regimes before the 1930s; what occurred after 1945 was first and foremost a restoration of those constitutional regimes. Iraq has never known constitutional, rule-of-law government.[140] The skills, traditions, memories, institutions, and, most of all, the professionals to build a constitutional state were available in both Germany and Japan but not in Iraq.

(4) Germany and Japan are ethnically homogeneous. Japan is also religiously homogenous, and the violent Catholic-Protestant conflicts in Germany ended in the seventeenth century. The ethnic and religious situation in Iraq is obviously different, to say the very least. Here the ascriptive cleavage structure is three-dimensional and highly antagonistic (Arab-Kurd, Shi'ite-Sunni, secular-religious—with six of the eight possible combinations in existence, even if not always salient).

(5) Germany and Japan were liberated or occupied as the result of the aggression of the latter two countries; Iraq was liberated or occupied in a war in which the United States was, like Napoleon's France two hundred years before, the aggressor.[141]

(6) German and Japanese elites and the Western, mainly American agents of democratization had a common enemy, whose support was relatively weak within their countries: the Soviet Union. Iraqi elites, in common with other Arab/Muslim leaders and opinion makers, have a major enemy that is a friend of the United States: Israel.

(7) The external boundaries of Japan were relatively secure; those of Germany could be threatened only by a new world war. The boundaries of Iraq, on the other hand, are porous and threatened by a plurality of states that have important allies within Iraq. Iraqi democracy is a threat to all of these states, some of them allies of the United States and therefore difficult to restrain by threats of force.

Looking at the matter from the point of view of international politics indicates some differences between Germany and Japan, which, however, further indicate their common distance from the situation of Iraq. The political transitions of Japan and Germany, because of the more complex occupation structure of the latter, took place in different international constellations, as Japanese writers were the first to point out.[142] Japanese constitution making occurred at a time when the United States was unchallenged in the Pacific, before the victory of the Chinese Communists, and before the outbreak of the cold war. The Japanese were not (yet, or mainly) thought of as potential allies, a fact explaining their relatively rough treatment compared to Germany. In (West) Germany, the making of the *Grundgesetz* was an intrinsic part of the cold war division (of the country and Europe), and it was clear that the new Federal Republic would have to be an important ally on the very frontier between West and East. It was, moreover, important to demonstrate the superiority of the American-supported autonomous democracy to the Soviet-imposed pseudodemocracy next door. Given this train of thought, we can see that in an epoch of unbalanced American dominance, Iraq is seen as its terrain rather than its partner. There is no other sociopolitical model around that would require the demonstration of the superiority of our model. Moreover, the outcome of a genuinely democratic process in Iraq is likely to be very different from the point of view of American interests than in Germany in 1948 or Japan in 1946 and 1947. Given the political forces in Iraq and their international alliances, the United States is, from the outset, more ambivalent about the Iraqi democracy it supposedly promotes than about the two earlier examples.

Thus, when compared to Iraq, the German and Japanese models lead to a strongly negative balance sheet consisting of two major components. First, the given internal and external conditions of the three countries during the beginning of their occupations were so different as to discourage almost any attempt to apply German and Japanese lessons to Iraq. The earlier cases do not justify at all the optimistic scenarios concerning the later one. But, second, if we insist on learning something nevertheless—and after the invasion there was little choice in the matter—the lesson should have been simple enough. The only imaginable basis for initiating an autonomous political process in Iraq was either ensuring the continuity of the central state, as in Japan, *or* abetting the rapid and thoroughgoing organization of elected local government, as in Germany. Because of the far less favorable starting point in Iraq, most likely a combination of these desiderata would have been important if at all possible.[143] Adhering to them would most likely not have been sufficient, but disregarding either and especially both would make the chances of disaster very high.

Since the German and Japanese "gold standard" (as Galbraith puts it) for occupation had only limited value for Iraq, it is not surprising that analysts supporting the war have sought other examples. In a study performed by the Rand Corporation[144] led by Dobbins, which made the rounds of the inner circles of government,[145] in addition to Germany and Japan, the cases of Somalia, Haiti, Bosnia, Kosovo, and Afghanistan were added. Subsequently, Dobbins was to argue much more strongly for the irrelevance of the German and Japanese cases, which his group still took seriously, and for the salience of the ex-Yugoslav cases in particular, and the conclusions of the original study support this focus.[146] The recent cases here all belong to an epoch in which the United States as sole superpower is in principle capable of exerting its will in the world on an entirely new basis. But as the failed cases (Somalia, Haiti) testify, such power in itself does not lead to the desired result. Undiscouraged, neoconservatives or "democratic realists" have argued that failure is inevitable unless vital national interests and political principle both justify the necessarily very high expenditure of the required resources.[147] Conversely, the Dobbins group seems to demonstrate that where the expenditure of resources (military and financial) is sufficiently high, the task can be accomplished even where the initial conditions are much less favorable than in Germany and Japan, where the society is much less homogenous, and where it is capable of further military resistance (for example, Bosnia and Kosovo, though Iraq is depicted as a still more difficult case than these two). Admittedly, in Bosnia and Kosovo the resources came in large part from Europe, and, based on these experiences and also on the Japan/Germany comparison, Dobbins's group favored international participation in shouldering the costs and in helping to compose the command structure. That would mean in Iraq that the United States, not willing to share the command, would alone have to shoulder the burdens. Based on Bosnian and Kosovo comparisons, the Rand report estimated for Iraq a minimum occupation force of 460,000 to 494,000 in 2003 and 258,000 to 526,000 in 2005 and an expense of thirty-six billion dollars over the first two years. (It is in this context that the report recommended the gradual dissolution of the established Iraqi army and the creation of an entirely new one.) But assuming the geopolitical stakes, it was assumed nevertheless that the costs could be managed and paid.

Disregarding recommendations like this, at least with respect to the size of the U.S. military force (the funds committed were very high, though not properly utilized), could only be described as an effort of calculated inexperience or a calculated attempt to learn not to learn.[148]

The assumption behind the Rand report's conclusions is the same as the premise of Charles Krauthammer's "democratic realism," even if they do not marshal up questionable examples such as the long dictatorship of South Korea to support it: "the single most important factor in the success of nation building is seriousness."[149] Everything thus depends on us; the other is a passive object for our experiment. The more difficult the case, the more we must do in terms of the commitment of resources. But what happens if our own actions make the problems worse, not better? More reflective conservatives tend to recall what happens when dictatorships dissolve in multiethnic and multireligious societies held together by authoritarian states. According to James Kurth, liberating a segment like Kosovo or Bosnia was thus less indicative of what was likely to happen in Iraq than was the dissolution of Yugoslavia as a whole or the breakup of the Soviet Union.[150]

As suggestive as the violence of some of Kurth's examples may be, given what is *now* happening in Iraq, it is not entirely obvious that they had to inevitably apply to this case. And there are two reasons for this. First, it is not axiomatic that the end of a dictatorial regime must mean the end of a state in a multiethnic but not federally organized society. All his examples were federal as well as multiethnic. While it is true that the Shi'ites have experienced Saddam's rule as very oppressive, interpreters tend to forget the historical importance of Iraqi nationalism as opposed to Arab nationalism and the historical desire of the Shi'ites to participate in an Iraqi state rather than to destroy it.[151] And second, it is not certain that an occupation state could not have been temporarily grafted onto the inherited state, preparing the ground for a new process of state rebuilding (whose burden would have to be carried by the constitution-making process).

State and Revolution

For an occupation to be represented as liberation, it would have to above all function effectively; paradoxically, it would have to be an effective occupation, one providing public security and basic social services on a continuous basis. To most people, this was more important than even the questions of the occupation's duration and whether that time was being used effectively to transfer governmental power and organize an autonomous constitutional process.[152] And, clearly, a longer but more effective occupation regime would allow in principle at least a more lasting transference of power and the building of stable institutions than a shorter but disorganized occupation. It is undeniable that this point was clear to the founders of the CPA,[153] but they did not understand the important corollary: an effective occupation regime would have to rely on an effective occupation state. As we have seen already, historically this problem was solved in two different ways. Here briefly: an effective occupation state could be grafted onto the inherited state (Japan) or it could be a function of its own effective forces of coercion, administration, and economic support (Germany, Bosnia, and Kosovo), the latter requiring the presence of much larger occupation forces per capita.[154] The most remarkable thing about the occupation of Iraq was that it followed none of the earlier patterns: unwilling to use a large enough American force and unable to mobilize a large force of allies to join the enterprise, the U.S. occupation authority proceeded both to disband the Iraqi forces that could have been used to provide security and to eliminate or reorganize the inherited institutions on which the occupation state could have been grafted. State destruction without the hope of creating an occupation state to replace it: that was the formula that made the failure of almost everything else highly likely, though I will argue not entirely inevitable.

Here some definitions are in order. For the purposes of this chapter, I will consider the *state* as the Weberian one: "a compulsory political organization with continuous operations [within a given territorial area, whose] administrative staff successfully upholds the claim to the *monopoly* of the *legitimate* use of physical force in the enforcement of its order."[155] When older German and French writers analyze the category in terms of *population, territory*, and a *form of organization* or "political organ" capable of producing a public power exercising coercion over them,[156] they are rightly adding only the element of membership, admittedly with the risk that "state" and "nation" may be wrongly conflated.[157] Their subtraction of *legitimacy* from the definition is only apparent, because it is contained in the idea of a *public* power. Nevertheless, I will leave open here whether a plausible claim of monopoly *produces* legitimacy or publicness or *presupposes* it.[158] Admittedly, other important features could be added for the modern state, such as its link to an order of positive law and legislation[159] and its role as an organ of communication in reflexively monitoring society.[160] Even if we distinguish between nation and state, as we should, it may be important to stress that a state's people are themselves *socially* (and not just coercively) integrated in a variety of ways, and this entails important state symbols and rituals at the state's end (communicated through a variety of socializing agencies) and entitlements on the members' end (administered through a variety of administrative structures).[161] It is, however, a mistake in my view to reduce the state either to the sum total of bureaucratic offices or to the territorial entity (or, for that matter, the people or the nation). The state must be seen as the operation of ultimately coercive political and bureaucratic structures on people (distinguishing between *a* people with some kind of collective "state identity" and *all* people, members and nonmembers both) within a territory.[162] Here, in the given context, I will concentrate on these three dimensions: coercive organization with a (legitimate) monopoly, territory, and people, the last in the sense of members.

In distinction to the concept of the state, I will understand *government* here in the American manner, to refer to all the functional branches of political power, not only the executive.[163] From the point of view of international law, government is the body of individuals that "by virtue of the effective constitution of the state, represents the State in relation to other States."[164] Government is the political center or political top of the administrative and coercive apparatus of the state; when differentiated, all three branches of governmental power have a relation of formal superiority to that apparatus. From the point of view of a formal action theory, government is the source of goals and objectives; administration is the instrument that carries these out. The reality, as organization theory has repeatedly shown, is far more complex, however: goals emanate from below as well as from above.[165] *Regime* is the institutional structure of state and government, including the rules and practices that govern the relations of governors and governed.[166] It is best understood in relation to the term *constitution*. Until the late eighteenth century, "constitution" meant the empirical structure of state and government, and, as in Aristotle's *Politics*, all states had constitutions in this sense. In the late eighteenth century, primarily through the American and French Revolutions, the term "constitution" was transformed to mean the legal rules regulating the establishment and practice of political government.[167] Not only did the term now mean secondary legal rules, namely rules of rule making, identifying, adjudicating, and applying,[168] but when differentiated, there was also the implication that constitutional rules would be made in a special procedure, included in a single document—a written constitution—and protected from amendment by stringent rules.[169] However, as Dieter Grimm rightly notes, the old notion of constitution in the empirical sense survives, and, together with the legal practices, customs, and conventions indispensable for any actual constitutional tradition, these can be understood as a kind of "constitutional reality" that still influences the law.[170] The actual political order is thus governed by a combination of institutionalized legal, unwritten legal, and empirical regularities, and it is this combination we should refer to by the traditional term *regime*. This term denotes little more than Aristotle's *politeia,* that is, one of the meanings of "constitution," as long as we realize that today a *regime* will be a complex combination of formal and informal, normative and empirical elements, all however requiring some level of institutionalization.

The three terms "government," "regime," and "state" imply three categories of political change that are, more or less, in the order of their radicalism: coups d'état, revolution, and (what I will call) revolutionary state destruction, one of whose forms is a not necessarily very radical revolution-secession.[171] Little needs to be said about the first. It is a form of illegal change in which merely the government is replaced, but the old rules of the political game remain in place despite a one-time violation of the key rule according to which the incumbents of government are supposed to be replaced. It is wrong to consider, as does Kelsen, such an event the equivalent of a revolution or even the demise of an old constitution (which would be discredited, though very possibly preserved). While in a very narrow technical sense one could argue that during a coup, with temporarily two contending armed forces, a state in the sense of a legal monopoly over the means of violence has ceased to exist, this is neither true in international law nor in terms of the important territorial, popular, or even administrative components of the state. Revolution is more complex. Generally it entails not only a replacement of the incumbents of government, but also a change in the *form* of government. Thus it contains a coup d'état, and sometimes it can look like a coup or begin with one. But more importantly, by attacking the regime as well as the government, revolution arguably smashes the old state structure as well. Such was the view and desire of Lenin before Russian conditions taught him the Tocquevillian insight of the partial survival of the old state and its bureaucracy even in radical revolutions.[172] Because regime and constitution regulate both state and government, it is difficult to see how a regime change can leave a state more or less intact. At the very least, it will imply a reform of the state structure and organization. In great revolutions, there have been certainly important tendencies toward the disintegration of one or another dimension of the inherited state apparatus: in France, the bureaucracy though not the army; in Russia, both until they were reconstituted from largely old elements.[173] Theoretically, however, three distinctions can be made. Even a radical revolution can use important segments of the old state organization, such as the army and the police, to build its own state. Here the objection would be that a radical revolution needs to reorganize the mode of operation of even these organs of power. Such an effort can be relatively complete when a revolutionary force has a very large, trained military force and incipient political apparatus at its disposal, as did the Chinese Communists. The counterargument is on the whole more plausible empirically: radical revolutions in particular immediately need state power to suppress class-based forces of the old regime and to impose their very likely elite minoritarian conceptions about the reorganization of society. Generally, they may have the forces to take the commanding heights of power but not to administer, control, and defend the country as a whole. Second, regime transformation is indeed likely to weaken a polity with respect to its external environment, and thus the mobilization of inherited state structures on behalf of the external defense of the revolution is likely to be necessary. Even a radical revolution would wish to preserve the territorial integrity and continuity of the state along with its international recognition, and in most cases the new regime would also wish to be perceived as the legal heir of its predecessor. Finally, even in a radical revolution, the same population or those speaking in its name could play the dominant role in the building of new institutions. Thus Carl Schmitt argued that in a democratic age, during some "revolutions," as in 1848 and 1870 in France, the (same) people retain their constituent power. From a legal point of view, he referred to these phenomena as "setting aside" or, more clearly put, "replacing" the constitution (*Verfassungsbeseitigung; Verfassungswechsel*), in contrast to its annihilation (*Verfassungsvernichtung*).[174] He called both types of events "revolutions," but only the latter, the annihilation of the constitution, involved state and regime destruction in the terms of internal and possibly even international law.

The combination of preserving some administrative and coercive organs, territorial integrity, and (reference to) the same political community thus implies that a radical revolution can and most likely will assume a conservative posture with respect to the state. Within a two-part distinction between revolution and coup d'état alone, this insight in an age of bureaucratization could lead to Weber's diagnosis concerning the passing of revolutions and their general replacement by coups, a diagnosis especially paradoxical at the dawn of the twentieth century.[175] Using my three-part distinction based on the differentiation of government, regime, and state, I should note only the state-strengthening character of revolutions not directed against the old state structure itself. [176]

The survival of the inherited state in revolutions in turn implies the persistence of a "minimal constitution,"[177] which French thinkers have rightly interpreted in terms of the survival of political organs that can help organize the constituent process even in the midst of revolutions.[178] In any case, there is a clear distinction between a revolution that builds on the existing state and the type of radical change that destroys a preexisting state, for example through a revolution-secession. Here the preexisting territorial integrity and the political community are destroyed, and whatever remains of administrative and coercive apparatuses can exercise monopolies only over parts of the former state, not the whole.

Important consequences follow from these distinctions—especially the distinction between revolution and revolutionary state destruction—for the problems of constitution making, the potential for civil war, and for the specific nature of an externally imposed revolution. Regarding constitution making, revolution proper no longer needs to be understood as creating a *tabula rasa* or creating a legal state of nature; only revolutionary state destruction has this consequence. And even in this latter case, if the state destroyed in a secession-revolution is a federal state with organized units, the constitution-making process can rely on their "state" organizations to avoid a legal state of nature. This is what happened at the beginning of the American Civil War, but there are many recent examples as well. Thus, state destruction is the most radical from a constitutional point of view when it occurs in a previously centralized state. From the point of view of radicalism, this is the most radical form of revolution. It is, of course, also the most difficult context in which to carry out the second stage Arendt insisted on: the constitution of freedom, as she called it, or less dramatically, the institutionalization of a new regime.

Civil war is a danger in all three forms of change, including the coup d'état, where two military leaders, for example, can have equal forces to contest the seat of the established governmental power. It is a greater danger in revolutions, because the prospect of regime change with important distributional and symbolic consequences is likely to mobilize politicized social forces along all important cleavage lines. This is an additional reason why revolutionaries, whatever their initial intentions, are likely to avail themselves of and strengthen the forces of the old state, and generally their success depends on their ability to do this effectively. Thus while revolution may almost tautologically imply civil war (as Tilly rightly notes),[179] the actual duration and depth of such a conflict may be manageable. The case of revolutionary state destruction, including revolution-secession, is fundamentally different. Here the old apparatus will be broken up or split. There will be no force available to contain armed political claimants to power, or the fragmented old state forces themselves will become part of a contest for power. A revolution-secession can lead either to the strengthening of the original unit-states that become independent or to the creation of new, weaker or stronger, federal or confederal structures, as was the case for both sides in the American Civil War.[180] However, to the extent the state breakup or the secession is contested, the result can be only an extended civil conflict.

Finally, it is very important for us that an externally imposed revolution has a freer hand in choosing among options than a classical internal revolution. When Lenin faced the problem of actually destroying the existing state, he had to realize that if he followed through his original ideas he would then have to face a still continuing external war and counterrevolution without the support and with the enmity of those sectors of the inherited military and administration that were now potentially loyal to the new regime. An external agent of revolution such as the United States, in its various attempts to impose democracy, had a choice at least when it faced an inherited state organization in an occupied country. It could act like MacArthur in Japan and build on the existing state. But with its own vast military resources, it could afford to be more like Lenin than Lenin himself. To the extent that it saw the inherited state and its administrative and military structures as part and parcel of an old regime that would always reproduce that old regime, even if the formal governmental structures were replaced, the idea of destroying these structures could be entertained supposedly without the fear of a scenario in which social order collapses because of missing state inputs and the emergence of armed political actors who cannot be controlled without the presence of much stronger state coercive forces. An occupation state could in theory replace the inherited state while an entirely new state structure was being created *ex nihilo*. This would involve creating a new army and police force as well as a state administration. Even de facto fragmentation of the territory could be permitted, as long as the agents controlling the potential breakaway region could not leave the political process of state rebuilding. The constitution-making process would thus serve as the context where both a new territorial state structure and new regime rules would be negotiated. It would not occur in a state of nature, because the occupying power (under its own interpretation or misinterpretation of international law) would supply the constitutional minimum needed for the process to move forward.

For the American occupiers of Iraq, only the third of these consequences was initially relevant. They only saw the availability of a choice, not the potential problems. Thinking in terms of historical analogies alone and relying on the German and Japanese models, they may have imagined that state destruction was a matter of choice without grave consequences for the occupier and that occupation with or without the destruction of the occupied state can allow for effective constitution making without the danger of civil war. Misunderstanding the Rand report, which stressed the greater similarity of Bosnia and Kosovo to Iraq, Bremer seemed to consider the Japanese and German examples especially relevant models to follow.[181] But the connection between the parts of these models seemed to have been entirely unclear to him and his colleagues, since bizarrely enough they adopted, as I will show, their initial constitution-making project from Japan, where the old state was preserved (and where its mechanisms could disguise their imposition), even though they were going to head the German way and destroy inherited state structures. Without a theory or any serious prior analysis—but with almost hysterical warnings from other American participants—the CPA, supported by the Pentagon, embarked on an experiment during 2003 and 2004 with consequences that are now almost universally recognized as devastating.[182] This they did despite a fundamental built-in flaw they were clearly conscious of, one called to our attention by L. Paul Bremer himself,[183] that there were not going to be enough American forces to monopolize the forces of violence, and that was going to be a problem, as the complete breakdown of public order and security as the Saddam government collapsed in April and May 2003 showed plainly. We will never know if having had enough American forces would have made the experiment work.[184] It is possible that such a force would have only increased the resentment and size of the insurrection. But it is also possible that a crucial period of time would have been gained to enable implementation of the rest of the project. We also cannot even know if having enough American forces would have worked if there had been an attempt to build on the inherited Iraqi state. What is clear is that not having enough occupation forces meant that the experiment in state destruction should have been abandoned before it was started. Jay Garner and others who had been a bit longer in Iraq were right; the new arrival Bremer was not.

In any case, CPA orders 1 and 2 proceeded to destroy the Iraqi administration (meaning both the top levels and large parts of the civil service) and the army. It is right to treat the two decisions together as the destruction of the Iraqi state in its administrative capacity, as long as we realize that its territorial integrity was already severely compromised.[185] There is more than ample literature on these two interrelated decisions, and there is no need to go into them in great detail here.[186] As to the army, the argument that it was already disbanded is clearly fallacious in light of the testimony of American officers already involved in trying to reconstitute it. Generals Abizaid (the new regional commander, the only one with local knowledge) and McKiernan (the highly professional first commander of American forces in Iraq) and Col. Pat Hughes, Garner's planning chief, were heavily involved in trying to create the core of a viable army from the old, including even the formation of a new general staff.[187] If the soldiers went home, they could have been recalled. Their officers were ready to reorganize them even taking into account the purging of their ranks that Americans would have in any case insisted on. The political risks involved in recalling the army were real, because the officer core was indeed a stronghold of Arab (Sunni-centered) nationalist power, but this could have been gradually altered by selective decommissioning and commissioning and by a new stress on an inclusive Iraqi nationalism (always a minority alternative).[188] That the survival of the army would have been politically resented by organized Kurdish and Shi'ite groups is certainly true,[189] but with all their expected benefits from the occupation these groups would not have violently resisted. Their capacity to do so was in any case doubtful. In the longer term, gradual reform, reorganization, and affirmative action for underrepresented groups could have dealt with the problems. Keeping the army and most of the old apparatus would have involved costs, but getting rid of them involved even greater costs. It was up to the occupying power to evaluate which cost was greater: keeping a more or less efficient state machinery in place or not and attacking the main symbols of the integrity of the Iraqi state or keeping in place a set of institutions the leaders of Shi'ite and Kurdish groups wished to see destroyed. It was not enough to weigh the costs (dissatisfaction of major groups, deceleration of the change) and forget or easily discount the huge potential cost on the other side (collapse of security, collapse of administration, collapse of symbols of stateness).[190]

And it was not just a matter of a static situation at the time the choice was made, because the choice was to affect profoundly the developments in Iraq. The destruction of the army by CPA order 2, "Dissolution of Entities"[191] (meaning army and all military formations, the ministry of defense and all security-related ministries, but not apparently the interior ministry), created ready recruits for the insurrection in the stratum most capable of fighting a long-term resistance against any new government. When the fired military men demonstrated against Bremer, they did so openly, some even mentioning suicide bombings, and there is no question that many were to join the insurrection, with devastating results.[192] The CPA's first two orders solved the most difficult problem for the insurrectionists—recruitment—for them.[193] Moreover, it has been estimated that dismissing about 7 percent of the workforce produced severe economic hardship for about 10 percent of the population as a whole.[194] Finally, having to organize a new army *ex nihilo* created a long-term security vacuum in which militias took over law-and-order functions. It was difficult to prevent them from then entering the new army in an organized fashion. Thus there would be no new national army at all except in name. The one historically anticolonial and statewide institution—the one remaining symbol of state sovereignty[195] that was considered the guarantee against the return of neocolonialism—was destroyed, and many Iraqis interpreted this as an act of deliberate imperialist policy intended to maintain the country's long-term dependence on the current occupying power.[196]

As to the administration of the country and the provision of professional services, de-Baathification (CPA order 1) as ordered by Bremer and as administered by Ahmad Chalabi had devastating consequences. Surprisingly, the army was not a center of Baath power and organization, but this was discovered only when it was dissolved. As a matter of fact, Saddam Hussein trusted neither the army nor in the last phases of his rule the Baath organization itself. Reduced in size, deprived of all ideological vigor, the late Baath was a tool for selecting "careerists and obliging technocrats, and providing a parallel bureaucracy to ensure the loyalty of the bureaucracy and armed forces."[197] However, most members of the bureaucracy at the upper levels still had to show their loyalty by joining, as did professionals including teachers, doctors, and university professors wishing to practice in their fields. In his book *My Year in Iraq*, Bremer speaks of ridding "the Iraqi government of the small group of true believers at the top of the party and those who have committed crimes in its name." CPA order 1 had to do with the top four levels of the party of two million, definitely far more people than the twenty thousand he estimates. Either deliberately or inadvertently he is confusing the figures and the Baath categories initially agreed upon in Washington with the much larger figures his own order entailed. Even more seriously, he glibly glosses over the important new distinction in his order, pointed out by Rajiv Chandrasekaran, between eliminating the top four categories of Baath from all jobs and eliminating *all* Baath members from the top three levels of government jobs. Based on a memo by Douglas Feith of the Pentagon, it was the two steps put together that generated the high numbers of firings.[198] Moreover, there must have been few true believers and even fewer actual criminals among them. On the other hand, the admitted "administrative inconvenience" involved was a pathetic understatement of the likely and actual results. Finally, government here meant civil-service employees in a country where the state was by far the largest employer, and "full Baath members" purged from the top layers of the management of every "ministry, affiliated corporation, and other government institutions, institutes, hospitals" would not be allowed government employment anywhere else. This meant teachers, doctors, managers, engineers, and so on. Ten to fifteen thousand teachers were fired, leaving only one or two teachers in some Sunni-dominated areas. Ministries lost the bulk of their staffs; Americans lost the partners they were already working with.[199] Some hospitals were in danger of being closed.[200] One American official fired 1,700 university professors and staff, and felt justified in doing so by the German analogy,[201] though the official does not seem to realize how idiotic that analogy was. Some estimate that 35,000 employees of the bureaucracy, mostly Sunnis, lost their jobs overnight, with 65,000 targeted.[202] The significance of this number is that it hides the fact that the people involved were probably the most expert and most able to lead institutions, including state-owned companies, which were severely affected.[203] But the most disastrous result may have been, according to a joint study of the inspectors general of the State Department and the Pentagon cited by T. Ricks, the complete decapitation and disorganization of the Iraqi police, which had been exempted from CPA order 2, which dissolved the security institutions along with the army.[204]

There is much evidence suggesting that the consequences of CPA order 1 were immediately far reaching, and Bremer's attempt to put the blame for this on Chalabi's de-Baathification commission in the IGC is only partly justified. On the other hand, Chalabi and his group's influence seems to have been crucial in making the original decision.[205] In the face of State Department opposition, it was Chalabi's group who apparently convinced the Pentagon with entirely mistaken analogies such as "de-Nazification,"[206] when the generally rejected idea of de-Communization in eastern and central Europe would have been the far better analogy given the respective lengths of Baath, Communist, and Nazi regimes and their types of relationships to society. It seems well established that it was supporters of Chalabi such as Feith who convinced Bremer of the idea of drastic de-Baathification, although he like all others continues to deflect the blame. There is some evidence that Z. Khalilzad, with whom Bremer was initially supposed to work, teaming with A. Allawi, fought for a very limited process of de-Baathification and sought to recruit the professional and expert strata for the new order. But Bremer made a special point of insisting that Khalilzad be recalled, and with Garner out, the Chalabi position became dominant.[207] It is thus no use to put the blame on Chalabi's later administration of the program. Moreover, interestingly, the de-Baathification order was announced to Chalabi and the ILC the same day they were told that power was not going to be handed over to them, as Garner promised. Bremer, who called his role that of first a good cop (before a bad one), seemed to believe, rightly, that de-Baathification would be the carrot that the seven leaders, especially Chalabi, needed in order to accept the stick of the CPA's dictatorship.[208] Bremer notes what he thinks is a contradiction, namely that Chalabi himself pointed out that some Baathists were forced to join. What in fact he was doing is indicating his objectivity and his suitability to be in charge of a process that would gain him influence over both those who replaced old employees and those Baathists who were after all allowed to stay. And indeed, to make the carrot even more tempting, Chalabi was put in charge of the de-Baathification commission, giving him immense potential power.

Some interpreters seem to feel that de-Baathification and the decommissioning of the Iraqi army would have worked less destructively if Bremer had a delivered on Garner's promise and put the ILC in charge of the provisional government.[209] Note that Garner's plan, even for that case, involved only very minor de-Baathification, and he would have reconstituted the old army. But the idea that the people in power, who pushed for the most radical reconstruction of the Sunni-dominated state—without adequate Sunni representatives—would be forced to negotiate with Sunnis was a nonstarter unless they lost the protection of American military forces: if, in other words, the United States withdrew from Iraq or threatened to do so. Even then, it is more likely that they might have opted for the drastic measures they themselves, namely Shi'ite and Kurd exile groups, pushed for the hardest, even at the cost of launching a civil war immediately. With the United States in Iraq, they would have felt even more confident to pursue their maximalist goals of revolutionary restructuring, which, given the small size of the American force, would not have been able to prevent civil war. If the goal was to produce a negotiated settlement between the real forces in Iraq, and that included the Iraqi military as well as Sunni Arab nationalists, the best way to accomplish this would be for a neutral monitor to force parties into contexts of inclusive negotiation and power sharing. The United States was in the position to play this role, and it is not clear why in the long term its hostility to a given side had to be so great as to inhibit its playing it. What is certain is that with CPA orders 1 and 2 the possibility of becoming a neutral referee was gravely compromised if not lost altogether.

That the experiment in state destruction was pursued meant several interrelated things for the Iraqi state, some obvious, some less so.[210] Best treated around the dimensions of the control over violence, population, and territory, the first three are directly connected to the combined problem of the small size of the American forces and the dissolution of the Iraqi army. The fourth is connected to the dramatic decline of the Iraqi state as the producer of goods and services.

(1) Most obviously, the state in the sense of any imaginable monopoly over the means of violence was gone. There was not enough of an occupation force to reestablish it. The Iraqi army was gone; the police force was severely compromised. If there was to be any order, Iraqis had to rely on themselves, their tribes, their mosques, and the various militia that emerged from mixed political, religious, neighborhood, and tribal foundations. The decentralization of violence, however, only added to the problem itself. Because the relationship of each of the forms of coercive organization to the occupation was different, and because there were traditional grievances against one another, it was only a matter of time before antioccupation activities released grave sectarian conflicts as well. An insurrection based in the Sunni Arab part of the population always had the

potential to produce a Shi'ite-Sunni civil war even without the deliberate provocations of the most radical Sunni Islamist factions. This potential was unavoidably released when most Shi'ite political groups, themselves no friends of the occupation, chose the strategy of coming to power not through open resistance but through elections the Americans in the end were forced to accept.

(2) The population of the country, another dimension of stateness, was increasingly fragmented on ethnic-religious lines. Perhaps there never was an Iraqi nation, or perhaps it was already severely compromised by Saddam's treatment of the Kurds and the Shi'a. But there was nevertheless common membership in a polity that provided a large variety of social (educational, medical) and infrastructural (communication, transportation, electricity, water, sanitation) services and enforced a variety of duties (military service, primarily) on that basis. To be Iraqi meant at least a minimum entitlement[211] to many things and a responsibility to perform certain duties that would apply across the board to different population segments. When the organization of violence took place on ethnic-religious grounds, penetrating the police and the new armed forces, this meant that people could expect state-type outputs only from "their own people," and that the others, even when wearing Iraqi uniforms, had become deadly threats to them. It was not only a matter of security and protection but also the provision of local services. The general insecurity, disorganization of the state apparatus, fall in revenues, and open attacks by insurgents meant a collapse of what used to be central state services, whether social or infrastructural. Many of these would now be supplied by local governmental organs under the protection of militias, both organized increasingly on ethnic-religious lines. Public services still supplied by the central state, such as water and electricity, were distinguished by their scarcity and poor quality. There is some evidence, however, that in mixed areas including Baghdad even central state infrastructural services are now provided on ethnic bases,[212] and the same is probably true for whatever is left of medical services and the increasingly segregated system of education. The trend toward ethnicization was also supported by the continued exclusion of organized Sunni forces from the political process and the establishment of ethnic-religious quotas whenever governmental structures were negotiated. Unsurprisingly, political parties when successful were also organized on religious-ethnic lines.

(3) The territorial integrity of the state was severely compromised from the outset. Admittedly, this was a function of the particular ending of the

first Gulf War, which left the Kurds with an autonomous area. But the paucity of American forces meant that Kurdistan was unoccupied by the United States in 2003, the CPA's control therefore could not be extended to all of Iraq's territory, and thus the Kurds could enter constitutional negotiations as agents of a de facto independent territory that as far as they were concerned might not reenter Iraq. Failure to secure Turkish support for the war, which would have led to a Turkish occupation of Kurdistan,[213] and the unavailability of American forces meant that the Kurds would be allowed to create more and more facts on the ground and could be entirely recalcitrant when it came to constitutional negotiations. Had there been an Iraqi army, any threat reinforcing the bargaining position of Arab parts of Iraq would have been far more credible.

(4) Despite some economic liberalization already under Saddam, before the war the Iraqi state was both the major producer of services and of (state subsidized) goods, including the all-important nationalized oil industry (the basis of all subsidies).[214] Under the American occupation, the decline of the state in its economic functions was in part the result of the security problem (hence of the destruction of the army) and of the disorganization of the state apparatus (through de-Baathification) and in part the consequence of other conscious efforts on the part of the CPA during the period of formal occupation. With respect to the oil industry, exposed to both sabotage and corruption, the resulting decline in potential revenues (somewhat balanced by the rise in the price of the commodity) affected all other dimensions of the effort to restore state activity. Here the culprit was primarily the security situation, a situation involving obvious negative feedback: less oil, less money, less security, less oil. It is not clear, however, that given the apparent inside knowledge of the industry and its infrastructure by the neo-Baathist insurgency anything can be done to improve the situation short of a comprehensive political bargain.[215] Other state industries were victims of reorganization schemes that produced factory shutdowns, bankruptcies, and unemployment. Here de-Baathification played an important role in getting rid of expert managerial staffs, though there are no exact numbers indicating the extent. Even more damaging were reorganization schemes starting with a privatization effort that failed in the face of international legal prohibitions[216] and the fairly general incomprehension of Iraqis, who blamed their country's lamentable economic situation on Saddam's wars and not on a structure that previously produced a high level of (admittedly oil-related) welfare. When privatization failed, mostly because there were

no buyers or even leasers for Iraqi firms under the given security conditions,[217] its apparently wholly amateurish American advocates shifted to a policy of "shrinkage" based on the elimination of subsidies that almost no Iraqi company was prepared to survive. Worse, a simultaneous elimination of all company debts and financial assets, which was supposed to help weaker companies with high debts that were still not in a position to resume production, in actuality deprived stronger companies with serious bank holdings of their ability to do so. Shrinkage there was, with most of the one hundred thousand workers of state firms left unemployed as a result; even now, plans involve rehiring only ten to fifteen thousand of them.[218] By the time the transfer of "sovereignty" brought these experiments to an end, the damage was done.

The four dimensions of state destruction certainly had independent motives, even if they might appear "rational" or "logical" in terms of some imperialist grand design to keep Iraq weak and dependent. The state apparatus and the symbols of statehood were victims of the revolutionary radicalism of the occupiers, goaded on, to be sure, by office seekers and Iraqi enemies of the older central state. Thus the state's people fell apart both because of the occupier's policies and because there were large groups that understood their identities in alternative and competing ways. The state's territory fell apart because the occupation was powerless to reunite it, despite some intentions to that effect, for example, the toying with the idea of Turkish destruction of independent Kurdistan. The state in its economic capacity fell apart both because of the security situation and the ideological antistatist proclivities of the occupiers. All these dimensions were mutually reinforcing, obviously, in their negative consequences. But in all of them, the failure of the classically Weberian dimension of the monopoly or near monopoly of the means of large-scale violence has pride of place, and it is a dimension that reinforces the connection of all the others. Given the extreme tenuousness of the assumption in this context that the small American forces were sufficient to provide security, a tenuousness understood by the leaders of the CPA, their destruction of the Iraqi army and civil apparatus can only be described as wanton state destruction.

Given state destruction, admittedly, it becomes true after all to describe the American project, eventually, as both regime change and state building. A very important part of both these burdens had to be assumed by the constitution-making process. Not only would a new constitution have to establish a new structure of government, it would also have to reestablish the territorial integrity of an Iraqi state, the political organization that could maintain it, and presumably a locus of services, rights, and obligations that could again produce a minimum Iraqi collective identity. Such a burden is a difficult one for constitution makers.

State and Constitution

Historically, all modern constitution making presupposes successful state making. It may be valid to argue, as did Raymond Carré de Malberg, that since all states have a constitution in at least the eighteenth-century sense or in the sense of Kelsen's material constitution, the state and its first constitution are co-original.[219] The continuity of the state in revolutions thus implies, as already argued, the continuity of a minimal constitution. This does not change the fact that even revolutionary constitutions are made in most cases for a preexisting, even if already minimally constituted, state. State making in revolutions then means the building or rebuilding of the state under a new constitution but on the foundations of a preexisting state. In a case such as Iraq, which was a state before the American invasion and occupation, it is hard to see how public power and public security, and therefore the *object* for which constitutions would be made and that it is meant to reorganize and regulate, could come from any other arrangement of the polity than a state. This theoretical point has been persuasively argued by Dieter Grimm, who has further maintained, in the tradition of Schmitt's *Verfassungslehre*, that the *subject* of constitution making as well as the object presupposes a state, in other words, unified public powers capable of being activated by a people or a nation as a constituent power.[220] Accordingly, if a state did not exist before constitution making, or if it was destroyed, the logically prior act of state making would have to proceed simultaneously with constitution making. That this is possible is shown by the historical examples of the formation of federations and federal states where a new subject (state) is constituted from old subjects (states) in some kind of constitutional treaty.[221] Even in such contexts, the perspective advocated by Grimm can be sustained, because as we see from the example of the United States both in 1776 and 1787, the units that formed the confederation and federal state in constitution making themselves had well-organized states with close enough approximations of public monopolies of the legitimate means of violence. Here both the subject and object of constitution making were public powers. Nevertheless, I believe in any case that the notion that private powers cannot be the source of constitutional authority is belied by the role of juridically private conventions in the American states in the period 1775 to 1780 and the round tables in the recent experiences of the new democracies. In these cases, *only* new forms of public legitimacy had to be generated for private organizations, and any agreements emerging from private spheres had to be approved in public political procedures. Of course, Grimm would answer that even these experiments presuppose "stateness" or public powers with the requisite monopolies either existing before or constituted during the constitution-making process, at least as the object of constitution making.

However, what the American invasion and occupation in Iraq did was to introduce both serious doubts concerning the legitimacy of the "subject" of constitution making and equally serious uncertainty about the "object" for which a constitution would be made. This issue of legitimacy I already discussed, but I can briefly restate it here. The foreign occupying power has no right under international law to give the occupied country a constitution. By implication, neither do its Iraqi agents such as the IGC.[222] Private organizations, like political parties, not organized in a public body, also have no legal right to do so, but they could, as set against a foreign occupier, generate political legitimacy under conditions resembling the round tables of Poland, Hungary, and South Africa. I will return to this point in later chapters, but I will say here that this has not happened in Iraq because of the narrow, exclusionary bases of the constitutional negotiating process under the shadow and influence of foreign imposition.

The situation is even worse with the "object" for which constitutions are made: public power. The issue of unresolved state structure goes so far as to have consequences for organizational choices on almost all levels, making the writing of a constitution that could be taken seriously extremely difficult. The problem was both dedifferentiation and disorganization of the Iraqi state. The differentiation and independence of something like that state both from an *external* power and *internal* private powers with their own armies allows considerable doubt. The occupation forces, now under simply the name of "coalition forces" or "multinational forces" (MNF), as well as a large number of private military contractors (that is, mercenaries of a new type), remain a state within the "state" not subject in any way to Iraqi law or constitutional restraints. These could be written into constitutions in general but did not apply to the major forces of violence and incarceration in particular. With the de facto Kurdish entity, which acts like a full-fledged state within its territory—and at times elsewhere where its forces are engaged nominally under an Iraqi flag—and the assertion of various uncontrollable forms of local rule, all with their own military forces, the boundaries of state authority or authorities are extremely poorly defined even if we forget the foreign forces. From this point of view, the insurrection may be particularly ugly and violent, but legally it represents more or less the same problem as the other violent nonstate organizations that control people and territory and cannot themselves be controlled. The organizations that in the modern world are called upon to enforce "stateness"—the "national" army, the "public" administration, and the "national" police—lay in shambles because of deliberate American policy. As to the issue of security and the control of violence, it is clear that the enforcement of any constitution in the legal sense cannot focus or rely exclusively on public authorities but must also and to an equal extent take into account the very private powers (and their good will) that are themselves the greatest threats to legality. The issue, however, is not only that of violence and security. Public services, enforcement of contracts, and in most areas personal relations too are under the control of juridically private organizations, in the latter case religious organizations. In such a situation, Grimm's question concerning the very meaning and possibility of a constitution makes a great deal of sense. One makes a constitution, but it establishes or regulates only a small part of political power in the country—and by no means the most important part.

Because Iraq *was* a state before the beginning of the American war to change its regime, in principle constitution making here could have followed the pattern established with the overthrow of *old regimes*, one relying on inherited state structures. Instead, there was a set of policies, coordinated or not, whose aim or at least consequence was to destroy the Iraqi state as well as the regime.[223] As a result, fragments of the old state went underground. The very same Sunni elites that were being deprived of employment in the state organs were also denied all representation in the political process, and they were being given an underground army or armies, fueled by powerful new resentments, in a context where there were no effective military forces available to control them or even to prevent their access to the enormous amount of ordinance stored in various parts of the country. The result was not only the insurrection and the collapse of public security but the impossibility of dismantling militias and private military organizations. In short, the effort to temporarily replace the dismantled Iraqi state by the occupation state was strikingly unsuccessful: no one established any kind of monopoly over the legitimate means of violence except for the political authorities relying on the Peshmerga in Kurdistan—the Kurdish quasi-state that was neither dismantled nor occupied but strengthened in its autonomy, and whose strengthening was a sign of Iraq's disintegration and of the difficulties of rebuilding its state.

To sum up then: the destruction of the state in Iraq placed tremendous burdens on the constitution makers of Iraq, whoever they were going to be, operating under whatever procedure. Their task was both the creation of the new regime and, logically prior to that, the rebuilding of the Iraqi state in its political and territorial integrity. Evidently, success would depend on other efforts, arguably even more important: the reconstruction of the forces of violence and administration. And all of these concerns were interconnected, because a unified military and administration was not possible without a general state bargain on the constitutional level, and a constitution could hardly be made for a country in civil war. Arguably, such a task was impossible, given both the bad faith of the Americans in ceding real autonomy and the security situation, which could be linked to state destruction. On the other hand, the emergence of autonomous, popular forces on the terrain of constitution making and the reluctant concession of the Americans to a stronger UN role in the process gave the constitution-making process at least a chance at becoming autonomous (Sistani's role) and inclusive (Brahimi's role). And if these forces had been successful in converting the process of constitution making into an autonomous, legitimate, national and inclusive effort, it was just possible that a significant part of the insurrection would have joined the political process at an early stage. Thus the security situation and incipient civil war that always threatened to reduce the political process to a mere sideshow could have been perhaps marginalized by a different political, constitutional process. This did not happen, because a convincing and broadly legitimate political process was subverted relatively soon. If anything, the failed constitution-making process became an additional source of conflict and violent confrontation.

As we now see, the margin of error on the part of constitutional negotiations dealing with state making is much smaller than it is in the case of constitution making in general. If, however, the state-making part fails, the possible "success" of the rest of the constitutional product becomes irrelevant. One cannot make a constitution for a failed or nonreconstituted state. I will argue that the model of constitution making adopted was actually suitable when abstractly considered for the double task of state reconstruction and regime creation. In the Iraqi case, compared to others, failure of a part of the process would have far more devastating consequences than elsewhere. To understand what could have been possible, I will now turn to a theoretical and comparative consideration of the specific model of constitution making adopted in Iraq.

[2]

Postsovereign Constitution Making

The New Paradigm (and Iraq)

> Of all regimes of which we know [modern democracy] is the only one to have represented power in such a way as to show that power is an *empty place* and to have thereby maintained a gap between the symbolic and the real. It does so by virtue of a discourse which reveals that power belongs to no one; that those who exercise power do not possess it; that they do not, indeed, embody it . . .
>
> —Claude Lefort, "Permanence of the Theologico-Political?" (1981)

When in my first article on Iraq I began to play with the idea of recommending the paradigm of constitution making drawn from central Europe and South Africa, I must admit that I did so with the gravest of self-doubts.[1] The model I will discuss in this chapter was one developed for indigenous, postrevolutionary transformations involving legal continuity. Iraq had an *externally* imposed, *revolutionary* rupture involving a complete break in legality. To accommodate this difference, my theoretical slight of hand, perhaps not even entirely clear to me, was to treat the Americans as the "Russians" and their Iraqi clients as the "Communists," so to speak, and I tried to imagine a negotiated transition under pressure from below, with the Shi'ites playing the role of the leading force of an ascendant civil society. Call it late cold war nostalgia, on my part, though mine was far less destructive than, say, Vice President Cheney's brand, which helped to produce a hopeless war. I merely tried to imagine a perhaps impossible peace. Remarkably, however, within a few months, by November 15, 2003, at the latest, and with some changes in early 2004, a version of the paradigm I had in mind was actually adopted in Iraq, under the strong pressure of the movement led by the Grand Ayatollah Sistani, the one cleric who arguably could count (back then) as *the* leader of the Shi'ite community in Iraq.[2] Yet my early doubts were also well founded: the model adopted was always a pathological or highly defective version. Despite Sistani's ultimate rejection, the fact that it was adopted and remained in place kept enough Shi'ite political streams within the process of transformation for the political process to somehow stay on track until the formation of a so-called National Unity Government in 2006. But the defective or pathological nature of the paradigm meant that it failed to produce a historical compromise among the main forces of society and thus the more general political legitimacy that would have allowed the *two* resulting constitutions to play the very difficult double role allotted to them: state rebuilding and the construction of a new, legitimate Iraqi regime.

When I say that Iraq adopted "the paradigm I had in mind," I am referring to a two-stage process of constitution making (and the making of two constitutions rather than one), with an interim constitution as its centerpiece and with relatively free, competitive elections between the two stages, the transition between them provided by the election of a *nonsovereign* constitutional assembly. This assembly is not a sovereign one in the sense of being able to produce either its own rules or a final constitution without any limitation whatsoever. In my view, the model adopted in Iraq was pathological in that the classical version, from Warsaw to Johannesburg, involved, under whatever name, round-table (or multiparty) negotiations of the main political forces of society concerning the making of interim constitutional arrangements and something like the famous South African "talks about talks" concerning the setting up and procedures of the round tables themselves. In Iraq, the process (the talks) and the metaprocess (the talks about talks) were replaced by one-sided imposition or pseudoconsultation, which was reflected in Sistani's rejection of the interim constitution. That would be equivalent to the hypothetical and absurd case of Solidarity or the ANC not accepting a round-table deal that the government in place enacted anyway.[3] This defect was not merely a question of details. It had to do with the absence of a central element of the model: the basis of its negotiated process and consensual legitimacy. Without it, none of the other elements could play their desired roles.

In this chapter, I will first discuss the elements of the new paradigm, their historical origins, their functions, and their interconnections. Next, I discuss the political contexts out of which the model emerged and the relationship of changing contexts to the eventual availability of the model as a solution to the fundamental dilemma: how to begin democratically where there is no democracy beforehand. I conclude by considering what was missing in the Iraqi case as a function of the new context and as the failure of constitutional learning.

Postsovereign Constitution Making and Its Elements

In the midst of the dramatic events of 1989 and 1990, it was the (West) German constitutional theorist Ulrich Preuss, expert advisor to the Round Table of the German Democratic Republic, who first called our theoretical attention to the transformation of inherited paradigms of constitution making.[4] In a series of articles and a book, he insisted on the obsolescence of the revolutionary democratic model as old as the American and French (and, in my view, even the English)[5] revolutions and on the emergence in central Europe, including the old German Democratic Republic, of a new model no longer based on or appealing to the *potestas absoluta* of the sovereign, unified, constituent power of the people. Preuss identified a multiplicity of constitution-making events and stages as the marks of the model he saw in action: legal continuity, changes through amending the old constitution, the organizing role of round-table negotiations, and the decline of constituent assemblies. With several years' hindsight, especially with the full unfolding of the new paradigm in South Africa and its subsequent adoption in Nepal, one should certainly add the negotiation of an interim constitution and the drafting of a final one by a freely elected assembly to this list. More controversial, perhaps, but still logically required would be the inclusion of a constitutional court created under the interim constitution during the process of generating the final constitution.

To understand the version of the paradigm adopted in Iraq and its inevitable problems, it should be helpful to present its basic elements as they emerged, starting with Spain in the 1970s, continuing with central European and some East European cases in 1989 through 1991, and culminating in the South African model of the early 1990s. Most of the relevant elements reappeared most recently in Nepal's democratic transition, admittedly with the twist of legal discontinuity. I will focus on the specific historical cases only when there are significant differences between a case and most others. Admittedly, I derive the paradigm from the most advanced case, the South African one, which certainly involved learning from previous history. But South Africans took some departures that were entirely unique, and it is risky to include them in a model or a paradigm. I do so for logical and normative reasons.

To sustain the claim that the paradigm is that of a *new*, contemporary democratic method of constitution making, I will make occasional comparisons with the great historical paradigms of the American and French revolutions, with the additional simplification that the former is treated under the eventually triumphant version first used in Massachusetts in 1780 (and in New Hampshire slightly later) and more influentially in Philadelphia in 1787 (the "American Model"), while the latter is considered under two variants that remained historically relevant ("French type I": 1791/1848, versus "French type II": 1793–1795), involving two interpretations of the role of the people in the constituent process.[6] Since the idea of the interim constitution in the sense used here was introduced in France in 1945 and 1946, I will have several occasions to refer to the making of the Fourth Republic, a marginal case of French type II.

Two-Stage Process and Interim Constitution

In a sense, of course, all constitution making involves many events, thus arguably several stages. What gradually emerges from Spain (1975 through 1977) to South Africa (1991 and 1996) is the new reliance on two fundamental stages that foresee from the outset the production of two constitutions, an interim one and a final one, where the rules of the first not only occupy some kind of temporary or provisional "space" but, more importantly, structurally constrain the making of the second. Such constraints play a highly important *double role* when they posit rules for the drafting and enactment of a final constitution. They limit the constitutional assembly and they affirm the merely transitional role and timeframe of the interim constitution itself.

The existence of a fully developed, explicitly interim constitution is the most important documentary evidence of the new paradigm of constitution making, and yet it appears to be somewhat exceptional if we take all the cases one by one.[7] There is *formally* speaking no such instrument produced until Hungary in October 1989 (amended in 1990), the third case.[8] Before then, we find only a Law of Reform (*ley para la reforma politica*) in Spain[9] and individual laws and constitutional amendments regulating the transition in Poland.[10] And even afterward, the Czechoslovak Round Table, concentrating on forming a new government, came up with very little legislation, constitutional or otherwise,[11] and the Bulgarian Round Table produced agreements only on three packages of documents, including important constitutional amendments, an electoral law, and some not very elaborate regulations for the process of the Grand National (constitutional) Assembly.[12] Conversely, the German Democratic Republic's Round Table produced a draft for a (never enacted) *final* constitution. In fact, even the Hungarian interim constitution, which never regulated the making of the final constitution, turned out to be "permanent," because the second stage of the process, left more or less to the ordinary and open-ended amending process, failed.[13] In contrast, the two-stage character of the Spanish and Polish processes was maintained without a full-fledged interim constitution, possibly indicating the undesirability of an overelaborate interim document that can make the drafting of a final one superfluous, especially if it does not regulate the final constitution-making process, as in the Hungarian case. Strictly speaking, an elaborate and complete interim constitution as part of a fully regulated two-stage process was produced only in South Africa and now Nepal, and so far, we can say only that it was in the former case alone that it successfully regulated the two-stage process and its culmination. If we disregard the successfulness of the attempt, the Iraqi Transitional Administrative Law belongs to this latter, in my view most advanced pattern, at least formally. The TAL was an elaborate and complete interim constitution, with provisions that were supposed to fully regulate the subsequent process of constitution making, at least in principle, something painfully absent from the Hungarian prototype, for example. (The TAL will be discussed in detail in subsequent chapters.)

This somewhat exceptional status of interim constitutions in the history of the two-stage model may be illusory and a function of an overly restrictive definition of "constitution." Whether we consider an interim constitution a regular feature of the new paradigm depends on the meaning of the term *constitution*. If by "constitution" we mean legal rules that establish and regulate the lawmaking, applying, and adjudicating process, namely Kelsen's material constitution or Hart's secondary rules, encompassed or not by a single, comprehensive formal document, then the answer is emphatically different than if we define "constitution" in the formal, documentary sense, insulated by distinct rules of revision.[14] All the various legal instruments produced in the first stage of the new processes had constitutional regulation in Kelsen's material sense as their fundamental goal, whether or not they were incorporated in a new formal document called the interim constitution, in an old constitution through an extensive set of amendments, or by a combination of these methods.[15] The (double) purpose of the devices was everywhere the same, successfully combining the necessity of some kind of provisional government with the requirement of subjecting this form too to constitutional limitations *and* combining the needs of constitutional learning and troubleshooting in the early stages of constitution making with the requirement that the new constitution be insulated against easy alteration.

CONSTITUTIONALIZATION OF THE PROVISIONAL GOVERNMENT

Provisional governments are ordinarily inimical to constitutionalism. They are needed in revolutionary situations, when incumbents have lost power altogether, or during other forms of radical change, when they are neither trusted nor strong enough to institute a series of political changes from above. The classical provisional government formula linked to sovereign constitution making, as in the two French models, operates either in a context of legal rupture, without legal limitations, or as a commissioner of the constituent assembly, limited only by that assembly. In either case, the sovereign authority, either the provisional executive or the legislature, is under no legal limitation whatsoever. The two-stage process is meant to remedy this state of affairs by negotiating with incumbents a transition to types of provisional arrangements where the new executive and/or the new legislature themselves will be under law, specifically constitutional law. That law, whether it is a full-fledged basic law, a set of organic laws, or a package of amendments, will be in fact (if not in legal form) the interim constitution of the transitional regime.[16] With respect to sovereign constitution making of French types I and II, this interim constitution applies constitutionalism, namely fundamental legal limits to the powers it establishes, also to the process and not just to the resulting political powers of constitution making.[17] By this highly innovative feature, the paradigm avoids the dictatorship that Carl Schmitt postulates as the political form of the exercise of the constituent power.[18] If the previous regime was a dictatorship, as in all the cases treated here, the shift to such an interim constitution is therefore already regime change (to an interim constitutional regime). At least on a symbolic level, a full, documentary, interim constitution, a constitution in Kelsen's formal sense,[19] expresses this state of affairs better than some political packages or a mere series of laws and amendments. The latter modify the existing constitution and retain the appearance of regime continuity (though in fact contradicting the reality of change on the most central point).[20] But as we will see, the reasons are not only on the symbolic level. A little exploration in the longer-term history of interim constitutions can help us see this more clearly.

The most important *normative* reason for adopting an interim constitution was strongly implied by the makers of the so-called *préconstitution* (or "*petite* Constitution," formally the *Loi constitutionnelle* of November 2, 1945), which helped establish the Fourth French Republic. That law[21] passed in a popular referendum that called for a new constitutional assembly,[22] provided for both clear limits to that assembly (in particular, a rigid timetable and the requirement of a ratificatory referendum), and required the provisional government to have some separation of powers uncharacteristic of "convention government."[23] Because there was binding of the constituent assembly in advance, and not only by the requirement of a referendum, the making of the constitution of the Fourth Republic represented a marginal case of French type II and already points to our two-stage paradigm.[24] However, because of the unfortunate history of that republic, the denunciations of its final constitution, and the frequent abuse of the instrument elsewhere (for example, in the Arab world), interim documents have had a relatively bad name until recently, when they played a dramatic and positive (if implicit) role in the Spanish transition, a more explicit one in the Hungarian regime change, and achieved the most developed form in the great South African transformation.[25] The original reason for creating the instrument was conditioned by the not unrealistic political fear of dictatorships of any kind, given that France had just endured a foreign-imposed dictatorship. Theoretically, provisional government after a rupture had to be disconnected from dictatorship, and it was the task of the interim constitution to accomplish this task. Given our political predilections, we can describe the interim constitution as antirevolutionary or as an attempt to domesticate revolution. Given French history, it was a highly plausible expectation that in an unrestrained revolutionary process one or the other side would dominate and either make a provisional dictatorship permanent or impose *its* authoritarian constitution. This was the source of the aspiration to apply the principle of constitutionalism not only to the result but also the process of making constitutions. Obviously, that would have appeared like a contradiction in terms to authors who believed in a fully unbound, unlimited constituent power that by definition had to be conceived "in the state of nature." Given that assumption, in the European (originally French) tradition of revolutionary constitution making, constitutional assemblies invalidate all previously constituted powers and unite in themselves the plenitude of all powers.[26] Schmitt was right in calling them *sovereign dictators*—even if he was not generally right in tracing modern dictatorship as such to this modality primarily.[27] An equally or more important threat that motivates actors to apply constitutionalism to the process of constitution making is the institution of provisional government that is legally unchecked before the meeting of the constituent assembly that justifies its existence. Such a government has a far better chance of transforming itself into a permanent dictatorship than a constituent assembly, which it would then be able to control in terms of its election and procedures. An interim constitution, if successfully enacted and enforced, represents a fundamental device by which the constitutional assembly and the provisional government both are subjected to quasi-constitutional rules for the duration of their tenure, possibly limiting that tenure itself in time (and punctuated by a new election).

The French *préconstitution* of 1945 was a minimal document involving minimal constraints. The French constitution-making process of 1945 and 1946 can hardly be said to be a genuinely two-stage one, except at the logical level. Moreover, the *préconstitution*, though enacted by referenda, did not escape the problem of the unconstrained government of the liberation imposing the rules for its establishment, and thus the problem of an arguably illegitimate or merely factual beginning that was to plague the Fourth Republic to the end. These two related problems show that the interim constitutions' true home is not revolutionary rupture[28] but, in terms of the scheme introduced in the previous chapter, coordinated or negotiated transition. (Iraq returned to the problems of the French prototype, perhaps unsurprisingly, because in both cases a previous authoritarian regime was eliminated in war, producing a legal rupture.) But what ties the two types of uses together is the issue of dictatorship and the desire to apply constitutionalism to the process of constitution making itself.

The problem of dictatorship during constitution-making efforts is not restricted to contexts of legal breaks, and therefore the antidictatorial, constitutionalist impulse has an important role to play in enacting interim fundamental laws where there is legal continuity. This is the case when the "old regime" is either a dictatorship or a highly exclusionary polity. In almost all such cases, at least recently, from Spain and Chile to Hungary and South Africa, one can document the efforts of previous power holders who can no longer avoid some kind of transition from authoritarian rule to create from above a "hard democratic" or "soft authoritarian" regime in which their social, economic, personal, and even political power positions are protected or favorably transformed. Elections held under their rules are likely to produce undemocratic results, and no democratic oppositions can or should accept such imposed solutions if they can help it. At the same time, democratic oppositions may be unable or unwilling to try the path of revolutionary transformation, as was indeed the case from the 1970s to 1990s. I will return to the empirical problem of how this situation typically leads to round-table negotiations, given a particular type of power balance along with appropriate expectations about the future. While the empirical outcome of a detailed interim constitution in the same contexts is not equally pervasive, logically the creation of such a transitional document is nevertheless very compelling.[29] As we have seen in Hungary, the attempt to restrict the constitutional product to mere organic rules (materially, a constitutional minimum) can be difficult in cases where the need for reassurance and guarantees of both sides (the veil of ignorance problem) is great.[30]

The key point is that in the case of a negotiated transition, as opposed to a revolutionary rupture, there are two projects rather than one that can lead to authoritarian solutions. The negotiations are between old-regime actors that have typically tried but failed to enact system-preserving reforms from above (soft dictatorship) and actors who by virtue of their total opposition to the existing system aim at revolutionary democracy, with all its very negative personal and institutional consequences for incumbents and their relations. In such negotiations, the opposition can protect itself from the attempts of old-regime actors to maintain their power openly or even in disguised ways, while these actors can in turn gain guarantees that there will be no revolutionary dictatorship that would treat them, collectively and individually, as enemies of the new regime. Given the complexity and potential vulnerability of agreements that would achieve these aims, the actors generally seek both formal protections in a constitutional type of enactment and ways of guaranteeing the survival of key parts of the interim constitution in the final document. Thus, while the French type of *préconstitution* involved only procedural limits on the constituent assembly, the new interim constitutions either have to seek to impose limits on its contents, along with procedural safeguards likely to preserve agreements regarding contents, or establish a very wide range of procedural safeguards and their institutional protections, which are likely to have substantive consequences and which will be difficult to eliminate in the final constitution. An example of the former are the famous South African "Thirty-four Constitutional Principles." An example of the latter is the assignment of final constitution making to a normal parliament working under a consensual amendment rule, as in Hungary. In both of these empirical cases there was, for logically very sound reasons, an institution safeguarding an interim constitution "worthy of defense"—a new and powerful constitutional court.

In these contexts, then, there are two (or more) sides that could potentially impose a constitution, and the purpose of the interim constitution is to fashion a "second best" solution each can live with, since no one side is able to achieve its preferred solution. Here too the antidictatorial or anti-imposition logic leads each side to desire (however reluctantly) that constitutionalist norms be imposed both on the process and the results of constitution making.

Understanding the purpose of interim constitutions in terms of the demands of constitutionalism almost tautologically indicates why such a constitution should be designed, if possible, in the formal sense as a documentary interim constitution and not only as a set of secondary rules that satisfy Kelsen's material notion. In fact, Kelsen already thought, despite the British example, that a constitution in the formal sense was an important way to serve the purpose of a material constitution, of safeguarding its norms from arbitrary alteration.[31] The point applies especially to contexts where one or two sides have strong motives to have a provisional government on their own terms. For example, an interim constitution that regulates government in a provisional period but is established only on the level of ordinary, individual laws would run the risk of alteration by ordinary legislation and would not protect minority political forces during the transition period. While preferable to a revolutionary provisional government, a mere statutory scheme could be easily transformed into one, without illegality. A provisional government with a documentary constitution is therefore preferable, and one with an amendment rule requiring more than ordinary legislation to alter it would be better still. One protected by an amendment rule and enforced by some separate authority, most likely a court—in other words, a constitution in the full formal sense of the term—would be best and most adequate in terms of the main purpose of the interim constitution. But here one must be careful, as overdoing the protection of the interim constitution and its insulation from change may interfere with its second purpose: the facilitation of normative and political learning.

CONSTITUTIONAL LEARNING

While the idea of applying constitutionalism to the making of constitutions is more or less conscious, that of facilitating learning between the two stages is not. Constitutionalism itself has been interestingly defined in the legal domain as "learning not to learn." Rigidly understood, that notion would ban amendment rules and would have disastrous consequences similar to those of the almost unamendable French Constitution of 1791, which survived less than a year. But amendment rules do mean that learning is to be made more difficult in the case of constitutional rather than ordinary legal norms; we do not amend the constitution as readily after disappointment. The two-stage process rightly constructed creates an intermediary site of learning, because it invites the constitution makers to learn between the two stages and apply the results when drafting the final constitution. For its own duration, the interim constitution should allow for its amendment more easily than the final constitution; the rule of ratification for the interim constitution should likewise be more relaxed than that for the final constitution. But it should also be more difficult to amend the interim constitution than to adopt ordinary legislation.

An interim constitution by its nature implies a constitutional learning process involving two fundamental stages. This claim is itself based on *learning* from the common historical experience of many constitutions (the U.S. Constitution, the French Constitution of the Fifth Republic, the *Grundgesetz*) that emerged after the dramatic failure of a recent forerunner whose problems became the occasions for important learning experiences and corrective efforts. While the same cannot be said about minimal preconstitutions such as ones adopted in France, the more detailed interim constitutions clearly attempt to institutionalize this kind of learning. Only a *detailed* constitution allows learning over a wide enough range. But only when that constitution is *interim* can it organize learning within a single process, making it less likely that specific constitutional problems will lead to revolutionary, totalizing breaks such as the one that occurred in France in 1792. If successful, they also make it less likely that experiments in less radical revision will lead to the replacement of all of the earlier achievements along with genuine problems, resulting in the replacement of the second constitution by a third, then a fourth, and so on, as occurred in France and many Latin American countries. The learning advantage of an interim constitution is that political formulas that are indispensable in the short term but very questionable in the long run (such as consociationalism, rigid power sharing, or great coalitions) can be included in interim constitutions, if carefully planned, without the fear of their transposition and insulation in the permanent document.[32] Thus the new type of interim constitutions have allowed—as they must—a broad learning process to take place across two interlinked constitutions.

There are many constitutional problems that learning across two constitutions can address. Most obviously, there is the possibility of incoherent drafting, where one article should be changed to make it consistent with another or with the rest of the constitution. More important and difficult are problems where there is no logical incompatibility but where the actual functioning of rules leads to undesirable results. Here the attachment of beneficiaries to a type of malfunctioning, such as dramatic and unfair overrepresentation, will be a problem more difficult to handle with a normal amendment rule giving some veto powers to minorities. Conditions of democratic transition may require a very high threshold of consensus, for example through consociational devices, which within a final constitution would have a self-freezing character. In the longer term, they may make a country ungovernable and lay the ground for future civil war, given inevitable changes in the original power and demographic constellation. The South African approach of mandating consociationalism in the first stage while not enshrining it in the second stage, allowing the freely elected assembly to move instead to *constitutional* protection of minorities, has been particularly successful in this regard.[33] Only a two-stage process involving a relatively detailed interim constitution allows for this clever, temporary use of consociationalism without provoking a revolt by the majority.

There are important prerequisites for constitutional learning to take place. Since experimentation must occur during the beginning of the process, as already stated, a considerably more flexible amendment rule for the interim constitution must be established than would be appropriate for the permanent constitution in the same sociopolitical setting.[34] More importantly, beyond the provisions or principles consensually agreed upon by the main participants, interim constitutions must not interfere with the learning processes involved in making the permanent constitution.[35] No interim constitution could violate its own purpose more obviously than one that through its own rules both inhibited learning and tended to make rules of ratification for a permanent constitution that are destined to fail. While some interim constitutions may legitimately become permanent (as in Hungary) when a relatively open final process repeatedly fails, we risk serious abuse when the rules provided by the interim constitution are so constructed as to make the failure of the final constitution extremely likely. Finally, for an interim constitution to work as a legitimate antidictatorial and learning instrument, it must be enforceable. In Hungary and South Africa at least, the provisions of the interim constitutions have been effectively enforced by strong constitutional courts.[36]

Again, it is worth stressing what is new in the two-stage paradigm. It is true of course that many successful constitutions, such as the U.S. Federal Constitution, the *Grundgesetz*, and the Constitution of the Fifth Republic, were parts of learning processes involving two constitutions with long or short crisis periods between them. However, none of the initial constitutions—not the Articles of Confederation, the Weimar Constitution, nor the Constitution of the Fourth Republic—were said or meant to be interim or provisional, and the successor constitutions were not made according to their rules of amendment.[37] With the new model, what we have to work with is a reflexively two-stage character rather than simply an ad hoc one. Thus the new two-stage model in its completed form self-consciously and deliberately incorporates the need to learn from one stage to the next, guaranteeing that a process like the drafting of the Bill of Rights, which occurred outside the original constitution-making process in the United States, could be still accommodated *within it*, something that many critics of the first stage actually desired. The critics in the United States did have their way in that instance, eventually, but they nevertheless were disturbed about the relatively passive role to which their participation was relegated after the meeting in Philadelphia. Ultimately, as Preuss hinted at but never fully explained, it is the reflexive character that replaces the sovereign claims of the classical efforts.[38]

Thus while it is possible to regard the making of a single constitution like that of the United States in 1787 as involving a plurality of instances (the Convention, the Congress, and the ratifying Conventions), this was true only in a limited sense. As the antifederalists specifically charged, only one of these instances could play a role in actual drafting, and the state conventions were denied the power to do anything but ratify or reject the document as a whole. In the new paradigm, there are at least two instances that play a fundamental role in the drafting process: the instance that drafts the interim constitution, typically a round table of major political forces, and an instance that drafts the final document, always a freely elected body that should probably not be called a constituent assembly (*une Constituante*) in the French terminology at least, because it must operate under definite limitations set out in the interim documents and because it must actually share constitution-making powers.

In my view, it is this two-stage character above all that is the key to the idea of *post*sovereign constitution making. It is therefore only this model that fully realizes the idea of democracy elaborated by Claude Lefort, which insists on the *empty place* of power and the gap between the symbolic (the people) and the real (the institutions and political organs through which the empirical people act). With respect to the French type I, there is no instance here that can represent in the absolute sense the sovereign will of the people. But also with respect to the French type II, there is no incorporation of the people in a "two-body" version, where the natural body of the people in a referendum or the organized body of the people in a convention registers through its "yea" or "nay" the compliance of the will of the assembly with the people's will. Even with respect to the main interpretation of the American model, the people, as Madison said in a different context (*Federalist Papers* 63), are not assumed to play a role in an embodied or collective capacity even at the level of ratification. If the people can be said to be present in the new type of constituent process, this is so in a plural, complex, and always limited way that has neither the possibility of the absolute "no" of the referendum nor the unlimited constituent power incorporated in an assembly.[39]

Round-Table Agreements, Free Elections, and Nonsovereign Constitutional Assemblies

The interim constitution helps with subjecting the process of constitution making to constitutionalism but not with the vexing problem of how to begin democratically or at least legitimately where there was no democracy before. This last problem can never be solved rigorously: the French constitution makers of 1945 tried to do so, desperately and creatively, by putting elections and a referendum at the very beginning of the process, but they were nevertheless open to the charge that they determined the electoral rule undemocratically.

The famous round tables from Poland and Hungary to Bulgaria and South Africa (under whatever name—in South Africa it was called the Multi-Party Negotiating Forum) and now Nepal are called upon to solve this problem, but they can do so only if they can solve their own very likely problem of legitimacy. They *partially* deal with the latter by substituting principles such as pluralistic inclusion of the main political forces, publicity, and adherence to the rule of law for the missing principle of democratic legitimacy. The round table is a more pervasive structure for the new model than the interim constitution, at least in the formal sense. Only Spain's history lacks a round-table episode, and there either informal discussions and consultations or the otherwise very rare existence of democratic aspirations by authoritarian incumbents seems to have substituted for an initial agreement or pact.[40] Regardless of the Spanish case, János Kis is exactly right when he states that while the round table is not empirically indispensable for the type of coordinated transition that occupies the conceptual field between reform and revolution, it is nevertheless the key and even characteristic political institution for this type of change.[41]

Evidently, the round tables are new institutions with respect to the drafting assemblies of the two French models and even the American one; they are not the makers of the final constitution. But they have been compared to the drafting convention of the American model nevertheless, an argument made plausible by their coexistence with the ordinary legislative body, which they do not supersede in its normal operations and whose formal consent they must secure even with respect to constitutional drafting. In fact, they are juridically weaker, though politically stronger, than the American convention in its last and final form of appearance, as pioneered in Massachusetts and Philadelphia. Legally, the round tables are only private gatherings with no public legal status. But given the role of the old ruling party in their negotiations, round-table agreements generally amount to much more than mere recommendations that can be turned down by ratifying bodies. The official parliaments that must approve the interim constitutions for the sake of formal legality have little ability to do more than to initiate marginal changes—and sometimes not even that.

All the round tables are conscious of, to varying degrees, the lack of representative status that only electoral legitimacy could provide, and thus to some extent labor under a fundamental legitimacy problem, which can affect the degree to which they can design constitution-making rules for a subsequent freely elected constitutional assembly.[42] In Hungary, the doubts on the side of the democratic opposition went so far as to prompt an initial rejection of constitutional change, a position that could not be sustained. Countries with much stronger oppositions, such as Poland and South Africa, with their Solidarity and ANC movements and their well-known and even charismatic leaders, did not face the same problems. But the point insisted on by Preuss in the case of the GDR round table applies to all exemplars of the model, from Poland to South Africa: whatever weakness of democratic representation the round tables, some of their participants, or even external critics considered significant, the resulting legitimation problem was to be everywhere dealt with on a double level: in the procedures of the round table itself and when clearing the path to free elections. The second alone is insufficient, because the assembly chosen by free elections is not intended to have unlimited sovereign status. Binding it had to be itself a legitimate affair that could not rest on the subsequent electoral authorization.

In any case, while the procedures of round tables did vary, a common element in this model is that the final constitution would have to be the work of a freely elected parliamentary assembly and not some commission chosen by the executive, as many constitutionalists today around UN circles seem to recommend. Nevertheless, such an assembly would not, minimally, dispose over its own constitution-making rules, and more maximally may be forced to adhere to substantive principles agreed upon by the round tables. Note the somewhat paradoxical two steps. The round tables, though aware of their initial legitimacy problem, hope to generate enough legitimacy to bind the constitutional assembly. But they know that they cannot become sufficiently legitimate to draft a final constitution, even assuming popular ratification of that product. They must produce rules for free elections, specifically for the free election of a body making the final constitution. But again, this body originating in free elections can be bound, and the degree of its limitation should depend on, at least in part, the level of legitimacy generated by a given round table. Or, if there is reason to bind it because of substantive considerations, such as the need to protect discrete and insular minorities, it is important that the agency doing the binding, the round table itself, have a relatively high level of legitimacy.

Note the return of the countermajoritarian difficulty as constitutionalism is being applied to the process of constitution making. The round tables produced constitutions, more or less detailed, that were to limit democratically elected constitution makers, occasionally in terms of the substance and almost always in terms of the procedures of their activity.[43] Because they had not been democratically elected, such a significant role for the round tables could have posed a challenge to exclusively liberal, constitutionalist justifications based on the idea of submitting the process as a whole to the rule of law. And the round tables, dramatically wrestling with problems of their own legitimacy, sought a plausible response to the paradox, a response other than merely the cheerful acceptance of being in the position to impose. They did not, in other words, consider the formally correct answer to this originary problem, namely that "where there is no democracy, a purely democratic beginning of democracy is impossible," sufficient.[44]

The key to resolving these problems of legitimacy lies in the two stages permitted by the interim constitution itself. During the first stage, normative principles other than electoral authorization and accountability must be rigorously honored to make up for the democratic deficit. The most important of these principles are plurality and inclusion, publicity, and legality. Adhering to these principles provides what Jon Elster has referred to as "upstream legitimacy."[45] If these principles are not adhered to, the normative integrity of the whole constituent process becomes difficult (though not impossible) to maintain. The interim constitution must then in turn organize a second stage allowing the rigorous fulfillment of the technical preconditions of democratic elections without the possibility of deformation by those organizing existing or provisional executive powers. Herein lies the "midstream legitimacy" of interim constitutions, which is supposed to compensate for inevitable weaknesses of upstream legitimacy.[46] Whereas upstream legitimacy depends upon the procedures of enacting interim constitutions, midstream legitimacy is more a function of its design, including its procedures. Extreme lack of upstream legitimacy may, however, interfere with the successful functioning of even relatively good constitutional designs (and thus the generation of midstream legitimacy), and it is for this reason that I stress the importance of plurality (including fair procedure), publicity, and legality in establishing interim constitutions.

Here I can give only a short summary of the relevant principles. By *plurality* I mean the requirement of drawing in as broad a range of significant political participants into the negotiating process as possible and, by using a (relatively) consensual decision rule, allowing all of their voices to count. By definition, inclusion on this level cannot be perfect or complete, since it will involve some group(s) choosing (and rejecting) others as partners when none of them has been tested electorally.

The question of establishing the round table itself is indeed a difficult matter, yet everything depends on how it is done, the resulting membership, and the rules by which they are to interact and decide things. It will be central to my argument here that Iraq had no round table and that the Iraqi Governing Council, which formally produced the Transitional Administrative Law, the interim constitution, was not a round table, and it is on this point that the adoption in Iraq of the new method of constitution making fundamentally failed. But where does the round table (or rather, its members) come from? How do the rules for the negotiations emerge? In a democracy, one does not shoot one's way into power, Paul Bremer liked to say, forgetting both that he himself had just done that and that, while he had supreme power, whatever Iraq was, it was not (yet) a democracy. Members of the round tables, such as Solidarity, the ANC, the Hungarian Democratic Opposition, the Inkatha Freedom Party, and the Nepali Maoists, have used and still use various forms of power and indeed violence as well as nonviolence to become members of the types of bodies from which Bremer excluded Arab nationalists, including the neo-Baathists, the Sadrists, and so on. But who decides who participates? The only answer is that round tables must aim at the greatest possible inclusiveness, excluding only those who would use their participation and the consensus requirements to subvert the process. In general, it is much better to err on the side of inclusion than on the side of exclusion, as the efforts of the architects of the two South African round tables (Codesa and the MPNF) have shown.[47] While the formal invitations may begin on the government side, the invited members themselves may then delegate new participants, and late new claimants may also appear, clamoring to participate. Then the only serious questions become whether the group represents a sufficiently important political segment of society and whether it is capable of relatively constructive participation on the formal level.

Ordinarily, it should not be difficult for a representative group of external observers to determine whether the main cleavages of a society are "represented" by groups having some genuine organization and support, and when in doubt, their advice should certainly be relied on to complete the process of the inclusion of at least the main groups. But it is not enough to include; those included must not be marginalized by the procedural and decision rules.

When it comes to the rules and procedures for the round tables, one runs into a problem of an infinite regress. In order to have adequate rules for round-table meetings, these should not be imposed, because then the results may be foreordained. A lack of rules can have the same effect, because without some kind of formal decision-making process, raw power will decide everything. In effect, one would need round tables to consider the procedures for round tables—or spend the first sessions on purely procedural matters, assuming that these would be decided consensually. In South Africa, there were the famous and seemingly unending "talks about talks."[48] But the rule of thumb must be that the rules for negotiation and decision must be neither left entirely implicit nor be imposed prior to the meeting of the round tables. One of the ways of ensuring the rules will be fair is either to publicly negotiate them or at least to publicly present and explain them at the beginning of the negotiations.

Publicity too cannot be complete or perfect, as Elster has well explained, if there are to be genuine negotiations. But providing for a sufficient number of public forums to present the state of the negotiations at various levels, and for sufficient time for the public to absorb information about them, certainly forces actors (as in 1787) to adopt many positions that can be justified by using arguments that appeal to groups across different particular interest and value constellations (in Rawls's terms, "public-regarding arguments").[49] Finally, *legality* under dictatorship may be fictional, but when participants in round tables take the law seriously, it shows that their work is rule constrained and never the product of the arbitrary wills of even a plurality of actors.[50] Elements of genuine legitimacy (as well as the mutual promises and commitment of major political actors) allow the interim constitution to limit the sovereign, unlimited powers of the constitutional legislature, which would typically be only a "convention" or even an ordinary parliament, not a (classical European) constituent assembly.[51] At the same time, the incomplete legitimacy of the interim constitution requires that the restrictions on a freely elected body be as limited as possible under the circumstances.

Evidently, the legitimacy of the two-stage model is only conditional until free elections can lead into the second stage. The longer the gap is between the various key events of the process (especially between the end of the old regime and the meeting of the round table, between the promulgation of the interim constitution and elections, and less so between elections and the promulgation of a final constitution), the greater the legitimacy problems of the model. Yet in a former dictatorship, one can rarely hope for ideal democratic elections in the second stage, and there are arguments (though often self-serving ones) for delay. In most cases, the greatest threat to genuine and free competition are undemocratic incumbents, and interim constitutions and other legal arrangements such as electoral rules, party rules, and disposition over public media must be so devised as to inhibit the holders of executive power from manipulating, deforming, and falsifying the elections. Of course, when the threats are multiple, coming from both the government and an insurrection, or from different actors in a civil war, it may be impossible to produce or enforce measures restraining the repressive apparatus of the executive. Pseudoelections may be worse than no elections at all, and the longer elections are postponed, the more important "interim" arrangements legitimated by a complex of justifiable principles become.[52] But in general, the model allows the postponement of elections to a lesser extent than reform, where the old regime is still legitimate, or where there is genuine revolutionary legitimacy.

The body making the final constitution in the model, the constitutional assembly (under whatever name: convention, constitutional assembly, parliament, or even conference) must be freely elected, and constitutional commissions under the provisional executive must be entirely eschewed even when legitimated by some kind of pseudoparticipation. However, the type of electoral rule that elects the new body is an eminently contestable matter. Democratic theory in the abstract cannot decide among electoral rules. For example, there are good arguments, such as the independence of representatives and enhancement of deliberation, for single-member constituencies and thus majoritarian or plurality rules, but on the other hand, greater inclusiveness speaks for proportional representation. For a constitutional assembly, it is fatal to exclude major groups, and it makes sense therefore to opt for proportional representation, as in South Africa. To enhance other democratic virtues and governability, a mixed system, as in Bulgaria and now Nepal, with, say, half proportional list-based seats and half single-member district seats may be workable. But it is important to choose the least aggressive electoral rule possible, precisely because the body establishing it has fundamental legitimacy problems from the point of view of democratic norms. It does not have the right to choose a system that would greatly structure the conversion of votes into seats according to desiderata that have not been and could not have been democratically decided upon. And, as it is well known, proportional representation is the most passive type of electoral rule. The choice of any other rule enhancing, for example, governability, should be up to a body itself chosen by PR rules—though, admittedly, electoral rules tend to freeze, and small parties elected by PR for the constituent assembly will want to keep the rules that elected them.

Thus, like the Pennsylvania Convention of 1776, the Massachusetts Convention of 1780, and the French assemblies in types I and II with the exception of the original 1789 Assemblée Constituante, the constitutional assemblies in the two-stage paradigm are freely elected for the purpose of constitution making. At the same time, the constitutional assemblies of the model differ with respect to these great democratic models because of the limitations to which they are subjected, even if they are given special names like the Grand National Assembly in Bulgaria or where the distinction between the terms "constitutional" and "constituent assembly" is blurred, as in South Africa. Where the old French Third Republic National Assembly formula is followed, as in Poland and South Africa, requiring the joint meeting of two chambers, the so-constituted constitution-making body does not thereby escape the limitations imposed by the interim constitutional provisions.[53] The limitations can admittedly be as little as having to work under the amendment rule of the interim constitution or under ratification rules provided by that constitution for the final process, but, in fact, much more can be regulated, including the voting rules, the composition of the constitution-making committee, their voting rules, the role of outside inputs, the length of time allowed for the process, mechanisms for new elections in case of failure, and so on. Some of these restrictions (especially timeframes) could be applied to traditional constituent assemblies like the two 1946 assemblies in France, but the number of possible procedural limitations and especially the restrictions on majority rule here are very new, even if we do not focus on the extreme South African case. Of course, we should not mistake these external and prior restrictions with ones that a sovereign assembly establishes entirely for itself after it first meets.[54]

I am assuming that the constitutional assembly would be the normal legislature as well, an idea that goes against the American model since the Massachusetts Convention of 1780 and was accepted even by Sieyès only reluctantly, at the beginning of the French and European models.[55] In France, however, the separation between the constituent and legislative power has been subsequently maintained only on the level of the amending power, which in the nineteenth century was a theoretical matter only, since constitutions up until the Third Republic were mostly changed by revolution rather than revision.[56] The new model has an interesting solution to this problem, in principle, though the practice is different than the form. During the first stage, the inherited legislative assembly and the round table exist jointly, and while substantive decisions are made by the round table, these have no legal force until the legislature formally enacts them. The assumption is that the government will control its legislature as it did under the dictatorship and fulfill the bargains it makes, but the assumption may not be always right.[57] The legislature may rebel, protected by the rule of law, or it can be used manipulatively by the government to violate its bargains. In the second stage, however, this legislature inherited from the previous dictatorship cannot be left in place. Even if one managed to create a co-opted legislature by appointment, as was partially done in Czechoslovakia, as was first suggested in Iraq by the November 15, 2003, "Agreement," and as was now done in Nepal, after the free election of a constitutional assembly it would be absurd to leave the appointed and concocted legislature also in place.[58] Other methods of differentiating the constitutional and legislative assemblies within a single body could model themselves on the Indian pattern in 1948,[59] and hopefully this is what will occur in Nepal, the only current case where the constitutional assembly has not yet been elected.

Legal Continuity and the Use of Amendment Rules

I now come to somewhat more contingent but nevertheless very characteristic elements of the new model. The first is legal continuity. The new model generally avoids both the legal and institutional state of nature in which one line of thought from Sieyès to Schmitt put the *pouvoir constituant* and the illegalities involved in the Philadelphia Convention's break with the amendment rules of the Articles of Confederation. All the characteristic cases from Spain to South Africa involve no legal break between old regime and new. This has several aspects beyond the matter of shoring up legitimacy to those with a legalistic orientation or more minimally ensuring some legal certainty and predictability to all in the midst of radical change. One is that the legislative activity of the first stage is under the aegis of a parliament inherited from the old regime, even if, as in Spain, it is used to rubber-stamp the decisions of a reformist government or, more commonly, the decisions of the round tables. The second is that one way or the other there is a reliance on the old regime's amendment rule to accomplish revolutionary change through legal means. Either that rule is directly used by parliament to make changes, or it is itself first revised (in a revision of the revision) to allow changes to be made more easily. While both approaches were logically possible, because of some always present theoretical doubt concerning the legality of revisions of the revision, it was generally the first approach that was seen and used as more appropriate to guarantee legal continuity.[60]

Two reservations need to be made regarding this important issue. First, it is the amendment rule of the formal constitution that is used, a rule that may not have ever been seriously treated as the old regime's actual rule of change. Indeed, the legality being preserved in many of the cases is fictional or created for the occasion, since the old regimes were dictatorships with paper constitutions that may have been routinely disregarded. Nevertheless, even a fictional legality or legal continuity can produce the element of predictability and stability needed for at least some legitimation in the sociological sense, and if not that, at least a stabilization of expectations. Second, when an amendment rule was used *for real* for the first time, there was also a risk that it would be unusable in practice. That certainly could be the case for previous rule-of-law regimes and dictatorships, as the cases of the Articles of Confederation and the Constitution of 1791 in the age of democratic revolutions, the Czechoslovak constitution inherited by the opposition in 1989 and 1990, and the European treaties of the present tend to show. In such situations, the example of the American framers seems to be a better one than that of the other relevant constitutional politicians, who blindly stick to legality. Or, at the very least, in Czechoslovakia the avoidance of a revision of the revision, whatever one thinks of that procedure, could be said to have led to the failure of constitution making in the Federal State.[61]

At the same time, one should be very careful with *both* the demand of complete legality and a permissive attitude toward illegality. As even the history of the first interim constitution, the French *préconstitution*, indicates, initial legal continuity with an old regime, though important, is not an absolutely essential prerequisite of the applicability of this instrument. The liberation of France from a foreign-supported dictatorship created a legal rupture and had to lead for at least a brief moment to what Duverger apparently was the first to call a *gouvernement du fait*. It was a very admirable act on the part of the government of the liberation to try as soon as possible to subject its own activities in the period of constitution making, along with that of the drafting assembly, to a set of constitutional rules, however minimal in that particular case. But even that move could not eliminate the initial *ex lex* situation in which things were decided under no law. As the government of the liberation, those who decided did so on the basis of revolutionary legitimacy earned through the act of liberation itself, a legitimacy later contested.

Granted, the French example from 1944 through 1946 does not fully belong to the paradigm discussed here. But very recently in Nepal, a version of the model was adopted involving (so far) multiparty agreements, the drafting and promulgation of an interim constitution, and hopefully free elections of a constitutional assembly bound in some procedural respects by that constitution. The origin of this formula, however, involved a legal break: the monarchy, exercising a kind of dictatorship that violated the constitution of 1990, was forced to extralegally reconstitute the illegally dissolved legislature. It was a provisional government responsible to that illegal legislature (a single-chamber body, moreover, and not the constitutional bicameral one) that participated in making the multiparty agreements that led to the interim constitution. Departing from all earlier precedents within the paradigm, the Nepali interim constitution used the legislature in place only for its ratification, and it generated a new provisional legislature by co-option until the election of the constitutional assembly.[62] Nepal had a revolutionary break, in other words, like Iraq, but tried to compensate for it by restoring an earlier parliamentary structure. As we will see, one of Iraq's most obvious deviations from the paradigm is the complete absence of any parliamentary structure from the overthrow of Saddam to the early 2005 elections of the constitutional assembly. There was an attempt to create an interim legislature by co-option (unelected caucuses), but it failed because the organs seeking to accomplish this could not generate sufficient authority in the face of great resistance. In Nepal, it first seemed that it was possible to appoint an interim legislature by party agreement, but even here subsequent charges of exclusion on ethnic bases indicate the difficulties of doing so in a legitimate manner. While politically inclusive, the parties making the deal were not ethnically inclusive at a time when identity politics cannot be disregarded.

In his typology of transitions, Kis has anticipated the possibility of a coordinated transition that may not involve legal continuity, though at the time he had no example to illustrate it.[63] He considered the option an unstable version of the type, because without legal continuity there would be no inherited parliament to formally enact changes, and the actors of the round table would be on an equal level and would have nothing but the scarce resource of mutual trust to coordinate their and other actors' expectations. If a co-opted or illegally recalled parliament was then constituted, as in Nepal, the danger was that the model could easily disintegrate in the direction of revolutionary duality or multiplicity of power. The procedure enacted by Nepali actors differed from the one Kis anticipated in that they relied on an inherited, originally elected even if not legally continuous parliament to approve the multiparty agreements, which in turn set up a new, co-opted parliamentary agency that was to exist until the meeting of a freely elected constitutional assembly. Under the considerable challenge of the emergence of ethnic politics, it is now the second co-opted legislature that is making all subsequent changes in the interim constitution. However, it is possible that it would have been better to leave the recalled (and originally elected) parliament in place, merely expanding it with new members (that is, Maoists), as was done in Czechoslovakia in 1989.

Note that when part of negotiated regime change, the model of legal continuity assumes that the old regime's actors remain in place and become parts of a negotiating process. When there is a rupture, as in Nepal, they are eliminated, at least initially. This creates a double problem if a model based on negotiation and legal continuity is subsequently superimposed. Governmental power is now in the hands of a force that claims some legitimacy (a "revolutionary" type) on the basis of having accomplished the work of liberation, and it may not be as conscious of the fragility of this symbolic resource as would be an old-regime actor facing a long-term legitimation crisis. On the other hand, an actor that may still represent very important social sectors may have been eliminated from the process altogether. Both of these issues were to be important in Iraq, with the already discussed proviso that an external force's claim of legitimacy through the act of liberation is made more difficult by its engagement in the occupation of the liberated country. Leaving that to the side for the moment, the success of the superimposition will then depend on an early recognition of two things difficult in revolutions whether internal or externally imposed: the weakness of revolutionary legitimacy based on liberation and the possible social representativeness of actors discredited for their political roles in old regimes.

The recognition that revolutionary legitimacy is a scarce resource leads to a stress on legality even where there was initially legal rupture. Whatever criticism could be leveled at the French Liberation Government concerning the imposition of initially self-interested rules—and many of the charges were in fact unfair and self-serving—what could not be said is that, after they allowed the French people to enact the interim constitutional rules, these rules were again violated in a subsequent procedure. The initial illegality and the problems involved in its substitution by an always precarious revolutionary legitimacy were not intensified by further illegalities. The model, in other words, is still practicable if superimposed on an initial revolutionary break, but only if once it is in motion legal continuity is staunchly preserved and enforced. The initial break cannot be an excuse for later ones; the revolutionary authorization must be treated as a very scarce resource that can only initially help with the ongoing problem of legitimation. So far in Nepal, after the initial revolutionary break (which is actually difficult to fully recognize and identify), there has been an attempt to adhere to principles of legality. In other words, legal discontinuity has not become the excuse for legal voluntarism, and this is as it should be within even a marginal case of the paradigm, one superimposed on a revolutionary break.

The Role of Constitutional Courts and Constitutional Principles

From the importance of legality, it follows that its enforcement is central for the model. Once an interim constitution is drafted, it must be enforced, if it is to be the type of constitution that can regulate the constitution-making process itself. For example, after opposing the premature setting up of a Constitutional Court, the Hungarian Democratic opposition consented once it had a constitution "worthy of defense."[64] Nothing like the role of a Constitutional Court in original constitution making exists in classical democratic models. Of course, in the new model neither do such courts play a in the making of interim constitutions. It is the role of the former to set up the latter, even if some primitive forerunner tribunal already existed. What happens then is truly extraordinary, though we have seen the full-fledged results only in the South African case. First, the interim constitution or the heavily amended constitution of the old regime is now under the control of a Constitutional Court, which, if what came before was a dictatorship, involves entirely new procedures by an entirely new institution signifying an entirely new regime. I am not arguing that such a change to a new transitional regime can be said to occur only where there is already a new, powerful constitutional court, because in fact rule of law can be enforced especially in a period of mobilization and international scrutiny by other, though less reliable, ways as well. But where there is a new constitutional court in operation, set up or transformed by an interim constitution, we have a sure sign of a regime change and the existence of a constitution in a new sense.

But there is an equally extraordinary second outcome, one that has only been actualized in South Africa but that logically belongs to the model. The constitutional assembly itself now falls under the control of the Constitutional Court, in the sense that its constitutional product could be challenged in front of that court as unconstitutional. Anticipated by some relevant theories (mainly Hauriou and Schmitt), actions by the German Constitutional Court (given the existence of unamendable parts of the *Grundgesetz*) and, most dramatically, the line of decisions by the Indian Supreme Court best known under the rubrics of the "Basic Structure Doctrine" and the Kesavananda cases[65] call a new legal option into being: the unconstitutional constitution.[66] But whereas in the case of all forerunners it was the amending process that could be declared unconstitutional in light of the "will" or "word" of the constitution's makers, here the constitutional assembly's own work can be challenged as to its constitutionality. Interested parties can sue to have the court declare parts of the constitutional draft unconstitutional, and the court can issue guidelines to the assembly concerning the forms of redrafting. Nowhere has anything like this been possible during the original constitution-making process.[67] The court, always a *pouvoir constitué*, here clearly becomes a part of the institutions through which the *pouvoir constituant* is said to act.

In South Africa, the powerful role of the court was made possible by thirty-four constitutional principles enacted in the interim constitution and themselves unamendable, many of them substantive, that allowed the court to play a very active role in constitution making through the certification process. But in principle, the new model implies such a possibility at the very least on procedural grounds, if the freely elected constitutional assembly violated the rules set out for it by the interim constitution. Note the reappearance here of the countermajoritarian difficulty, but without the ability of a Hamilton or a Marshall or a Hayek or an Ackerman to argue that the court is denying the majority of an assembly in the name of the majority of the people, since the makers of the interim constitution had no link to the will of the electorate. The limitation of the freely elected assembly thus cannot gain its legitimacy from the will of a higher, sovereign authority. In South Africa, that legitimacy is derived from the solemn promise the Constitutional Court saw as the foundation of the interim constitution.[68] But a solemn promise made by who and to whom? It could not be by one imposing authority to itself, to its clients, or vice versa, nor could it be made by two social forces to one another while other major social forces were left outside the process. The connection to the legitimacy of the round-table agreements here is undeniable.

Departures in Iraq

Let us quickly consider where Iraqi constitution making departed from the paradigm as presented here (later chapters of this book will go into more detail). The process set up was a version of the two-stage model, with an interim constitution. This interim constitution, the Transitional Administrative Law, was a detailed one, dealing with all of the issues of institutional life, rights, and constitutional change that a normal constitution would. It already included a highly decentralized "federal" (in fact, closer to confederal) structure of the state. It had a well-developed amendment rule, in my view one too stringent for an interim constitution, but one quite significantly omitting any rule of change before the election of the constitutional assembly. Like the South African interim constitution, the TAL had extensive regulations concerning the enactment of the final constitution, but with a very peculiar consociational structure of approval that allowed either the (Shi'ite) majority or one of two minorities (the Kurds)—but given the high two-thirds threshold most likely not the other minority (the Sunnis)—to veto the final product.[69] Note that ratification through referenda is ordinarily not part of the process as it has historically developed; for good or most likely ill, this was an Iraqi innovation for which there was no logical reason. The key democratic component of the model is the election of the constituent assembly that plays the double role of both drafter and ratifier, precisely the option desired by the American Anti-Federalists for the ratifying conventions of their day. Referenda, unlike elections of representatives, suggest that the will of the people can be fully grasped by one phase of the process, a claim in any case belied by the consociational structure of the referendum. That consociational element could have been secured more directly in the decision rules of the freely elected assembly, though then it would have been hard not to give a secure veto to the Sunni Arabs as well. That would have been only fair, since the Kurds were given what was in effect an iron-clad veto power.[70] Nevertheless, the instrument of the referendum was most likely adopted because it was a part of the initial Bonapartist scheme of the CPA and the opposed populist democratic model of the Grand Ayatollah Sistani.

However, the ratification rule did mirror the structure of exclusion. Iraq had no round-table negotiations, and the body that adopted the TAL systematically excluded the political representatives of the main part of the Sunni Arab segment of the population, which in the judgment of UN officials were evidently Baathist or neo-Baathist or Arab Nationalist, at least in the first few years of the occupation. Compared to other such processes, the "party" of government, the American CPA, represented a much larger force and had a greater input in the production of the interim constitution than any example elsewhere, with the exception of the first Spanish case. Their actions were neither cushioned by an inherited legislature with public sessions nor streamlined by an inherited amendment rule. There was an attempt to establish the international legality of the effort by a series of UN Security Council resolutions (1483 and 1511), but this effort was abandoned at the last moment when it came to the final ratification of the TAL by UN SC Res. 1546. But the earlier resolutions contained no legal guidance of any sort, and nothing stopped parts of the interim constitution from being rushed through in a couplike fashion without any real discussion, although the Iraqi Governing Council had a fairly expert and independent Constitutional Committee previously welcomed by the UN Security Council. But all of the formal Iraqi bodies were treated as advisory, and power was in a single set of hands alone. While it is true that there was a very important element of bargaining built into the making of the TAL between the CPA and the Kurdish parties concerning the structure of the state, the results of this bargain were imposed on the IGC, the body that was to formally approve the interim constitution and that was playing the role of the postwar Japanese government and Diet. Thus it is fair to treat the interim constitution as ultimately an imposed rather than negotiated one. At the same time, even among the included groups there was significant inequality in access and decision-making power: hence it is fair to treat the process as both exclusionary and hierarchical.[71] By the time there was an attempt to bring in previously excluded forces, it was too late; there was, in other words, a fundamental (though in the end unavoidable and desperate) confusion of what was appropriate at one stage of such a process (the negotiated one) and the other (the postelectoral, constituent assembly stage). Finally, regarding legality, it is admitted by advocates of some of the strongest forces that made the interim constitution that their side did not adhere to the terms. Legality was also severely compromised when the final constitution was drafted, enacted, and ratified. While a constitutional court was provided for by the TAL, it was not set up, itself a fundamental legal omission that allowed other illegalities to remain without any conceivable remedy. And serious legal omissions and commissions there were, when it came to enacting and ratifying the final constitution.

One may, and I actually will at least in part, chalk up these absences and departures from the standard to historical specificities. We have seen already that other countries within the paradigm differ from one another, and it is not surprising that Iraq, inhabiting a different time and space and subject to a different causality, differs from each and every one as well as from the abstract model. But we should not underestimate the internal relation of elements of the model and forget that absences and departures had consequences elsewhere too, for example in Hungary, where the interim constitution not regulating the process of final constitution making significantly contributed to the failure of the second stage. In Iraq, that problem was solved much better, based on South African precedents, probably. The missing round table and the exclusionary practice meant that the legitimacy problem was never solved and that the constitutional assembly and its leading forces considered themselves bound by the rules only to the extent that the rules suited them, and this was true even for the groups that otherwise benefited the most from the TAL. Thus a lack of legitimacy led to illegality that could not be sanctioned in the absence of a court or a procedure and thus led to more illegality. All this I will show below.[72]

What we need to understand is (1) the specificities of the Iraqi context that led to the pathological form of the adoption of the model, and (2) whether these specificities could have been nevertheless adequately dealt with had there been a sufficient understanding of the type of constitution-making model being adapted—that is, had there been sufficient constitutional learning from other relevant cases.[73]

Sociohistorical Preconditions and a Key to Pathologies

It is safe to say that there is considerable enthusiasm today concerning the application and further development of the new paradigm in its South

African version, the case that can be regarded as the most developed and characteristic one despite some unusual features.[74] It is more relevant here in that there has been far too little work in political science concerning the conditions of its possibility, after the early and outstanding analyses of Adam Przeworski and Janos Kis, which however did not focus on the constitutional output of negotiated transitions.[75] The paradigm has by no means become universally preferred; even today, authoritarians everywhere continue to favor top-down, imposed forms of constitution making, while democrats and democratic theory still tend to argue for traditional American and especially French models of sovereign constitution making. Yet it is exactly this clash of constitutional ideas, when there is a strategic balance of forces behind them, that provides the most likely context for the adoption of the new method.

One might very well ask why this new method only emerged in the 1970s. Kis rightly traces both reform and coordinated transition to legitimation crises, but such phenomena were obviously not new in the 1970s.[76] Why did they lead to revolutions before then, and more often than not to coordinated transitions after? Was there no such clash of ideas *cum* balance of political forces before? The answer probably lies in the ideological changes of the 1970s, the emergence of a postrevolutionary consciousness on most of the left, and a new acceptance of constitutionalism on the right, at least until the more recent revival of religious fundamentalisms. Both sides now tended to be more receptive to a second-best type of negotiated solution on the question of constitution making than their historical forerunners had been. Finally, the new model emerged in a step-by-step fashion from its beginnings in Spain to its culmination in South Africa, and there is plenty of evidence that activist-theorists learned from those previous experiences.[77] Thus not only general democratic commitment but democratic learning in specific areas played an important role.

Both ideas and forces are important. A balance of forces may point to the plausibility of a compromise, a second-best formula no one initially values as their first option. But would a balance of forces alone lead to the required outcome, or are ideas necessary? How much of a difference do ideas make?[78] The Spanish case indicates that when the new model was not yet available, informal substitutes were sought, substitutes whose success depended on democratic intentions on the part of incumbents. Furthermore, must there be an actual balance, or is the actors' belief that there is one enough? It seems that a belief or perception on the part of the actors is more relevant, though the belief itself should be influenced by reality. Actors, however, could be mistaken, especially when a sector within either side ("reformers" or "moderates")[79] sells its allies the need for negotiations by claiming that they cannot together force through their preferred solution. In such a case, obviously, belief in negotiations as at worst a second-best outcome may replace an actual balance of forces and can lead a stronger side to negotiate rather than stubbornly stand firm. Such an outcome would be all the more plausible if a stronger side became convinced that the new model is preferable to its imposed solution, something that may have happened in Spain and that may be increasingly possible with the growing prestige of and knowledge about the negotiated transitions of the 1980s and 1990s. But when political sides are too unequal and there are radicals on the stronger side, it is in general difficult to completely stop them from pushing through a program of imposition.

We know that actual intentions to institute the new paradigm are initially not in the driver's seat, because almost everywhere the process begins with an attempted top-down reform.[80] Assuming that regime leaders foresee the need for structural changes, they try to accomplish these on their own terms, providing all the institutional continuities and guarantees they need. The goal is to change things so that things can remain the same. While it is hard to precisely specify the identity or essence or structure or imaginary significations that constitute the core of a regime, the initiators think they have a pretty good idea of what they are, and their goal is to save them. The method is liberalization, or *abertura*, or *perestroika*, or *glasnost*, what I have described as the electoral road or more generally political reform, and its initiators are aware that they are embarking on a hazardous path. An early settlement on a semiauthoritarian constitution, as in Chile in 1980, belongs to this trajectory.[81] To succeed, authoritarians must marshal enough public support and enthusiasm to gain sufficient time for their structural program, but they may also run into difficulties with their own coalition if the response is too much mobilization and activism. In general, those who argue that under dictatorships the method fails are correct, though there are great historical exceptions, such as for many decades Mexico.[82] When the method threatens to fail, reformers, as Przeworski argued—though not very clearly—can be recaptured by hardliners within the regime or can escape forward and try to make an entirely new type of alliance across the political divide. This can they do if, either because of the earlier reform process or independently, there are forces on the other side of or within civil society desiring a regime change but lacking the force or optimism to initiate a revolutionary process on their own. Reform would have been best for the reformers; democratic revolution the supposed best for the forces of civil society. Defeat by hardliners, anarchy, or outside intervention are all considered unacceptable by these two actors or groups of actors. So according to the model, they opt for a second-best solution, a process of negotiation in which each side has a fair chance to get relatively close to a desired alternative if things work out well and to at least get some guarantees if they work out badly. And in this ideal-typical four-actor model, they have to be strong enough, Przeworski adds, to bring others on their own side ("hardliners" and "radicals") along to work for a deal. It is not that among the actors constitutionalism is anyone's ideal, but that constitutionalism is the system that can provide the bottom-line guarantees.

On the other hand, I would add that it would help if constitutionalism were itself valued, for whatever reason, and this is why. First, because the actual equality of two sides or an equal lack of faith on both sides in their own ability to push things through is possible but unlikely. A stronger side (or a side that imagines itself to be stronger) would oppose guarantees, at least extensive ones. Here ideas would be the great levelers. We have seen this in Czechoslovakia and South Africa, where the electorally stronger sides agreed to electoral rules that would greatly diminish their results (PR versus plurality), for reasons of principled pluralism or ideology. Moreover, the positive role of ideas increases as the model itself becomes better known and as there is imitation across cases. In general, practical examples have more effect than abstract theory, but both can matter. It is ultimately impossible to believe that the central European cases wound up with the types of constitutions they did only because of a power balance, which in fact varied more from case to case than did the institutional designs, rather than because of the general expectation that in Europe one chose institutions within a given set of possibilities only. Thus ideas matter even more when there is sufficient international pressure to back them up.

To sum up then, the succession of cases that applied our paradigm do not indicate identical political contexts. Most of the time, the initiative has been on the side of regimes, but even this was not the case in Czechoslovakia. There is usually a rough balance of forces, which stems on the one side from a loss of legitimacy of ruling regimes and their resulting inability to repress and on the other side from the inability of oppositional forces, which can block reforms from above, to carry out revolutionary programs of their own. But the actual balance of forces varies, and here ideas and imitation across cases tends to play a major role. This is how we can explain the adoption of the model even in a case such as Nepal, where the legitimation crisis of the old regime led to negotiations among entirely new forces and where the restored parliament could have but did not claim to govern alone and without restraints until free elections and without the negotiation of an interim constitution with a Maoist insurgency. The idea that interim arrangements should be constitutionalized and that the interim constitution should come from negotiations was thus adopted even though there would have been alternative (restorationist) claims around which a transition could have been organized. Admittedly, such claims may not have been able to sustain a joint challenge from civil-society forces and the Maoists. But the alternative of negotiations leading to an interim constitution was available from previous experiences to deal with this potential problem.

Iraq, like Nepal, began with a full legal break, with the added difference that this was produced by a foreign power. That alone could have rendered the new paradigm irrelevant, but it did not, however surprisingly. In principle, Iraq could have had an early constitutional conference or convention or whatever, Afghan style, with international supervision of the process and with the United States letting the chips fall where they may. Obviously, this was unacceptable to the Americans. The war was fought neither to strengthen international institutions nor for a completely uncertain outcome; the process had to wind up somewhere specific, at least within a range. Initial military control would have to be followed by some kind of U.S. control of the political transition; there was no question of farming out this part of the process to the United Nations or anyone else. Thus in Iraq too there is a point in speaking of a top-down reform attempt, presumably guided by the desire to transform an initial structural relationship of complete American dominance (military rule followed by Bremer's dictatorship) into a different system that nevertheless preserved something essential in the initial arrangement. It does not matter for my purposes what that "essential something" is, and I leave it to others to characterize the shift as one from direct to indirect control, or from imperialism to neoimperialism, or from a complete American dependency to either an American client state or to a friendly democracy. Undoubtedly, some critics of my argument will point out that the American occupiers were trying to institute a formally complete democracy from above, while the other cases of top-down reform to which I compare them involved attempted creations of hard democracies or soft dictatorships. But with an external power, the stakes are different than with an internal dictatorship. While the latter can only preserve itself in a top-down reform by preserving elements of dictatorship, an external power can preserve its influence also in a weak and dependent democracy.[83]

Whatever the goals of the originally intended imposition, it was the countermove by the Shi'ite clergy that opposed and halted the original process without being able to put into effect its own revolutionary-democratic process of transition and populist constitution making. The two-stage alternative that emerged was a compromise between these forces: there would be one imposed stage and one popularly generated stage. But as we clearly see even in Bremer's memoirs of the crucial year, the imposed stage would have to structure the popular stage to a very large extent.[84] In my previous writings, I have pointed to the following paradox: one has good reason to assume that the greater the legitimacy of the first stage of the process, the greater the possible restriction of the freedom of the constitutional assembly in the second stage. In Iraq, however, the results of a first stage *without* much legitimacy were supposed to greatly restrict the actors of the second stage.

The key difference here between the general model and its Iraqi adaptation was that though the abstract model had the form of a series of compromises, neither its beginnings were negotiated as such (in some "talks about talks") nor were subsequent steps ever consensually arrived at. The governmental party, in effect the CPA, thought itself and indeed was strong enough to impose the whole process. For the moment, only the theoretical presuppositions interest us. The governmental side in other cases were instances like the Suarez government in Spain, the CP-dominated governments of central Europe, and the NP government of South Africa. Only the first of these was able to impose a solution, and two things must be said about the Spanish case. It was the first such case, and thus the negotiated model as we know it was not known or available.[85] And Suarez was able to act on behalf of a new monarch and to partially separate himself from the Franquist forces that had controlled government in the past. Moreover, he chose rules of the game that opposition forces could accept, and indeed many of them did accept, in informal consultations. In all the subsequent cases, partners from the opposition were needed to negotiate broadly acceptable compromise solutions.

The American government was not the first, if we look at it from the point of view of the recent sequence of democratization, to face the question of constitution making in a transitional polity. It could have clearly learned much more than it did from previous models and examples. But in its own eyes it may have been the first, because it was an external agent and moreover a superpower accustomed to regard itself as representing all that is good in geopolitical life. Supremely confident of its own constitutional heritage and values, it was not accustomed to taking constitutional lessons from others. It had no doubts as to its legitimacy, at least in the moral sense. While formally occupiers, the Americans regarded themselves as liberators, some in the more demanding but most in the less demanding sense, as I have discussed in chapter 1. Though they would not have used the term and would not have recognized it, they were convinced they had a type of revolutionary political legitimacy in Iraq itself. For all these reasons, they could not have seen themselves at the moment of initiating a process of top-down changes as reformers trying to save the core of an existing system. The old regime was Saddam's regime, and they obliterated that one more radically than had most revolutionaries had in the past. Conveniently disregarding that they had already established a power position for the United States and that they meant to preserve it, they did not see themselves as trying to conserve anything, but only as interested in creating a pluralist, liberal constitutionalist democracy, something entirely new in the region. Or so they acted, whatever some of them may have thought. Internally, this meant far greater unity, at least in the CPA leadership in Baghdad, than in the cases to which I am comparing the process. There were no hardliners or reformers, or rather it was hardliners who undertook the reforms, and the reformers who opposed things such as state dissolution and de-Baathification were entirely marginalized. The four-actor model Przeworski sees as the ideal-typical condition for a negotiated solution could not emerge, because of the unity of the American side.[86] They did not doubt their legitimacy, the element stressed by Kis, and did not seek therefore to increase it via a truly inclusive process. Being in the position of incumbents, however new, they saw no need to include any of the old incumbents, however many Iraqis they may have represented. Yet while an external observer could see them in the position of the foreign sponsor of incumbents required by the model I am using, they could not see themselves that way. Seeing themselves as the democrats, it was also hard for them to identify as democratic or as possible partners any external force that opposed them in any way. If they were opposed by a social movement from below composed of forces that were also enemies of the Saddam regime, this could have been only because of a new particularism or lack of understanding.

Interestingly, the constellation of forces, sufficiently balanced in terms of strength and expectations, did produce a compromise result of two stages—one that no one intended from the outset—but from the American point of view, this was never a principled compromise. Moreover, the goal remained to structure the first stage in such a way as to make the second turn out properly. And this could only be done if the parameters of the whole process were imposed in the first place and if no elements were included in negotiations (such as they were) that could have made trouble about the whole structure or some of its significant details. Only Sistani continued to create difficulties from the outside, because he also had important agents within the process, but by co-opting UN participation, which also could have made trouble but didn't (and effectively dealing with the so-called Shi'a House in the Interim Governing Council), Sistani too was sufficiently neutralized by the Americans. If all these successes made the Sh'ia complicit in the logic of the occupation, it would be so much the worse for them, but of course no one could predict the disasters related to that inevitable perception in the Muslim world. But it remains the case that the paradigm came about as a result of the clash of two forces. One force, the Americans, hoped to instrumentalize the result and assimilate it to its initial top-down goals, and the other force, Sistani's movement, never accepted the compromise as a compromise at all.

The only thing that could have made a difference was constitutional learning. At the moment when it was decided that there would be an interim constitution[87] rather than a move to a final one approved by a plebiscite, the CPA faced a lot of choices. One choice concerned the type of interim assembly Iraq would have, either elected or co-opted, and this was much discussed. But there were others, the main one being who should draft the interim constitution and under what procedures. Even if one strongly believed in one's own legitimacy and power, it was not obvious that the prudent course was to apply that power to simply use Iraqi agents to impose an interim constitution, however attractive its projected contents. After all, that belief was hardly shared by many key Iraqi elites, the minimum condition of legitimacy in the sociological sense. Thus the process started out with severe legitimation problems whose extent and depth had to be serious however difficult to measure and whatever the Americans thought of their own legitimacy. One-sided imposition was only a way of exacerbating this legitimacy deficit, which would grow into a full-fledged legitimation crisis under Sistani's challenge.

Certainly, all international experience spoke against an external governmental power going about the matter by way of such imposition. Adopting the idea of an interim constitution and a two-stage process could and should have initiated a process of discussion and reflection concerning just what the creation of such an instrument might entail if it is to work. There was enough international expertise to help in the process, but to the extent it was used, it was used only as window dressing.[88] Undoubtedly, it was felt that accepting a two-stage process was compromise enough, not understanding that if imposed, the two-stage process would lose its virtues in the eyes of those whom they needed in the process of coming to a fundamental agreement.

Let me sum up: it was not after all wrong to worry about the initial implausibility of the new method of constitution making being adopted in Iraq, a method that was to begin with an externally produced revolutionary break rather than a legal continuity of regimes. More important was the related fact that discredited old-regime forces did not merely lose their legitimacy, a significant precondition of the new model,[89] but, as in all revolutions, were eliminated from a position of formal power altogether. Thus, to the extent that a negotiated transition would have to be grafted onto a revolutionary model,[90] it would have to be arranged among new actors. This led to a serious problem of underrepresentation, which the United States responded to like a typical revolutionary authority, that is, by enforcing the exclusion of the relevant group previously implicated in the business of ruling understood in a very wide sense (encompassing government, party, and state), rather than acting as an old regime–supporting actor seeking to expand legitimacy through new inclusion.

Assuming that fateful and disastrous exclusion, which I will consider in detail in the following chapters, why was the model adopted at all, and why was it adopted in a pathological form? Again, the key problem was that the actor in the position of de facto power, the United States occupying authority, was stronger and arguably more legitimate (at least to itself, a few important internal groups like the Kurds, and, after two UN Security Council resolutions, in a narrow sense internationally)[91] than were the discredited old-regime actors of this model. While there was no legitimacy in either the sociological (the supporting elite groups were too few; only in the case of the Kurds was their support based on anything more than instrumental considerations) or legal sense (the UN Security Council resolutions were narrow and could not really make up for the illegality of the war and the invasion itself), there were sufficient confirmations for the self-understanding of the occupying authority, which was already highly disposed to believe in the justification of its actions. That gap between self-understanding and self-evaluation of authority and how it was understood and evaluated by most if not all relevant others was a huge disadvantage for the adoption of the model in question, and especially for its adoption in a normatively and politically adequate form. For the model to have a chance to be adopted, one would have to compensate for the difficulty, either by a very strong opponent on the other side pushing for classical democratic options or for ideas on the side of the de facto power strongly influencing the process in the direction of such adoption. There was such political opposition, led by the Shi'ite Grand Ayatollah Ali al-Sistani. But it was not strong enough to impose a revolutionary solution if a negotiated model was not conceded. And there were (we are told) such ideas on the American side, but they were much less important than projects of imposed constitution making. The result: the model was adopted because of the presence of these factors, but it was adopted in a version deformed by continued efforts at external imposition, because of the insufficiency of these factors even in combination.

[3]

Sistani Versus Bremer

The Emergence of the Two-Stage Model in Iraq

> These [occupation] authorities do not have the authority to appoint the members of the constitution writing council. There is no guarantee that this council will produce a constitution that responds to the paramount interests of the Iraqi people and expresses its national identity of which Islam and its noble social values are basic components. The [constitution writing] proposal is fundamentally unacceptable. There must be general elections in which each eligible Iraqi can choose his representative in a constituent assembly for writing the constitution. This is to be followed by a general referendum on the constitution approved by the constituent assembly. All believers must demand the realization of this important issue and participate in completing the task in the best manner.
>
> —Ali al-Husaini al-Sistani, June 25, 2003[1]

The model of constitution making used in Iraq was initially planned by no one; it was the result of the clash of major political forces. Thus it could be said to incorporate a compromise. Yet while there were important negotiations and even international mediation, ultimately the formula for the process and a good part of the contents of the Transitional Administrative Law were imposed by the occupying authority. However, there were two distinct dimensions to this imposition. The clash with the forces led by the Grand Ayatollah Sistani led to the compromise formula of a two-stage transition imposed (rather than in any serious way negotiated) by the Coalition Provisional Authority on the Interim Governing Council as a whole, and through them on Iraq itself. That process is the theme of the present chapter. There was no clash with the Kurdish Regional Government or the two parties that controlled it, but the CPA conducted serious negotiations with them—entirely outside the IGC, to which these parties indeed belonged—regarding the structure of the Iraqi state as it would appear in the interim constitution. The results were then imposed on the rest of the IGC when other important contents of the TAL were worked out. Chapter 4 will deal with this second process of imposition and bargaining, which also involved genuine give and take concerning American positions not assumed to be sufficiently fundamental (or deemed impossible to impose) to the CPA.[2] Interestingly, the second process to a significant extent vitiated the elements of compromise contained in the first, and this is why the Grand Ayatollah Sistani was confirmed in his determined antagonism to the TAL, which never would have emerged without his political movement in the first place. Thus these two chapters together deal with ultimately failed attempts to deal with the legitimacy crisis through constitution making.

The Protagonists and Their Plans

The Americans

From the outset, the Americans wanted to impose a constitution. The motives may have varied greatly, from a neoimperialist desire to get a friendly government to liberal democratic distrust in the political cultures and political forces they encountered.[3] Whatever the motives, they could be justified by a logical self-assurance that since where there is no democracy the only way to begin is by imposition, thus it does not matter much whether the imposition is uni- or multilateral, internal or external, especially if the end result can be justified in terms of "universal" values. We cannot untangle the real motives, and the later testimonies of those involved (full of self-justification) are unreliable. For whatever it is worth, among these statements the idea that stands out is that only by American imposition could sufficient respect for rights, a degree of separation of religion and state, protection of minorities, and federalism be assured.[4] A more skeptical interpretation would represent this as a public-relations attempt to retroactively justify the war by eventually being able to point to Iraq "as an example of enlightened democracy in the Arab world," as manifested in constitutional documents.[5] But once the question of not immediately transferring power to some Iraqi provisional government was decided, so was the question of constitutional imposition. In principle, it was possible just to impose enough to jumpstart full autonomy, but that would have had unpredictable consequences, which the Americans in Iraq were never prepared to live with and were warned not to do even by realist opponents of the war such as Scowcroft. That such a thing as "imposed constitutionalism" was possible was indicated by one and only one successful historical example, the occupation of Japan, and this is why I think the figure of MacArthur was so important for Bremer and his circle.[6] It did not matter that partly because of historical givens and very soon because of their own grave acts of commission the Japanese situation was very different than the one in Iraq. What they learned from the occupation of Japan—but did not unlearn even under Sistani's challenge—was that a determined group of American politicians and supposed experts could use whatever available political façade for making and imposing a constitution that could be, if done right, successfully presented and legitimated as a highly progressive and indigenous achievement.

Thus I simply do not accept at face value the continued insistence by Paul Bremer[7] that in his scheme at all stages Iraqis were supposed to write their own constitution. When Bremer was confronted by the charge, apparently from Sistani, that Bremer planned to imitate MacArthur and impose on the Iraqis a constitution written by American experts, he gave a response quite literally worthy of MacArthur. Such a thing was furthest from his mind: "the Coalition has no intention of writing the constitution."[8] While it is impossible to say whether or not at all moments he and his advisors expected American experts (of Iraqi origin or not) to do the bulk of the drafting (as they actually were going to do in the case of the TAL), what they had in mind, indeed for the writing of the permanent constitution itself until Sistani's victory on this point, was that officials appointed by the CPA directly or through the IGC but under the former's sovereign authority would write and enact the basic document. Only what the CPA wanted to pass could be passed in such a model, whoever the literal drafters and their expert advisors were.[9] They assumed, in other words, the legal authority to impose, and from the retrospect of the TAL we can infer that this intention referred to both the contents of the document and to the one-sided structure of authority.

Of course, the intention to impose made the adoption of the postsovereign paradigm discussed in the previous chapter in a fully legitimate form impossible, because that would have presupposed a many-sided rather than one-sided structure of authority and control. But before that choice could even come up, there were serious problems with a model of straight imposition. Unlike in Japan, where state and governmental continuity provided a ready-made formal process behind which the act of imposition could be veiled, in Iraq nothing like that was available. Thus a process had to be constructed rather than inherited—one that looked legitimate (that is, Iraqi) but that would not get out of hand. This turned out to be impossible for the initial constitutional project of the CPA.

Initially, there was much confusion about how policymakers wished to proceed, but it was definitely assumed that it would be an Iraqi body ("a conference") *selected* by the CPA that would be formally in charge of the drafting.[10] Once the IGC was formed, it was assumed that the selection process would operate through it or formally by it, but always under the CPA's strict supervision. Any plan generated by the IGC or its Constitutional Preparatory Committee, as it is clear in Bremer's memoirs, had to be thoroughly negotiated with and approved by the CPA. It may be true that Sistani's first fatwa quoted above was initially entirely disregarded,[11] but in any case, under his pressure or not, the CPA's plans developed in what could be claimed to be a more "democratic" direction. Bremer in particular later claimed he was impressed by the 1925 Iraqi Constitution having been ratified in a referendum, and he believed he was following that example when he linked the idea of a selected conference to popular ratification.[12] Quite amazingly, he does not seem to have realized even when writing his memoirs that the 1925 Constituent Assembly was *elected* and that this was probably one of Sistani's models in the fatwa of June 25.[13] It is possible that the idea of the referendum was a detached part of Sistani's wider proposal. In any case, simply adding a referendum or a plebiscite to the CPA's ideas was a characteristic attempt to shore up the democratic legitimacy of a constitution-making process that would be in the hands of the executive branch. It would have been the mark of Bonapartism, in quite a strict historical sense, especially because under conditions of foreign occupation the plebiscite in question, once a constitution was previously approved, would have to be regarded as highly constrained.[14]

That last suspicion is amply demonstrated by looking at Bremer's seven-point program published in the *Washington Post* on September 8, 2003, under the revealing title "Iraq's Path to Sovereignty." Here the argument was repeated that in Iraq, elections presuppose a constitution, a new and permanent constitution. The steps relevant to constitution making were said to be (1) the creation of the IGC, (2) the creation of a Constitutional

Preparatory Committee of the IGC, (3) the writing of the constitution by a process recommended by the Constitutional Preparatory Committee, and (4) popular ratification of the constitution.

The process was represented as the first time (perhaps Bremer was unaware of the 1925 constituent assembly back then) that "Iraq will have a permanent constitution written by and approved by the Iraqi people." How the document was supposed to be written by "the" Iraqi people was unclear, given that there was no formula under point 3, and in any case a co-opted conference could not be said to be representative of the Iraqi people. However, what approval by "the" people meant was clearer. Steps 5 and 6, namely the election of an Iraqi government and the dissolution of the CPA along with the recovery of Iraqi sovereignty, could follow only if the popular response to step 4 was positive. The recovery of independence was linked to one and only one outcome of the plebiscite, thereby foreordaining the result whatever the voters thought of the constitution itself.

As I have said, the motives for imposed constitution making in Iraq, though convergent, were probably plural, complex, and difficult to reconstruct. It was a little different with the problem of justification. The CPA did not take the position of John Yoo,[15] who argued in clear violation of the Hague and Geneva conventions that an occupying power had the right to make a constitution for the occupied. The constant stress, also there in the seven-point program, that it would be Iraqis that would make their own constitution indicates something different. As ambiguous as UN Security Council resolutions 1483 and 1511 may have been, and deliberately so, they seem to have pointed to a combined responsibility of the CPA and Iraqi actors to manage the political process of the transition. I am quite certain that the CPA's lawyers believed that all of their various formulas, including the one eventually adopted, satisfied this rather vague demand, which does not deal adequately with the precise structure of authority, and indeed there was never a significant challenge of CPA constitution-making formulas from international sources. With respect to Iraqi actors, the argument had to be made repeatedly that an elected constituent assembly was not possible on empirical and even logical grounds. The empirical grounds, as weak as they were, had to do with the absence of an electoral law, electoral rolls, and census data, and insufficient time to organize such things. These arguments were in part spurious, because a single-country PR system like the one eventually chosen could be legislated in a day and requires no prior census data, only proofs of age and citizenship. Being a passive electoral system, its imposition would not be seen as trying to construct a particular outcome. Since this was very well known on all sides,[16] the empirical arguments could only arouse the obvious suspicion that the United States feared the victory of those who were likely to win.

The arguments on logical grounds were somewhat better, but they pointed to a very different type of process than the one chosen. In terms of the legal regulation of all the processes needed for free elections, from private security to media access and various other rights, Iraq was under an old political regime in many respects, or an occupation regime, or their combination, and none of these was conducive for a democratic transition. To have elections, Bremer rightly and repeatedly argued, new laws, some of them constitutional laws, were needed, and thus for logical reasons free elections could not be expected to produce them. However, when this dilemma has arisen in other situations (for example, in the South African and some central European cases), the actors working for democratic transitions arranged inclusive round tables of all the important groups—and even the "talks about talks." Even transitional rules have distributional consequences, and it creates enormous problems to impose them in a one-sided manner. That is precisely what the CPA intended to do, directly or through Iraqi proxies, and indeed initially for permanent rather than transitional rules. The logical argument was thus correctly employed against holding early elections, but it could not justify the alternative that was chosen.

The Ayatollah Sistani

The original perspective articulated by the fatwa of June 25, 2003, was maintained by Sistani with amazing consistency. While the exact formula advocated, a freely elected assembly plus referendum, seems closest to the French model first practiced in 1793,[17] Sistani was obviously aware of the rhetorical power of advocating a democratic alternative against the Americans' imposed model, who were evidently quite vulnerable to this type of "immanent criticism."[18] Nevertheless, it is highly likely that Sistani's constitutional ideas come from his own tradition, even if that tradition itself absorbed classical European ideas of democratic constitution making.[19] The tradition of the Iranian Constitutional Revolution undoubtedly strongly influenced him, as did some turn-of-the-last-century Shi'ite scholarship. But the former did not yet have a freely elected constitutional assembly,[20] and he follows the latter more in calling for limited government and accountability than for a council of guardians.[21] He certainly has a more authentic claim to the heritage of the 1924 Iraqi Constituent Assembly than does Bremer. But this example was a complicated one for the Shi'a clergy to exploit, because it was during the 1923 elections that the leading Shi'ite mujtahids organized a boycott that led to the temporary expulsion of many of them from Iraq, the reduction of their political influence, and the overwhelming Sunni control of the Constituent Assembly (already guaranteed to some extent by the electoral rules).[22]

It is often said that Sistani advocated a program calculated to bring to his forces the power of the majority. And indeed whatever plans he had for actual constitutional arrangements, a constitutional assembly elected before any provisional agreements, an interim constitution, and so on would only be under rules it chose to impose upon itself. If it had a narrow Shi'ite majority (and that is what the overall demographic distribution indicated), such a body could enact by simple majority simple majoritarian decision rules both for itself and the following national referendum. There would be no limits in principle with respect to religious and ethnic affairs, administrative centralization, and control and distribution of national resources that such a majority, however small, could not arrogate to itself. The intentions of Sistani and close supporters such as Hussain Shahristani, most likely relatively humane and tolerant, might not matter, because such a majority could fall under the sway of its most militant elements. Even before that happened, given Iraq's strongly divided society, the minorities would reject the process, and instead of majority tyranny the more likely result would be constitutional and civil crisis. When Bremer and his colleagues referred to these issues in their attempts to block Sistani, they were not only being self-serving or demagogic. They were also articulating the views and interests of all non-Shi'ite groups in Iraq.[23] These perspectives were possibly reconcilable with Sistani's positions, but he himself was not in a position to do the reconciling. However, it is also true that he showed no sign whatsoever of being aware of any constitution-making approaches that could unite constitutionalism and democracy and the rights of a majority with the needs of minorities.

However, the CPA was in the driver's seat, not Sistani, and it was up to the CPA to offer formulas of reconciliation. Sistani's opposition to imposed constitution making was clearly right in terms of what it opposed, and the mantle of democracy he assumed projected him for a while into a position of national leadership. However, because of his view that clerics should not play a direct political role, and because of the divided nature of Iraqi society, increasingly manifested in the Sunni insurrection, Sistani could not assume the national political stature that would have best fit his constitutional challenge. However, there is little in his later political statements to indicate that his view of Iraqi politics was highly exclusionary or narrowly majoritarian. Had he been offered a better deal than he eventually received, perhaps he would have been able to play a more integrative role. As things happened, he found himself outside, and in a peculiar way the moderate Shi'ites whom the Americans did in the end use to make the final deal were more hardline on the divisions of Iraqi society than Sistani might have been.

The First Round of the Battle

With a large popular movement behind him—but one with a relatively narrow ethnic-religious definition—it is quite amazing how far Sistani was able to deflect the Americans from their original goals. He stopped them from writing the permanent constitution and he received from them a commitment for a freely elected constitutional assembly. He got them to bring elections closer by about a year if not more. He got them to restore sovereignty, though only in a formal sense, a year and a half early. But his defeats are also significant, given how much more difficult he could have made matters for the occupation.[24] He had to accept elections much later than they could have been held. He had to accept the imposed TAL, even if he could block its UN Security Council authorization. He had to accept an interim government that would not be composed of the elements he wanted and that could not do its job effectively.

Aside from his own popular forces, his strength also depended on the ideological power of his message. If the occupation of Iraq was for the sake of democracy, he wanted that democracy to operate in the most fundamental political process of all: the making of rules for the political process. He quickly became a favorite of reporters and politicians from all over the world, even though he would not see them or give interviews.[25] But his limitations were obvious too: having taken a deeply and fundamentally political stance, he refused to enter politics, acting only through weak and often unreliable intermediaries. Of course, even these weak intermediaries were better than nothing, given his unwillingness to play a direct role. As things unfolded, it was unexpectedly the Constitutional Preparatory Committee rather than the main leaders of the IGC who proved receptive to his message. Most likely in this formally subordinate body, religious allegiance and expertise reinforced one another.

Without the large popular demonstrations in Najaf, Karbala, and, with the greatest effect, on five consecutive days in Baghdad, Sistani would not have achieved much.[26] His theoretical priority as the first among equals among the most senior clergy "worthy of emulation" (*marja' al- taqlid*) or his leadership of the *marja'iyya* in Najaf[27] became really significant only when he demonstrated his power, and the constitutional issue gave him a great vehicle for this. It is possible that the crowds were moved by the combination of religious leadership and the discovery of his political attitude, reflecting that of the Shi'a masses, who disliked the occupation but wished to benefit from it if possible. Nonviolent public protest was the perfect means for this and was a better alternative for most than Moqtadah al-Sadr's armed resistance. They could now demonstrate for something that was neither possible under Saddam nor given to them by the foreign occupiers: a freely elected constituent assembly. It was humiliating to have to be liberated by the Americans, but some of the shame could be redeemed if that liberation could be turned in quite a different direction than the liberator-occupiers themselves had chosen for Iraq. To the constitutional scholar, Sistani's challenge was about democracy. To the Shi'ite masses, it was probably more about dignity. Regardless of what it was "about," they marched and demonstrated in very great numbers, under Sistani's picture and chanting Sistani's slogans.

Part of the battle was fought in the streets, the other part in the IGC, especially its Constitutional Preparatory Committee. If these two bodies were meant to be a mere façade for the rule of the CPA, Sistani's challenge temporarily put some life into them. It is highly amusing today to read Bremer's cynical description of the plans to make it look like the IGC had created itself, by "immaculate conception," and his indignant refutation of press charges concerning the lack of independence by members of the council.[28] The IGC was put together mostly by Bremer and his advisors, with some help from Sergio de Mello, the UN High Representative.[29] It is right to call the IGC exclusionary and lacking governing powers, but its members nevertheless were not puppets. Regarding representation of the country ("the most representative government Iraq ever had," according to Talabani at the inauguration of the IGC), the representative character of the IGC was asymmetrical and incomplete but not for that reason entirely nonexistent. On a political level, Shi'ites and Kurds were represented in the twenty-one-person council by individuals with important ties to political or religious organizations in Iraq, the earlier exile status of some of the representatives notwithstanding. But as a result of the strict de-Baathification program, the five Sunni representatives had very weak ties to important constituencies.[30] Conversely, most important Sunni constituencies tainted by Baath, ex-Baath, post-Baath, and in general Arab nationalist associations were unrepresented, despite repeated efforts to the contrary.[31] The Iraqi Islamic Party, a branch of the Sunni Islamic Brotherhood, was there, but it was not an important force in Iraq, at least not at that time. Significantly, the more radical Association of Muslim Scholars was absent. Regarding issues, the religious-ethnic structure and cleavages of Iraqi society were well represented—one might say too well. It was this representation that was to make the imposition of American-style separation of church and state impossible, but it was also the same representation that in the eyes of many Iraqis helped to harden the ethnic-religious divide of society.[32] From a political point of view, it is clear that the IGC was grossly unrepresentative of a society that had a significant antioccupation segment from the beginning, one that became a quickly growing majority.[33] That opinion was politically absent from the council, whatever the private views of a few members. On the other hand, there was significant resentment within the IGC, whose key members expected to be part of a provisional government, to the way the occupation was being conducted and especially to Bremer's policies. Here there were significant differences, however, since the Kurdish members could exercise their autonomy and leadership in their own provinces and had no problems with CPA interference on that score.

The constitutional issue was a good one for the IGC to use to make a small stand against the CPA, against which they were otherwise powerless. To begin with, this was one issue where they were assigned some power in Bremer's formal scheme of things, power they could ideally employ for gain. Second, as a group, even the Shi'ite clerics among them could play the moderates to Sistani's hardliners, and they indeed continued to assure Bremer they could moderate and channel the Grand Ayatollah's demands.[34] This was not just a tactical matter. For some of them, even before they were appointed to the IGC, contradicting Sistani's fatwa was almost impossible unless Sistani himself opened the door to compromise.

Bremer should have realized this at the latest when he appointed the Shia cleric Mohammed Bahr al-Uloum to the council, and it is quite interesting that he then assured the candidate (who would certainly report to Sistani) that he would do nothing to contravene the fatwa.[35] Finally, they could hide behind their expert Constitutional Preparatory Committee, and it was that body that was to take the strongest stand against the Americans, with or without encouragement from IGC politicians. Expected by the Americans to produce a report choosing a co-opted conference to draft Iraq's constitution—and a method of selecting it—that body, with a secular academic majority, voted (initially) twenty-four to zero to go with Sistani and elect a constituent assembly.[36] When this was not approved (by Bremer), the Constitutional Preparatory Committee simply deadlocked around three plans (election, selection by the IGC, and caucuses doing the selection). According to Bremer, this happened because twenty members he claimed favored his proposals for unelected caucuses could not overcome the pressure from Shi'a Islamists.[37] More likely, however, was that the majority supported elections and did not think that they could push through that option in the face of Bremer's resistance.[38] But either way, the seven-point program that required that the IGC and its Constitutional Preparatory Committee produce a method for drafting a constitution came to an end without Sistani able to push through his alternative solution.

It is tempting to analyze this ending as a step toward a supposed compromise solution in terms of a simplistic four-actor model, where ultimately American moderates reached out to deal with Iraqi ones. In this scheme, Bremer would be the hardliner who stuck to his guns and kept trying various ways to ram through the original, top-down, seven-point program. For him, Sistani's opposition seemed to be only about getting a Shi'ite majority at a "convention," and that could be arranged in a selection process. But even he was slowly realizing that Sistani was not amenable to any version of that, though his idea that somehow the cleric "operated on a different rational plane than we Westerners" did not let him grasp why.[39] As the very reliable Chandrasekaran describes it, National Security Advisor Rice, her advisor Robert Blackwill, and Secretary Powell came to the conclusion that Bremer's plan had shipwrecked but that waiting for free elections would extend the formal American occupation for an unexpectedly long period. Thus an entirely new approach was needed. In order to facilitate this, the Iraqi Stabilization Group was formed under Rice on October 6, 2003, bypassing the Pentagon, and it was that group that at the latest between October 27 and 30 told Bremer to go back to the drawing board. There was also pressure from the Pentagon for an early transfer of sovereignty to the IGC or a body appointed by it *without* a constitution, a position entirely unacceptable to Bremer.[40] Back in Baghdad, his advisors (again according to Chandrasekaran) had already prepared the alternative of promulgating an interim constitution, by the CPA and through the IGC, under which free elections could be held.[41] This idea had the virtue of blocking a Pentagon proposal of transferring sovereignty to the IGC without a constitution, an idea Bremer adamantly and rightly opposed, but it required at the same time that the IGC accept it and this time get at least Sistani's grudging acceptance. One carrot for the IGC, including its Shi'ite members, was that it would be the IGC itself that would write the interim constitution, with some expert help, not some new body created who knows how, producing the constitution according to who knows what procedure.[42] Another carrot was that this CPA-by-way-of-IGC constitution writing was a way for IGC members to enter the interim government, since sovereignty would not be given to the IGC, even in an expanded version. The interim constitution would be called a "fundamental" or "basic" law or a "transitional administrative law" (the final term had not yet been decided on), so as to avoid a term with negative implications in Iraq[43] and most likely not revive the Sistani bloc's earlier objections against imposed constitutions. When the plan was approved in Washington, the so-called November 15 Agreement was born.

AGREEMENT ON POLITICAL PROCESS (NOVEMBER 15)[44]

1. **The "Fundamental Law"**
   - To be drafted by the Governing Council, in close consultation with the CPA. Will be approved by both the GC and CPA, and will formally set forth the scope and structure of the sovereign Iraqi transitional administration.
   - Elements of the "Fundamental Law":
   - Bill of rights, to include freedom of speech, legislature, religion; statement of equal rights of all Iraqis, regardless of gender, sect, and ethnicity; and guarantees of due process.
   - Federal arrangement for Iraq, to include governorates and the separation and specification of powers to be exercised by central and local entities.

- Statement of the independence of the judiciary, and a mechanism for judicial review.
- Statement of civilian political control over Iraqi armed and security forces.
- Statement that Fundamental Law cannot be amended.
- An expiration date for Fundamental Law.
- Timetable for drafting of Iraq's permanent constitution by a body directly elected by the Iraqi people; for ratifying the permanent constitution; and for holding elections under the new constitution.
- Drafting and approval of "Fundamental Law" to be complete by February 28, 2004.

2. **Agreements with Coalition on Security**
   - To be agreed between the CPA and the GC.
   - Security agreements to cover status of Coalition forces in Iraq, giving wide latitude to provide for the safety and security of the Iraqi people.
   - Approval of bilateral agreements complete by the end of March 2004.

3. **Selection of Transitional National Assembly**
   - Fundamental Law will specify the bodies of the national structure, and will ultimately spell out the process by which individuals will be selected for these bodies. However, certain guidelines must be agreed in advance.
   - The transitional assembly will not be an expansion of the GC. The GC will have no formal role in selecting members of the assembly, and will dissolve upon the establishment and recognition of the transitional administration. Individual members of the GC will, however, be eligible to serve in the transitional assembly, if elected according to the process below.
   - Election of members of the Transitional National Assembly will be conducted through a transparent, participatory, democratic process of caucuses in each of Iraq's 18 governorates.
   - In each governorate, the CPA will supervise a process by which an "Organizing Committee" of Iraqis will be formed. This Organizing Committee will include 5 individuals appointed by the Governing Council, 5 individuals appointed by the Provincial

Council, and 1 individual appointed by the local council of the five largest cities within the governorate.

- The purpose of the Organizing Committee will be to convene a "Governorate Selection Caucus" of notables from around the governorate. To do so, it will solicit nominations from political parties, provincial/local councils, professional and civic associations, university faculties, tribal and religious groups. Nominees must meet the criteria set out for candidates in the Fundamental Law. To be selected as a member of the Governorate Selection Caucus, any nominee will need to be approved by an 11/15 majority of the Organizing Committee.
- Each Governorate Selection Caucus will elect representatives to represent the governorate in the new transitional assembly based on the governorate's percentage of Iraq's population.
- The Transitional National Assembly will be elected no later than May 31, 2004.

4. **Restoration of Iraq's Sovereignty**
   - Following the selection of members of the transitional assembly, it will meet to elect an executive branch, and to appoint ministers.
   - By June 30, 2004, the new transitional administration will be recognized by the Coalition, and will assume full sovereign powers for governing Iraq. The CPA will dissolve.

5. **Process for Adoption of Permanent Constitution**
   - The constitutional process and timeline will ultimately be included in the Fundamental Law, but need to be agreed in advance, as detailed below.
   - A permanent constitution for Iraq will be prepared by a constitutional convention directly elected by the Iraqi people.
   - Elections for the convention will be held no later than March 15, 2005.
   - A draft of the constitution will be circulated for public comment and debate.
   - A final draft of the constitution will be presented to the public, and a popular referendum will be held to ratify the constitution.

- Elections for a new Iraqi government will be held by December 31, 2005, at which point the Fundamental Law will expire and a new government will take power.

FOR THE GOVERNING COUNCIL:	FOR THE COALITION PROVISIONAL AUTHORITY:
______________________	______________________
Jalal Talabani	L. Paul Bremer;
______________________	
David Richmond	

Agreement or Imposition?

I first called the above "Agreement" a Bush-Sistani compromise, but in fact it was not exactly that. Clearly, on the American side important concessions were made. Bremer himself considered the move from a one-stage process of constitution making to a two-stage one and the abandonment of a longer occupation before free elections to be a significant diminution of his plans ("at the outer edge" of American interests in Iraq) and a reduction of the chances of success. Yet whatever the new plans were, they were the CPA's plan in their own mind, their "plan B" so to speak, and Bremer makes fun of A. Pachachi, who presented them as his own to the IGC.[45] Things were different on the other side. First, as great as Sistani's political role in producing the new approach in general was, his actual role in approving it was minimal and ambiguous. Bremer tells us that the new formula was checked with Sistani before it was taken to Washington, and that he approved.[46] We don't know what was actually shown to Sistani, but whatever it was could not have been the final version. In the original version, an interim constitution would have been drafted by March 2004, elections for a Transitional National Assembly would have been held by the summer of 2004, and an Iraqi government would have been chosen by that assembly.[47] While it was not explicit, the interim constitution itself, despite some obvious problems of circularity, could have then been approved by the elected Transitional National Assembly. It would have been illogical, perhaps, to do this, but from the sociological point of view very useful nevertheless.

(Sistani himself was to demand exactly such approval, as we will see.) Be that as it may, it was this plan more or less that was sent to Sistani for approval via Talabani, then president of the IGC. It is also clear that it was this plan he approved, if he approved anything, as reported by Abdel Mahdi on November 14, who himself found out about very significant changes in the plan only at that moment or on the next day.[48]

The first version of the plan was changed in Washington on November 11 at an NSC meeting at the behest of Rice and Powell, who doubted the feasibility of elections by June. Late summer 2004 would be "a little too close to another election." Bremer and his team then returned to the caucus option, in order to save the new framework.[49] While telling the NSC principals that Sistani was probably supportive of the plan according to Hakim and Jaffari (the leaders of SCIRI and Dawa) and that this was being double checked, neither he nor anyone else noticed (or said anything if they did notice) that this could have been the case only with respect to the version involving earlier elections.[50] This was obviously not some minor matter, however, but rather the very issue around which Sistani organized his whole challenge. The governance team in Baghdad was extremely unhappy when they found out about the change, Bremer admits.[51]

In fact, the altered final version was not checked with Sistani at all. Moreover, it was rammed through despite objections, after a discussion of a mere two and half hours, with four dissenting votes from Shi'ite representatives. The previous night, Bremer refused to describe details of the plan.[52] Obviously, the arrangement was based on the support of the rest of the IGC, something that was not achieved for the previous seven-point program. However, as far as Sistani and his followers were concerned, the new plan had essentially been forced through the IGC. This was certainly a valid assessment, given the alterations, the short time period for discussion, the fact that the plan was leaked to the press before Sistani's group had a chance to examine it, and the threats from Bremer that accompanied the whole charade.[53] So much for the Iraqi "talks about talks."

Structurally, as already argued, there was a lot about the agreement that was indeed a compromise, allowed by the adoption of the two-stage model and the plan for two constitutions, one to be produced the American way, the other to be produced Sistani's way. This compromise ultimately seemed to favor Sistani, because it was his constitution that was to be the final one. The question, however, was about how these two stages were to interact. In

Bremer's later recollection, "our objective would be to embed these points [basic principles of individual rights, federalism, and checks and balances] so thoroughly in the interim document that they would stand a chance of surviving into any permanent constitution."[54] If successful, this view of the project would vitiate the compromise, because although there would be a freely elected constituent assembly, it might have nothing important left to do with respect to producing the final constitution. With different means perhaps than via the seven-point program, the project of imposed constitutionalism would have remained.

Before the new project could succeed, there was one big hurdle to overcome. On November 26, the Ayatollah Sistani denounced the November 15 Agreements and renewed his call for free elections:

> First of all, the preparation of the Iraqi State (Basic) Law for the transitional period is being accomplished by the Interim Governing Council with the Occupation Authority. This process lacks legitimacy. Rather the [Basic Law] must be presented to the [elected] representatives of the Iraqi people for their approval. Second, the instrumentality envisaged in this plan for the election of the members of the transitional legislature does not guarantee the formation of an assembly that truly represents the Iraqi people. It must be changed to another process that would so guarantee, that is, to elections. In this way, the parliament would spring from the will of the Iraqis and would represent them in a just manner and would prevent any diminution of Islamic law.

He added: "Perhaps it would be possible to hold the elections on the basis of the ration cards and some other supplementary information."[55]

A closer look at the November 15 Agreement ultimately explains and in part justifies his rejection. Yet what was agreed upon was also to an extent Sistani's product. The new fatwa insists on the version of the plan that was apparently first presented to him and adds only the requirement of the ratification of the TAL by the elected assembly. However, was this not a possible return to the one-stage model after all? At the same time, the highly ambiguous status of what was agreed upon—or rather imposed by the CPA—had to do with the simultaneous presence of the innovative two-stage model, which was the result of the clash and implicit compromise of two projects and the attempt to guarantee the original goals of one the projects, that of the occupying power imposing rather than genuinely negotiating the fundamental terms. These contradictions and Sistani's (imagined and actual) response to some of them are worth examining.

The Source of Authority

The problem of authority arose because the CPA only made the November 15 Agreement (which was to be the foundation of the whole subsequent process) with its own creation and agent, the IGC—which was, legally speaking, an entity authorized entirely by itself.[56] In terms of international law and in particular UN SC Res. 1511, which recognized the CPA (point 1: temporarily exercising sovereignty) and the IGC (point 3: embodying sovereignty) as somehow jointly sovereign, this procedure could arguably be interpreted as legally valid. Its political legitimacy in Iraq was an entirely different matter. There was no question here in this externally imposed revolution, any more so than in other revolutions, of legal legitimacy in Weber's sense. The legal order was dramatically ruptured. In indigenous revolutions, the instance that authorizes the drafting of Kelsen's "first constitution" can typically rely on revolutionary, democratic, or charismatic forms of authority, but these were also unavailable to the parties to the November 15 Agreement. Finally, as I have shown in chapter 1, as a foreign occupier, the CPA's claim of authority as the liberator of Iraq was always weak, and it became weaker every day the occupation continued without solving fundamental problems such as employment, public services, and especially physical security.

Thus, from the internal Iraqi point of view, the CPA-IGC agreement rested on brute force alone, on facts rather than norms. Given this state of affairs, it is striking that this agreement assigned almost all the crucial tasks, and not only ultimate authority, to the two contracting parties themselves. The task of creating the unamendable body of rules, referred to in the agreement as the "fundamental law" but elsewhere as the interim constitution or the "transitional administrative law,"[57] was given to the current IGC itself, "in close consultation with the CPA" (heading 1).[58] This was strictly speaking not a violation of UN SC Res. 1511, which called for the IGC's Constitutional Preparatory Committee to prepare for a constitutional conference that would draft a *permanent* constitution. The IGC-drafted constitution would be *interim* or *transitional* and would not be called a constitution. However, the fact that it was to be unamendable by more representative bodies, including even the elected convention, was a remarkable postulate, given the low legitimacy its enactment (and the agreement itself) would have in Iraq. Other interim constitutions, for example in Hungary, South Africa, and now Nepal, have had relatively easy amendment rules.[59]

Further important tasks were delegated to the selfsame agents, notwithstanding their low levels of authority and legitimacy in Iraq. Agreements concerning security—that is, the future role of U.S. military forces—would be agreed upon by the CPA and the IGC by March 2004, three months before the transfer of power (heading 2).[60] After a misleading introductory statement to the contrary, the IGC was given a crucial role along with the CPA in choosing an "Organizing Committee" in each "governorate," which would select the caucus of notables of that province ("Governorate Selection Caucus[es]"). The latter would pick that province's representatives to the Transitional National Assembly, to which the CPA would transfer sovereignty in June and that would elect a transitional executive (headings 3 and 4). Finally, the very procedures for the adoption of a permanent constitution by a freely elected ("no later than March 2005") constitutional *convention* would be provided by the fundamental law produced by the CPA and the IGC by February 28 (heading 1). It is worth noting here one unusual aspect: the dates of the first and subsequent free elections (by December 31, 2005; heading 5) were already provided by the agreement, without waiting for the fundamental law that by this wording could bring the dates closer but not delay them.[61]

Those accustomed to coherent legal hierarchies immediately noticed the irksome problem with all this: instances of potentially higher political legitimacy—the supposedly representative caucuses, the transitional assembly, and the freely elected constitutional convention—are here authorized by an instance, or two of them jointly, with little legitimacy in Iraq. They were even forbidden to amend or revise the instance that would hold them in thrall, the fundamental law.[62] The issue was not just an abstract one, and it may indeed have played a role in Sistani's reservations. When at the intermediate stage of the process the Transitional Legislature and later the Transitional Executive would have been formed, these bodies could easily have considered themselves more legitimate than the process that created them and the original source of authorization, the will of Iraq's conqueror. They could have been tempted to do what the Estates General did in France at the famous tennis courts: namely, sever themselves from their source of authorization, declare themselves the representatives of the Iraqi nation, and proceed to establish new rules for constitution making or even give Iraq a new constitution themselves. The Transitional Legislature was especially likely to do so, since it was, paradoxically, supposed to be sovereign and yet was denied any role in the constitution-making process. The fact that it was not even allowed to amend the interim constitution under which it was supposed to operate for a year and a half could easily have led to the rejection of the document as a whole.[63] But if the new, handpicked legislature subverted the planned procedure in any way, that would have compromised the concessions to Sistani, who would find it much more difficult to oppose an Iraqi legislature than the foreign CPA.[64] Given the projected timetable, this would have happened presumably only *after* the American elections, when Sistani's probably effective call for massive Shi'a protests would no longer have worked on the occupation forces, which would be on hand to protect their clients.

Constituent Assembly or Constitutional Convention?

It is also true that the constitutional convention, if and when elected, might also not have considered itself bound by the procedural rules of the interim constitution—or the constitutional decisions of the interim legislature, for that matter. But that would have happened only (if elections for a constitutional convention took place at all) at a later stage of the process, when new power relations may already have been frozen. Nevertheless, this danger also existed, especially if the legitimacy of previous stages of the process remained questionable.

Note that here the choice of terminology mattered a great deal. Sistani and his circle seemed to have in mind, at least by implication, a constituent *assembly* as in Iran and Iraq in the early twentieth century. Indeed, since there would be no other legislature, in their model the body to which sovereignty would be transferred after free elections could only be a classical, European-type sovereign constituent and legislative body with the plenitude of powers. The fact that Sistani's fatwa called for a referendum to ratify the constitution confirmed that he was operating with the European radical democratic conception, where the only recourse against usurpation by the drafting assembly is an "appeal to the people." The November 15 Agreement, however, spoke of a constitutional *convention* (heading 5).[65] In the American (and Latin American) tradition, "convention" denotes a legislative body with the one and only function of drafting and proposing a constitution, and it exists side by side with a normal legislature that continues to function as such. We have no reason to assume that the drafters of the agreement were ignorant of this distinction. They thus wished to devalue and possibly provide a way to control the freely elected body conceded to Sistani[66] by providing an interim legislature that would hold sovereign powers during the whole drafting process.[67] They did say, however, that the "Fundamental Law," that is, the interim constitution, would expire only with the elections of the new Iraqi government under a new, permanent constitution. A convention in American theory is neither an organ that exercises sovereignty nor is it the foundation of the executive power. Thus the implication was that both the unelected interim legislature and the executive branch rooted in it would stay in power until then. If so, only two outcomes were imaginable: either the interim government would be able to control the constitutional convention, or it would not. In the former case, the concession to Sistani of democratic elections for the constitution-making body would turn out to be meaningless. But if the latter happened, Iraq would have a classical situation of dual power,[68] where only force can decide the issue, as in Russia in 1917, in 1918, and again in 1993.[69] The U.S. example of the Confederation Congress peacefully submitting to the extralegalities of the 1787 Convention is entirely unusual.[70] More common are the examples of Argentina under Perón and Venezuela under Chávez, where originally American-style conventions claimed and successfully asserted full sovereign powers. In Iraq, it is hard to say which assembly would have won this type of conflict, which could have become especially intense because of the probably quite different social bases of one body chosen in carefully regulated provincial caucuses and another by democratic elections. But it is understandable that Sistani would have wanted to avoid such a confrontation—in other words dual power with civil war—as its very possible outcome, no less than outright rule by forces he suspected.

The Interim Constitution

No major player seems to have doubted in November 2003 that forces supported by Shi'a clerics could win free elections for a constitutional assembly under just about any democratic electoral rule.[71] Sistani's demand for such a procedure, however, came not only out of self-interest. He had good reasons to believe that Iraqi politics suffered from a dramatic legitimacy problem, and it was to his credit that he sought the answer in democratic legitimacy.[72] In his view or that of his advisers, an interim constitution such as the one proposed by the November 15 Agreement failed this democratic test. They could not have been taken in by the shifting name "fundamental" or "provisional administrative" law, or even "Law of Administering the Iraqi State for the Transitional Period," and they knew even if not immediately (who knows what they were first told or shown!) that an interim constitution was actually at issue.[73] It is possible that Bremer and the CPA made a huge mistake, as Peter Galbraith argues, in not projecting a very minimal document able to take the country to free elections for a constitutional assembly.[74] For that, perhaps the small amount of legitimacy they could draw on would have been enough. But if so, the mistake was natural, because as Galbraith very convincingly continues, "the Bush administration was desperate to leave its mark on Iraq's constitution and the TAL was now its only chance."[75] But when it came to a *constitution* under any name, Sistani's position was that it could gain its validity only from a freely elected assembly. Moreover, his advisers had to understand, given Iraqi precedents, the high likelihood that an interim constitution would become a large part or even the whole of the permanent one. In the entirely reasonable view of Sistani and his advisers, such an outcome—here too subverting the apparent concession to their side—would be intolerable, especially in the case of an *imposed* interim constitution or its creation by an unelected body controlled by the Americans. Thus they retreated to the idea that, whoever drafted the interim constitution, at the very least in order to be valid it had to be *ratified* by a freely elected assembly. The first version of Bremer's "plan B" was thus marginally acceptable for them, but only marginally, because ratification is not the same as drafting. But when the United States backed away from a freely elected transitional assembly, the interim constitution too became unacceptable.

Nevertheless, the idea that an interim document can gain its validity from an assembly elected under it is circular and therefore procedurally flawed, and there are important substantive considerations against it. Procedurally, free elections can be held only under some framework of rules that are not exhausted by an electoral law. If democratic legitimacy means electoral legitimacy, as it did for Sistani and his followers, this framework must come before there are elections. There can be no purely electoral beginning to a democracy.[76] Moreover, conditions of free electoral competition require basic civil and political rights and rights of access to all relevant media. These arrangements need enforcement as well. When one begins to produce interim "organic rules" that contain these, however, there is a tendency to produce something like a detailed interim constitution. So let us assume that an interim legislature is elected under an interim constitution and proceeds *not to ratify it*, a possibility if Sistani's demands were met. Either the country still remains under more or less the same interim arrangements and the point becomes irrelevant, or, more likely, the interim legislature is forced to become a constituent assembly, which is what Sistani wanted to begin with for the first freely elected legislature. The two-stage process would collapse into a single stage, without the assembly being limited in any way.

It is worth noting that the idea of legitimating the interim constitution through a broad social agreement of the main political forces, reaching well beyond the IGC, was just as foreign apparently to Sistani as to his American opponents. Neither side had a reliable proposal for generating legitimacy for an interim settlement that would have binding force (and possibly enforcement, probably international) with respect to the subsequent stages of the constitution-making process. While Sistani was right in insisting on the original formula offered to him involving an elected transitional assembly, his new proposal still missed the essence of the two-stage formula he helped produce.

The CPA drafters, on the other hand, were right to propose an interim constitution, something that never occurred to Sistani's side, which did not fully understand this instrument in its contemporary form. Even the choice of a nonsovereign convention bound by preexisting interim rules had a lot to recommend it. Here I come to three *substantive* desiderata that may be compromised if free elections were held without prior, legitimate agreements on interim arrangements: the rights of minorities, federalism, and (relatively consensual) procedures for the making of the permanent constitution. In terms of substance, Bremer was right to worry about these desiderata. But he chose the wrong and I think strategically ineffective procedure to guarantee them.

Of course, neither Sistani's sovereign constituent assembly nor a freely elected ratifying assembly that turned down an interim constitution could be bound in these three or any other substantive respects. But the problem was that neither could the freely elected constitutional convention of the November 15 Agreement, if it chose not to be bound by instances of weaker or entirely missing legitimacy. Whatever the interim constitution would enact, such an assembly, functioning through majority rule, could indeed *legitimately* if not *legally* reject establishing Western-type protections for minorities, possibly strong federalism, and very likely an independent, strong, and secular constitutional judiciary needed to enforce these rights. It is easy to speculate about the disasters that would result, which in the political and military sense may not differ much from the consequences of the clash of jurisdictions by assemblies also implied by the CPA proposal. Whatever Sistani and his circle wanted, once they had an overwhelming majority they might not have been able to control their own most radical tendencies unless self-binding occurred previously under conditions deemed legitimate.[77]

Let me repeat the paradox. Both the choice of a nonsovereign convention and of interim minority and regional protections along with an independent judiciary, all present in the November 15 Agreement, were intelligent and innovative. The crucial point, however, remains that neither the procedural nor substantive parts of the agreement could stand up to the claims of a breakaway transitional legislature or constitutional convention. In other words, an interim constitution resting on little more than American fiat was open to repudiation from the first moment that either a transitional legislature of a freely elected constitutional convention or assembly were formed. This meant that it could not be used in a manner that would risk such repudiation by the electoral majority. For the Allawi government, which was to operate under the TAL, this was to mean the loss of the freedom of action needed to deal with the Sunni insurgency.

As we know from previous negotiated transitions, the alternative to the imposition of interim arrangements was not immediate free elections but a genuine and comprehensive historical compromise on interim arrangements. By excluding not only remnants of the Ba'ath (perhaps justified, as far as top echelons are concerned) but also all Arab nationalist parties and Sunni and Shi'ite radicals from the IGC and therefore the process leading to the agreements, Paul Bremer deprived the outcome of even this type of *pluralistic* rather than *democratic* legitimacy.[78]

The Interim Government

What Sistani found in the November 15 Agreement was in any case not a program of historical compromise but rather a top-down model for creating a transitional legislature and, much more importantly, an executive created by it, both based on co-optation and, potentially, clientelism.[79] The agreement's most obvious flaw was indeed its formula for constructing an interim legislature that would be the repository of political sovereignty for a year and a half. Here journalistic attention has focused mainly on Sistani's demand for a freely elected body, rather than the formula he opposed. It was one eminently deserving strong opposition. The caucuses the CPA and the IGC had in mind evidently could not resemble the direct democratic procedures of, say, Iowa—open caucuses in which citizens (or members of each party) can participate if they wish. The Iraqi provincial caucuses were meant to be *closed* meetings of notables rather than open ones of citizens. The last thing the Americans could have permitted is the voluntary participation of those most intensely concerned, perforce the most militant. Moreover, the provincial and local councils that would receive a role in organizing them were all picked by American military commanders, who still provided protection, and their independence was questionable at the very least.[80] What would have been especially problematic, however, was the ability of the current IGC and CPA to control participation. The IGC did receive, despite inconsistent denials, a formal role in selecting members of the caucuses, and, because of the three-stage process, its members could easily wind up being picked, as specifically permitted. In each governorate, the IGC was to pick five individuals to serve on an "organizing committee"; five others were to be picked by current provincial authorities, and five more by the authorities of the province's five largest cities. Note that the provincial and city authorities were clients of the CPA. In each province, the organizing committee of fifteen would then pick the notables for the Governorate Selection Caucus, and the latter would elect the province's representatives in proportion to its population.[81] In case the method was not foolproof, the interim constitution (produced by the IGC and the CPA) would regulate eligibility on these three levels and undoubtedly exclude unstated categories from participating in any of them.[82]

There was thus every reason to believe (even if some members of the IGC did not, at least according to outside testimony) that if the proposed procedure had been followed, the interim legislature would have been composed of friends, clients, and even members of the IGC. Nothing would have stopped such a legislature in that case from reappointing the council, its leading figures, and the ministers and state secretaries they had already named to every important executive position! The post–November 15 call of a few IGC members to preserve their own body contrary to the agreement arose either from an excess of caution or, more likely, a transparent ploy to deflect from the expected state of affairs.[83]

Elections

The Americans (along with the part of the IGC closest to them) continued to adamantly oppose either free elections in June or postponing the transfer of sovereignty. The November 15 Agreement put off elections until March 2005.

But why did they not just accept the Sistani demand for free elections? The U.S. administration's and CPA's stated reasons have to do with a lack of time, relevant laws, and adequate voter rolls. Time was mostly a function of the law and the voter rolls, as far as they were concerned. Admittedly, it would have taken time to negotiate electoral, party, and media laws, but it would have taken no more time to impose them than it did to write the November 15 Agreement. Moreover, the United Nations could have been asked to write laws at least for the first election, as it eventually was, avoiding another American imposition. It has further been demonstrated in November by Iraqi Ministry of Planning officials that a census could have been completed by the summer of 2004.[84] Other plans had been offered as well. A single-district (the whole country) PR (the rule eventually adopted for the first elections) would not even have required a prior census of the population. So the CPA argument then shifted toward security considerations. It was alleged that the insurgency in the Sunni heartland in particular would depress participation there, and this could lead to an unfair result, in the case of a single-district PR (presumably favoring the Shi'a, who needed no extra help with their probable 60 percent of the voters). But a territorially based PR electoral system (the rule adopted for the second elections), with representatives assigned according to population and not participation, would not have had this unfair result. If elections were by district, as in the United States or United Kingdom, low turnout in some districts would not affect their representation. To be sure, both systems would have required a rough prior census for accurate apportionment of seats, but as was demonstrated in 2006, this was possible.

Thus, it was difficult to avoid the impression that the Americans opposed free elections now because a dramatic Shi'a victory that summer would have made mincemeat of the American justification for the intervention in Iraq, in an American presidential election year. It would indeed have been a tough sell to the American electorate that all of the country's sacrifices and illegalities had the purpose of putting yet another Islamic government in power, the friends of Iran no less. Four of six justifications listed by Bremer for opposing Sistani's demand, jotted down supposedly in late November 2003, all focus on the fear of a Shi'a victory.[85] The most organized group, the Shi'a Islamists, would win, and in Sunni districts, the winners would be perhaps the Baath in some incarnation. Giving in would encourage further radical Shi'ite demands, who would now appear superior to the CPA and the IGC. The Sunnis (to whom he was not reaching out anyway) could not be brought into the process if the Shi'a were seen as dominant.[86] What all this amounts to is that the CPA was clearly aiming at democracy with a certain outcome, excluding the possibility that one of America's many enemies come to power in Iraq, and most American commentators are not disturbed unduly by this *contradicto in adiecto.* Democracies, however, are systems where any party (here including the Americans) can lose elections.[87] Postponing elections just because one's side would lose them is certainly the wrong way to begin a democracy. It was never very clear how postponement could do anything else than delay the inevitable result.

Nevertheless, even if the U.S. administration's and CPA's rationalizations and actual reasons for opposing free elections before the transfer of sovereignty were highly questionable, nevertheless free elections too soon could have been a bad idea.[88] This was the view of knowledgeable UN officials (though not de Mello, in the beginning). If there was a serious reason to oppose early elections for a constituent assembly, it had to do with ensuring ample time to organize public discussions and participation regarding the meaning of a constitution and the choices involved in creating one, and to establish fundamental rights, including minority and regional rights, which could fall by the wayside in a majoritarian constitution-making effort.[89] The issue was not, in my view, primarily that of time but rather of the fundamental difference between two- and one-stage constitution-making processes. A two-stage process would be more time consuming, of course, but it need not have been as delayed as in the November 15 Agreement's formulation. However, it would have had to allow for social negotiation and compromise concerning the fundamental rights of individuals, minorities, and regions before the majority got its say. Moreover, a two-stage process could have involved enforceable limitations on the powers of a *constitutional convention*, which would be impossible in a one-stage variant involving a sovereign *constituent assembly*. But this could not be achieved by the illegitimate formula of an imposed interim constitution and co-opted interim assembly.

Rights and Security

Interestingly, when making the case for delaying elections, the Americans did not focus on the problem of personal security. This may have been because the November 15 Agreement is itself particularly vulnerable on this question. Granted, the Fundamental Law was meant to incorporate a variety of equal freedoms, including political, minority, and due-process rights along with an independent judiciary to enforce them. A gaping hole in the agreement, however, was its lack of rights against the power that was likely to monopolize (or dominate) the means of state violence, namely the U.S. military authorities. The transference of sovereignty (illogically) had to do only with the dissolution of the CPA, the civilian arm of a coalition that is fundamentally a military dictatorship. The agreement (heading 2) spoke of security arrangements to be made between the CPA and the IGC that would give coalition forces "wide latitude" to provide for "safety and security" for the indefinite future. Sistani had good reason to believe that such an agreement could be made only by fully legitimate representatives of the Iraqi people, and undoubtedly he and his followers would not have considered arrangements made before the end of March binding. But the fact is that U.S. troops were likely to stay in Iraq for some time; they were engaged in counterinsurgency as well as police work, and therefore rights of assembly, association, press, and speech as well as due-process rights had to protect private and public actors from the American forces if they were to protect them at all.[90] No really free elections could be held unless the relevant rights were secured against all capable of repression—and that included the coalition forces, who held in November 2003 between eight thousand and fifteen thousand people, according to different estimates. None have been charged, and, given the likely presence of many noncombatants among them, astonishingly few have been released. The human-rights situation in Iraq was thus dismal, and it is difficult to see how the Fundamental Law planned would provide any remedies. While repression was then mainly directed at the Sunni militants, there was understandably much suspicion concerning this state of affairs on the Shi'a side as well. The November 15 Agreement, along with its projected addendum on security, did not recover Iraqi sovereignty in a meaningful way, and Sistani's call for free elections and approval (or rejection) of all interim documents only by a freely elected assembly was thus also meant to be a more effective formula for its recovery.

The Second Round of the Battle and UN Mediation

Any illusion concerning the viability of the November 15 Agreement as it stood was dispelled a few days later, when on November 26 the Ayatollah al-Sistani himself denounced it and renewed his call for free elections. The new fatwa demanded two things, the creation of a transitional assembly by election and not by co-opted caucuses and the approval of what he recognized as an interim constitution behind the phrase "basic law" by such an elected assembly. Sistani, in other words, was not, at least explicitly, going to battle against the two-stage process that was in effect his unintended achievement, but rather, his fight was against an illegitimate process of drafting an interim constitution and the establishment of an illegitimate legislature. In both interrelated cases, his opposition was about *democratic legitimacy*. Nevertheless, we can assume that he counted on a Shi'ite majority in any freely elected legislature and thus, as the best-case scenario from the point of view of the two-stage process, the prior framing of an interim constitution that he at the very least could live with. After all, as in the case of all ratification, the process of drafting should be affected by knowing who will be the agent that will have to ratify the document. (As I already explained, there was also a worst-case scenario, which would arise when an elected assembly—now the repository of sovereignty—rather than the electorate was the agent of ratification, and it rejected the interim constitution. This would have meant the reemergence of a one-stage process dominated by a sovereign constituent assembly!)

How far ahead Sistani was thinking we do not know. How his opposition to the November 15 Agreement came to pass has been described by at least two authors, but I do not fully buy these accounts. According to Bremer as well as Chandrasekaran, it was the SCIRI leaders Adel Abdel Mahdi and Abdulazziz al-Hakim who went to Najaf to gain Sistani's opposition to the scheme on November 25. Sistani obliged but surprised them by not simply denouncing the caucuses but also advocating instead an elected interim parliament that supposedly SCIRI did not want at that time.[91] I am not sure why they would not have wanted such a thing, but the claim here is that they preferred the IGC simply creating a co-opted legislature directly, an idea Sistani did not support. What is hard to believe is that they expected Sistani to support that particular preference if they helped sell him the whole scheme with elections for a transitional assembly in the first place. Did they also think that he was only interested in a Shi'a majority, as perhaps arranged by the IGC, a solution that Bremer would have been glad to offer much earlier? I think rather that they knew Sistani was going to be furious about the change of plans and they wanted to rally to his side—a very smart political move.

According to Bremer, everyone was betrayed by Sistani, who "moved the goalposts" because he had already accepted that the interim government would not be selected by free elections.[92] But this charge is nonsensical by Bremer's own account. As I have shown, at the time when Sistani was first consulted about the new interim arrangements, the scheme still involved free elections for the interim parliament, and it was only afterward, on the demands of Washington—and reluctantly as far as the Governance Team in Baghdad was concerned—that Bremer and his close advisors gave up the idea. If the goalposts had been moved, the Americans had moved them. What that move allowed Sistani to do, admittedly, was rethink his attitude to the proposal, in particular concerning the enactment of the basic law. It may be that he assumed that the elected transitional legislature was supposed to have something to do with enacting it, though this would have been both a mistake and illogical on his part. Thus the dropping of the electoral formula would have been doubly wrong in his eyes. Moreover, even if the transparent cover of a basic or fundamental law for an interim constitution was not going to fool Sistani long, it may have fooled him for a brief moment. It soon became clear that this was not a matter of agreeing only on a few common principles, as Bremer warned Talabani right in the beginning, with the latter quickly adding the need to include federalism in the interim document. Thus everyone knew they were engaging in a subterfuge, and the responsibility was theirs and not Sistani's when the real intentions became clear.[93] What the Americans gained thereby was a determined enemy of what came to be known as the TAL.

The most important thing about the November 15 Agreement for the Americans was the timeline. Formal exercise of sovereignty had to be restored by June 2004, in time to affect the U.S. elections.[94] As a result, two strategic tracks had to be followed roughly at the same time: (1) dealing with Sistani and (2) beginning work on the interim constitution, now to be called the Transitional Administrative Law. There was no time to do these things in order. As a result, the second battle with Sistani, which ended through mediation and which will be the last theme of this chapter, would not be the last one. Just as a new deal was fashioned with him concerning the problem of unelected caucuses and the timing of elections, an interim constitution was being drafted (as I will describe and analyze in the next chapter) that reaffirmed his suspicions and reinforced his doubts concerning the process of which he now became a significant outside actor.

The mediation in question had to be accomplished by another prestigious outside actor, one whom Sistani was willing to see, and only a high representative of the United Nations would obviously qualify for the role. The Secretary-General and his ambassador, L. Brahimi, who were chosen for the task, were opponents both of the war and the Saddam dictatorship, as well as of any neocolonial aspects of the occupation, including the authoritarian steering of the political process, but they were, as we have seen, also on record with the opinion that a transitional society, in particular Iraq, should not be rushed into new elections.[95] Brahimi, quite critical of the IGC, which had now disappointed Sistani as well, was thus perfect for the job of convincing the latter that early elections were not possible. Yet his mission would only be a success if he could also convince the Americans that in return for such a concession from Sistani, one that he actually attained, a more legitimate process of drafting the TAL than the in-house procedure concentrating on the old IGC and some additional American and Iraqi experts was needed.[96] Neither this concession nor a convincing process of picking the interim government was arrived at after several consultations.[97] In the end, the only thing Sistani got in return for accepting late elections was the dropping of the idea of a transitional legislature along with the caucuses he objected to. But this left the other problem, the legitimacy of the TAL, entirely open.

UN officials were entirely clear concerning both the actual shortcomings of the November 15 Agreement and the potential problem with the TAL's legitimacy, and they did not hide their views.[98] As Jamal Benomar put it: "instead of a detailed interim constitution, it would have been wiser to develop a consensus among all Iraqi stakeholders before producing a general set of principles, consistent with international law, to guide the transition."[99] But these same officials sincerely believed that elections should not be held early, and by the time they arrived in Iraq on February 6, 2003, they found it difficult to shape issues other than that one. Although they had ideas regarding how the overall process could have been significantly improved, they found it difficult to introduce them into the negotiations at this late stage. The TAL was already being written in a matter they did not like, but that could be altered—if at all—only in open conflict with both the IGC and the CPA, which the United Nations would not risk. Since such a conflictual perspective was no longer viable, the UN officials adjusted their priorities, and since what they objected to most in the November 15 Agreement was the caucuses choosing the interim government,[100] they concentrated their fire on this *bete noir* of Sistani, hoping to arrange a tradeoff. They succeeded, but this was to be their only success. Upon mediation, Sistani gave up on the early elections and Bremer let go of his caucuses.[101] There would be no elections before the ones for the constituent assembly, and there would be no transitional legislature of any kind.[102] But since now there was no plan at all for picking a transitional government, Brahimi converted a part of what he had brought with him, namely ideas for a national conference, a round table, or a suitably expanded and pluralized governing council, into options for selecting a transitional executive.[103] These plans would have been more suitable for negotiating the interim constitutional arrangements but perhaps also could have served in the more restricted capacity. In fact, as the UN report makes clear, in line with an aspect of Sistani's last fatwa, either a national conference or a round table could have amended and then approved the fundamental law, if it were given an amendment structure as opposed to the November 15 arrangements. But these ideas were all opposed by the IGC in either case, and given the uncertain support to any of the options by either Brahimi or Bremer,[104] none of them were picked, leaving the issue of choosing a transitional government to whom sovereignty would be transferred unsolved for the drafters of the interim constitution, who were not given the power to solve it. Among American policymakers, an option favored especially by R. Blackwill, namely that Brahimi should come back and in consultation do the job himself, vaguely came to be established as the only possible option if the IGC's direct role was to be avoided.[105] The issue of the legitimacy of the fundamental law was placed on the back burner, even though UN officials predicted that the actual drafting (in part by the CPA) and enactment (by the CPA), arguably violating international law, in secrecy and without public consultations of any kind, was likely to give rise to a serious crisis in a "postdecolonization era."[106]

Conclusion

Before the Iraqi constitution-making process settled on what I would call a pathological or at least deficient version of the two-stage postsovereign model of constitution making, other possibilities were tried out, at least ideally. First came the model of top-down imposed constitution making, which was justified, if at all, on realistic, liberal, or formal-logical grounds. This model was an insult to the occupied country, neoimperialist even in its most sympathetic liberal guise, and reminiscent of the colonialist's white man's burden. No one would think it appropriate today for a European country, the United States, or even a U.S. state, and it was not appropriate for Iraq, where even in the 1920s the British used a far more democratic method, at least in appearance. The Ayatollah Sistani's successful challenge to the implementation of the top-down model calls to mind Paine's famous slogan: "The constitution of a country is not the act of its government, but of the people constituting a government."[107] While enlightened monarchs, reforming dictators, and colonial powers have historically imposed constitutions on passive populations and weak political forces, the legitimacy and therefore stability of such an enterprise is highly doubtful. But what democratic procedures would today satisfy Paine's maxim?

As I have repeatedly argued both here and elsewhere,[108] Sistani's choice, the revolutionary democratic European formula involving a sovereign constituent assembly with the plenitude of powers and, supposedly, purely democratic beginnings, has become dangerous and undesirable today, especially in deeply divided societies. Such a democratic beginning under nondemocratic conditions is logically impossible, because free elections themselves require a prior, quasi-constitutional political framework. The choice of the first electoral rule cannot be the result of an election that presupposes it. A sovereign constituent assembly is possible but undesirable. It practices exactly what Carl Schmitt called *sovereign dictatorship*: nothing stops it from making itself permanent but its own good will or strong popular resistance.[109] In addition, a majority in a sovereign assembly cannot be stopped from or even faulted for adopting majoritarian decision rules. Such an assembly, not dependent on the votes of or agreements with minorities, may very well choose to adopt few or no protections for them. It has little reason for not adopting its first preference among constitutional models, and that preference may not be democratic in a broad sense of the term. Again, only self-restraint or external resistance could control a sovereign assembly's majoritarian tendencies, but the first factor may be absent, and the second, if present, could lead to massive repression or civil war.[110] We are accustomed to thinking that majority rule in a constitutional democracy needs to be limited by fundamental rights. This recognition needs to be extended to the constituent process, and it speaks against the sovereign constituent assemblies of the European revolutionary tradition.

Grudgingly, I have to admit, either for self-serving reasons or because of a genuine concern for the rights of minorities and women, the CPA group around Bremer saw these problems in Sistani's model even if they had not studied comparative constitutional theory and history—as they evidently had not. When they were forced to abandon the imposed, liberal alternative to the democratic populist proposal and chose in its place the two-stage paradigm with the centerpiece of a interim constitution, they had an opportunity to substitute a legitimate, democratic model recently tried out in several countries for Sistani's model, in essence one of two French revolutionary models. But they did not seem to know anything about the history and character of the model they were adopting. Thus they grafted on what they knew or were instinctively familiar with: the American model of a convention that admittedly also dispenses with a sovereign unlimited instance of constitution making. But that requires the coexistence of a constitutional convention specializing in constitution making alone with an ordinary legislature in which the executive is rooted and that deals with all other political tasks. In America, where the constitutional change was from a republic to a republic, legitimate legislatures inherited from the previous constitutional arrangement were available and could be used. In Iraq, this was not the case. Thus the CPA spent an inordinate amount of time in trying to put together a long-term interim legislature before Brahimi, unfamiliar with American constitutional assumptions, made them call off the quest.

In fact, in most places, and especially during transitions from dictatorships, the American formula of a nonsovereign constitutional convention has preconditions that may make this option either impractical or dangerous. Even where there is some kind of inherited legislature, as in Russia in 1993, the specter of dual democratic legitimacy and dual power may surface with explosive results. That was, as I tried to show, the danger inherent in the November 15 Agreement's formula. Even if the drafters of this agreement had been more careful and ended the tenure of the Transitional Legislative Assembly the moment the constitutional convention was convened, they would have had no way to block either of these bodies from violating or changing the rules delivered by instances less legitimate than themselves.

It is important to note that the concession that eliminated the caucuses and along with them the Transitional Assembly also converted the constitutional convention of the American formula into a constitutional assembly of the European and indeed, the early twentieth-century Iranian, Iraqi, and Indian type—an assembly that doubled also as a regular parliament. Note, however, that the November 15 Agreement was not abandoned but rather altered in yet a new compromise. The survival of the interim constitution implied potentially, and in the TAL quite explicitly, that the constitutional assembly though freely elected would nevertheless not be a sovereign one, checked only as Sistani wanted by a subsequent referendum. It was now the contemporary two-stage postsovereign paradigm that was adopted, but since the interim constitution itself was still to be imposed, that paradigm was destined to be implemented in a pathological version. Here the first point of the Agreement on Political Process of November 15, by far the most important one, remained entirely unaltered.

The UN officials who had the comparative knowledge to understand all of the implications also had the final opportunity to straighten the matter out, and unlike the Americans (who should have had the motive but it seems lacked the knowledge) and Sistani (who may or may not have had the knowledge but lacked the motive),[111] they understood what needed to be done and were committed to doing it. But unlike Sistani and the CPA, Brahimi's team lacked the power. Or, more precisely, they had a little power, given the fix in which the Americans found themselves, but the timing was wrong. As I will show in the next chapter, by the time they arrived in Iraq, on February 6, it was probably too late to seriously alter the formula and the timetables of November 15, which were linked to the American elections. Round tables and national conferences would have meant delays in producing the interim constitution, and to Bremer's bosses in Washington, timing and speed became crucial. The choice was either to take a big stand and risk being able to do nothing or to concentrate on the things that could be certainly accomplished. Being diplomats, the UN officials chose the latter option. In my view, they should have tried the former, but I am no diplomat. In any case, marginal corrections and successful short-term mediation of the conflict between the CPA and Sistani could not significantly improve the process or do better than delay the next battle over the interim constitution. The process remained pathological, and when the interim constitution was actually crafted, its contradictions were to have serious consequences. Iraq was to miss its best if not yet its last chance for state rebuilding through constitution making.

[4]

Imposition and Bargaining in the Making of the Interim Constitution

> We're going to follow two parallel tracks: the Governance Team will continue to work on details with the Arabs on the [I]GC while I tackle the difficult issues directly with the Kurds. Then all the parties will get together to hammer out an interim constitution that would withstand the stresses of sovereignty beset by a stubborn insurgency. And we need to do all this by March 1. . . .
>
> —L. Paul ("Jerry") Bremer, late December 2003, according to *My Year in Iraq*

In this chapter,[1] I will argue that at the heart of the interim constitution, the product of the first stage of Iraq's constitution-making process, was a state *bargain*. This idea is a clarification, not an abandonment, of my earlier stress on imposed constitution making, which others who once disagreed with me have since made their own.[2] The bargaining in question was highly exclusionary, more so than even political participation in occupied Iraq, and the exclusion was imposed. The results of the bargain would never have survived the various levels of negotiation and could not have been ultimately insulated by a very difficult rule of change had it not been for constantly renewed threats, in effect acts of force, on the part of the American occupiers. On the other hand, it is also true that what was imposed was not the Americans' own initial preference but was the result of a genuine bargain with one agent, the only agent they treated as an equal, the Kurdish parties that controlled the Kurdistan Regional Government and who were more or less completely united during these negotiations.

Below, I will contest the notion that the bargain was a historic compromise between Arab and Kurdish positions. The idea of a genuine American-Kurdish bargain, where the CPA negotiated in effect for Arab Iraq, may imply something like that, so I will respond to any possible confusion and criticism in advance. The position the Americans began with in the negotiations was indeed very close to Arab civic or postnationalist positions (the terms will be explained below). But they abandoned that perspective relatively early, and the deal they made was not a fair compromise between the initial positions. It could still be represented as a fair American-Kurdish bargain—after all, the two sides, understanding all the circumstances and power factors, entered into it freely—but it was not a fair Arab-Kurdish bargain, because Arab positions were abandoned, in their name, by others who would not have to live with most of the consequences. Indeed, this was done without using the considerable threat potential of the American government and the CPA, the factor Arabs in the process relied on to the extent they accepted the two-sided structure of bargaining in the first place.

Thus it would be misleading to treat the central phase of the process of making the Transitional Administrative Law, the process of bargaining over the territorial structure of the state, as *mere* imposition. It was and remained imposition vis-à-vis the Arabs, but it also involved bargaining with the Kurds. The transformation of the Arab-Kurd relationship into a purely strategic one on which no stable new state structure could be based was one important consequence of this asymmetrical way of proceeding.

Arguing, Bargaining, and Imposing

In general, we must assume the presence of all three forms of coming to a collective decision in constitutional negotiations. Undoubtedly, *imposition* and *bargaining* both involve threats and the willingness not to carry them out in return for concessions. But it is worthwhile to distinguish the two categories. Imposition is relevant to the extent that (1) an actor's *credible* threats cannot be met by effective counterthreats, (2) threats play a much greater role than promises, (3) the bargaining relation becomes monological rather than genuinely interactive, and (4) the result involves no *exchange* of concessions. In fact, remembering a warning from Max Weber, insisting only on the inevitable presence of both imposition and agreement,[3] we should always keep in mind all three terms. Persuasion ("agreement") must be present in order to keep one's own side together, the "friend" portion of Carl Schmitt's famous couplet, which would become too unstable and prone to defection if based solely on interest, fear, or having a common enemy, or even all three together. Imposition is always present, because no two or more sides are ever completely equal, and the stronger always gets to impose to some extent. As long as there is voting on a final draft, and there should be, the winners impose at least part of their constitution on the losers. The same is true when two or more sides make a compromise that excludes a third or fourth on whom the constitution or at least a part of it is then imposed by a majority or qualified majority. It is equally unthinkable finally that different sides should be able to persuade one another on *all* issues and that there would be no need for compromise. But it may be difficult to imagine a legitimate process where there is no persuasion at all (at least implicit persuasion concerning the fairness of the procedure itself) if compromise processes are to have any success. There are indeed many issues that lack a single legitimate solution, and there is no normative reason to expect one of the two sides in every debate to be persuaded. But only persuasion can lead to an interactive framework that could be the basis of fair bargaining, and only the latter allows parties to generate a minimum of trust, if not in each other then in the framework, and to regard their compromises as more than simply strategic and temporary.[4]

Thus there is imposition, persuasive arguing, and bargaining in all *successful* negotiations, especially including constitution-making processes. Of course, the weight of each element need not be the same. If Elster's emphases concerning 1787 and 1789–1791 could be rightly put on persuasive arguing and bargaining, in Iraq, according to my underlying hypothesis, everything shifted to imposition and bargaining. Ultimately, there were two reasons for this: the amount of force available to one primary actor, the U.S. government, and the repeated and continued insistence of that actor to accomplish constitution-making tasks according to rigid, artificial, and accelerated timetables. The presence of open force and an apparent lack of time make the use of persuasive arguments a highly implausible way of advancing one's interests in a negotiating situation. I doubt that at the Iraqi venues of negotiation there was a great deal of arguing in the sense of attempts at mutual persuasion based on principles, but it is difficult to tell given the dearth of records and credible testimony.[5] At some of the venues, as I will show, we can assume the presence of persuasion based on participation in a common struggle and the obligations that would arise from that. Even here, the instrumental use of public-regarding arguments was the thing that must have been feared the most, namely that the supposedly weaker party will go public with a story of trust and betrayal. But the overall negotiation process had little relationship to publics other than an engagement in the most crass and transparent public-relations operations. Indeed, again following Elster, both imposition and bargaining were often presented to the press in public-regarding forms (and even imposition was masked as genuine bargaining). Under Iraqi conditions of trust, however, hypocrisy rarely had the desired result. Very likely, on the contrary, even genuine public-regarding claims inevitably appeared to be hypocritical. This is a serious matter, because coming to agreement by using public-regarding arguments that authentically could be presented to the outside as such is an extremely important element of the legitimacy of a constitution-making process. It is also part of the "glue" that makes the actual bargains something more than merely strategic ones that could be renounced at the slightest excuse or opportunity.[6]

I will on the whole avoid evaluating the few claims of justice on the part of the actors, which mostly dealt with past injuries and their proper contemporary and future institutional redress. As far as I am concerned, all of the sides have suffered enough by now, and many though by no means all of the arrangements they seek (for example, a postnational or civic-national state on the part of some Arabs and bi- or multinational arrangements in the case of many Kurds, if they accept "Iraq" at all) could all be made compatible with the demands of justice, even if in different ways, as long as they were promoted in liberal constitutionalist versions. In my view, there is no *single* just solution to the problem of defining the *demos* or *demoi* of a divided society over a given territory, but it is not the goal of this work to demonstrate that rather obvious normative claim. The various solutions to this and other problems that were to concern the Iraqi constitution makers were, however, greatly tied to the past and present structure of inherited memories, ideologies, interests, and power positions of the various actors. The question throughout the process of constitution making was whether these memories and ideologies allowed actors with diverging interests and power positions to compromise their different ideas about institutional solutions. While it is possible but by no means certain that the particular memories and ideologies made mutual persuasion unlikely, in my view they certainly would have allowed principled compromise solutions if a fair bargaining framework had been provided. In relation to the four pressing issues I will discuss, state formation, government structure, rules of constitutional change, and the relationship between state and religion, there is enough to indicate the outlines of where second-best solutions could have been (and, in the last case, were actually found to an extent). The reason why this did not happen in all four cases and for the overall constitutional package was not first and foremost because of the failure of persuasion, which probably never had a chance, but because of the triumph of imposition and its timetables over fair bargaining.

That at least is my thesis in this chapter. To demonstrate it, I will first try to consider the venues and actors in the processes of making the TAL. Then I go on to discuss, as ideal types, the positions the main actors could draw on regarding questions of state and government formation and where the possible intellectual lines of compromise between them lay. Next, I will describe the actual process of the making of the TAL, moving through the venues and making the case for the centrality-of-the-state bargain amid the various phases. Then, switching perspectives and looking at the TAL itself, I consider the three most important areas of constitution making, where there were sharp divergences of positions, to evaluate whether the outcome should be understood as a historic compromise or ultimately the imposition of the perspective of one side. Finally, after considering the deep legitimacy problems of the TAL and its creation, I will consider Sistani's final battle against the interim constitution and the provocative but inaccurate suggestion that the Grand Ayatollah actually managed to invalidate, and not just delegitimate, the TAL. I end with a discussion of the failure of state reconstruction in the TAL.

The Venues and the Actors

The Transitional Administrative Law was made in four venues, and people who assume that it was one or the other that produced the whole thing are mistaken. In chronological order, but definitely not in order of importance, these were, first, the ten-member Drafting Committee of the Iraqi Governing Council founded in December 2003, under the chairmanship of Adnan Pachachi,[7] which may have actually dominated the process very early and produced at least one draft in January[8] but later was reduced to a clerical function. This group, in terms of its power to do anything, was the least important, and we know the least about how it worked. It may very possibly be the case that here initially attempts were made to make principled arguments for positions. It seems, however, that when serious disagreements manifested themselves, the Pachachi Drafting Committee hopelessly deadlocked.[9] The second venue, in order of importance, was the Interim Governing Council itself. It is hard to say when exactly this body began to discuss TAL drafts and amendments, probably very late if Bremer's recollection can be trusted.[10] But if the Crisis Group is right, its members attended the drafting committee earlier, and the line between the two bodies was fluid.[11] Equally important, the IGC did not have a constitutional secretariat or expert staff to preprocess the issues and were entirely dependent on the other venues to prepare the discussions, materials, and drafts for them, and this was a very serious weakness. There was only one exception to this, the issue of state and religion, where many of the members had comparative knowledge and both settled and sharply differing views. Here the sources indicate, as I will show, that there was genuine discussion and give and take in this body, with the political principals playing direct roles, and even the great power holders, Bremer from within and, the sources say,[12] Sistani from without, paid close attention and exercised influence. In my view, however, this issue was construed in largely symbolic terms on whose outcome, as I will show, very little was to hinge in the end, except that one side, the Shi'ite clerics, were to sacrifice a lot of negotiating capital over it.

In my view, two other venues were more important. It is commonly said that American experts drew up the TAL, which was originally written in English, not Arabic.[13] This is also how one of the insiders, Larry Diamond, seems to describe it, with two qualifications. First, the American drafters did work on a draft submitted to them by the Pachachi Drafting Committee, and second, they included two important expatriate Iraqi (nonconstitutional) lawyers, Feisal Istrabadi and Salem Chalabi, both members of that committee, with the former beginning his service by translating and rewriting the Pachachi draft.[14] Thus there was considerable overlap between what I will call, using Bremer's language, the Governance Team and the Drafting Committee.[15] Altogether, the Governance Team, an informal subcommittee of the Governance Office of the CPA (the latter name aping MacArthur's Government Section, which sat as a "constitutional convention"), had five members, according to Diamond: himself; Istrabadi; Chalabi; a British foreign service officer, Irfan Siddiq; and an American political appointee, Roman Martinez.[16] Very likely others including Scott Carpenter, Meghan O'Sullivan, and unnamed lawyers and bureaucrats went in and out of the group. But there was no constitutional lawyer.[17] According to Diamond, they worked tirelessly for many weeks.[18] From all descriptions, that could not be said of the other three venues, so it is likely that the actual drafting did occur mostly here. However, drafting should not be confused with making, and the Drafting Committee should not be confused with the overlapping Governance Team, which is what Chandrasekaran seems to do, with Chalabi, Istrabadi, and Diamond as his main informants.[19] Thus even if the five-member Governance Team "made" most of the TAL—which it did not, as I will try to show regarding the essentials—this would not make it an Iraqi, nonimposed product.[20]

From Diamond's own description, it seems to me that the basically American Governance Team had its actual political influence in the area of governmental structure. While it seems that some members of the group had very strong, well-formed opinions on some subjects, for example Istrabadi in his opposition to any ethnic federalism and consociationalism and Martinez in his opposition to judicial (constitutional) review, these ideas were easily eliminated not as much by their internal debates as by the political and ideological trend of the general proceedings. It was when technical solutions were sought to previously made political decisions that the drafters had some freedom, even if at times they wound up (as in the case of the veto powers of the members of the Presidency Council) going against, whether deliberately or not, the original political intentions of actors who may not have understood what the "experts" actually did. Thus they had considerable power, and they had this power on rather less symbolic issues than the plenary of the IGC as a whole.

Where the five-member Governance Team (and especially the Iraqi Drafting Committee) had no power at all was on questions of state structure.[21] "The federalism issue was temporarily quarantined while Bremer and other top CPA officials negotiated directly with the Kurds."[22] That negotiation was to last until the bitter end, and was to be no mere "conversation among friends." According to Paul Bremer (whether or not these words were actually said), a two-track strategy was decided on early in the game: "We are going to follow two parallel tracks: the Governance Team [his use of this term may have been somewhat different in terms of its personal composition than mine] will continue to work on details with the Arabs on the [I]GC while I tackle the difficult issues directly with the Kurds."[23] These trips to Kurdistan continued from January 2, 2004, through at least the middle of February,[24] and there were discussions with the Kurds as a caucus in Baghdad[25] and with them alone up until the last day before there was a final agreement on the TAL. One such meeting was also held with the "Shi'a House."[26] The "I" in the Bremer quotation, of course, was not quite accurate, even if it revealed a weakness that the Kurds or their advisers discovered how to utilize.[27] Bremer went to Kurdistan a number of times, with either Ron Blackwill,[28] the British diplomat Jeremy Greenstock, or two young aides, Martinez or O'Sullivan,[29] but there is little sign that he ever took anyone along with even the slightest expertise on issues such as federalism, natural-resource allocation, the conversion of the militias, and governmental structure. On their home turf in Kurdistan, in Erbil or Salahuddin as the case may be, Massoud Barzani and Sami Abd-al-Rahman of the KDP and Jalal Talabani and Barham Salih of the PUK, themselves well experienced in governmental-institutional matters (unlike their U.S. counterparts), had great reserves of expertise to draw on, including a very talented group of American, Irish, Canadian, British, and Kurdish exile experts in law, political science, and negotiation.[30]

As I have already suggested, these Kurdish negotiations were the most important. This was true first because only here did power and issue significance come together. Elsewhere, the participants of the other venues did not have the ultimate power to decide (the draft committee and the Governance Team) or were not given the time and supporting expertise to really discuss the fundamental issues (the IGC as a whole). The Kurds knew exactly over which issues there could be no compromise, but beyond that they were willing to be quite flexible, in particular regarding Kirkuk and the distribution of oil resources. In return, they expected two things and got three, the last the most important. First, whatever compromise was going to be made in Erbil, it was going to be *the* compromise, and the Americans were expected to impose it on the rest of the IGC.[31] The Kurds themselves were not similarly bound. They could and did try—and this was the second thing they expected—to turn their concessions on federalism into gains on the governmental structure being drafted by the five-person governance subcommittee. And they could and did ask for entirely new things in the final short plenary mode, and they expected the Americans still to support them substantively and procedurally. These actions radiated out from the state negotiations and made the Kurds the dominant force next to the Americans in the process as a whole.

And that outcome was perhaps foreordained by the structure of the negotiations over the state structure. It was only here that Bremer and the CPA treated another actor, or two united actors, as an equal, in a genuine bargaining situation without an attempt to impose or to use threats that could not countered (with respect to the Kurds, the threat would be that of an American or Turkish invasion). While I was not there and cannot say for sure, I would not be surprised if the two sides used real arguments to persuade each other on the basis of common interests, common earlier support for each other, and even shared values, along with, most likely, common opposition to the Islamists, or "Black Turbans," as the Kurds referred to the Shi'ite clerics. With the historical mistrust of the Kurds and the likely prejudices of the Americans, this could have been a context in which some trust was built.

Much more important was the fact that whereas all other negotiations were multilateral, if highly exclusionary, this process was bilateral. The Americans, in other words, accepted the most fundamental premise: Kurdistan was one and Iraq was one, and the two were negotiating their federation and not, as Galbraith supposedly explained, the ways and means of the devolution of power in a united state, in the form of a new autonomy.[32] The operative phrase for the Kurds became "voluntary union between the Kurdish and Arab peoples," which had already appeared in an article by Massoud Barzani on December 21, 2003.[33] Of course Iraq, not having a de facto state, could not negotiate with a quasi-state on an equal basis, and this is why Bremer took it upon himself to deal with the Kurds while "mere technicians" did some drafting with the Arabs. Bremer himself claims that all this was "suggested by several Arabs on the IGC." Diamond says that it was Pachachi's idea[34] to send the CPA boss to Kurdistan, and if so, the elder Sunni statesman must have assumed that only the American leadership had the power and authority to negotiate with the Kurds.[35] Indeed, when (apparently meaninglessly) selected Arab participants were invited to join a meeting in Erbil or when the Drafting Committee went there for a session, nothing much was accomplished.[36]

But what was at stake was incredibly serious and went beyond occasional Arab presence here or there.[37] The Kurds were consistent supporters of a selected rather than elected body to draw up a constitution, and they consistently opposed early elections. This was hardly because their parties needed time to prepare themselves, since they were politically the best organized and most experienced in Iraq.[38] What was anathema to them for very obvious demographic reasons was a sovereign body, elected by a one-person-one-vote principle, drawing up a constitution for the whole of Iraq on the basis of even a qualified majority decision. They immediately grasped the significance of the November 15, 2003, agreement, and Jalal Talabani was entirely right to sign it from a Kurdish point of view, despite later criticisms he received for accepting language vaguely having to do with territorial eighteen-province federalism.[39] That issue could be and was dealt with later; the choice of the negotiating forum was far more important!

What Talabani or his advisers grasped, unlike their Arab counterparts most likely except for Sistani, was the significance of the IGC under the CPA producing an unamendable interim constitution that would significantly preempt and structure the work of the constituent assembly and the final constitution. But even an interim constitution and its negotiation involved hidden dangers for them. If the process was constructed fairly and inclusively, the Kurds would be only one-fifth of the forces present. Their military strength would be neutralized by the referee, the United States, and could not be used as a threat. Secession was a threat but not a fatal one, unless they could take Kirkuk and the oilfields with them, and the Americans had reoccupied that part of Iraq after its early Kurdish conquest in 2003.[40] Secession also risked deep problems with Turkey, especially with Kirkuk involved. To be sure, the structure of the IGC was not fair to begin with. With Sunni exclusion,[41] Kurdish strength in the IGC was greater than it would have been in a truly representative co-opted body. But their view on nationality, state structure, and governmental institutions was a distinctly minority view, especially initially. They would have received concessions, but the tendency would have been to grant them cultural autonomy in the context of eighteen-province federalism. So it was crucially important for them but unacceptable to everyone else involved to change the format from a round table of, say, four major and a number of minor participants (major: Americans, Kurds, religious Shi'ites, and secular Shi'ites; minor: religious Sunnis, independents, and other ethnic groups) to a figuratively two-sided table of Kurd-Arab negotiations. This was not possible because it clearly would have incited the resistance of all those who opposed the sectarian redefinition and possible division of the country. But it was equally good to get the same structure via a separate set of negotiations in which the Americans represented Arab Iraq; in fact, as it turned out, it was much better, because of the unexpected cooperative attitude or weakness of this substitute partner.

Once the premise of a special bilateral venue was accepted, it would have contradicted the negotiating situation itself to ask the Kurds to give up just those things that led the Americans to accept them as an almost equal partner.[42] Letting the Kurds keep those things, however, made them entirely unequal to all the other Iraqi participants in the negotiations, and it required the Americans to enforce precisely this inequality.

Finally, it was important that those who would have objected most vociferously were kept far from the most important negotiations. This was certainly true for the relevant members of the IGC and the Drafting Committee. Equally or even more important, just at the time that Bremer and the Kurds were bargaining the most intensely, the return of L. Brahimi to Iraq was also being negotiated, and he struck his compromise with Sistani around the time the Americans finalized their state bargain with the Kurds. Because of the demands of international law, UN officials were almost unanimous in their opposition to negotiating and especially altering state territorial structure under conditions of an occupation, and to Brahimi and Benomar, being liberal and secular Arabs, the idea of a division of Iraq on an ethnic basis was hardly appealing.[43] They were, however, not part of the crucial negotiations with Talabani and Barzani, though of course in February they could have been included. What they knew of the emerging deal is hard to reconstruct. In effect, however, they were offering a bargain to Sistani based on delaying the free election to the constituent assembly at a time when the very significance of that assembly was being reduced by a deal concerning the state that, having been arranged before the elections, would thus be one less thing over which Iraq's elected representatives would have decision-making powers. No wonder that Brahimi felt cheated and undermined afterward.[44]

But the UN could in no way reverse or even modify the result of the state deal. Only Sistani could attempt to do that, and in the end he failed as well.

The State Bargain I: The Positions

Having destroyed the Iraqi state in its territorial and organizational integrity and having contributed to the division of the state's people on ethnic grounds, the Americans clearly understood that part of the constitution-making process would have to do with state making. Most of their bilateral discussions with Kurds were focused on this issue, and it was these negotiations in Erbil and in the end in Baghdad that decided the question regarding at least the territorial structure of the state. They also touched on, less inconclusively, the related question of the possession of armed forces within the state.[45] While the reconstitution of the state's people as two nations along with protected nationalities was also discussed in the bilateral talks, these matters were handled fairly consensually by the other three venues. Given the territorial structure negotiated by the Kurds and Americans, however, it is difficult to believe that the issue of binationalism (language rights in particular) was as open as it may have seemed to some participants. To understand the connection, it may be worthwhile to briefly sketch, even if as ideal types, the main positions present in the controversy. These positions have particular representatives in Iraq, but they cut across parties and in their pure form do not represent party positions.

Ethnic Nationalism (Kurdish)

The ethnic nationalist position ascribed to many Kurds, usually without further qualification, sometimes to the Kurdish "street" and rarely to a specific individual, periodically surfaces in the statements of main leaders and even some foreign advocates.[46] It is based on the more or less correct historical premise that Iraq's originally patched-together territory has always been the homeland of two major "nations," both quite recent imagined communities, of which one, the Kurds, have never accepted attempts to "Arabize" the whole territory, despite repression, assimilation attempts, ethnic cleansing, and forced deportation. According to the Kurd ethnic nationalist, it is both a matter of justice and unfulfilled historical promises of the great powers that twenty-five to thirty million Kurds, the largest nation in the world without a state, receive their own nation-state.[47] For the ethnic nationalist Kurd, there "always" was a Kurd entity in the sense of a people and a territory, and all it has been missing despite relevant promises was a state organization covering the *whole* territory and administering the *whole* people.[48] For the ethnic nationalist, here as elsewhere, ultimately there is a choice only between (1) Arabic (and Turkish) ethnic nationalism along with the repression and even elimination of the Kurds as a people and (2) Kurdish ethnic nationalism. There is no room here for multiple identities, for example, a Kurdish national one within an Iraqi civil "nation."

Given their history in Iraq, this position sees only three acceptable institutional solutions for its aspirations. In order of desirability, the first would be a greater Kurdish state incorporating also the Kurds of Turkey, Iran, and Syria, an option everyone regards as impossible in the short and middle term. The second would be a smaller Kurdish state carved out from Iraq, encompassing both the three governorates plus the fragments of two others in the present Kurdistan region and all Kurd-majority areas or even Kurd-plurality areas in Iraq, including Kirkuk. This option would be undesirable *without* the added territories and may be currently impossible *with* such additions, so there is also a third formula, a binational state with a more or less independent Kurdistan within it. This is seen by the ethnic nationalist as a huge concession from the point of view of his or her first and second options, a mere third best, and in return there is a definite expectation of the territorial expansion of the Kurdish part of the binational structure to include all Kurdish majority and even plurality areas, including Kirkuk province and Kirkuk city. As we have seen, in this view of things, such a confederation or federation (not really a state) should be negotiated bilaterally between Kurds and Arabs. Ideally, it would have two symmetric parts, one Kurdish, one Arab. But the organization of each should be up to its own constitution, and in theory it would be acceptable that the Arab part organize itself subfederally, in terms of, say, thirteen to fifteen provinces or governorates. Thus an asymmetric structure on a Canadian model (the Arab part would not have its own regional government, only the federation government; the Kurds would have two governments) would be acceptable, depending on the status of the whole and the powers given to the parts (great) and the whole (very limited).[49] As long as each part—that is, first and foremost, Kurdistan—retains a veto over all constitutional legislation, foreign and military policy, and possibly all national decisions of any importance, even a three-part organization (Kurdistan, a Shia region, and a Sunni region) or a five-part one would be acceptable. The stress is on the veto power.

The ethnic nationalist perspective to the extent it accepts Iraq at all sees it as a treaty organization, a confederation, or a federation (not federal state) only somewhat more centralized, if an asymmetric structure is conceded. At the same time, the ethnic nationalist will tend to accept the empirically false and logically somewhat incoherent idea of Brendan O'Leary (himself a liberal nationalist) that there is some kind of deep structural link between three dimensions: ethnically defined federations, powerful units with weak centers, and power sharing in the center.[50] And, in fact, the linkage is more logical from the ethnic nationalist point of view than otherwise, though it is not completely clear why someone who wants to separate would still want to rule the unit one is separating from. However, the motivation is fairly understandable. If the ethnic nationalist cannot have his independent state, he will want a three-fold guarantee against the "state" that is conceded to the federation, which will make the unit itself a quasi-state. Note, however, that in this version power sharing means a device to weaken the central federation by a system of rigid vetoes.

Civic Postnationalism or Republican Nationalism (Arab, American)

There is no question that this relatively well represented position in the IGC and the Drafting Committee in terms of individuals lacked a power base and may have appeared extreme and ideological.[51] Its advocates accepted Kurdish claims that pan-Arab nationalism has resulted in great oppression of and crimes against the Kurds. But replacing an ethnic national state with a binational state or by ethnically based federalism in their minds would be no solution. When Arabs such as K. Makiya make the argument, they often use an Israeli analogy. In Iraq, like Israel, ethnic definitions of the state or of units of the state would be in the end incompatible with democracy, because those not part of the relevant ethnic group would be lesser citizens of the state or the unit.[52] Iraq (and its units) should be a state (and units) of all its (and their) citizens, and they should all receive the same rights and obligations as citizens of Iraq. Federalism is here favored not as a way of instituting special identities but as another set of checks and balances against arbitrary government ("separation of powers" and "protection of minorities"), but federal units organized on an ethnic basis could themselves become small-scale but equally potent threats to individual and minority rights as could an ethnically defined national state.[53] Ethnic federalism would lead to the complete ethnicization and, in Iraq, the sectarianization of politics, which would threaten the survival of any kind of statehood. One answer is therefore comprehensive separation and division of powers, where *all* the different branches and levels—central and decentralized—control, monitor, and correct one another. Another is fiscal federalism (central control and equitable sharing of a large share of the resources to the units) complementing the territorial one that splits up ethnic fiefdoms.[54]

There are two possible versions of the civic model, a postnationalist and a republican nationalist one. The difference has to do with the thickness of the nonethnic collective identity that is affirmed and its resulting openness (of the postnationalist) or suspicion (by the republican nationalist) toward claims of subethnic nationalisms when restricted to demands for cultural autonomy. It could be said that while the postnationalist could live with a "state nation" concept as proposed by Linz and Stepan, involving multiple identities and multicultural rights, the republican nationalist still imagines a "nation state" but with all requisite *individual* rights.[55] It is very hard to say where Iraqi liberal advocates on the Drafting Committee would have defined themselves in relation to these two positions. Most likely, the republican conception may have seemed a little too close to Arab nationalism (see below) and was not considered to be worth advocating under the circumstances and given the way the IGC was constituted. But it is also possible that all civic nationalists were also committed or strategic multiculturalists, given the atmosphere of our times, especially in the patron country.

However that may have been, although advocates and even states may not be entirely coherent on these matters, a whole variety of federalist arrangements are compatible with the two versions, granting stronger or weaker powers to the units and to the whole, which could be a centralized or a decentralized state with provinces, a federal state, or a federation, but not a confederation or an asymmetric federation with one "federacy" that has a confederal, treaty-based status. Of course the model allows for the possibility, as in India, of a highly (though diminishing over time) centralized federal state, with some or even most of its territorially defined units having an ethnic majority, but the units themselves not being ethnically defined and therefore a consolidation of units on merely ethnic grounds not easily permitted.[56] Disincentives to such consolidation[57] can be established, or they would need to involve constitutional amendments if not outright bans. Amendment rules would involve participation by federal state organs and legislatures or electorates of the units, according to various possible quantitative proportions, but outright vetoes would not be allowed. The question of whose powers are enumerated and whose would be the reserved powers need not be solved in the American way, for example, and current theorists tend to favor enumerating both sets of powers as well as shared powers. With respect to Iraq, this position in its postnationalist and some republican versions would affirm or allow a federalism based on eighteen provinces, with significant powers devolved to them. Evidently, it would have to accept the fact that each province would have an ethnic majority or plurality. The postnationalist at least could offer cultural autonomy to all the main nationalities of the country, which could go so far as establishing two official and several other protected languages, allow public use of several above a certain threshold of population, establish institutions of higher learning in at least Kurdish and Arabic and other schools in all protected languages, and so on. But the constitution in the postnational version would not define the state as that of one or of two nations, and it may not mention the word nation at all. Or alternately, in a more republican version (coming closer to Iraqi nationalism, see below), it could define the Iraqi nation in terms of all of its citizens, whatever their ethnicity, religion, or gender.

Liberal Nationalism (Kurdish)

The liberal nationalists are clearly different from both the ethnic nationalist and the republican nationalist positions, because they think in terms of the possibility of multiple identities. They would not go so far as to adopt the category of "state nation" for Iraq. Thus liberal nationalists postulate the possibility of two or even more national identities within a single nonnational state identity, for example "Iraqi identity."[58] Its advocates say they are liberals but "not difference-blind liberals." The position even prefers a relatively thin civic definition of nation, but it argues in that case that in Iraq two such nonethnic definitions are needed, one Arab and one Kurd, or possibly three, one Iraqi, one Arab, and one Kurd.[59] The argument for this cannot be theoretical, since theoretically either one (Iraqi) or three such identities fulfill the same civic purpose, and indeed the two-part Arab-Kurd division threatens to reethnicize the civic conception. (One could be Iraqi and Arab, Iraqi and Kurd, or just Iraqi, but never Arab and Kurd.) The reason for making their particular choice (aside from latent ethnic nationalist sympathies) is historical: the bitter experience of perhaps the largest "nation" without a state, the Kurds, at the hands of Arab nationalism requires separation if any common state framework is to be preserved. Here the example of Israel is used in quite a different way than it is by Makiya: genocide helped produce a *Jewish* state, not integration-minded Jews.[60] That is a fact, but so are the consequences, good and bad. Makiya's point regarding some of the outcomes of an ethnic definition of the state in Israel is not thereby diminished, especially to an Arab audience, but apparently that is not to whom the liberal nationalist is speaking.

Admittedly the model, unlike that of the ethnic nationalist, goes beyond the leading Israeli paradigms today. While the Kurds, like the Israelis, simply cannot and will not trust Arabs in any framework that does not make them the center of a distinct statelike formation, that formation can however "federate" on the basis of mutual need and interest with an Arab statelike entity called Iraq (or in the least nationalist version, even "in Iraq"). Thus for the liberal nationalist too the maintenance of the Kurdistan region is not negotiable, and its geographical extension is a highly desirable goal. While important Kurdish politicians such as Mahmoud Othman and Hoshyar Zebari seem to hold fairly consistent versions of this position, it has been developed in the greatest detail by several foreign advisors, who use it to reply to the charges made by the civic nationalists and postnationalists against the ethnic nationalist perspective. However, the distinctness of the position when compared to ethnic nationalism comes into question. Understanding the Kurdish perspective as a civic rather than ethnic nationalist one, O'Leary and Salih defend the position against charges that Kurdish nationalism could be as repressive over a smaller territory as Arab nationalism was over a larger one.[61] The historical experience of Kurdistan since 1991 partly bears out their claim, although Kurdish rule in Kirkuk more recently has left a lot to be desired as well.[62] But the real question concerns the future rather than the past. Here even the foreign advisors of the Kurds differ, and there is much more willingness on the part of some (such as O'Leary) to see the guarantees for individuals and minorities in a future Kurdistan also in terms of state- and federation-wide relations of checks and balances. Others (Galbraith) push for a kind of confederal status that leaves Kurdistan, when expanded in territory, part of a larger integration in name only.

There are, I think, important strategic differences between Kurdish perspectives, differences that roughly correspond to the ethnic and liberal nationalist positions even if inconsistently. They do in the case of O'Leary, the most consistent thinker on the side of the Kurds. The liberal nationalist also trades Kirkuk only because he must. But, despite the fact that he may accept some kind of link between ethnically based federalism (strong powers for the regions and power sharing), he is willing to see these devices as functionally interchangeable protections for the region and the ethnic group.[63] He wants power sharing not only to weaken the federal state but to retain a strong federal state for the purposes deemed legitimate or shared. Thus he should be more willing than the ethnic nationalist to trade some powers of his ethnically defined region, because he wants a somewhat stronger organization than mere treaty-based integration.[64] In return for what is given up, the liberal nationalist seeks to have greater powers in the federation, which as a minority the Kurds can get reliably through consociational structures of power sharing and less reliably through a federal chamber either suitably, that is proportionally, or, in their favor, disproportionally organized (but not according to a system of eighteen governorates of which the Kurds have three, or one-sixth, as opposed to their one-fifth share of the population). In order to constrain his own *ethnos*, the liberal nationalist can even affirm a strong constitutional judiciary with a strong Kurdish presence.[65] Here the problem is only that enforcement mechanisms in other federal states or federations involve strong executives, federal interventions, federal police forces, strong federal military, and the like—the very institutions the liberal nationalist opposes creating, along with his ethnic nationalist colleague. Finally, logically, seeking a stronger integration than a treaty organization would suggest an amendment rule perhaps between those of the civic postnationalist and the ethnic nationalists' veto, but here too the actual positions of liberal nationalists and the ethnic nationalists on the Kurdish side tend to become indistinguishable.

Other Positions (Arab and Iraqi Nationalists)

Ethnic nationalism has obviously existed among Arabs too, as pan-Arabism or Arab nationalism, and it has always interpreted and fought for Iraq as a Sunni Arab country that should grant cultural rights to Kurds and Shi'ite Arabs very reluctantly and sparingly—and territorial rights not at all. The perspective is thus constitutionally strongly centralistic, in line with Iraqi traditions (at times compromised vis-à-vis the Kurds). It was entirely excluded from the negotiating process, despite its continuing political popularity in Iraq among Sunnis. What is obvious is that even if the perspective had been present its chances of winning would have been nil. Its exclusion nonetheless had some consequences. Paradoxically, had Arab nationalists been present, it would have been easier to see the postnationalist position as a possible basis of compromise. Otherwise the IGC would have had to face the internal prospect of a polarization on the lines of ethnic nationalisms, followed by the inevitable breakup of the country itself, which at the time most of the members would not have relished. The best way to avoid this would have been to eliminate the question of national definition from the discussion altogether. At the very least, the postnational or a compatible Iraqi national position could have been strengthened. Thus the exclusion of an undesirable perspective both weakened its role and shifted the whole intellectual balance of the discussions. Still, centralism had its advocates among the Shi'ite clergy, the potential beneficiaries. This, however, was a very weak position because among the exiles and their American sponsors "federalism" was always accepted as a magic mantra that could not be compromised. Moreover, the Shi'ites too have suffered because of Arab nationalism, from which they were excluded as "Persians" or because they follow a supposedly non-Arab version of Islam. The form of nationalism that has periodically appealed at least to more secular Shi'ites (and many Kurds, during the Bar Sidqi experiment, with the Communists, and under Kassem) was "Iraqi" nationalism, which was a nonliberal version of the civic republican form; according to this, Iraq was an Islamic nation of all its ethnic and religious groups.[66] Perhaps understanding their relatively narrow majority, they were not interested in explicitly redefining Iraq as a Shi'ite Arab nation. But they were nevertheless allergic to liberal postnationalist or even civic republican definitions of the political community, which to them in any version reeked of secularist, antireligious biases and traditions well known in the region.[67] In any case, they were both too distracted and divided to strongly represent Iraqi nationalism against the Kurdish gambit in either its ethnic or liberal version. As I will show, identity issues for them came to be focused on the role of Islam in the state, which was rather irrelevant constitutionally because here local control rather than constitutional formulae was going to decide things. But they did not seem to care too much whether Iraq was Arab or Arab and Kurd or just Iraqi as long as it was Islamic. Second, the more politically savvy among them early on saw the differences among alternative federal proposals that were functionally equivalent to the Kurds, namely whether the "rest of Iraq" would be one or two or four regions in a symmetric structure or merely fifteen provinces in an overall asymmetric one. And depending on party and geographic constituency, they either opposed regions altogether or supported them because they too wanted one or two of them in oil-rich areas with large Shi'ite majority populations. Until the final round of negotiations, their own choices or their divisions excluded them from this part of the discussion, and the basic agreement concerning the Iraqi state was thus made without them. When it was crowned with a ratification rule that protected the new arrangements, they woke up much too late.

TABLE 2
Varieties of identity positions on Iraq

1. Ethnic nationalism	2. Liberal nationalism	3. Civic post-nationalism	4. Civic republican nationalism	5. Iraqi nationalism	6. Ethnic nationalism
Kurds	Kurds	Secular Arabs and Americans	Secular Arabs	Shi'ites, Secular Arabs	Religious and secular Sunni Arabs

Purely intellectually, the weakness of positions 4, 5, and 6 in the process (and especially the absence of 6, which would have been the most aggressive) tended to make Kurdish liberal nationalism rather than postnationalism the natural basis of compromise. Moreover, because of their harsh disagreement over Islam, secular nationalists and postnationalists and Shi'ite Iraqi nationalists had trouble finding common ground; in fact, each side seemed to be more comfortable with the Kurds, who were flexible on the big symbolic issues. They were Islamic but not fundamentalists. "Socially" (and such issues influenced even the highly sophisticated UN delegation), that put them between the liberals and the "Black Turbans," who did not as a result see that as far as the main issue was concerned they were together on the opposite side of the Kurds. Aside from the structure of bargaining, the intellectual positions of the Kurds, especially the ones who did not argue on the grounds of ethnic nationalism, could begin to occupy a middle ground. Two things should be noted. Organizationally, as I already explained, there were two fundamental choices (rather than three): (1) a bargaining situation involving two parties, Iraq and the Kurds (a two-sided table), or (2) one in which the Kurds would be one actor among several (round table). On this point the two Kurdish positions were in agreement, and in fact both adopted the ethnic nationalist premise of "Iraq as a voluntary union." Even more importantly, they managed to have their way. Just as the American negotiators, who originally started out with simple but reasonable versions of the postnationalist federal conception (eighteen-province, genuine federalism with full cultural autonomy), were brought into the Kurdish framework by accepting the negotiating model, the same process also blended the two Kurdish perspectives even closer together. To an extent, the ethnic nationalist position became the long-range objective if not the bottom line, and the liberal nationalist governmental schemes and statements of values became either public-relations tools or strategic bargaining ploys. Even if this is a slight exaggeration, the weakness of the opposing perspective pushed the supposedly compromise position, the Kurdish liberal nationalist one, in a more ethnic direction. Here are my hypotheses concerning the intellectual causal scheme that, in itself of course, could not have been decisive: the American exclusion of the Sunni nationalists led to a Kurdish center in the spectrum of positions. The weakness of the Shi'ite Iraqi nationalists and the secular postnationalists, who could not form a real alliance, made the other extreme, the Kurdish nationalists, stronger, and this made the center, the Kurdish liberals, move toward their positions.

Political outcomes, however, do not take place first and foremost on the level of ideas. Undoubtedly, the surprisingly weak pressure of the Americans on behalf of a civic postnationalist perspective they were expected to favor was to be an even more fundamental reason for what was to happen, and it is to this dynamic that I will now turn.

The State Bargain II: The Process

The Creation of the First Drafts

Looking at all the negotiating venues and their products, it becomes clearer how in the end a Kurdish amalgam of ethnic and liberal nationalist elements triumphed. I will here focus only on questions of state structure and political identity. In the Drafting Committee led by Adnan Pachachi, the civic nationalists and postnationalists were apparently strong, mainly because of the role of the chairman. Whatever Pachachi himself represented during his first governmental role (before 1968), he was now an Iraqi (rather than Arab) secular nationalist[68] opposed to ethnic federalism, provincial control of oil resources, and forms of power sharing based on ethnicity.[69] He worked mostly through Feisal Istrabadi, who held similar views and who as a drafter and advocate seemed to have been quite accomplished and impressive.[70] I do not know if at this level persuasive arguments of the type we see in Makiya's well-known piece were attempted on behalf of civic postnationalism or Iraqi nationalism. Given the strong convictions of the chair and his top representative on this ten-person committee, there were certainly some frank exchanges of views. Whether or not there was any serious attempt to persuade, strong threats were certainly used on both sides, using external instances to pressure the drafters.

In December, according to Diamond, "Washington" informed the Kurds that they would have to give up their region and their regional government and would have to accept a federalism based on eighteen provinces. This was certainly based on a common opposition in the Pentagon, State Department, and White House to ethnic federalism, which they saw as a formula for the unacceptable breakup of Iraq.[71] This converges with both O'Leary's view that the U.S. authorities interpreted the November 15 Agreement in the sense of territorial or eighteen-province federalism (though this is not really supported by the agreement's rather vague wording) and with evidence that the Kurdish signer J. Talabani came under strong pressure in Kurdistan for even signing the document.[72] In reality, the agreement was vague on the question of federalism and did not exclude a Kurdish region or a special status for the Kurds.[73] In any case, the Kurds responded with very strong threats of their own, including secession.[74] On December 20, 2003, the five Kurdish leaders on the IGC submitted a draft "bill" in which they outlined their vision of federalism.[75] In Barzani's summary, directed against both Iraqi and "foreign" interlocutors, the main principles were the voluntary union of two peoples (Iraqi and Arab used interchangeably for the other side), no surrender of anything in the existing situation including the Kurdistan Regional Government, the rejection of the separation of the Kurdish governorates from one another and at least to this extent province-based federalism, and the inclusion of all other "Kurdish areas" in Kurdistan, including Kirkuk.[76] Finally, the Kurdish members of the Drafting Committee (among them Fersat Ahmad) submitted a list of specific demands, based on "draft constitutions" adopted by the Kurdistan National Assembly in October 2002, for inclusion in the TAL. Among them:

> the establishment of a federal Kurdish region, recognition of Kurds as one of the two main nationalities of Iraq, recognition of Kurdish as an official national language alongside Arabic, recognition of the Kurdish (regional) flag and anthem, reversal of Arabization in mixed areas and a highly evolved form of decentralization that would give Kurds a significant degree of autonomy and control over resources in their federal region. Proposed language concerning non-Kurdish matters proved rela-

tively noncontroversial but everything having to do with Kurdish aspirations led to stalemate in the committee, which operated by consensus.[77]

At this point, the different venues interact. All sources indicate that Bremer went to Erbil to break the deadlock in the Drafting Committee.[78] But he did not really get any results until later in the month (January 7, at the earliest, but that was only an outline conceding the existence of a Kurdistan Region), since the deadlock at first continued in Erbil, as we will see. Meanwhile, obviously not unaffected by the American-Kurdish negotiations, and with some possible help from the Governance Team, which was focused on other issues given Bremer's instructions to remain hands-off, it is nevertheless possible to argue that the Drafting Committee produced a compromise (or at least "amalgamation," according to the Crisis Group)[79] of its own, based on its earliest draft (which we do not have) and Kurdish submissions. According to Diamond,[80] during the first days of January there was already a draft he could read, written by an unnamed advisor of Pachachi and translated as well as redrafted by Istrabadi. This text has never been published, but from Diamond's critical description we can tell that it strongly resembled what has been called the Pachachi draft, which was published in Arabic on February 1.[81] It did not seem to contain a formula on federalism, however—at least Diamond does not mention such a thing. This can be taken in terms of the emerging formula for all of the early versions: leave the status quo as it is for the transition period and let or even require the elected constituent assembly decide most but not all the issues linked to the ultimate meaning of federalism in Iraq. The one issue I think the drafts did decide (possibly and even likely because of Bremer's deal on January 7) was that there would be a territory called Kurdistan beyond provincial federalism if that was the scheme ultimately chosen. And this was a concession to the Kurds, even if it fell well short of the idea of a voluntary union. I will rely on the one published version to make the argument and will use O'Leary's commentary as a partial corrective.

The Pachachi Draft seems amateurish next to the finished TAL, but that is in retrospect a very misleading impression. It has been rightly said to be "deliberately short on detail" and this, I think, was a matter of both democratic and international legal principle. Given the legitimacy problems of the CPA and the IGC, due to Sistani's demands for a freely elected assembly, the idea of significantly binding a body with much higher legitimacy than the drafters of the TAL may and should have seemed unacceptable. Given international law, the idea of seriously transforming Iraq's state structure and indeed irreversibly altering its regime under and by the authority of a foreign occupation also could and should have seemed unacceptable. But it was exactly the latter that was sought by the Kurds, who rightly recognized that a detailed interim constitution would help create or legitimate facts on the ground that would be very difficult to reverse later in a permanent constitution. Thus all the Kurdish proposals were highly detailed in all matters that concerned them.[82] This invited "compromise" solutions that would be themselves highly detailed, as the TAL eventually was, and therefore this structural issue of the type of interim constitution represented not a compromise but the adoption of the Kurdish preference of neutralizing the constituent assembly reluctantly conceded to Sistani, one elected on the basis of a one-person-one-vote principle.

According to the Pachachi Draft published on February 1, 2004, Iraq is an independent and sovereign state with a democratic, parliamentary, pluralist, and federal "system," but it is neither said to be Arab, or Arab and Kurd, or multinational, or any other kind of "national" (art. 3). In line with a postnationalist conception, or because no decision was possible, "nation" is not mentioned in the draft. Language is, and it is, in line with a more republican model, Arabic (art. 3). Regarding both these provisions, it is said that *in the transitional period* the current special status (regarding statehood) *of* Kurdistan and current special situation (regarding language) *in* the territory of Kurdistan shall be respected. The name Kirkuk is not mentioned in the draft, but respect for current special status would not in any way include Kirkuk city and Kirkuk province in Kurdistan, which after being captured by the Kurds from Saddam's forces have been, unlike Kurdistan, occupied by the Americans—at least formally. Thus the draft does not meet any Kurdish demands regarding Kirkuk nor does it promise that the constituent assembly would even deal with this question. For the transition period, federalism is discussed only indirectly, with references to the eighteen provinces (one of which is Kirkuk) and the applicability of the TAL itself in all of them, and by outlining the powers of central government: foreign policy; defense; guarding of borders; peace and war; monetary, currency, and development policy; public budget; and citizenship affairs (art. 3). However, as this draft contains some ironclad principles for the drafting of the permanent constitution, one of these is relevant to federalism: the final constitution must include "a democratic, pluralist federal system including a unified Iraq and organizing the relationship between the territory of Kurdistan and the central government." While this language again does not include Kirkuk, in one respect at least this version of the TAL would seem to preempt the elected constituent assembly: there would have to be in whatever federal formula chosen a place for a territory called Kurdistan, and not just three or four Kurdish majority provinces or governorates (art. 42). However, it is not clear who would control adherence to the constitutional principles, and whatever formula emerged in the final constitution would have to be approved in a referendum that without further elaboration seems to be a countrywide vote requiring only majority approval.

O'Leary is working with either a later version, a different translation, or a somewhat arbitrary interpretation of the Pachachi Draft.[83] That is why, surprisingly, he detects a harder-line position on the Arab side than I have. Either his polemical reading style, the translation, or the then current state of American-Kurdish negotiations could be responsible. There are crucial differences between our readings. The control of integrated armed forces and natural resources seem to be new, and could have been included at the behest of Bremer, to counter relevant Kurdish demands. The declaration of the Kurdistan Regional Government as a "subordinate level of government" seems to be new, but instead of a denigration, this seems to have been rather an acceptance of the Kurdish demand that the KRG would not be abolished. I note that the supremacy of the Federal State is not as O'Leary thinks "a wholly antifederal" but only a "wholly anticonfederal" mode of thought. There has been such supremacy in the United States, (West) Germany, India, arguably the European Union, and even Canada, though not recognized by those in Quebec who seek a confederal status. Other features of the two drafts regarding federalism seem to be the same, though interestingly O'Leary does not mention what would have been for him strongly in the "minus" column, Arabic as the official language, and, on the "plus" side, the limitation of the constitutional assembly by a constitutional principle that seems to enshrine the territorial integrity of Kurdistan. Perhaps these elements were now gone. There was a trend among the drafters of the TAL, because of the legitimation problems of the whole process, to eliminate constitutional principles binding the constitutional assembly in the South African manner. The powers of the constituent assembly were, however, still there, and O'Leary explicitly mentions the (implicitly or explicitly?) majoritarian ratification rule for the final constitution.

The CPA-Kurdistan Regional Government Bargain

I think it would be a great mistake to see the early drafts emerging from the IGC Drafting Committee as the basis for the eventual compromise with Kurd positions. Of course, one can put various proposals next to each other, extrapolate some such relationship, and argue that the TAL created something like the Pachachi model in Iraq and somewhat modified versions of Kurd proposals for Kurdistan.[84] This very dualism, however, was itself the heart of the Kurdish proposal and therefore should not be understood as some kind of compromise. Whatever real bargaining occurred after the Drafting Committee deadlocked was between Bremer and the Kurds, and thus if anyone compromised it was them, around their own positions, which in the case of the CPA were constantly shifting. Initially at this venue too there was deadlock. But the point of this negotiation from the very beginning was that neither side wanted to act on or even fully articulate its most potent threats (which would have been fundamentally unequal), and as a result there was genuine give and take. After the January 2 "acrimonious and unproductive session," when each side presented its hard-line position, Bremer returned in seventy-two hours with Ron Blackwill, and the two sides made an effort to avoid taking inflexible positions.[85] Bremer seemed to understand the history that had led to the special position of the Kurds, appreciated their military alliance, and supported their demand for federalism, but only within a unified Iraq. Moreover, he rejected settling the most difficult questions (for example, Kirkuk) in an interim document, and said the United States would not accept a federalism based on ethnicity, which he very rightly recognized as "a central feature of the Kurd's draft."[86] Thus the Kurds gained very little at this point. But Bremer realized at the same time ("Barzani remained silent") that they were not going to simply give in to the American positions. He "left Irbil with a sense of apprehension."[87] According to Diamond, before they left, they decided to defer the question of ethnic versus provincial federalism and concentrated on the powers of government. The idea was that if the Kurds agreed to a strong central government with sufficient protections, maybe they could have their ethnic federalism after all. I think in the end the opposite happened, but the strategy made a great deal of sense. With the most important issues left undecided, the Kurds were willing to entertain the possibility of a relatively strong central government with exclusive control over defense, oil and water resources, fiscal and monetary policy, and borders.[88]

By January 7, the Kurds got Bremer to return to the theme he was avoiding. In return for conceding a relatively strong central government, they wanted him to accept that they could not retreat to where they were before the war in 2003, and therefore accept the principle of a "voluntary union with Iraq." This time what was always their truly fundamental principle was not completely rejected.[89] They also got Bremer to accept some modest action on Kirkuk and the establishment of a property-claims commission to adjudicate longstanding disputes due to the policies of Arabization. At the same time, the leaders of the CPA heard but did not (yet) give in on other Kurd demands, notably the nullification of federal laws, the retention of the Peshmerga, the banning of federal troops from Kurdistan, and a binational definition of the state. Nevertheless, in Diamond's not implausible view at these January meetings, which continued through the month sometimes with and sometimes without Bremer, a "historic bargain" was struck between the CPA and the Kurds, based on the tradeoff of significant central powers and the preservation of a unified Kurdistan region with far greater powers than the eighteen provinces (or rather fifteen, because the three in Kurdistan would have no powers). Advocates of the Kurds do not see matters this way. According to Galbraith, on January 27, 2004, Barzani and Talabani met alone with Bremer, a disastrous mistake on the part of the Kurds, as he earlier explained.[90] At that meeting, the three seemed to have agreed to a formula that sounds like Diamond's "historic bargain": Kurdistan as a federal unit and a central government with great powers, including military and judiciary powers. The Americans thought they had an agreement, but according to Galbraith the Kurds later claimed they did not. It is difficult to know whom to believe. Given the power difference, one would have to go with the Americans, ordinarily, because they could insist on the deal being honored. But these were not ordinary times, and the United States did not have an ordinary government during them. In any case, even Galbraith says "fortunately" it was the Americans themselves who abandoned the deal.

At this point, the accounts of Diamond and Galbraith merge. According to Galbraith, it was on February 6 that Bremer informed Barzani that all references to the Kurdistan Regional Government would have to be struck from the TAL at the insistence of the White House, along with Kurdish as a second official language.[91] While this set of events is interestingly missing from Bremer's otherwise pretty complete memoirs, they are confirmed from the other side by Diamond. Chandrasekaran specifically mentions

Rice and Wolfowitz as both being behind the order to Bremer.[92] The Kurds, feeling double crossed (a different story than Galbraith's, because this would indicate initial adherence to the January 27 agreement), retreated to an extreme and even more truculent position. Now even moderate leaders, including the remarkable Mahmoud Othman, joined the chorus of more extreme demands.[93]

The so-called Kurdistan Chapter, submitted for inclusion in the TAL on February 13 but first discussed on February 10, 2004, was clearly a unified Kurdish response to the new American position. It was neither an initial bargaining position nor primarily a response to a Pachachi Draft, as O'Leary and the Crisis Group claim.[94] Galbraith, who along with O'Leary seems to have been one of the authors of the Kurdistan Chapter, makes a much more convincing case for the chronology and the politics of this proposal, though it is surprising that these sophisticated operatives, working so closely together, have not gotten their story straight.[95] For the moment, I wish to only summarize this proposal and consider its details in comparison with the final TAL arrangements themselves.[96] Only a few matters would be the province of the federal government; otherwise Kurdistan's laws would be supreme in the region. Kurdistan would have its own army and own its oil resources, but it would not manage fields currently in operation. Iraqi troops could enter Kurdistan and taxes could be collected there only with the permission of the Kurdistan national assembly. The permanent constitution would apply in Kurdistan only if approved by a majority of its voters.[97]

We have only Galbraith's testimony for what happened at the next negotiating session, with Bremer back in Erbil. That he supposedly insisted on the January 27 agreement is hard to believe, since the White House repudiated it. But anything is possible; perhaps he already got his bosses to backtrack, since they in reality only had the option either to come up with a credible set of threats or make concessions. He refused to discuss the "Kurdistan Chapter." Then or at a subsequent session, he got the Kurds to give up recognition of the Peshmerga and agree to its formal dissolution (which the Kurds would certainly not go through with) and to federal control of resources in the TAL.[98] Meanwhile, having persuaded Washington of the necessity of preserving the Kurdistan Regional Government, this key institution was again conceded to the Kurds, along with Kurdish as an official language and some partial measures for reversing the Arabization of Kirkuk before the final settlement of this question.[99] Note that a key result was, despite many strong words by Bremer to the contrary, an asymmetrical form of federalism that established the most powerful unit on entirely ethnic grounds. The other parts of Iraq would be under the system of provinces; only Kurds would possess a powerful regional government to protect their interests. All others would only have one government, the federal one, and how strong that would be was again made dependent on the Kurds. Somewhere along the line—I cannot tell when—a new balance sheet was drawn (most likely by the American experts of the CPA, or the experts of the KRG, or somehow the two together) among the powers of the federal state and that of the region, and, amazingly, the right of nullifying (amending, not applying) federal laws in all but a few enumerated areas was conceded to the Kurds as well. It is because of this structure that people began to speak about a "historic bargain" or a "historic compromise." To me it looks rather like a compromise well tilted in the direction of the Kurds, but that outcome, already prefigured in the bilateral structure of the negotiations, would not be fully visible until somewhat later, when the Kurdish-CPA bargain was processed through the body officially responsible for enacting the TAL, the full IGC.

Imposing and Negotiating at the Interim Governing Council

Consider the position of the IGC. Its own Drafting Committee, having recommended the bare outlines of a provincial federalism but conceding some undetermined special status for Kurdistan as a constitutional principle, left the actual work of producing a model (in accordance with both democracy and international law) to a freely elected constituent assembly that would be no longer under foreign occupation. Now they were suddenly given a "compromise" model of asymmetrical provincial-ethnic federalism hammered out in a state bargain by the Kurds and Americans. Did they have the power to resist this deal, especially when the strongest opponents of ethnic nationalism, the secular postnationalists, were weak on the council, and when the Iraqi nationalists among the Shi'ites were distracted by religious issues? One response, the line of least resistance, was that the Drafting Committee and especially the American Governance Team proceeded apace to fashion a TAL consistent with the basic idea behind the bargain. Indeed, as I will show, under the false assumption propagated by the Kurds that it was they who had surrendered the most because of the signature issues of "Kirkuk" and "oil," a governmental structure was negotiated that would have made sense only if the powers of the federal units were much weaker, in line with the very early strategy of the CPA.[100]

But then three new things happened. The Kurds decided to insist on the "Kurdistan Chapter" as a formal submission to the TAL, despite the fact that they did not get Bremer's assent to this. Some of the Shi'ites became attracted to a symmetric model of purely ethnic federalism. And third, everyone became sidetracked by the mainly, but not exclusively, symbolic issue of the relationship of Islam to the state.

The Kurdish challenge came first, inviting the Shi'ite move on federalism as a response. What was originally a response to Bremer's repudiation of a prior agreement now became a stake in Kurd-Arab negotiations, renewing the possibility of deadlock. And this released the Arab, mainly Sunni and secular members of the IGC, who now roundly attacked ethnic federalism and the danger of dividing Iraq.[101] This time, however, a deadlock did not occur, for two reasons. One is that Bremer, though he did not formally accept the Kurdish laundry list not previously agreed to, given his bargain with the Kurds, also did not renew his own earlier strong stand against ethnic federalism in any way; thus in effect he switched sides. And a new and unpredicted division occurred on the Arab and even the Shi'a side: some of the Shi'ites, mainly around SCIRI, became interested (or revealed their interest) in an entirely ethnic-based, symmetric form of federalism where they could "have everything the Kurds have."[102] While the Kurdish idea of a voluntary union made most sense with a two-member Kurd-Arab treaty organization or confederation, it could be made compatible with an asymmetric structure negotiated with Bremer as well as three-member or five-member "federations" or "confederations,"[103] always with the proviso that the Kurds would retain a veto over all constitutional changes (preferably for all Iraq but at least as they concerned Kurdistan).

Once it became clear that only Kurds were getting a potentially strong regional government to protect their interests, in a setting where the federal government might be weak, the disadvantages of an asymmetrical structure for the Arabs became clear. This was especially true for some of the religious Shi'ites, who had a primarily southern base and who, like the Kurds, could hope to control large oil resources in their territory, whatever early arrangements for resources were to say on the matter. One could have assumed that the religious Shi'ites had the greatest interest in a strong majoritarian central government, because they could control it. This was so if they were united, but they were not. Regions with oil had different interests than regions without it, and the attitude to Iraqi nationalism was also different between the various parties (the SCIRI, Da'wa, and, outside the IGC, the Sadrists, to whom one did not want to lose the oil-poor urban vote). Moreover, now the Americans were helping to remove Kurdistan from central authority, and the negotiating process began to favor power sharing, as I will show, and thus a weak government no one would exclusively control. Thus having what the Kurds had made a lot more material sense, especially for those for whom symbolic issues of identity were increasingly articulated on a transnational rather than national level, concerned with Islam rather than nation. It may even be that this turn from Iraqi nationalism made their demands on behalf of Islam, the other possible center of identity, all the more vociferous. But more likely it was the other way around. Interest in the transnational allowed them to focus more on the homogeneous region than the heterogeneous state.

When demands surfaced from SCIRI (the Supreme Council for the Islamic Revolution in Iraq) for the ability of other provinces to form regions, the Kurds were, most likely, happy to oblige. They did not propose the idea, but among acceptable solutions this was for them marginally better than an asymmetric structure that might unite rest of Iraq, centrally organized against them, depending on the type of voting. A symmetric, ethnically based federation or confederation could effectively be the same as an outright two-unit confederation, where a veto by one is automatic.[104] More immediately, they were getting new and unexpected allies and supporters for the regional idea, their opposition was being split, and the TAL would be even more restrictive with respect to the freedom of action of the constitutional assembly. Indirectly, if the Shi'ites dropped their focus on the federal government, it would be more likely that the latter would be weak. Only the secular nationalists and the Iraqi nationalists among the Shi'ites, who may have recognized that the goals of Sistani were being undermined, objected.[105] Given the relative disinterest of the Kurds and the Americans concerning this particular outcome, genuine negotiations and compromise did follow, with the surprise ending of a separate meeting between the Kurds and the Shi'ites, on February 28, where Kurdish support for new potential regions (which they did not mind) and for some formula acceptable to the Shi'ites on Islam (more on this below) was traded for Shi'ite support for two official languages in the state.[106] It was probably because of such a deal, and not merely because of a concern in the IGC for greater equality among parts of Iraq, that it was finalized that the TAL (after the initial elimination of this provision) wound up allowing new region formation in the transition period, but only for three provinces, and with the permission of the majority of the national assembly, which was perhaps unlikely but hardly impossible for say three Shi'ite regions (and one Sunni region) if they wished to do so (a large Sunni region would be another matter, or a united, oil-rich Shi'ite region!).[107] None of this, however, would have happened if the asymmetrical structure was not first separately negotiated and then treated as a given by the CPA. At any rate, now the possibility of an Iraq composed of quasi-independent regions was established, and equally relevantly, the Kurds almost until the very end had a free ride home. But that was because the IGC, including the religious Shi'ites, still did not realize that while compromising on some details, they were also well on the way to accepting the deeper Kurdish scheme for the new Iraq as a voluntary union.

Finally and fatefully, the organized group on the IGC with the greatest popular backing, the Shi'a House, which had been rather uninvolved in most of the constitutional negotiations,[108] now mightily distracted itself in the middle of the critical, final possible negotiations over the state structure and wasted the remaining time (given the highly artificial American deadlines) to solve a largely symbolic issue in a largely symbolic way. This was the problem of Islam as an official state religion, and it was negotiated largely within the IGC as a whole. Admittedly, this issue was intertwined with the very important question of a Personal Status Law, which in principle would have a very significant effect on the lives of men and women all over Iraq, determining whether questions of marriage, divorce, custody, and even some property matters would come under religious or civil courts. But while the latter question was being resolved, an inordinate amount of attention was paid to wholly symbolic issues mattering far less.

It is probably true that the overall discussions concerning Islam and the state probably represented the most genuine, open-ended, bargained segment of the negotiations over the TAL, with several actors exerting strong pressure both inside and outside the formal negotiations, and to some, this particular part of the negotiations was evidence that the interim constitution was not ultimately an American-imposed one, or at least was not imposed unidirectionally, whatever that may mean.[109] To "neoconservative and evangelical voices within the U.S. political sphere" and Senators Santorum and Brownback, Iraq's constitution had to be secular, even though all the Iraqi forces on the IGC, including the Iraqi Communist party, noted that every constitution in the Arab world made Islam the official state religion.

As a matter of fact, as the same author well knows, Bremer indeed helped to "impose" by his standing veto threat the withdrawal of a potentially new status law passed by the IGC on December 29, 2003, as resolution 137, which (voiding a law from 1959) was to make the Shari'a the foundation of family and civil law. The new regulation was to have been incorporated both in a so-called Personal Status Law and in the TAL, but neither happened. As far as I can reconstruct, during the first half of January this proposal was strongly challenged in the streets of Baghdad by a series of women's demonstrations ranging from hundreds to thousands of participants. Undoubtedly, the anger of the demonstrators was fueled by the dramatic worsening of the conditions of women in many parts of the country, the return of honor killings, the enforcement of strict Islamic dress, firings from many jobs, and reprisals and threats against female political activists.[110] While up to eighty-five groups were said to participate,[111] the leading role was played by two civil society organizations: the OWFI (the Organization of Women's Freedom in Iraq)[112] and the Women's Alliance for a Democratic Iraq (WAFDI).[113]

It was above all the larger and more radical demonstrations led by the OWFI that began the process that in the end led the IGC to revote and repeal resolution 137, although Bremer's veto threat also must have played a major role. That threat may have been influenced by the appeals of the Women's Alliance, and it is even likelier that the requirement that one-quarter of the National Assembly be female was written into the TAL as a consequence of their demand. Assuming that the figure represented a compromise between two factions of the IGC,[114] Bremer's changing one-quarter to every third person on electoral lists when writing the electoral law was probably influenced by demands addressed directly to him.[115] On the electoral guarantees for women the Shi'ites were surprisingly pliant—or not so surprisingly, given their later ability to control their women MPs.[116] It was different regarding the question of the status law. When on February 27, 2003, on the "surprise" (to whom?) motion of a secular Shi'ite female member of the IGC (obviously prompted by Pachachi, cleared by Bremer, and backed by a crowd of women allowed into the chamber) resolution 137 was withdrawn, prompting a walkout by religious Shi'ite members and their allies, there was outrage, even though the idea of getting a new status law into the TAL was probably already dead.[117] My evidence: it was not even once again raised by Shi'ite members in negotiations over the TAL. However, the event was almost certainly timed if not engineered as a response to a Shi'ite consultation, the day before, with the Ayatollah Sistani, concerning the question of Islam in the TAL, and the Shi'ites interpreted it as an frontal attack.[118]

Thus the walkout, prompted probably as much by high-handed strategy as substance, was very real, and it sought, among other things—much too late in the game—formal bilateral negotiations with the CPA, like the Kurds had for a long time.[119] When this was granted, there were only two issues left to negotiate: making sure the Shi'a could have in principle what the Kurds had, namely the right to form regions in oil-rich areas and the symbolic issue concerning Islam. With the first demand quickly granted given the prearranged support of the Kurds,[120] all energy was expended on the second. And here the CPA was unwilling or unable to act entirely on its own. Initially the question was whether Islam was to be "the" or "a" source of legislation. The first idea was clearly nonsensical for the very modern constitution the TAL was going to be, and the second did not require of the lawmaker much of anything. In the case of passing the first formula, everything would depend on the kind of constitutional court Iraq would have to enforce it. For the TAL, the Drafting Committee and the Governance Team had already settled on a mixed framework, despite some fundamentalist antijudicial views of one American member (oddly enough for a civil-law country), namely a "Federal Supreme Court" of nine (!) members (in reality a constitutional tribunal that shared the powers of a highest court of appeal with the Federal Court of Cassation: TAL art. 44b) who had to be picked according to difficult consensus requirements by a three-member Presidency Council from nominees drawn from higher and lower *secular* juridical councils. This body could rule laws and lower legal acts of any type unconstitutional, but it is doubtful if it ever would on the basis that Islam was not the source of the act in question, whatever that is even supposed to mean, beyond perhaps natural-law principles of justice (TAL art. 44, 2–3).

According to N. Feldman, Shi'ite Islamists, because of unfortunate promises made to Brownback and Santorum by Bremer, which "reeked of imposed constitutionalism," upped the ante. They now demanded a new formulation: no law should be able to "contradict Islam."[121] Most likely, the Shi'ite Islamists simply realized that it was easier to show in a court a contradiction between a specific law and a specific Islamic tenet than to demonstrate that some law, any law likely to be proposed, did not have some relation to some kind of Islamic rule, practice, pedigree, or interpretation. This is pretty much the picture I get out of Bremer's and Diamond's converging but not identical retelling of the events. When, instead of returning to the IGC plenary, the Shi'ite House finally forced Bremer to negotiate with it directly on February 28, it got him to at least entertain the possibility of the new wording, as long as a totally redundant proposal concerning no law being able to contradict the table of rights was added as well.[122] This was then sold as a compromise, having received the "green light" from Secretary Rice at Camp David and "cleared in advance with the Ayatollah Sistani" in Najaf.

So it went. I think if Sistani told the Shi'ite politicians anything, he may very well have told them that the new wording would be more effective anyway. But even the new formulation was going to achieve little without the right kind of body to enforce it, one that the Islamists were not going to get in the TAL at any rate, and there is no evidence that they were even asking for it. Still, if Sistani really was involved, the matter was now enormously important in their eyes on a symbolic level. The fact is, the matter was equally important for the secular side in the negotiations, and the Kurds who did not care one way or the other apparently joined them. Thus there was yet another fight in the IGC in the final hours before Bremer's March 1 deadline, with the Kurds supporting the Shi'ites, who would not change anything but in the end agreed to add yet another meaningless phrase: legislation could not contradict "democratic values."[123] The end result was actually a verbal compromise, if a quite meaningless one: not only laws contradicting Islam and the rights provided for in the TAL were to be forbidden in the transitional period (art. 7), but also laws contradicting the principles of democracy, whatever those principles were deemed to be. This, of course, was an entirely superfluous and redundant addition, since legal acts contrary to democracy or enumerated rights would be unconstitutional under other paragraphs of the TAL. The whole provision was moreover useless to either side until a Federal Supreme Court was created, which never was to happen, however "unconstitutionally," during most of the life of the TAL. The most important thing about this whole incident was the amount of time wasted on it, the fact that it divided the secular (civic) and religious (Iraqi) nationalists on a very emotional issue, and, as we will see, that it involved so much time, energy, and divisiveness in the last crucial hours of negotiation over the TAL. And this is the case because, as the Shi'ites would realize very soon but still too late, something much more important was happening at the same time.

The Final Act: Inventing and Imposing the Ratification Rule

The American-Kurdish bargaining over the state did not stop with the special sessions in Kurdistan. The Kurds were supremely conscious of one flaw in all that they had achieved: a freely elected constitutional assembly could take it all back. Thus it was very important in their eyes that, of all their proposals, one was clearly not accepted, nor was its inclusion in the TAL seriously considered, namely, the provision of the "Kurdistan Chapter" (art. 5) that would allow the permanent constitution or any law replacing the TAL to apply to Kurdistan only if approved in a referendum of the region.[124] This was not a potential veto of the permanent constitution but, in line with the idea of voluntary union, the affirmation of one entity to agree to the replacement of one state treaty by another according to its own *sovereign* or quasi-sovereign decision. The issue was not raised as far as I can see during the February 28 Shi'ite-Kurdish talks, because the talks very likely would have fallen apart if they had. At any rate, Bremer does not mention it. I will initially follow his very revealing testimony, which is as interesting for its revelations as for its symptomatic omissions.

After the Shi'ite walkout was diffused, at 2 a.m. on February 29, according to Bremer, the Kurds suddenly presented a two-page set of demands, including demands for money, the legalization of the Peshmerga and, most crucially, "the right to veto the ratification of the constitution." Since Bremer says these were the issues presented three weeks earlier, I am assuming that the last provision was still referring to a veto that would apply to Kurdistan only. It is at this point that Bremer supposedly convened the Kurds "in a small, dark work room," complained about last-minute demands, and said they threatened (not *he* threatened, as Galbraith says, but the result is the same) the Kurd-U.S. special relationship.[125] It is this that Galbraith considers "more brutal" treatment, when very likely he was one of the people to help the Kurds understand the possible utilization of the weakness of the Americans generated by their own artificial deadlines.[126]

Despite his complaining, Bremer nevertheless decided to sit down with the Kurds alone, before the IGC plenary, "to get agreements on the demands they had sprung the night before"[127] and, unsurprisingly, given the same structure and the lack of time on the American but not Kurdish side, the results were again the same. The Kurds, appealing to American political and public-relations interests, expressed their fear of a constitution that the "black turbans" (the Shia clerics) would write. Then they[128] proposed a new idea: ratification of the constitution by simple majority, as long as two-thirds of the voters of three provinces did not reject it. Bremer is quite right (along with almost everyone else) to interpret this as a Kurdish veto,[129] but he did not seem to notice or remark that this veto pertained to the ratification of the constitution for Iraq as a whole and not just for its validity in Kurdistan. Thus it went *beyond* even the veto contained in the "Kurdistan Chapter." He may have been misled by the fact that in this formula voting would be by governorates and not by the region as a whole. The Kurds were thus asking for formally less but substantively more than before. It was a brilliant move.

According to Galbraith, the Kurds made the acceptance of the provision a condition of their supporting the TAL, a document that he repeatedly alleges represented a bad compromise for them.[130] I will try to show below that with the default provision already built into the TAL in case of the failure of ratification, this could not have been true whatever anybody said. The ratification veto would be no gain for the Kurds over the TAL without it, because all it would get them in case they hated the new constitution was the preservation of the TAL itself. Thus what they were trying to do in reality was enshrine their old gains and create the foundation for additional ones.[131] But if this is true, then the claim that they would not accept the TAL, involving great gains, unless they got even more, was perhaps a huge bluff. Nevertheless, it is quite likely that the Kurds did tell Bremer that without the ratification rule they would not accept the TAL. If they did, given his self-imposed deadline and his own desire to limit the black turbans in advance, Bremer fell for what may have been only a negotiating ploy. He promised to consult Washington about the proposal and got Condi Rice's agreement at 3 p.m., February 29, the last day.

The Kurds were told the good news at 5:15 p.m. At this point, in Bremer's recollections something strange happens. According to him, between 6:45 p.m. and 4:20 a.m. (March 1), the plenary of the IGC met. "Much of the text was agreed on the day before," and thus it could not have contained the ratification rule. For much of the night the question of Islam in the TAL was discussed, and the compromise—including its attendant redundancies discussed above—was finalized. This happened by midnight. After that the compromises were easy. At 2:15, Bremer managed to get the idea of reconvening anew quashed. There was a short debate, also quashed, on security arrangements with the United States. Finally, a unanimous vote, at 4:20 a.m., on the TAL as a whole was held. There was not one word of discussion on the central question of a dramatically new ratification rule.[132]

Diamond, probably incorrectly, puts the IGC all-night plenary on March 3, but he supplies the missing details.[133] According to him, on February 29 Bremer was not able to finish as planned and was forced to allow "a seventy-two-hour marathon struggle to conclude the interim constitution."[134] The decisive event described or rather omitted by Bremer supposedly came on the night of March 3, rather than February 29. At 4 a.m., an hour that corresponds to Bremer's timeline, when all else was done, Massoud Barzani offered an amendment to TAL Article 61c that contained the new ratification rule. Without anyone really considering or certainly discussing what they voted for, the IGC adopted the change and the TAL was finished.[135]

According to another version, SCIRI's Adel Mahdi did raise an objection to the ratification rule, saying that Sistani would never accept it, but when asked for an alternative he could not provide it and instead asked for a day's delay, which Bremer would not grant.[136] It is then that the text was unanimously accepted. This version does not make the event any different than Diamond's description, though it makes voting for the TAL as it stood even more questionable on the part of the Shi'a House. A third version explains the voting by arguing that it was Mahdi himself, as the "Kurds' advocate," who persuaded the other Shi'ites, "who had not done their homework," to go along with the plan, arguing that they could not afford to alienate either the Kurds or the CPA.[137] In any case, over the next day or two, when the Shi'ite leaders and especially Sistani's circle realized the full meaning of what they had done, they strenuously and vociferously objected to the procedure and to the ratification rule, but too late. The Kurds would not budge, because now they had what they wanted, and Bremer refused to reopen any negotiations dealing with the TAL. The ratification rule was successfully imposed on the IGC as a whole—though that was not to be the end of the story.

This may be the place to ask why the Americans, the world's one and only superpower, proved so weak with respect to the Kurds. It cannot be, as we have seen, because their positions were identical. Initially at least, Washington understood the demand for a Kurdistan Region in terms of ethnic nationalism, to which all sections of the U.S. government were opposed;

moreover, they foresaw some of the disastrous consequences of going down that road.[138] So in this context at least we cannot speak of ignorance, only a lack of will.

First, there was a question of the bargaining strategy. This was evidently delegated to Bremer and his team, who were inexperienced and outgunned by the Kurds and their advisors. The CPA team never understood the significance of the two-sided structure, which they never should have granted, and this in itself must have cost them some concessions. Bremer may have chosen his approach because of his repeatedly documented desires both to personally micromanage and to do it all very quickly. The first desire, anchored deeply in his personality, he could not satisfy given the messy IGC format in Baghdad, while the second was imposed on him by the Republicans, with an eye to the U.S. electoral timetables. The two factors partially explain why so much was conceded. The experienced leaders of the Kurds were not ashamed to rely on real experts, and they had much more time—as far as they were concerned, they had been waiting since the treaty of Sèvres. As their advisors must have explained to Talabani and Barzani, the Americans meant Bush, and Bush had to have results quickly if he wanted to be reelected. But even so, threats of secession or of not signing any version of the TAL were all pretty hollow, and at the very least Bremer could have called the Kurds' bluffs or held out longer when his bosses tried to do so.

There had to be other things also at work. Consider the fact that while the Sunni-led insurrection was already unfolding, the Shi'ites led by Sistani mounted a series of tough constitutional challenges that forced the Americans to back down or compromise. Not only in the war against Saddam but in all these later fights, the Americans and the Kurds were on the same side. They also shared more or less their opposition to the Islamization of the new Iraq, whether this fear was real or imagined. For Bremer, these issues and fights were intensely personal, and his distrust and dislike of Sistani seems to have greatly increased over time. Was it therefore the Americans' far greater trust in the Kurds than in any of the Arab factions that made them their prisoner, or was it a common desire to stop the "black turbans," the friends of Iran, from inheriting the prize the war was about to give them—or did the Americans, in classical imperial fashion, actually aim at a weak Iraqi state open to influence and penetration?

The several failed attempts from Washington to deprive the Kurds of their Kurdistan Regional Government, whose potentially negative consequences for the integrity of Iraq as a whole were obvious, is consistent with the first or second but not the third interpretation. Even if initially American positions on the structure of the state were opposed to those of the Kurds and implicitly at least were closer to those of what seems to be Sistani's Iraqi nationalist position, that initial preference was altered precisely because of the Americans' very serious conflict with Sistani. The Kurds were able to successfully represent a position according to which even a relatively united Iraqi federal state (which is what territorial federalism implied) would easily fall under the domination of the majority and thus the "black turbans." In order to prevent such an outcome (which probably also would have been seen as a victory for Iran in the region), the American negotiators first softened their stand and then accepted the basic Kurdish demands, toward which the negotiating format was already predisposed. Finally, when it came to the Kurdistan veto, the Americans were predisposed to accept this simply because of their own desire to limit a constituent assembly they would not be able to control as easily as they could the makers of the TAL. Very likely the change of form from an ethnic veto to a three-governorate model, whoever thought of this move, was also helpful in gaining the incredibly rapid acceptance by Bremer and Rice. That was partly a function of time, but given the radicality of the proposal, we have to assume that the experts on the National Security Council decided that the combination of rules of change corresponded to the American interest in controlling the Shi'ite majority.

With the eventual convergence of interests between the Americans and the Kurds, it seems to me nevertheless very important finally that the Americans could not occupy Kurdistan, because of the Turkish refusal to allow an invasion from the north, and thus did not have any obvious military means to force the Kurds to do anything.[139] This led to the mistaken view that they had to be treated completely differently than those who were supposedly under their full physical control and "tutelage." Thus the origins of the two-sided negotiations, which came to resemble a pact between two holders of state power in two independent units, conceding the most fundamental point to the Kurds right from the outset, may have had more of an effect than even Bremer's very real mistakes in strategy. And, given such a bargaining structure and the Bush administration's time constraints, the Kurds' ability to outwait the Americans always proved decisive. But whatever the reasons, once the deal emerged among Bremer, Barzani, and Talabani, to put the matter crudely, it became their consensual position, and the rest of the IGC or the drafting committee of five was in no position to do much about it. At best what could still be done, if inconclusively, was to generalize some of the concessions given to the Kurds to the Shi'ites as well, with provisions such as the ability of any three provinces, potentially, to form a region, and the firm intention to hold on to other militias under the same cover given to the Peshmerga. These concessions only confirmed the fears of those who thought that conceding an ethnically defined, asymmetrical federal structure to the Kurds would keep Iraq on the path of state destruction rather than lead to a model under which the state could be rebuilt.

A final note on this point: had there been an Iraqi state and an Iraqi army, the negotiations with the Kurds could not have taken the form they did. In that case, most likely the Americans would not have been bargaining in the place of Arab Iraq, and even in the unlikely case that the Americans had been, they would have had a very powerful bargaining chip that the Kurds could disregard only at their own peril. Whatever compromise was struck, it have been struck taking this factor into account.

The TAL: Historic or One-Sided Compromise?

Another way to examine the process is from the point of view of the result, the Transitional Administrative Law itself. Ultimately, even if the process failed from a normative point of view, had the interim constitution itself nevertheless embodied a "historic compromise," as some of its defenders claim, it could have contributed to its own effectiveness and legitimacy during the course of its roughly year-and-a-half existence. Here I wish to examine the question of to what extent the interim constitution represented such a substantive compromise, with respect to three areas where the TAL did have great deal of *material* constitutional relevance during that period: the territorial dimension of the state structure, the model of government, and the rules of constitutional change. I will not repeat my discussion of the relations of state and church and the significant symbolic compromises made, but rather I will focus on where local power rather than the TAL's prescriptions were to decide, for example, what kind of status law Iraqi citizens were going to live under. Many readers, especially those who interpret all constitutions in terms of their tables of rights, will find it strange that I will not pay any attention to the impressive and well-drafted table of constitutional rights in the TAL. This I do for several reasons. First, during the life of the TAL no apparatus of courts (until the end, almost no constitutional court) was created that could imaginably enforce such rights against the "state." Second, I consider it a laughable proposition that such protections were enacted while they were not meant for a moment to apply to the main actual holders of the means of violence, the military forces under coalition command.[140] Third, and most important, rights against the state and rights to state outputs are relevant only if there is a state, and the TAL failed, as I will show, in its attempted reconstruction of any plausible state in terms of territory, people, or form of organization of the exclusive means of violence. Of course, the rights of the TAL also did not, do not, and could not apply to the decentralized forces holding the means of violence in Iraq, the insurgencies and the militia, the latter having infiltrated the new army and the police, and thus it is hard to see what the relevance of constitutional rights is supposed to be, outside of a symbolic and public-relations one. Let me note finally that given my interest here in negotiation and compromise I detected no debate, conflict, or need for compromise concerning the table of rights outside of some technical suggestions made by American participants to Arab drafters. No one thought it worthwhile to spend a lot of time on this; it was permissible to let Mr. F. Istrabadi, using American, international, and Middle Eastern precedents, just go ahead and draft.[141] To his credit, he seems to have wished for the extension of rights protection to the American forces, which was equivalent, however, to wishing the occupation to end, because the United States has never made such guarantees of putting its forces abroad under a foreign constitution and foreign courts, even if they actually existed and were viable. I do not discount the symbolic and programmatic importance of asserting the rights of the TAL, but I fear that they now are also infected by the interim constitution's illegitimate origins. The future possible role of these rights in Iraq and the Middle East depends much more on the solution of the other problems that were treated in the TAL and the permanent constitution. It is to them I now turn.

State Structure

The TAL's solution is the asymmetric structure composed of Kurdistan, still containing formally at least three provinces and two fragments, and fifteen other provinces, with only Kurdistan having a regional government.

But as I already detailed, any three provinces could form a region if their electorates and the National Assembly approved (art. 53c). Thus a bridge was provided to a symmetrical system of a federation of ethnically based regions. To be sure, this bridge explicitly and doubly excluded Kirkuk (and Baghdad too) for the transitional period as far as Kurdistan, already composed of three regions, was concerned. But that in general was the result of the CPA-Kurdish bargain, the *status quo plus* solution, that led to the TAL delaying the final resolution of the territorial question of the disputed province and the city for the final constitution. The adjective *plus* was now really earned (it is unclear to me when these provisions were agreed on and why there was no strong Arab response),[142] because the TAL undertook a series of measures that had the effect of beginning the reversal of the Saddam-era ethnic cleansing, by altering the property and demographic structure of especially Kirkuk city, the latter not only by resettling Kurdish expellees, which is understandable, but also by expelling individuals (read Arabs) "newly introduced" (art. 58a 1 and 2). Here the TAL went well beyond the "Kurdistan Chapter," which was silent on all Kirkuk-related questions. In line with that spirit, while the resolution of the final territorial status of Kirkuk was left to the permanent constitution, this would now mean a period after the completion of the measures dealing with demographic and property transfers. Only then would the relevant population, reconstructed by these measures, be finally consulted.

As to the division of powers, the TAL takes over the formula of the "Kurdistan Chapter" (art. 1, sec. 3) of assigning all unenumerated powers in Kurdistan to the Kurdistan Regional Government except those powers where the "Provisional Government of Iraq," now called the Iraqi Transitional Government, has exclusive (enumerated) competence.[143] But the TAL again goes beyond the "Kurdistan Chapter" in one respect, by giving a nullification right, "the right to amend the application" of all federal laws, with the exception of laws within the exclusive competence of the federal government and decisions of federal courts in the areas of that exclusive competence (TAL art. 54b). Where the TAL did not satisfy maximal Kurdish demands was in its enumeration of the very short list of exclusive federal competence, which included the uncontroversial areas of foreign policy, fiscal policy, monetary policy, weights and measures, citizenship, and immigration; the very controversial areas of defense, securing borders, and resources (national management and ownership); and the somewhat controversial area of public communications (TAL art. 25). The "Kurdistan

Chapter" sought a recognition of the Peshmerga and its transformation into a Kurdistan national guard (art. 2) as well as the "non-deployment of other Iraqi armed forces in Kurdistan." These were not granted, and by implication, Kurdistan's borders too would be guarded by federal forces. Moreover, the TAL expressly required the dissolution of all militias (art. 27b), and in the eyes of the Americans and Arabs the Peshmerga was a militia. Note, however, that from the Kurdish point of view the Peshmerga was Kurdistan's national army and not a militia, and there was never the slightest intention to dissolve them or cede the defense of Kurdistan's borders to any other force.[144] As to oil, the Kurds were not in a similar bargaining position. Present resources were around Kirkuk, which they did not control militarily. Moreover, they wished to battle the impression that they wanted the city for its oil.[145] It was not even completely clear (the Kurds said) if they would gain or lose from national ownership, given the greater reserves of the south.[146] Thus they sought a formula in the "Kurdistan Chapter" (art. 3) that would grant Kurdistan ownership, but management of current fields could still be left in federal hands as long as the region received its just share of the proceeds. The TAL did not grant this mixed formula, for the moment keeping the ownership and management of all fields and not only the management of current fields in federal hands, promising only some affirmative action to areas previously unjustly deprived of the proceeds (art. 25e).

There are various ways of speaking about this package concerning the territorial structure of the state. Galbraith seems to treat it as a defeat of Kurdish positions ("Bremer got most of what he wanted in the Transitional Administrative Law")[147] but then goes on to describe the far more essential things conceded to the Kurds. All the later outcry, when the TAL seemed to be under the threat of abrogation, is wholly inconsistent with this perspective. Others more convincingly speak of a historic compromise[148] or of the TAL as a compromise between strongly divergent Arab and Kurdish proposals.[149] Undoubtedly in terms of contents, the matter can be looked upon this way: both sides got some but not all the things they wanted, leaving aside the matter stressed by Galbraith that the Kurds never intended to or could be made to fully deliver on their side.[150] What is deeply unconvincing is to say that the compromise consists of the asymmetrical model itself, with Arabs getting the type of state they wanted for Arab Iraq, a centralized federation, and the Kurds getting what has been called a "federacy" for Kurdistan.[151]

The asymmetrical model itself was an expression of the fundamental Kurdish drive to understand the new structure as a voluntary union. Let Arab Iraq be organized one way and Kurdistan be organized the other way, and we can arrange a few remaining common affairs by something like a treaty. That was the position of the Kurds before the beginning of the bilateral negotiations with the Americans (and this was conceded by the CPA by the structure of those negotiations, though never in so many words), and now the TAL projected a state structure much more compatible with this assumption of a voluntary union than with any conceivable notion of a coherent state organization. Granted, there was already a way of making it coherent in the TAL, at the risk of its disintegration.

The new term "federacy" expresses a quasi-confederal enclave in what is otherwise supposed to be, but in my view cannot be, a true federation and especially a federal state. At issue here first and foremost is not how the parts (Arab Iraq and Kurdistan, the supposed two halves of the compromise) are organized but how they are related. O'Leary has defined "confederation" as that type of "federal" system where the units retain sovereignty.[152] Less legalistically, we might say that a confederation is a system where the political center has no one area where it is relatively autonomous in making policy with respect to the whole country, while in a federal state both center and units have autonomous policymaking powers.[153] Kurdistan is supposedly a federacy, not a unit of a confederation, because in international law at the very least it is not sovereign; Iraq as a whole is so recognized. Moreover, the Iraqi government does have or seems to have autonomous policymaking powers. A federacy, O'Leary says, is semisovereign, but that term is entirely meaningless.[154] And here is where formal understandings of sovereignty lead us completely astray. Kurdistan has its own army, under its own control, and is unoccupied. Iraq does not, and it is. Kurdistan has its own constitution and its own government; Arab Iraq does not, only the federal government does, that is, the government of Arab Iraq. This is, of course, the very asymmetrical arrangement itself, but more is involved than that. As for the TAL, it has given very few powers to the central government that are enforceable in Kurdistan, but it has given all unenumerated powers and rights of nullification to the KRG. On the crucial question of the constituent power, Kurdistan can veto any constitution that would apply to it and indeed to the rest of Iraq. It is the only such veto from the ethnic point of view. The Shi'ites have the majority, that is, *more* than a veto, and the Sunnis have *less* than veto power, as we will see when we examine both the amendment and the ratification rules. Thus while the whole is not a treaty organization formally, the Kurdish "federacy" comes close to being a unit of a confederal state or confederation whose constitution is actually a treaty that can be made and altered only with the full consent of the contracting party, a "voluntary union." The reason why Iraq does not appear to be a confederation formally is because its "federal" government does have autonomous powers. But in reality it has them only with respect to Arab Iraq, and this is what allows Kurdistan to be a federacy, also formally indicated by its powers and veto rights.

According to O'Leary, when there is a federacy within a federation, neither side has the right to unilaterally alter the division of powers between the units and the federation—that is, the constitution that entrenches these—thus the implication is that there is neither federal constitutional supremacy as in a federal state nor the right of secession as in a confederation. Today, however, the unilateral right of secession is no longer the right of members of treaty organizations, whether or not we want to retain the term "confederation" for a treaty organization where such a right is spelled out.[155] Thus a federacy still can and does signify membership in a kind of treaty organization. The peculiarity of Iraq is that this is a one-sided relationship according to the TAL, because the Kurds, who have to agree to all changes of the constitution and thus can consider it a treaty from their point of view, alone have the requisite autonomy of the federal government, even as they participate in both governments in Iraq, regional and federal. No other part of Iraq has the same autonomy, at least formally speaking, because in reality the federal government is an extremely weak one with respect to all parts of the country. Reality is more symmetrical than the formal relationships. Despite the formal asymmetry, the structure encourages the three major ethnic-religious groups to treat the constitution as a treaty, though the Sunnis do not alone dispose of a veto power over it. They too, however, like the other two ethnic groups, have the actual power to control large parts of the country.

Thus we do not have to go to Arab authors to get a wholly different evaluation of the TAL than "Kurdish defeat" or "historic compromise." Amazingly enough, sometimes in the very same texts a few pages later, advocates of the Kurdish cause go on to say that what is much more true is that the same TAL "marked an overall defeat of the integrationists, the national, centralist, and majoritarian federalists of Iraq."[156] An overall defeat is very different than a great compromise. But the reason why the first formula is right and the second wrong can be understood only if we look at the other parts of the TAL, especially its governmental, amending, and ratificatory formulas.

Model of Government

From both the Kurdish ethnic and the liberal nationalist positions, powerful regions needed to be linked to Iraqi government through models of governmental power sharing, preferably of the consociational type. In my view, both empirically (think of India) and logically the links between the three dimensions (ethnically based federalism, strong powers for the units, and power sharing in the center) are tenuous, though there are many cases admittedly when all three vary together.[157] The most I would concede is that ethnically based federalism in a context of strong divisions may require the additional protection of *either* strong unit powers *or* participation in the government of the center. Being protected twice over can be at times necessary but can also be superfluous. It can even be the source of strong new resentments, when a minority nationality that has successfully separated itself nevertheless controls the lives of the rest through guaranteed participation and vetoes.

The motives of the two major Kurdish positions in seeking power sharing could be slightly different to the extent that the ethnic nationalist seeks only to weaken while the liberal nationalist also actually wishes to participate in "Iraq." Thus typically federalist forms of interlocking the region and Iraq could be more interesting for the liberal nationalist, if the proper formula for a second chamber could be found, a difficult task given the provincial organization of the rest of Iraq. For the TAL at least, the Kurds thus sought consociationalism. This was all the more so[158] because the TAL did not grant their region all the powers they wanted, and thus they needed more powers in the transitional federal government. But perhaps because they did not all seek it for exactly the same reason (weakening versus participation), here their bargaining power was somewhat diminished. It was also diminished because the governmental structure, unlike the state structure, was produced by American drafters with some prejudices for strong government (the Governance Team) in interaction with the IGC, rather than in the two-sided format between Bremer and the Kurdish leaders.

Why did the latter not hold out for their preferred negotiating structure with respect to the institutions of the federal government? I can only offer some hypotheses here. First, this issue was far less important. Implicitly, the Kurds too must have realized that they were now seeking a third level of protection for their ethnic federalism. But the issue had some import, and the creation of a purely majoritarian central government for Iraq could have represented a great de facto danger to regional independence won *de jure*. Second, it is also very possible, though I have no proof, that since Bremer was going to impose the results of the state bargain on the IGC, it was understood explicitly or implicitly that some kind of balance between imposition and bargaining had to be kept if the Shi'ite majority was not to bolt the process. Thus either Bremer refused to give the Kurds more or the Kurds and their advisors knew where the limits of the possible lay and thus did not even ask to include the government institutions in the two-sided negotiations. Most likely, the latter possibility actually happened, because there is no trace in Kurdish proposals of a governmental structure for Iraq. We know, however, that they eventually did seek to recoup some losses on this level and that they also believed that when it came to the final constitution, they could trade back some prior concessions on governmental institutions that made Iraq potentially ungovernable for even more regional independence than was provided in the TAL and for movement on Kirkuk.[159]

We know how allergic Pachachi, the chair of the Drafting Committee, and Istrabadi, the active link between that body and the Governance Team, were to power sharing, especially on an ethnic basis.[160] The latter even wanted to introduce a second parliamentary chamber early, with incentives against region formation. This proposal was totally unacceptable to the Kurds, who could not accept such a body on a provincial basis at all, and in any case it was not common for constitutional assemblies. We also know that American advisors such as Diamond strongly (and rightly) pushed for a parliamentary rather than a presidential form of government, which is not as easily open to power sharing. Formally speaking, this side left a strong impression on the TAL. Iraq's transitional government both before and after elections was to be parliamentary, and after the election of the *single-chamber* Transitional National (Constituent) Assembly the prime minister and his ministers (individually) had to get and retain the assembly's confidence by a (simple) majority vote (TAL art. 38a). The prime minister could also dismiss his ministers on his own, with the majority of the National Assembly behind him (TAL art. 41). But this parliamentary institution was surrounded by a series of partially presidentialist and quasi-consociational structures. There would be a three-person Presidency Council, first selected (TAL annex) and after free elections elected by the National Assembly, on a single slate, by a two-thirds vote (TAL art. 36a). While it remained unspoken, everyone understood that this had to mean conventionally one Shi'ite Arab, one Kurd, and one Sunni Arab member, even though a Shi'ite deal with one of the other groups could possibly subvert that imagined convention. The Presidency Council, having to act unanimously, would then select the prime minister, and this meant that a president or vice president of any of the three groups could veto the choice (TAL art. 38a). Unless a candidate presented a power-sharing cabinet, he could be vetoed. The same would happen after a vote of no confidence in a prime minister, when a new government had to be appointed, which would make the parliamentary majority think twice about whether to use the instrument at all (as of this writing three years into Iraqi "parliamentarism" there has not been even one such vote, not to speak of removal). Even the prime minister's removal of ministers runs into the problem of reappointment by full consensus: it could not be used to transform his government in a majoritarian direction, as I once thought. Only if the three "presidents" could not agree for two weeks would parliament be able to nominate and elect a prime minister and a cabinet, but only by two-thirds vote. This might overcome the veto of one group, but not of two, and it certainly is not a majoritarian or parliamentary device.

I believe that the presidents, each of them, were also meant to have veto power over legislation. But the postulate that they have to act as a unit in this case leads to the possibility of "a veto of the veto" by any of the three members. Was this result intended? Was it a result of a compromise? Was the trick of substituting one negative concept ("may veto") for a positive one ("must sign" or "must approve") (TAL art. 37) the revenge of a majoritarian drafter on a consociationalist bargainer, unnoticed by the experts of the Kurdistan Regional Government? Or did the liberal nationalist experts notice but forget to mention the fact to their ethnic nationalist colleagues? When the amendment rule was crafted (TAL art. 3), the drafters did know how to write the positive phrase "unanimous approval of the Presidency Council," but in that case, with three-fourths of the assembly concurring, the device was redundant. The fact is that "the veto of the veto" somewhat vitiated the consociational character of the structure and would have made the transitional assembly more capable of legislating by simple majority (!) if it really wished to do so (which in fact it did not). The supposed power, a kind of impeachment after "due process," of the Presidency Council to dismiss the prime minister or ministers also runs into a veto of such a decision by a single member (TAL art. 41).

On the face of it then, the governmental structure is a bargained compromise between majoritarian parliamentary, consociationalist, and vaguely presidentialist forms, even if it is hard to know just how it was negotiated. Again, however, the structure does not indicate what the Kurds claim, namely that the Arabs, or more exactly the Shi'ites, got a strong, majoritarian government for the Arab part of Iraq while the Kurds got safeguards to preserve their freedom in Kurdistan. While the latter half of the sentence is undoubtedly true, the former is not. In the process of getting some consociationalist safeguards that would make it hard to form a government that would attack the rights and powers of the Kurds, the rest of Iraq got both a mixed and weak structure. Given a plurality of parties, it would be hard to form a government under it, and the government formed would contain too many built-in vetoes. It would be very hard to replace an ineffective government. And as we will see later, it would be almost impossible to change the constitutional structure that caused all this except in the direction of making the same built-in problems even more serious.

Rules of Change and Constitutional Identity

Reasonable people can and will disagree concerning the type of compromise between Arab and Kurdish positions that went into the state and governmental structure of the TAL. One's judgment will inevitably depend on what one takes to be the real initial positions of each side, and that is not fully knowable because these are always disguised for negotiating purposes. If we assumed, for example, that the Kurds really wanted to secede, there would be merit to the position that they sacrificed the most in the TAL, which does not even grant them the right of unilateral secession. I of course make the contrary assumption and think they must have been really surprised at how easily the world's last remaining superpower conceded their fundamental understanding of Iraq as a voluntary union, which was against its own interests as most of its policymakers initially understood it. My case cannot be made foolproof by referring to the bargaining structure in general nor even to the bargains themselves as they pertain to the state and governmental structure. That is because there was some (I think mainly two-sided) bargaining, there were some (I think too few) concessions to Arab positions in these two areas, and it may all come down to what one chooses to emphasize and sometimes which sources one believes.[161] In my view, the issue can be fairly definitively decided when we turn to the topic of constitutional change and the deeply related one of constitutional identity. Here the key rule has been imposed, I will argue, producing a constitutional identity that fully incorporates the Kurdish view of a "voluntary union" and enshrines it against future *legal* alteration.

The interim constitution was to govern Iraq for a transitional period, but more importantly it was also to govern the making of the permanent constitution. Here the political reasons for adopting this instrument and its historical meaning fully coincide. The idea is both to apply constitutionalism to the transition period and to constitution making itself, both processes being open to the possibility of dictatorial concentrations of authority.[162] While it is the governmental and state structure that regulate the transitional period, it is through its rules of change that the interim constitution regulates the making of the permanent constitution.[163] These rules of change are not just the ratification rule, whose imposition I already discussed, but three rules, the amendment rule, the ratification rule itself, and what I called the "failsafe rule," which O'Leary and his colleagues have called, even more correctly, the "default rule."[164] Let me treat them in that order and then evaluate the package in relationship to the problem of constitutional identity in the TAL.

The Amendment Rules of the TAL

Contrary to the intentions of the American framers of the November 15 Agreement, who probably sought to maximize thereby their own input into the permanent constitution, the TAL was in the end not made unamendable. I should emphasize again that interim constitutions seek to accomplish two apparently contradictory things: to impose constitutionalist restraints on government and to allow learning during the period of political transition.[165] Formally speaking, an unamendable interim constitution would sacrifice the second goal for the sake of the first. Indeed, contrary to a published view of Feisal Istrabadi, this duality would generally call for amendment rules somewhat less difficult than those of permanent constitutions.[166] Because of such considerations, and not because of a conflict and compromise in the IGC, the TAL abandoned the initial prejudice of its planners on this point, but incompletely and partially. In fact, all of its amendment rules belong to the most difficult set of types among the world's constitutions, and they are significantly more difficult than the amendment rules of the interim constitutions I know of, including South Africa's, a country en route to being a federal state, a condition generally associated with difficult amendment rules. They "reflect" not so much the initial American intention but more the establishment of a Kurdish quasi-confederal enclave or a federacy in Iraq. Whatever their reason, these rules were nevertheless a serious impediment to legal constitutional learning and an implicit invitation to illegal learning.

There were in fact *four* distinct amendment rules in or associated with the TAL. Of these, the first and second below were mentioned in the document, the third follows from the language, and the fourth, soon moot, was only implied by the conditions of its authorization:

1. A good part of the TAL was amendable by a vote of three-fourths of the National Assembly and the unanimous consent of the three-member Presidential Council (art. 3a), who were conventionally assumed to be one Shi'ite Arab, one Kurd, and one Sunni Arab.

2. However, there were extensive unamendable provisions according to the same article (3a): rights covered under chapter 2, the timeframe of the transition as defined by the interim constitution, the powers of regions and governorates, and regulations having to do with Islam specifically and religions in general. Regarding both 1 and 2, after free elections, this self-referring rule could be used to change itself *before any other part* of the constitution could have been changed through the new rule.[167] Politically, such a "revision of the revision" is always explosive and rarely wise.

3. Since there would be no National Assembly until free elections could be held between late December and January 2005, the interim constitution was by implication unchangeable for the period from June 1 to some time after the elections, when the new National Assembly first met and chose a Presidential Council, as required by 3a.

4. What was not mentioned but was probably inevitable was that the CPA itself as the sole source of authority could have changed any part of the interim constitution before its full entry into force, that is, between

March 8 and June 30. Since the CPA never acted in a constitutional capacity on its own, the latter date was probably June 1, when in fact the IGC used the very last opportunity to add the short annex.

Rule 4 was soon moot. As to the third "rule," also unstated formally, it requires no analysis to show that unchangeability during the period between June 30 and, say, January 31 meant extreme rigidity for at least seven potentially crucial and difficult months. How bad an idea this was may be a matter relevant only to future constitution makers, because there were no important projects to revise the TAL in that period. Strictly speaking from the legal point of view, an unamendable constitution can only be replaced in its entirety, though of course politically speaking partial illegality regarding its application (through creative interpretation, disregard of the amendment rule, and so on) is also possible. In either case, the transitional legal order that interim constitutions are meant to establish and protect would be severely endangered. As we will see, it was largely the latter (disregard of the amendment rule) that occurred in Iraq.

The situation only gets worse during the period when amendments become possible (rule 1), because now there was a freely elected assembly that could run into governability problems and could still not easily modify the rules that caused them. Again, the rigidity of the rule encouraged full abrogation or illegality (and their anticipation as well, as preemptive moves) during a potentially extended period, especially long if the TAL were preserved because of the failure of constitution making. The formal amendment rule constituted an extreme consociational limit (as opposed to the confederal limit of the ratification rule) on the changing of the interim constitution. Theoretically, three-fourths of the National Assembly and the agreement of all three members of the Presidential Council could actually pass amendments to the interim document (except its unamendable sections) in the potentially extended period during which the permanent constitution was being drafted. Practically, the representatives of any of the three ethnic-religious (Shi'a Arab, Sunni Arab, and Kurd) groups were likely to have over one-quarter of the seats and possibly, if the convention held, one member of the presidential council. Thus any of them could veto any amendment twice over. It is very possible that Iraqi nationalist deputies, or strongly secular deputies, or deputies from Baghdad, or deputies from oil-rich regions, or any other combination could also have one-fourth of the votes in the assembly. Thus the possibility for vetoes of amendments could be greater than the framers of the rule initially imagined. Of course, some amendments might still pass through bargaining and compromise. But when in the face of a little less than three-fourths of the deputies and let us say all three members of the presidium, or, alternately, 95 percent of the deputies along with the president and one vice president, an important amendment could be blocked, the likelihood of a "runaway convention" that refused to be bound by the will of the illegitimate Governing Council or the foreign CPA would be great indeed. Or alternately, the provision encouraged unconstitutional amendments made by lower legal acts that could not be reviewed if a Federal Supreme Court was not set up or, alternately, could be passed with such a court's connivance. Again, all these solutions would encourage a culture of "illegality" on the governmental level and preemptively so on the regional one.

All the same, the amendment rule was for potentially a short period, and the design of the institutions already described was not so disastrous that it would have to be used repeatedly. Their importance is great only in relation to the ratification rule, which, unlike the amendment rule, was imposed in an entirely indefensible manner and was greatly resented by almost everyone except its Kurdish proponents and beneficiaries. The amendment rule meant that either this rule could not be changed at all (because it related to the powers of regions) or could be changed only if the Kurdish parliamentary faction and a Kurdish member of the Presidency Council both agreed, the second being relevant in case of a split in that faction. The same amendment rule guaranteed that the TAL as a default position would not be changed, thus strengthening the threat of nonratification. Thus the three rules discussed here very much belong together. Without this amendment rule, the following two rules would be useless to their beneficiaries, because without it a new constitution could be adopted as a single amending act.

The Rules for Passing the Final Constitution

Here we are dealing with two very important rules:

1. The TAL states only that the National Assembly "shall write a draft of the constitution of Iraq" and that this draft will be "presented for approval in a popular referendum." It was not said by what vote the assembly had

to agree on a draft. The most convenient way of reading the text was that the draft of the permanent constitution fully replacing the interim one had to be approved by 50 percent plus one vote of the National Assembly,[168] and then, as clearly stated, by 50 percent plus one of the population as a whole in a national referendum, as long as two-thirds of the voters of three governorates did not vote against ratification (art. 60–61a–c). Having to do with governorates, this rule may have been meant to be unchangeable, but that restriction would be useless, since the amendment rule was not enshrined.

2. In case ratification failed (61e) or the National Assembly failed to produce a permanent constitution initially by August 15, 2005, without changing that deadline through constitutional amendment, the National Assembly was to be dissolved, new elections called, *and Iraq was to continue to operate under the TAL* with all deadlines changed to keep the making of the new constitution within one year. Since nothing else was to be changed, I interpret this provision as depicting a scenario that could have happened over and over again, making the TAL the default or failsafe constitution of the whole process.[169]

The first rule will be called the ratification rule, and the second the default rule.[170] I consider the issue, discussed above, of whether the Sunnis could have used the ratification rule to their advantage no longer worth debating, because even O'Leary and his colleagues contradict themselves (or rather, they contradict O'Leary and Galbraith) on this point and because the actual referendum bore out the view of most participants, from Bremer to Sistani.[171] Sunnis had nothing to do with introducing the measure and ramming it through as a veritable coup against the rest of the IGC. Since they did not like the TAL, they had no interest in a veto that would make the TAL a default position. Thus the ratification rule did nothing else (at least originally) than give an absolute veto to the Kurdistan Region (acting through the three Kurdish provinces) over a constitution passed by the majority, which could be either an absolute majority or a very high, qualified majority of the National Assembly. Whether it was ironed out between Bremer and the Kurds or introduced by the Kurds only after Bremer rejected a veto for the Kurdistan Region as a whole, the three-province structure was a very formal concession to the Americans. The Kurds, who were intent in eliminating their governorates (regarded as "Trojan horses") and their administrations, now could not do so until all the referenda on the final constitution were over.[172] Three votes were needed to defeat the constitution, whatever the overall vote of the region was. But the voting difference here was always based on an illusion, a pure formality. There was no chance that a three-province vote and a Kurdistan Region vote would produce different results. The rulers of the region, who were united on Iraqi constitutional issues and who knew how to operate by democratic centralism, controlled both.

Thus regardless of its formal concession to provincial federalism, the rule treats the creation of a new constitution like the making of a treaty between two partners, which needs the complete agreement of the two as wholes and not just some of their population (one-third of each Kurdish province could agree with say, 100 percent of the rest of Iraq, and still the constitution would fail). A federal law (such as U.S. Article V, an amendment rule rather than a ratification rule) could have involved the passing of the constitution by a high, qualified majority, and its ratification (like Articles VII and V) by nine-thirteenths or three-fourths of the provinces.[173] In appearance, this is what TAL article 61c does, since if the majority were joined by just one of the three Kurdish provinces the constitution would pass. But this would have been like asking South Carolina, North Carolina, or Georgia of the original thirteen states to vote for a constitution banning slavery, an illusory hope regarding even far less momentous issues. As long as the two Kurdish parties stuck together, the uniformity of voting in the three provinces would be guaranteed (and if they did not stick together, their federalist and confederalist aspirations would be finished anyway). Thus the rule was and was meant to be a quasi-confederal rule for a treaty organization or at least for an asymmetrical structure that has a "federacy," that is, a confederal enclave attached to it by something like a treaty. With respect to the ratification rule of the "Kurdistan Chapter," which was frankly and openly treatylike, the new rule gave the Kurdish parties everything the original rule had and more, because now they could actually deprive the rest of Iraq of having a new constitution. This was going to be an important source of power when it came to negotiating the final constitution, as O'Leary and his colleagues openly foretold.

The amendment rule and the ratification rule one attaches to a constitution gives important clues to how the rulemakers regard that constitution. The more rigid the rules of change, the more attached the rulemakers are to the constitution. The rules discussed here indicate the high regard the Kurds had for the TAL and belie the interpretation that they regarded it as a defeat and only accepted it because of the ratification rule itself. The proof is the default rule. In case the Kurds were forced to defeat the new constitution, they could always go back to the TAL and its rigid amendment rule. To their opponents, that would be a threat, but to them it had to sound like a pretty good fallback position—"BATNA," as O'Leary and his colleagues called it. In fact, they already seemed to regard the TAL as pretty close to a treaty protected by a consociational amendment rule and a quasi-confederal ratification rule. That puts them in an admirable position, as I have explained, and I am well supported: "the Kurds could gain more autonomy under any new arrangements but would never have to accept less."[174]

I used to think that the confederal ratification rule and the default rule were as inimical to learning as the amendment rule.[175] But as I now see it, they do allow learning, but in a predetermined (that is, always more confederal) direction. If anyone wants anything new put in the permanent constitution, say a new status law, a new structure for the courts, or a new law for region formation, and wants to make sure it will actually be enacted, they can have it, but each time only in return for a new concession for the Kurds, who did not in the TAL get everything they desired from the point of view of regional autonomy—though they got the next best thing: a constitutionally built-in procedure for eventually getting it all.[176]

Rules of constitutional change are not just rules. For some, they indicate the ultimate locus of sovereignty, a perhaps too metaphysical way of looking at the matter, especially where the relevant provision, for example, Article V of the U.S. Constitution, would indicate a rather frozen document.[177] Undoubtedly, however, a fundamental power or dimension of sovereignty is here involved: the ability of a political community to fashion its own fundamental rules. Whatever a constitution says, the amendment rule and the ratification rule control a process through which everything could in principle be otherwise. But that is not all. Aside from powers of sovereignty, what is at stake is also the entity or subject to which sovereignty is imputed,[178] the identity of what Americans call "we the people," which, according to Sujit Choudhry, is the (symbolic) identity of the political community.[179] As he explains, the amendment rules and constitution-making rules, by determining which individuals can participate in the most fundamental form of boundary determining and potentially radical decision making, determine which individuals and communities can participate in political decision making. If a fundamental rule of change gives individual members of the legislature and individual voters the exclusive role, then the political community is defined as unitary in line with what I called the postnationalist or civic-republican nationalist conception. If a fundamental rule, on the contrary, gives veto power to individual communities already organized in a highly autonomous or independent manner, then it defines the country as the voluntary union of those communities, as the ethnic nationalist wishes. Finally, if a rule would compromise between these options and produce a synthesis where qualified majorities based on both individual and unit voting could make or change the constitution, but without vetoes, then it would come close to the multiple-identities model proposed by the liberal nationalist (and perhaps also be acceptable to the postnationalist). For Iraq, one such rule would have been a constitution-making procedure requiring the assent of two-thirds of parliament and three-fourths of the governorates.[180] But rule 61c together with 61e and 61g of the TAL were not this rule but rather ones in line with the aspirations of the ethnic nationalists. It finalized accordingly what the latter group sought: a definition of Iraq as a voluntary union of two ethnically defined peoples.

In several articles, Choudhry persuasively argues both that the amendment rule/ratification rule are not neutral rules and that there is no neutral process to generate them. Not only do they presuppose a political community and a political identity, but the rule according to which they would be made also would, and so on with infinite regress. I extended this argument with respect to procedure, when speaking about the shape of the table. A two-sided table (Kurds versus Iraq) presupposed the model of voluntary union; a round table with the Kurds as one participant at best allowed only devolution. Ultimately, such choices can be made only according to power relations as filtered through ideologies. But a legitimate way of making the choice would assume prior informal bargaining among the relevant actors themselves. The problem in Iraq was that the choice was made by only one of the parties together with the agents of the external, occupying power. And then on top of it all, that external power turned out to bargain incredibly weakly, even in the two-sided structure of negotiations. When the relevant ratification rule was introduced at the last minute, the U.S. managers accepted it in a wholly unthinking way and went so far as to manipulate the whole meeting so as to make sure the most important item in the TAL would be passed without any discussion at all. Thus the American occupier, without reflection perhaps but decisively all the same, imposed not only an interim constitution but a well-enshrined *constitutional identity* on Iraq.

Legitimation and Response: Sistani's Last Struggle

I believe I may have been one of the first to argue that TAL would have deep legitimacy problems due to the exclusionary and imposed nature of its origins, and now several well-known interpreters have come to affirm that perspective.[181] I did not, however, claim that it would lose its validity in the narrow legal sense, a position that since then has also found its advocates. My argument was originally based on interrelated domestic legal (instances with lower legitimacy trying to bind freely elected assemblies with higher, democratic legitimacy), international legal (Hague Prohibitions imperfectly overcome by UN Security Council authorization), political-sociological (the exclusionary structure of bodies that participated in process, especially with respect to organized sectors of the Arab Sunni part of the population), and procedural (the role of open American imposition in the process) dimensions.[182]

To this list has now been added the significant issue of the absence any public openness or consultation before or during the making of the TAL, a consideration I must admit I omitted because I thought it too utopian under the circumstances. But Diamond's analysis shows that to some extent it was possible to organize a *subsequent* sales or public-relations effort for the TAL, one that could only lead to anger and resentment of course, and this means that, yes, even in Iraq, the process could have been much more open and public.[183] But this, of course, would have been incompatible with what really was going on at the actual venues of negotiation, which was not merely an elite bargain needed to be initially shielded from the public but involved the active exclusion of some elites, the humiliation of others, the letting of still others play with the symbolic issues that happened to concern them the most, and the exaggerated role of the occupying power and one domestic actor among all others, the latter because it was the only one with a military capability, due to acts of the occupying power. None of this was fit for public discussion or even consumption. But the absence of the latter certainly contributed to the legitimacy problem, which is amazingly enough frankly admitted by the advocates of the greatest beneficiaries, the Kurds.[184]

Legitimation problems do not automatically turn into a loss of legitimacy. For this to happen, there must be an important social actor that will plausibly challenge the old claims of legitimation and offer a serious alternative. This actor was once again the Grand Ayatollah Sistani. I cannot tell whether he was equally concerned with the issue of Islam in the state as were his supposed representatives in the IGC. I have my doubts, because on this issue he seemed to always support various compromise formulas—not that they really mattered. On the contrary, when he found out about the final text of the TAL, the day after it was rammed through, his opposition to it was nearly complete, even if he concentrated on two provisions only, article 61c, with the Kurdish three-province veto, and the consociational three-person structure of the Presidency Council, where he may have thought that one member had a veto (accurately, for government formation, but erroneously, for legislation).[185] The fight is entirely misconstrued, I think, if we see it as a challenge of the Kurdish demand "for minority rights" on the basis of the Shi'ite "quest for majority rule." As advocates of the Kurds recognize, at issue were two structures of the state, one with and one without a Kurdish "federacy" with veto powers over all constitutional matters. Between such an asymmetrical federation and a purely majoritarian democracy there were a lot of alternatives, including federations involving all manner of minority rights, and there is no justification in claiming or implying that Sistani was against them all. All we know for sure is that he had to consider article 61c an abrogation of the concession of the freely elected constitutional "convention" made to him on November 15 and accepted by him in the compromise with Brahimi in the form of a European (and Iranian, Indian, and Iraqi) type of constituent assembly. Would he have rejected a solution that limited this assembly by any procedural rules at all? We will never know, because the three-province veto was a very extreme limitation, by one national minority, which gave its representatives a very high level of control over the assembly.[186] It would have been totally inconsistent with his previous modus operandi had he accepted it.

The Kurdish response to the challenge was predictably tough and unyielding; Sistani could not threaten them directly. The CPA's response was irrational, uncompromising, and probably driven by timetables. It was the Shi'ites who chose a very sophisticated double strategy, to sign and not sign the TAL at the same time, which was to have very negative consequences for the constitutional development.[187] They probably opted for this because they both wanted to get to their elections as scheduled in the TAL and to retain the rights of the constituent assembly when elected, as against the restriction of the TAL. In brief, they wanted to "have their TAL and eat it too."

The Shi'ite members of the IGC were to be in charge of the first, TAL-friendly dimension of the process. After demonstrably not signing the TAL on March 5, hugely embarrassing the Americans, they signed on the next day—and then announced that they considered it undemocratic, they had signed only to preserve the unity of the country (!), and that they would work to have it amended.[188] Sistani was evidently going to be responsible for the second dimension of the process, which involved working to delegitimate the TAL. On the same day (according to Juan Cole's translation, on March 9), he released a fatwa: "any law prepared for the transitional period will not gain legitimacy except after it is endorsed by an elected national assembly. Additionally, this law places obstacles in the path of reaching a permanent constitution for the country that maintains its unity and the rights of its sons of all ethnicities and sects."

Note that Sistani did not clearly say the law was null and void and that it would be wrong to obey it, nor that it could not be confirmed and repassed by the freely elected assembly if that assembly so wished. What he was disputing was legitimacy (which could only be democratic in his eyes) and not legality, whether or not he clearly articulated this distinction. After all, political actors supposedly in close consultation with him signed the law even if they then appended reservations, including the intention to amend it. But it is certainly true that he strongly believed that the freely elected assembly could not be bound by the TAL unless it chose to reaffirm it, and this could be (would have to be, in fact) done initially according to its own rules rather than the TAL's.[189]

As to legitimacy, he was concerned especially with an international-law legitimation of the TAL, which could conceivably bind the elected assembly, and thus he took immediate steps to block it. With the elimination of the caucus scheme, the TAL no longer had a method for choosing a government. "There was no plan B."[190] The job, the American authorities reluctantly agreed, would have to be done in consultation by Ambassador Brahimi, based on his earlier success with Sistani. Sistani was not opposed to this, but he hoped to use it as leverage against the TAL, all the more so since he too had had some success with Brahimi before. In a March 19 letter to Brahimi,[191] two weeks after the signing of the TAL and shortly before Brahimi was to come to Iraq once again, Sistani specifically mentioned the TAL's nullifying the usefulness of the free elections conceded to him, and he warned Brahimi of total noncooperation with his visit if the United Nations in any way legitimated the TAL.[192] He was not complaining about the concessions his side was forced to make about Islam[193] but rather about the state and governmental structure conceded to the Kurds and enshrined by a series of limitations on the constitutional assembly: namely, the rules of change. There was in fact nothing else in the TAL that limited that assembly, since the earlier tentative constitutional principles in the Pachachi draft were gone. But Sistani was evidently smart enough to understand that these particular rules of change in fact enshrined the default position of the Kurds, the imposed TAL, which involved their quasi-confederal enclave and the consociational structures of government that could not be changed without Kurdish consent, whatever the freely elected assembly and the immense majority of the people of Iraq wished. His concern was thus state and governmental structures, not minority rights more generally, unless we think that it is a minority's inalienable right to have a "federacy" and "consociational" democracy. His fears of these, beyond the loss of power for the assembly, had to do with the breakup of Iraq and general ungovernability, and these were hardly unreasonable fears in the given region in relation to an ethnically defined confederal enclave (think of Bangladesh) or consociationalism (think of Lebanon).

With Brahimi, Sistani found a partner ready to share his fears concerning the making of fundamental decisions before the country had a legitimate elected government.[194] We know that UN officials did not like the way the TAL was being produced, and though they did not share Sistani's majoritarian aspirations, they could have been happy to promise to deemphasize the interim constitution. We do not know what Brahimi promised to Sistani, and what relevant promises he extracted from the U.S. government, but we do know that they all fully cooperated in the choosing of the interim executive, where Sistani did not get his first choice for prime minister but at least got a candidate acceptable to him. It was actually Brahimi who wound up hugely disappointed here, because he was not able to construct a government of technocrats and was forced to basically transmute the old IGC into a new Interim Executive. He blamed Bremer, the "dictator of Iraq,"[195] for not supporting him, and it seems pretty clear that Bremer did get the candidate, Ayad Allawi, that he and his bosses wanted, as opposed to a "black turban," which would have looked bad for the U.S. elections and who supposedly would never say "thank you" to President Bush!

Few people noticed that while Sistani made no great stand for the black turbans (supposedly because he could not choose between SCIRI and Da'wa, which is ridiculous), in the process he had to follow the TAL's scheme for governmental offices and drop his objections to the three-person presidency, at least for the time being. The whole process strengthened the TAL as the legal framework on which they operated. Nevertheless, Sistani continued to battle for the freedom of his constitutional assembly, and thus against the legitimation of a document that would bind it. Thus when the government *was* formed in a way that was not his first preference but was at least acceptable to him, he renewed his campaign vis-à-vis the United Nations. First, he got Brahimi, a true gentleman, to deliver on what could have been an earlier promise, and he pronounced the TAL to be an interim document that could of course not bind the freely elected constitutional assembly, which was exactly what the CPA, the Kurds, and the document itself were trying to do.[196] Then, in case the message concerning the TAL was getting lost because of his own earlier cooperation, on May 7 Sistani addressed the following letter to the UN Secretary-General:

> It has reached us that some are attempting to insert a mention of what they call "The Law for the Administration of the Iraqi State in the Transitional Period" [i.e., the TAL] into the new UN Security Council resolution on Iraq—with the goal of lending it international legitimacy. This "Law," which was legislated by an unelected council in the shadow of Occupation, and with direct influence from it, binds the national parliament, which it has been decided will be elected at the beginning of the new Christian year for the purpose of passing a permanent constitution for Iraq. This matter contravenes the laws, and most children of the Iraqi people reject it. For this reason, any attempt to bestow legitimacy on it through mentioning it in the UN resolution would be considered an action contrary to the will of the Iraqi people and a harbinger of grave consequences.

What the grave consequences might be was already relatively clear, as the intifada of Moqtada al Sadr was gathering strength. It was crucial that Sistani did not support any such option—or even large peaceful demonstrations—against the interim arrangements, now very close to the U.S. elections. Unlike Brahimi, it seems, Sistani fully understood the vulnerabilities of the Americans. So did the Kurds, who felt their superpower patrons wavering. Thus they too decided to play the same game: In a June 4 letter to President Bush, Masuod Barzani and Jalal Talabani specifically asked that

> The Transitional Administrative Law (TAL) be incorporated into the new UN Security Council Resolution or otherwise recognized as law binding on the transitional government, *both before and after elections*. If the TAL

> is *abrogated*, the Kurdistan Regional Government will have no choice but to refrain from participating in the central government and its institutions, not to take part in the national elections, and to bar representatives of the central Government from Kurdistan.[197]

Four days later, UN SC Res. 1546 approved the formation of a "sovereign" Interim Government of Iraq, its assumption of full authority ("transfer of sovereignty") by June 30 with the end of the occupation and the CPA, a timetable (proposed by the TAL) for elections, and the formation of a Transitional National Assembly and Government, which would draft a permanent [*sic*] constitution leading to a constitutionally elected government by December 31, 2005. But 1546 did not refer to the TAL. Thus Sistani rather than the Kurds succeeded in this final round: the TAL did not receive international legitimation by the UN Security Council, and it can be said that in the end the U.S. government did not fully support its product. Nevertheless, 1546 did not detail an alternative method and scenario for government formation, moving toward elections, and writing a constitution, concepts it affirmed, leaving open only one of two possible alternatives. The more likely one was that these matters would still be regulated by the TAL, whose scenario was being followed, and certainly this is what the American government assumed. But a very narrow way of reading 1546 was also compatible with the idea of a provisional government, now established, that could fill each item with content as it went along as long as it adhered to the timetable, which was now enacted in international law (assuming the very contestable priority of international over domestic law in a formally nonoccupied country). To some extent then, arguably, 1546 left it up to the Interim Executive itself to decide whether Iraq's transition would be regulated by a classic quasi-revolutionary provisional government or a genuine interim constitution. Allawi's government then decided this question in favor of the latter, but without encroaching on the freely elected assembly's prerogatives. Sistani won his last battle, but the straightjacket for the constitutional assembly was not thereby removed. Nor were most of the other results very positive.

The Survival of the TAL and the Failure of State Reconstruction

Some supporters of the Kurds argue (on rather self-interested grounds, as we will see) that the TAL was indeed abrogated as Barzani and Talabani warned.[198] The most sustained version of this argument was made by Peter Galbraith, even if he later toned it down. Accordingly, under UN SC Res. 1483 Iraq was under "belligerent occupation": "Occupying powers are not allowed to make permanent, or irreversible, changes in an occupied country.[[199]] Occupying powers cannot *cede territory* [my emphasis], sell assets, or make permanent law. Accordingly, all law made by the Coalition Provisional Authority (CPA) expired when the occupation ended on June 28."[200] The United States could have secured Security Council authorization for lawmaking before making the TAL, but it did not. It could have secured Security Council authorization for the TAL (and other CPA-passed laws) afterward, before the end of the occupation, but it failed to do so. Not doing so signifies rookie mistakes on the part of Bremer and his inexperienced team, in the first instance, and an abandonment of the TAL by the U.S. administration in the second. Ergo, the TAL is legally null and void.[201] Relying on Galbraith's claims about what went wrong, the same argument about the rights of occupying powers are less precisely repeated by O'Leary.[202] In his view, the U.S. government had two choices to save the TAL (and CPA legislation): either get UN recognition or set up an interim government that could recognize these laws. It did neither, and therefore Iraq was left with no "formal interim constitution, and in consequence no recognized ground rules for the negotiation and ratification of the permanent constitution."

Written in September 2004, the last lines were surprising ones to write from the Kurdish point of view, but there was a method behind the apparent madness: if they are not bound, we are not bound; what is sauce for the goose is sauce for the gander. Kurdistan will apply those provisions of the TAL that it approves and ignore those it does not.[203] And then in retrospect we are told that "the Kurds never implemented the provisions of the TAL they did not like. They never gave up control of their international borders with Iran and Turkey and continued to develop their oil resources without reference to Baghdad. Of course, they kept the peshmerga."[204]

This self-righteous attitude justifying illegality and (from their own point of view) treaty violation is built on a house of cards. I was one of the first to discuss the deep legitimacy problems of the TAL, its delegitimation by Sistani, and the possibility therefore of a repudiation by the constitutional assembly, which, by the way, would have been a legitimate but revolutionary repudiation that no UN Security Council resolution could have blocked. This, however, is by no means the same as to claim the absence of legal validity. Certainly, Sistani's protest, no matter how legitimate, was an entirely political one, which could acquire legal force only if a public law organ, say the Interim Government or the Transitional National Assembly, repudiated the TAL. Though clever, the international-law argument made by Galbraith is not foolproof. To say a body cannot legislate does not mean that its laws, if they have already been followed, are null and void.[205] After June 28, for example, the de-Baathified civil servants or the dismissed military officers were still without their positions (because of CPA orders 1 and 2). They could not just return to work, and it would have taken another legal decision of some kind, a court order or a new piece of legislation, to give their jobs back to them, even under Iraqi legal conditions, such as they were. Of course these orders, later modified, remained in effect. Conversely, though they got their jobs under the TAL, I. Allawi, his ministers, and the Presidency Council could not suddenly lose them because of the supposed abrogation of the law on which they stood. And so on with all the many laws of the CPA, including the Electoral Law (CPA Order 96, June 7, 2004) and the Electoral Commissions Law (CPA Order 92, May 31, 2004), which were used to regulate the elections of January 2005. Thus the TAL rightly pronounces a necessary legal fact, even if a self-referring one, that all these orders remain in effect until repealed by or derogated from by some other law (TAL art. 26c).

Moreover, the terms "permanent, or irreversible, changes in an occupied country" do not apply in a completely obvious way to an interim constitution or transitional administrative law. Whatever we may think of the lawyers of the CPA and the U.S. government, they understood and worked with the Hague requirements in Iraq no less than their predecessors in Japan and found in each case a different way to disguise or legalize their imposition and their desire to make permanent change under the guise of transitional ones.[206] If we are to focus on where the TAL actually violated international law, it would have to be on the question of state structure and its insulation through the amendment and ratification rules. In the face of repeated warnings and criticisms from UN sources, the TAL did make changes here that would be difficult to reverse and made sure through the rules of amendment and ratification that they could not be reversed even when the occupation ended. Thus it is understandable that the Kurds wanted international legal recognition for American illegal actions in which they were deeply implicated. But to the extent the rules now existed, it was nevertheless strange that it was its beneficiaries who now claimed they were invalid and that they were free to follow them or not as they pleased.

Admittedly, the Kurds could claim that they were responding to Sistani's challenge to have his constitutional assembly abrogate the TAL, even if preemptively. Anticipating repudiation, they repudiated. The situation is the same with the now famous preventive or supposedly "preemptive" war. In fact, they were simply committing illegalities. But that is not all. They also assumed that the TAL was in effect and thereby recognized it. They did not follow through the threats contained in the Barzani and Talabani letters. They assumed their positions in the Iraqi interim government, accepted the financial grants due to them, fully participated in elections according to CPA electoral rules(!), counted on the provisions regarding Kirkuk being carried out, and never forgot about their amendment and ratification rules, through which they could get many more concessions in the future, all under the TAL. They had their TAL and were feasting on it too. This could probably be said of the Shi'ites too, who kept and developed their militias and undoubtedly introduced religious-status law wherever they controlled local government to a sufficient extent. But illegalities, even when committed by provincial or regional governments, should not be confused with abrogation. Only a national body on the same level as the authors of the TAL could be said to abrogate it. And this never happened, as weak as the interim constitution's legitimacy may have been.

First and foremost, after taking office, the TAL was a matter for the Allawi government to uphold. It is hard to understand both O'Leary's claim that the Americans should have set up an interim government capable of recognizing the TAL (which would have to be a government also capable of not recognizing or abrogating it) and his (inconsistent) complaint that Allawi, despite the Kurds' relevant demand, refused to legislatively enact it. As both O'Leary and Galbraith admit, Allawi did agree to abide by it until the first meeting of the freely elected Transitional (constitutional) National Assembly, but this limitation only meant that he did not feel he had the right to preempt the relevant decision of that body nor the power to challenge Sistani (supported by Brahimi) on this score.[207] As both O'Leary and Galbraith should have known, Allawi could not reenact it as a genuine piece of legislation, simply because he had no legislature.[208] But because he could declare (executive) orders *with the force of law* (annex, sec. 2), he actually did confirm the TAL in one of these, his Order Safeguarding National Security (July 6, 2004), which was about the most he could do.[209] Thus in this respect, he gave little justification for any other group's wholesale violation of agreements incorporated in the TAL or even for disregarding substantive provisions, all while adhering to the schedules contained in the TAL.[210]

There is only one justification for what the Kurds did, but it is a serious one. The Shi'ites were the first to reduce their relation to the TAL to a double, strategic one, inviting others in effect to follow them. Kurdish spokesmen (for example, Barem Saleh) have rightly pointed out that the TAL was unanimously approved by the Shi'ite leadership in the IGC. Thus it is disingenuous to say, as did Mowaffak al-Rubaie, one of the signers, "that you cannot control the will of the people [in the constituent assembly] . . . whatever they will do, they will do," when the same parties hoped to control the popular majority in the very same assembly.[211] The same criticism would be invalid with respect to the initial agreement the night TAL article 61c, the ratification rule, was introduced and hammered through by Bremer without discussion. But the two days of formal signing were another matter. The Shi'ites first refused and then proceeded to sign after extended deliberation, understanding the consequences. That they announced and even "attached" reservations is immaterial. They signed. And they signed precisely with a dual strategy in mind. They wanted the TAL to deliver for them what it could (elections) while remaining free to go beyond it when they got what they wanted. Now the Kurds were about to adopt the same double attitude, with the difference that in their case partial repudiation could only be in the form of "illegality," whereas the Shi'ites, when in control of the constituent assembly, could repudiate the TAL by establishing a new legality. But that difference could be seen in terms of the type of power each side had, not as an ultimate normative difference.

Nevertheless, I believe the Shi'ites had a better reason to adopt a double attitude to the TAL, even if the Kurds could be hardly expected to understand that. That reason had to do with negotiating and bargaining within an ultimately imposed structure, under the gun, where the Americans were in the position to use the continuation of the formal occupation, the restoration of formal sovereignty, and having democratic elections as bargaining chips. This put the Shi'ite leadership in a double bind almost every step of the way, and they were continually reminded by Bremer of the examples of the Shi'ite electoral boycotts in British Iraq, if they needed to be reminded of what happens when one chooses the alternative of simply withdrawing from a process seen as badly deformed by an occupation. Back in the 1920s, the Shi'ite mujtahids were to lose political influence for many decades as a result of choosing the clear and honorable path of resistance. As they now must have seen, they could neither withdraw nor not withdraw, even when they were very severely provoked, for instance with the adoption of 61c. Signing and keeping options open was a rational response to a very deformed political process, even if in retrospect the results proved devastating.

The Kurds understandably interpreted the TAL signing as an agreement among the signers. The Shi'ite double attitude was one addressed to the Kurds, as far as the Kurds were concerned, threatening what the Kurds had achieved—and the Kurds conveniently forgot how they achieved it. Thus to counter it, the Kurds assumed a double attitude as well. Despite their threats, they entered the Interim Government and played along with the TAL on the "federal" level. But on the level of their (con)federacy, the Kurds illegally continued to solidify all their positions as a quasi-state. All this is undeniable, since their defenders say so themselves, though denying any illegality, since the TAL was supposedly null and void. But this position is untenable, as I have argued, and in the light of subsequent developments those who have argued that the TAL was null and void have backed away from that assertion. The illegalities and their results are there to stay.

What the Kurds and their defenders wound up admitting is that the state bargain, the heart of the TAL, the only real bargain in it, a kind of treaty between a superpower and the quasi-state of Kurdistan, broke down before the ink was dry. The United States, the superpower, after having destroyed the Iraqi state, did not manage to use the constitutional process, in its first stage at least, to reconstruct that state in its geographical-territorial capacity. It negotiated an asymmetrical political structure of a federation for Iraq and a confederal enclave or "federacy" for Kurdistan, and overall "stateness" was to inhere in a very few powers the federation was to retain in and over that confederacy. Those powers were now recovered by Kurdistan, with the very partial exception of foreign affairs (controlled in fact by the United States), leaving a fractured territorial entity in place.

If that left the rest of Iraq a federal state, as the Kurds sometimes argue, perhaps state formation could still be pronounced a success. But the concessions to the Kurds in the TAL and the illegalities they committed despite the TAL were among the reasons why this was also not possible, and to his credit the Ayatollah Sistani was aware of this set of problems too. Let us recall that his objections were not only to the confederal but also to the consociational features of the TAL. In fact, consociationism, by no means a logical necessity if there is an ethnically based confederation, produced very a weak government for Arab Iraq, allowing all sorts of Kurdish vetoes over it (constituting or replacing government, amending the constitution). Even more significantly, as Sistani explicitly said (by then it was no longer a prediction), it sectarianized or ethnicized politics, with each group now looking to imitate the Kurds' success in gaining regional and veto rights. Here the second dimension of stateness, that of having some kind of unified status for the citizenry (the "people" of the state, not to be confused with the ethnic or even the republican idea of "nation"), was profoundly endangered, despite the TAL's provisions for a unified Iraqi citizenship. Finally, and deeply related, the concession to the Peshmerga, while certainly not the only cause, made the survival of other militias unchallengeable. And with militias in control, the third (and perhaps most immediate) dimension of statehood, already severely compromised by CPA orders 1 and 2, the organizational dimension that produces a monopoly over violence, was shipwrecked. A so-called Iraqi army and police could be built, but these would be based on militia units serving en masse, in organized fashion, keeping their primary allegiances, with the consequence that the population could encounter "foreign" and very much hated militias in "Iraqi" uniforms.

All the other supposed achievements of the TAL become irrelevant in terms of this failure of state making. If there is no state, government as the political organization that is supposed to control such an entity cannot function. At most, as early pluralists have thought, it becomes one competing organization among many, local and regional, civil and military, secular and religious. If there is no state, there are no state and confessional relations, and religious authorities will occupy the space of jurisdiction that government is unable to operate in. If there is no state, there are no rights against the state nor are there rights the state can positively guarantee. In failing at its most fundamental task, state rebuilding, the TAL failed at them all—with one exception. While it could not provide a serious constitution for the interim period, it did provide a framework for negotiating a supposedly permanent constitution. Its rules of change, which were a very important source of its failures, also turned out to be the most successful in achieving their purpose—if at the cost of more devastation. Despite claims of its abrogation, the TAL remained a highly constraining blueprint for Iraq's subsequent constitutional process.

[5]

The Making of the "Permanent" Constitution

> "We're short of time—it's the fault of the Americans," Kurdish politician Mahmoud Othman said. "They are always insisting on short deadlines. It's as if they're [making] hamburgers and fast food." Othman added: "If we'd had more time, it would have been possible to get Sunni participation. When October 15 comes, many won't even have seen the constitution."[1]

In light of subsequent history, there are striking and surprising differences of opinion concerning the "permanent" Iraqi constitution (ratified in October 2005) and how it was made. While some analysts (the Crisis Group)[2] consider the process and its result disastrous, others (Peter Galbraith)[3] find both to be much superior to what took place and was achieved in the case of the American-imposed Transitional Administrative Law. I tend to agree with the former view, and I share its advocates' concern that a constitution in several important respects worse than the TAL was eventually achieved. But I continue to think that the TAL remained a straightjacket in part responsible for the failure and many of its political consequences. At the same time, in two respects the making of the permanent constitution involved positive dimensions as well. First, a partially successful attempt at legitimation through national elections did occur, one that could have provided a completely new basis for democratic constitution making. And, second, an attempt was made, a seemingly serious but certainly an inconsistent one, to include important political actors of the Sunni Arab part of the population. This too was a very important departure from previous practice, even if it came much too late in the game. The very sad story is that the interaction of these two positive dimensions of the process exacerbated its negative features, which were already deeply embedded by the results of the previous stage. This produced a pathological constituent process, a constitution that once again was unable to solve the elementary problem of state rebuilding, and provided for the transition of the country to the civil war in which it finds itself at the time of my writing these lines.

The Elections for the National (Constitutional) Assembly

In our normative universe, democratic elections are an irreplaceable part of modern, legitimate constitution making. Very early in the history of democratic constitutions, in the cases of the Federal Convention and the Assemblée Constituante, the delegates were not directly (in the first case) or homogeneously (in the second case, with its original estates) elected, and some critics and even some of the framers themselves considered this a serious problem.[4] For different reasons, two of the most successful modern constitutions, the *Grundgesetz* and the Constitution of the Fifth French Republic, also did not involve *new* elections. Yet as a norm, new, direct elections of the constitutional assembly is nevertheless almost universal today, more so than the idea of ratification in a democratic referendum, for example. Empirically, the immense majority of constitution-making bodies have been democratically elected, at least in the twentieth century. Interestingly, the new two-stage method of constitution making described here and followed in Iraq complicates the picture. It involves the writing of an interim constitution by an unelected body, an interim constitution that will constrain to various extents the makers of the permanent constitution. Nevertheless, in every single example of the model, the assembly that makes the final constitution is freely and democratically elected and retains considerable freedom. Thus, while the model involves two constitutions, one made by a democratically elected body and one made by a different type of agent, the final product that comes out of the process is still supposed to be one made by a body consistent with the demands and recommendations of democratic theory.[5] Electing a constitutional assembly specifically charged with drawing up a new constitution but under the rules of the interim constitution is the specific formula appropriate to the two-stage model.

The democratic legitimacy of this model depends therefore on relatively early, competitive, and inclusive elections, and this step at legitimation can only come in the second stage.[6] That is why I write "relatively early," despite many opinions that in conflictual societies after the collapse of dictatorships elections should be delayed. The first stage of the process always has legitimation problems, even if they are rarely as deep as they were in Iraq. In the second stage, the temptation that the newly elected assembly will vote to disregard the limits placed upon it will always be there, though remarkably such a repudiation, common, for example, in the case of the American type of constitutional conventions in Latin America, has not yet been seen in the two-stage model. Early elections may have something to do with this. Had the time period between the making of interim constitutions by bodies of elites regarded as not fully legitimate been greatly extended, this would have been popularly regarded in many cases as a usurpation, potentially dragging down the authority of the interim constitution in the process. Conversely, in several countries the fact that assemblies elected in relatively early voting chose to accept (explicitly or implicitly) the interim constitutions when they could have (either legally or in a revolutionary manner) amended or repudiated them helped to legitimate the overall process.[7]

In Iraq, free elections did take place as scheduled, and, as we will see, the TAL, the interim constitution, was confirmed with only a partial relegitimation being the consequence. The explanation of this outcome starts with the analysis of the elections themselves. To begin with, they were Sistani's victory, despite many later claims on the part of the American government.[8] Good thing too, otherwise the legitimation process I have in mind, partial as it was, would not have occurred at all. Sistani, as already shown, wanted an even earlier date than January 30, 2005, but he managed to get one early enough given his need to organize Shi'ite groupings as a single electoral list, which (working through his agents) he did successfully. The United Iraqi Alliance (UIA) brought together the SCIRI, Da'wa, and several smaller factions under a banner widely associated with the Grand Ayatollah himself. And the result that Paul Bremer tried to desperately avoid was indeed achieved: a Shi'ite victory in the general elections. The UIA received 48.2 percent of the votes cast, somewhat under their expectations but still receiving over 50 percent of the seats. Because of the two-thirds needed to elect a Presidency Council, they could not govern alone, but they were now clearly the major political force in Iraq, at least from the electoral point of view. And for the moment, the Kurdistan Coalition List, or the Democratic Patriotic Alliance of Kurdistan, with 25.73 percent of the votes and seventy-five seats, was by far the second strongest force in the country. They alone were in a position to block amendments to the TAL, even before the election of a Kurdish member of the Presidency Council.

TABLE 3
Summary of the January 30, 2005, Iraqi legislative election results

PARTIES AND COALITIONS	VOTES	%	SEATS	LEADERS
United Iraqi Alliance (UIA)	4,075,292	48.19%	140	Abdul Aziz al-Hakim, Ibrahim al-Jaffari
Dem. Patriotic Alliance of Kurdistan or Kurdistan Coalition List (KLC)	2,175,551	25.73%	75	J. Talabani, M. Barzani
Iraqi List (or Iraqiyya List)	1,168,943	13.82%	40	Iyad Allawi
The Iraqis	150,680	1.78%	5	Ghazi al-Yawer
Iraqi Turkmen Front	93,480	1.11%	3	
National Ind. Cadres and Elites	69,938	0.83%	3	

To explain this somewhat inflated result, I first turn to the electoral rule and then to the problem of the Sunni boycott. The making of the rule was farmed out to a UN electoral team led by Carina Perelli.[9] They chose a single countrywide district list PR for two reasons. First, and probably less important, they chose it because such a system is very proportional, and for a constitutional assembly governability issues should recede to an extent behind those of fair representation of political groups, interests, and streams of opinion that could become important in the foreseeable future. If it is true that the CPA went for the rule because of its desire to limit the vote of large Islamist parties and get smaller parties represented, for once they rather than Sistani's circle had justice on their side.[10] Excluding small parties via an electoral rule when the fundamental rules of the game are being negotiated is not fair, and it is indeed true that many small territorial lists could have had that effect.[11] The problem of course for a constitutional assembly like the one to be elected in Iraq was that it would also be the legislative body in which the executive would be based, and thus governability problems probably should have been considered by the makers of the rule. A single-country-district PR can produce extreme party fragmentation, and a mixed rule that then would perhaps enable the assembly to create both a more inclusive constitution-making panel and a more governmental legislative panel, as in India in 1948 (where they so proceeded on the basis of a single rule inherited from the colonial period), could have served all purposes better. But—and this was the second and more important reason for choosing the rule—a single-country PR did not require a prior census of the population, a problem raised against early elections.[12] Both first-past-the-post voting and multidistrict PR would have required a prior determination of the number of people in each district, with equal districts in the first case and seats proportional to population in the second case. But this problem was perhaps a red herring, since Iraqi experts had long assured both the IGC and Sistani that a reasonable estimate of the population could be made on the basis of ration cards. Since a first-past-the-post rule of the British or American type was not considered, there was thus a choice between multidistrict and a more proportional one-national-district version of PR, and the UN experts chose the latter, with the CPA then decreeing it as Iraq's electoral rule (CPA Order 96, June 7, 2004).

Note that, unlike in the case of the TAL, no one ever made the absurd point that this purely CPA-enacted rule was abrogated because UN SC Res. 1546 or Prime Minister Allawi did not legislatively confirm it. I note, but without making too much of it, that there was little reason why especially Kurdish constituencies should have objected to this rule, nor was there a possibility, as in the case of the TAL, to have the rule and violate it too. Defenders of the Kurdish cause somehow forget to say that it too was abrogated with the demise of the CPA. It was, all the same, a disastrous rule and a disastrous choice. It was unfortunately foreseeable that a single-country-district PR would be turnout dependent in a way that a multidistrict PR would not be.[13] Iraq was a country in insurrection, and insurrectionary violence was another reason people used to argue for delaying elections. Of course, according to this logic, such a delay could make the violence even worse, and then one might never be able to have an election. But what one needed was an electoral rule that would be as little affected by the insurrection as possible. The insurrection was geographically concentrated in some areas and not in others. Where it was raging, electoral turnout would be low. In a single-country-district PR system, parties strong in these very areas would be strongly hit by low turnout, and in the single national comparison they would get a lower percentage than their actual support. And this would happen whether or not the insurrection formally discouraged electoral participation.[14] In a multidistrict PR, on the other hand, comparisons would be within each district, and presumably violence would affect the turnout of parties within a territorial district equally. There would be a smaller total turnout, but the seats would correspond to the percentages and the latter thus more or less to the actual support.[15]

To understand the Sunni boycott, one must start out with the elementary situation created by the electoral rule: under it, the Sunni part of the population would be dramatically underrepresented and, equally important to the actors, even undermeasured. The Sunni parties and associations only had the choice of being underrepresented or not being represented at all. There were thus also two fundamentally different types of reasons for the boycott: the "expressive" reason of the fundamentalists, who wished to denounce the political process no matter what, and the "instrumental" reasons of less radical forces, who hoped thereby to achieve greater representation. What was obviously spectacular about the call to boycott, its rhetoric and timing, admittedly seems to have had little that was instrumental about it. Linked to a fundamental situation that was not soon going to alter, namely the American occupation, and to events like the second, devastating set of attacks on Fallujah, the boycott seemingly could not be associated with any other set of political goals other than to rally the faithful.[16] Clearly, the calls of the Iraqi Islamic Party to postpone the election pointed in an instrumental direction, especially when coupled with demands for the change of the electoral rule. Since postponement was not going to affect the security situation, only the two demands together made sense. When neither demand was met because of a convergence of American and Shi'ite views on the matter,[17] the Iraqi Islamic Party almost relented. When it finally persisted in its boycott plans,[18] joining the more radical Association of Muslim Scholars and the Sunni Endowments, this clearly did not mean the abandonment of the instrumental goal. Rather, the Sunni moderates calculated that more representation could be achieved through the boycott and through the threat to the legitimacy of the new constitution than through participation in and thereby legitimation of elections that produced very little representation.[19] All the Sunni strategists had to anticipate was a strategic shift of American policymakers under the combined effect of the insurrection and the lobbying by influential Sunni states, especially Saudi Arabia, but also Jordan and the United Arab Emirates. If in the end the strategy did not work, in fact it did work in the intermediate term.[20]

In the short term, the parties that won the elections gained new legitimacy, especially because the American authorities openly and materially supported the loser, Prime Minister Allawi's secular Iraqi List. However, the victory of the UIA was not so overwhelming as to revive any plan (if one was still being considered) concerning the extralegal abrogation of the TAL. Very likely a deal concerning this and other matters was already well in the works with the Kurdish parties, even before the elections that were fought out between the UIA and the American-supported Iyad Allawi Iraqi List.[21] Before the elections, Allawi was already too much of a centralizer for the Kurds and too secular for the Shi'ites, some of whom were already tempted by ideas of regionalism. The Kurds were ready to make concessions on the religious issues, as long as these would not affect Kurdistan. After the elections, the Kurds and Allawi together would have been in any case too small to form a government; indeed, no government could be formed without the Shi'ite UIA. Even the Shi'ites and Allawi did not quite have the two-thirds of the seats necessary to elect a Presidential Council, which was needed to form a government. They had also fought a rhetorically bitter campaign, and the heterogeneous UIA would have been more difficult to keep together if an alliance with the pro-American Allawi was attempted. We can also assume by this time that a section of the Shi'a was thinking in terms of a Kurdish alliance, depending on their interests, either because of regionalism or hoped-for religious concessions, possibly even both.

In any case, the Kurds and Shi'ites together were powerful enough that it was superfluous to add other partners to a coalition that would not have to depend on even some of the unreliable members of the UIA. Thus given the compatibility or compromisability of their interests and the results of the election, the Shi'ites and the Kurds were more or less destined to run the transition government. This also meant that, in line with the strongest Kurdish demands, they had to formally agree to fully abide by the transition rules of the TAL.[22] That was probably a greater sacrifice to those closer to Sistani than for others interested in bargaining with the Kurds.[23] But despite their new electoral legitimacy and coalition agreement, they were not quite yet in the position to alone dictate the terms of the permanent constitution.

The Problem of Sunni Inclusion

The Sunni boycott, along with the intimidation of potential voters by the insurgency, was devastatingly successful in the most immediate sense. In the end, only seventeen Sunni Arabs were elected to the National Assembly, and with the Iraqi Islamic Party gone, none of these represented viable political organizations outside parliament.[24] This dramatic underrepresentation, whoever was responsible, only highlighted the exclusion of representatives of what were still very important social strata of Iraq's population, having more social, cultural, and professional weight than the 20 percent figure usually mentioned in this context. Most importantly, the military insurrection was almost entirely Sunni, and whatever propagandists tell us about their composition, the foundation for the insurrection was and is largely domestic. To the extent its small foreign part was the most nihilistic and destructive, its separation from the Iraqi Sunnis remains an important and viable objective. Thus Sunni exclusion from the political process, though never complete, has been and remains to this day one of the key problems that makes state and regime construction in Iraq next to impossible.

Ali Allawi is nevertheless right: despite early and sporadic recognition of this problem, the U.S. government only started to focus on it after the January elections. Whether the boycotters actually contributed to this shift or only anticipated it (or both), the arrival of Zalmay Khalilzad and even more his determined actions on behalf of Sunni inclusion signaled a dramatic shift in the perspectives of the constitution-making process.[25] Allawi speaks of the shift as inaugurating a third stage in American policy in Iraq, a little too neat a conception for something as incoherent and internally conflicted as this policy has always been.[26] What I would rather speak of here is a reluctant recognition of the elementary requirements of state rebuilding in a divided country with three very strong and armed political forces struggling for mastery.

State building or rebuilding in Iraq was not in principle impossible.[27] On some level, a state is only the knowledge, skill, and competence of a large number of actual or potential agents, and in Iraq this is all readily available. What no longer exists in Iraq is some kind of coherent set of public controls over coercive powers in the country as a whole, especially the means of violence. Bracketing the issue of limited sovereignty because of the occupation,[28] since a state with limited sovereignty is possible, whatever control was left to Iraqi governmental powers by the occupier could have been coherently organized only if there was either a fundamental, binding agreement over a state structure, one power forcibly bringing all other powers under its lasting control, or a binding agreement between some of the powers capable of bringing the others under their control. The second of these options presupposed the viability of long-term compulsion against all actors but one, and the third presupposed the viability of long-term compulsion against at least one such actor. In retrospect, the Sistani-led protest shows that pure compulsion was impossible with respect to the Shi'a segment of the population, and the insurrection showed, I believe, though the jury is still out, the same with regard to the Sunnis. Therefore, effective state building as the object of constitution making[29] presupposed, both at the time of the writing of the TAL and after the free elections, a comprehensive, inclusive agreement of all the major actors.[30] Before any further work on the structure of the regime, the top priority of negotiation would have to be the working out of a state structure acceptable (not preferable) to all sides—obviously, some kind of federal state or federation, but what kind? It is this type of agreement, which some rightly understand as a peace treaty or peace-building agreement, that had to be accomplished before the construction of a new regime.[31]

Another way of putting the matter was that the insurrection had to be brought into a process of constitution making that was partially transformed into a (peace) negotiation. This was a tough problem for Iraq's occupier. The insurrection was mainly against the occupation (and only later focused more on its supposed beneficiaries), and the occupation continued, supposedly, because of the insurrection. Could this vicious circle be broken? The occupation was now also there to police a state structure negotiated in an imposed, exclusionary bargain, and the insurrection was also protesting that bargain. Sunni elites were against that bargain for the formal but very good reason that they had no part in making it and did not receive any tradeoffs, as did the Shi'a. Nor could they hope for an electoral victory under it, which the United States very reluctantly recognized in the case of the Shi'a. But they were also against it for the generally recognized, solid, and substantive reason that the arrangements were very dangerous for the Sunni provinces in particular. First of all, the ethnic cleansing needed to create the state or region the Kurds really wanted would be in part at the expense of Sunni Arabs, involving a huge refugee problem for the provinces further south. Even more seriously, the asymmetric confederal structure of the bargain already in the TAL established the possibility for a more symmetric one (art. 53c), with any three provinces having the right to form a region, possibly with powers like Kurdistan's now or then. Assuming regional control over significant parts of the oil resources, which the Kurds have always demanded and at least some of the Shi'a would have an interest to concede if their provinces got the same privilege, the oil-poor Sunni provinces would be impoverished. They had a much better chance to fight such an arrangement early, when they still had the men, arms, and expertise. Aside from ideological and traditional Arab commitments to a more unified Iraq, which were probably very passionate for some, there were also solid material interests supporting such a position.

Again, the problem was foreseen in Washington very early on. However, the answer was not an IGC with memberships arranged according to ethnic quotas.[32] Once the United States presided over an exclusionary deal that it refused to reopen, it was this deal that had to be enforced. But enforcing this deal was not possible without the indefinite continuation of the occupation. It gave two reasons for the insurrection to continue, and thus the seemingly vicious circle, the occupation and the arrangement it guarded, could not be broken. Since the occupation could not be ended immediately or even in terms of a realistic timetable without admitting defeat, which would have political and U.S. electoral consequences, the only thing the U.S. government could try to do is change somehow the deal that the occupation continued to preserve. After negotiating a state deal with the Kurds and giving the Shi'ites the election that produced a governmental majority for them (modified, of course, by the results of the state deal though consociational controls), the United States now had to arrange some kind of Sunni inclusion, real or illusory.

There were four great roadblocks in the way. The first was the TAL. With its amendment, ratification, and default rules, along with its concessions to a quasi-confederal structure, it was not clear what, if now included, Sunni representatives totally dedicated as they were to Iraqi unity could actually change in the structure of decentralization conceded to the Kurds. And even if they could live with a Kurdish "federacy," if the Kurds kept what they had, the Shi'ites would ask for the same, and with their majority they could push it through, if they were united (admittedly a big "if"). In that case, the Sunnis would effectively be helping preside over the final dismemberment of the Iraqi state. Doing so would discredit them in the eyes of their constituency and the insurrectionary forces, and aside from endangering their lives (already in some jeopardy) the result would not lead to any diminution of the insurrectionary challenge.

Second, the process was not under American control, as the making of the TAL had been. Due to his style, personal gifts, and linguistic and regional knowledge, Khalilzad ought to have been a much superior negotiator than Bremer, but all this could not make up for the legal weakness of the American position and their increasing loss of political leverage with respect to their clients. And this was especially so after the Shi'ites and Kurds reached a *modus vivendi* that replaced the earlier "special relationship" between the United States and the Kurds. In particular, the new majority, the Shi'ite UIA, opposed anything more than a symbolic inclusion of unelected Sunni representatives or members.[33]

Third, inclusion would only work if the parties (clearly former enemies) had a sufficiently long time period to bargain and negotiate with one another, try out different alternatives, and slowly develop a minimum amount of trust. The TAL, however, had a very specific timetable for the process as a whole. A draft would have to be "written" by the National Assembly by August 15, a ratificatory referendum would be held by October 15, and new parliamentary elections by December 15. Admittedly, the same TAL permitted a six-month extension of the process, if applied by for by August 1 (art. 61f), and even subsequently all the dates could be amended by article 3 of the TAL. However, U.S. representatives insisted, implausibly, that the insurrection could be dealt a serious blow by the constitutional process only if all the dates were kept. Thus an unusually short time period was provided for the making of the permanent constitution (seven months), some of this was eaten up by the problems of government formation and the formation of the Constitutional Committee itself (three and a half months in all), and it took another two months to include Sunni representatives. Despite this disastrous shortening of the actual timeframe, unforeseen by the TAL and its framers, there was continued strong pressure from the Americans and the largest Iraqi parties not to use the legal possibility of extension according to TAL article 61f.[34] Once again, the artificial timetable interfered with the workings of the constitution-making model, this time making the new, more inclusive strategy, which came too late in the game in any case, all the more difficult if not entirely impossible.

And finally, most importantly, whereas in the first stage of the process all the participants were co-opted by American fiat, now the leading parliamentary parties had full electoral legitimacy. Only the Sunni representatives could be portrayed as having been co-opted or imposed. Bremer's adage that in a democracy you don't shoot your way into power finally could be applied without self-contradiction, if the Shi'ites and Kurds wished; now, only the Sunni representatives were shooting. But those Sunni representatives *weren't* shooting, they would be useless, since their whole purpose was to bring the less radical parts of the insurrection into the political process to produce a kind of peace agreement. Yet it could be said—and it was—that a group shooting its way into power may not be the one that really represents the aspirations of the broad Sunni masses, which may or may not have chosen these individuals to negotiate for them in the constitution-making process.

All these problems were pointed out relatively early, but the American side did not seem to be fully aware of them, or they wished to go ahead with the project of Sunni political inclusion regardless of the difficulties, some of which were caused by their own inflexibility. There were also some favorable factors that the Americans could take into account. The insurrection was now raging, and bringing at least some of it under control also had to be in the interest of the now-dominant Iraqi parties. Most of the Shi'a parties also wanted to end the occupation, and that too required that a role for the U.S. military be no longer needed. The prospect of forming a new Iraqi army that could and would effectively counter the old one, now partially underground, was remote. This too suggested the need to include some important Sunni forces in the political process and perhaps eventually in the new army. Finally, the Grand Ayatollah Sistani himself repeatedly called for new openness to Sunni participation,[35] and occasionally so did the Kurdish leaders, probably for quite different reasons.[36] Thus initially at least, Khalilzad's efforts to try to engineer Sunni participation did not have to be seen as merely an American project. It remained, however, a technical problem as to how one would accomplish it, given the fact that Sunni representatives could not now be elected in a regular process.

Many schemes were offered to remedy the situation,[37] but the one eventually chosen, after intensive prenegotiations with a new umbrella group, the Sunni National Dialogue Council, was entirely satisfactory in my view and from the point of view of nonpartisan observers.[38] Fifteen new Sunni members were added to a fifty-five-member parliamentary Constitutional Committee, plus ten advisors, with the larger group renamed as the Constitutional Commission. Technically, the smaller body would still have to confirm the product of the larger one, but since a consensual structure of decision making had been decided on, this should have been automatic. In other words, members would be asked to confirm the second time around what they voted for in the first place. There were some disputes concerning who the Sunni representatives would be and whether de-Baathification rules would be applied, but finally the decision was left to the National

Dialogue Council, which chose fifteen delegates and ten expert advisors from groups including the Association of Islamic Scholars, the Iraqi Islamic Party, the Sunni Endowment, and its own members.

I think it is safe to say that some of the fifteen new members (and their advisors), most likely a majority, sympathized with at least some wings of the insurrection, with some perhaps having political ties and channels of communication to armed groups. But that was an advantage, not a liability, if the whole process was to work. When they were picked, and subsequently, many charges were made concerning their rejectionist mentality and obstructionism, especially in the case of the neo-Baathist Saleh al-Mutlah, leader of the National Dialogue Council, and Adnan al-Dulaimi, leader of the Sunni Endowments.[39] The work of the Constitutional Commission, as long as it was allowed to function, does not bear out that there was such obstructionism, a charge made by highly biased parties, which of course does not automatically exclude its possible veracity. The charge of their nonrepresentive nature was much more serious, because it seems that the whole Sunni delegation was indeed picked by the leaders of these two groups plus the Iraqi Islamic Party, and they made no effort at consultations.[40] But in light of the short timetables, even this mode of selection was less surprising. As it turns out, insistence on these timetables made Shi'ite and Kurdish politicians reject the idea of drafting Sunni members through multiweek, regional caucuses.[41] Perhaps they also did not wish to add legitimacy to the new representatives, but in any case this rejection made their later objections based on a lack of representative character less than fully authentic. Moreover, advocates of the Shi'ite and Kurdish parties forgot that a short period earlier, their leaders too had been co-opted into the Interim Governing Council by the very same Americans whose intervention now included the Sunni delegates, and that incumbency in the IGC meant a positional advantage in all subsequent attempts to be elected and to form a government. Finally, given the fact that the negotiations were to assume the function of peace negotiations in the eyes of some of the same critics, it was a serious question of whom the Sunni members *should be* representing. If the negotiations were to be effective, it was probably more important that they have channels of communication to armed groups than to the grassroots opinion of their ethnic groups. However, through the network of mosques, the latter was hardly absent. The Crisis Group goes so far as to stress the "tacit community support" for the fifteen and their generally representative nature in terms of their views and composition.[42] Assuming that subsequent voting is a test for representativity (admittedly a big assumption), the referendum and elections of 2005 bear out the Crisis Group's assessment.[43]

With all this said, it remains true that these serious considerations could not change the fact that the type of representation involved by the Sunni presence was now out of sync with the democratic-electoral credentials of their Shi'a and Kurdish negotiating opponents. What was probably missing was a determined effort on the part of the electoral victors, perhaps Sistani himself, to lead the effort at national reconciliation and to lend their own legitimacy to the process of inclusion. In a strange way, what the Americans wanted could have best succeeded in the form of a national, nonpartisan, inclusive antioccupation effort. This is certainly so for the Sunni side. It is unclear how much credit Sunni representatives would have with their community if their main sponsors in an inclusion process were the Americans. For the Shi'ites, it was hard enough to accept Sunni representatives into the political process when violence against the Shi'ite community at the hands of insurgents was already taking place without (as yet) any retaliation. The fact that the Americans were imposing such participation made it even more difficult to go along with it, however rational it may have been even from the Shi'a point of view. Only a determined Shi'ite leadership that turned in a nationalist direction could have changed the picture, but unfortunately the zeitgeist tended toward religiously defined and sectarian identity politics. On that basis, no genuine overture to the Sunni would be forthcoming, unless we count Moqtadah al-Sadr's occasional flirtation with the AMS, which did not stop his militia from engaging in anti-Sunni acts of retaliation. The project of inclusion remained an American one, and although completely justified, its legitimation problems were probably insoluble. What this project demonstrated, however, is that inclusion *could* have been possible early in the game, when all the parties were on an equal footing.

Attempted Compromise in the Constitutional Commission

Aside from the goal of making a deal around everyone's notion of a second- or third-best outcome, one crucial experience of negotiated transitions is that deals that can be made and have a chance to last are based on agreements among the opposite sides' moderate forces, who can control or win the assent of their respective sides' more radical elements.[44] Thus there are, abstractly speaking, two types of agreements required: one among the sides and one within each side. In Iraq there were three sides—four if we count the Americans—and thus four or five necessary agreements. And it is not difficult to identify more moderate and more radical forces on each side, even if the picture shifts depending on the issue and if not all of what we have experienced can be easily fitted into any such neat scheme.[45] In any serious deal, there were two types of agreements to worry about: the deal across the sides and the deal within a given side. No deal would be worth much if the dealmakers on any side were denounced by (all) their radical allies as traitors. At the same time, in a polarized situation the risk of some such denunciation must be accepted, even if the consequences could be deadly. It was important, in other words, for the moderate partners to give each other enough in the negotiations so that they *and* the deal survived the bargaining process.[46]

This meant that the presence of Sunni players should have dramatically changed the bargaining process. That presence signified that on the *procedural* level, Iraq now almost had a genuine forum for negotiating a new state bargain. Though not quite. While a great number of details could be handled by the new Constitutional Commission, the really fundamental questions could not. This became a serious problem as the deadline for a possible six-month extension (as permitted by TAL art. 61f) approached. Strong pressure was put on the members to come to an overall agreement within that deadline,[47] but they could not, since those belonging to hierarchical leadership parties such as the Kurdish delegates did not have the authority to concede anything really important. First, there were some unfortunate attempts to divide the package into two and leave the most important and divisive questions until later, to be decided by majority votes. But this actually would have been equivalent to either (1) not getting the job done and replacing the TAL with an inferior product or (2) to delivering the crucial questions to a future parliamentary procedure with fewer restrictions than the current constitution-making one. It is hard to see, for example, why even the Kurds would accept majoritarian insecurity over the security provided by the TAL. Certainly, the Sunni representatives could not accept any such "compromise."

Almost all round-table settings presuppose that, aside from the more formalized meetings, there is a possibility for a meeting of the political principals of the really important groups, who would be capable, if anyone is, of making fundamental decisions on the spot, in one or several sessions. With the deadlock of the Constitutional Commission on the really fundamental issues, such as the structure of the state and the place of Islam in it, just such a meeting of principals was called for the weekend of August 6, 2005. This move was important for two reasons. First, the negotiation of the final constitution would take place in three important venues, at least in principle: the inclusive, formal Constitutional Commission; the informal meeting of principals, which was called the "Leadership Council" or the "Kitchen," presumably equally inclusive and consensual in terms of participation and decision making as the Constitutional Commission;[48] and finally, the (constitutional) National Assembly itself. This was the right structure, but there was an important proviso and limitation. Because of the artificially imposed time limit and the refusal to extend it, there would not be enough time (less than a month) for the first venue, in effect the "round table," where expertise and international advice could play its greatest role, to adequately look for and arrive at compromise solutions.[49] Given the same time limits, it was even more difficult to see what substantive role the third venue, the National Assembly, could play in fashioning the constitutional product. The danger of its becoming a mere rubber stamp was extremely real—not a good precedent for future representative government! Moreover, the National Assembly and its imagined discussions and hearings would be the obvious forum for, on the one side, making the process public and visible to the population and, on the other, permeable to a variety of democratic inputs. Such a public process was foreseen by advocates of some of the political forces, enshrined in the TAL (art. 60),[50] and promoted by UN representatives, but the time constraints now rendered almost impossible the chances of a public, participatory process focusing on the National Assembly.[51]

Second, the kind of constitution-making venues Iraq now had meant that for a fleeting moment the country had the inclusive negotiating format it should have had two and a half or one and a half years before, when the United States and the United Nations respectively could have pushed through a round-table negotiation, involving all the major political forces of Iraqi society, to negotiate an interim constitution, including a state deal, that was instead bargained by the Americans with the Kurds exclusively. Thus it appeared that all the elements characteristic of recent two-stage constitution making were now in place, though certainly not in their proper sequence. The cart was before the horse. This meant, first of all, that Iraqis were now supposed to negotiate, very late in the game and under extreme time pressure, a state structure and, at the same time, the governmental institutions appropriate for that structure—as well as a symbolic national identity—in a final, no longer merely interim package. And second, the change in sequence meant that at best this deal would be a deal among elites, and it would come very late in the overall process, with little opportunity for genuine parliamentary or public discussion. Once a draft emerged, there would be few opportunities and forums left in which to correct it, and it would be hard to treat a "final" constitution as another "interim" one, though not impossible, as the actual history would show. For example, the rejection of the draft in a constitutional referendum could supply yet another opportunity for correction. But such a rejection, with popular choice and input reduced to a simple yes or no, would not be based on experience with malfunctioning, and the corrective would be more a function of a new electoral arithmetic (about which more below) than of constitutional learning. If it happened, the consequences of rejection in a referendum were politically unpredictable and potentially explosive. Finally, sequencing also mattered, because now there was a freely elected parliamentary body in place. The temporal conjunction of a round-table, elite leadership format with a constitutional assembly allowed the parliamentary majority the freedom to manipulate, if it wished, these venues according its perceived interests. The majority was not compelled to make a deal because it reserved the right and had the contemporary opportunity to pass its own option. As opposed to the initially dominant forces of round tables elsewhere, which usually occur much earlier in the constitution-making process, the leaders of the Iraqi governmental parties had electoral legitimacy.

Nevertheless, though out of sequence, an inclusive round-table format was established, and with it a logic toward a fair political compromise first asserted itself. What such a fair deal would have been like is not difficult to reconstruct. As a *second, substantive* implication of serious Sunni participation in the negotiations, the outcome, this time, in order to really work, had to favor *their* bargaining position to whatever extent still possible. The point of inclusive negotiations within a proper timeframe was emphatically *not* to bring the Sunnis to understand better that they simply had to accept a state bargain first negotiated by the Americans and the Kurds, the structure of which was now to be extended to the Shi'ite governorates as well. No time would have been enough for that.[52] Since the previous state bargain and the subsequent political tradeoffs under Sistani's pressure favored first the Kurds and then the Shi'ites, one had to find some areas where the Sunnis could make gains, even if many of the results of the earlier arrangements were now no longer reversible. Clearly, given the TAL the Shi'ite majority of the National Assembly would not pass any arrangement that would take away the establishment of Islam as the state religion and the majoritarian, parliamentary structure of the central government. Similarly, the three Kurdish provinces would not ratify a significant diminution of the special rights of the Kurdistan Regional Government. Yet, important compensations had to be found for the Sunni delegates for them to be able to play their proper role, which consisted not only in coming to agreement with Shi'ite and Kurd moderates but also in convincing significant sectors of the radical Sunni insurrection that the deal was a good one or at least the very best one that could be achieved under the circumstances. It may be that Sunni elites still hoped for a fully centralized state, and some insurrection leaders may have even imagined that a new dictatorship could be erected on such foundations. This is the position continually ascribed to them as a group, in a rather self-serving manner, by some supporters of the Kurds. Such a state was now excluded as a possibility, both because of the special status of Kurdistan and because the Kurds would not accept the rest of Iraq being so organized and waiting to bring them again under Arab control. It is therefore much more worthwhile to pay attention to the Sunni bottom line, which was that they could not accept being an impoverished region in the center of Iraq, which was what the various breakup and confederal plans had in store for them. Thus, it was up to the other side to offer them arrangements that would involve guarantees against this worst-case outcome. The guarantees would have to come on three levels: the organization of the state, the organization of the government, and the disposition over natural resources (that is, oil). Substantively, it was important that the Sunnis receive with respect to all three areas a perceivably better deal, and certainly not a worse one, than they did in the TAL, in whose making they did not participate at all. Otherwise, they would have been co-opted into the Constitutional Commission and would be, both in their own eyes and in that of their dangerous constituency, mere window dressing.

There is no need to generate my own idea of a fair constitutional settlement, because, before the consensual process broke down, there were some clues in the press and in the documents of the expanded Constitutional Commission that its members were possibly developing at least important elements of such solution. Surprisingly, many of the crucial steps were taken even before the new Sunni delegates joined the Constitutional Committee, or rather the Constitutional Commission, on July 13.[53] This could have been because of the role of experts, international advisors, or because Sunni participation was already seriously discussed before their arrival, or because no Shi'ite group had yet made an irrevocable decision for a generalization of ethnically based federalism. Whatever the reason, in retrospect it seems clear that the solutions as they stood (and were interpreted) in early July could have, if there was sufficient time, gained Sunni acceptance if perceptibly clarified and modified according to their proposals. As to the structure of the state, it was clear that the Sunni delegates now accepted, however reluctantly, that the Kurds were not going to lose their special status, and this meant having a fully autonomous region, with a regional government, constitution, and a regional militia, all in a bilingual Iraq where they would play a strong (but not consociational or power-sharing) role in national government. But it was not likely that they were going to get to expand their region, with the possible exception of Kirkuk, and gain the exclusive right to dispose over the natural resources in their territory. Most importantly, they were not going to get to extend their quasi-confederal regional formula to the rest of Iraq under the misleading name of "federalism." It is true that the early draft of the permanent constitution available to me[54] contains regions as well as provinces and allows region formations in addition to the region of Kurdistan, which in this draft is not explicitly mentioned. But there is no sign in that document of a formulation that would restrict the federal government to a few enumerated powers and of nullification rights of the regions regarding most federal laws. On the contrary, it is the regional constitutions that must conform to the federal constitution (chap. 4, art. 18). While the mechanism of region formation seems undecided, the constitutions of the regions would be produced by the National Assembly (chap. 4, art. 7). According to press reports, the constitution was certainly going to establish a second legislative chamber based on the geographic principle of provinces, and there is some trace of this in the draft, which does not, however, provide a scheme for such a body.[55] The draft has a single-person presidency[56] rather than a three-person council and thus has no place to involve decentralized units in the management of the federal government other than in a second parliamentary chamber. Thus the political role of the Kurds in the federal government of Iraq would have corresponded to their numerical weight in two chambers and not according to consociational, power-sharing arrangements within the executive. In this sense, the journey from the TAL to the permanent constitution would have been, had things gone right, from consociationalism to constitutionalism, as it was in South Africa.

The direction of change regarding the structure of government parallels this, though for reasons of ideology rather than demography. The changes were in the direction of a more parliamentary government based on the rule of the majority, and that favors the Shi'ites and not the Sunnis. The latter, however, were ideologically committed to all measures that tend to strengthen central government. Paradoxically, in order to deny the confederalist Kurds consociational rights of participation in the executive, the Sunnis must accept the consequences of that same denial with respect to their own participation. Under the TAL (and in practice after the January 2005 elections), it took the consent of the Kurds (and potentially the Sunnis), again assuming a Kurd (and a Sunni) in the three-person presidency, to name a prime minister, making the formation of government if not its later composition dependent on their will. The first constitutional draft no longer contained any trace of this particular cumbersome power-sharing arrangement, which could have made government formation impossible at some point even with a parliamentary majority, an unacceptable state of affairs for a parliamentary government. Not only does the draft have only one president, a more ceremonial one elected by a two-thirds majority of parliament, he *must* also first offer the leader of the largest party the powerful position of prime minister. The overall relationship between government and state substitutes a federal state with a confederal enclave (Kurdistan), whose center-unit relations are mediated by a geographically based second parliamentary chamber, for the TAL's uneasy mixture of a centralized government and a confederal state mediated by badly designed consociational elements. Everything would depend on the composition of the upper chamber and its powers and its decision rules. But assuming either a purely provincial upper chamber (with three or four Kurdish provinces) or one based on a combination of regions and provinces, it would have been possible to give sufficient guarantees to the Kurds (and the Sunnis) against any tyranny of the majority at least on the level of lawmaking. There was, to say the least, a potential here for a better federalist formula concentrating more flexibly on the ongoing political decision making than ones focusing, with great rigidity, on the very beginning of the governmental process.

As argued in the previous chapter, amendment rules tend to indicate the nature of the state, and therefore in the case of the TAL indicate an ultimately confederal plus consociational structure from the point of view of the Kurds. In the early drafts, this was going to change. Now minor amendments would take two-thirds of the vote of one national assembly, and major amendments (Netherlands style) would take two-thirds of two assemblies, with an election in between. In both cases, a national referendum would have to approve an amendment by simple majority, but there is no provincial veto of any kind. While there was a need for the president to approve amendments, this again was in the place of the unanimous (that is, consociational) approval of the presidential council.[57] Nothing was stated to be unamendable this time around, including the rights of regions. In short, large minorities, regional or ethnic, unless they controlled over one-third of the parliamentary seats, would lose their control over constitutional change. This would be the amendment rule of a federal rather than a confederal state. However, from the point of view of majority and minority relations, note that one kind of equality has replaced another. Under the confederal or consociational rule, one group out of three, whether minority or majority, could veto any amendment. Now, it would take either two groups to pass or two to veto an amendment. From the point of view of the Sunni Arabs, they would need an ally either to amend or to block an amendment—but the same would be true for all other groups. But a major amendment would take the alliance of two national groups to accomplish, with the electorate getting to vote on it as well.

Finally, on an issue especially important to Sunni Arabs given the experience of the January 2005 elections, it was almost certain that the electoral rule was going to change in the direction of provincial lists. While not strictly speaking the competence of the Constitutional Committee or Commission (no subcommittee was assigned with this task), clearly it was in this forum that Sunni representatives could strongly advocate their preference for change in this crucial area. While to some extent some Shi'ite representatives held out for the old system, perhaps as a bargaining chip, no deal was possible with the Sunnis without basic reform of the rule.[58]

Such was at least one possible package that was emerging or could have emerged from the Constitutional Commission deliberations. There were alternative drafts, and there no consensus around any of them was achieved in the short time period. All the drafts, moreover, had areas left open for subsequent codification. Many critics of the process overlook that on the most important questions the decisions were political, and since the leaders of the political parties were not part of the commission, the fundamentally disputed issues ultimately had to be brought to them. Because of the pressures of time, undoubtedly, the switch of venues occurred too soon, though it had to occur at some time or another. Every negotiated constitutional process has its "Magdalenka," "bosperad," or other informal venue as the basis of the ultimate political compromise. The only problem in Iraq was that the "Kitchen" came both too late (it should have come in the first stage, for the interim constitution) and too early (the Constitutional Commission needed more time) in the process, and it dramatically excluded some of the most relevant members. If Iraq was still, however regrettably, making a peace treaty (which should have come in the first stage), amazingly enough they were now going to make that treaty without the participation of the side they were fighting!

Collapse of the Consensual Process in the Leadership Council

We will never know for certain whether the Leadership Council or Kitchen came to exclude the Sunni side only because of the extreme time pressure they were working under or because the purpose of the meeting of the principals from the outset was to seal a Shi'ite-Kurd exclusionary deal that the Constitutional Commission or Committee were afraid to complete on their own. That the latter option seems more likely is the opinion of the Crisis Group, who say that the goal was to both speed up the process and to confirm that whatever the commission structure and its procedural rules, "the real power to take durable decisions lay with the heads of these two communities."[59] Similarly, Jonathan Morrow argues that "scrapping the Committee [formally the Commission] on August 8 meant that the Sunni Arab Committee members, after no more than one month of trying to develop and assert a coherent constitutional position, were retired en masse."[60] I initially gave the Shi'ite and Kurdish leaders more of the benefit of the doubt, perhaps wrongly. What seems shameful is that all this happened in the presence of the American ambassador, Zalmay Khalilzad, who up until this point was presumably working on a three-sided fair deal some of his own principals in Washington considered essential.[61]

What seems to have happened in rough outline is more or less this: Sheik H. Hamoudi, the Chair of the Constitutional Commission (and Committee) made a determined attempt (supported by Mahmoud Othman and other senior members) to get support for an extension of the constitution-making process, and thus for the work of the commission, but he failed in the face of American opposition and the resistance of his own party (UIA) leadership.[62] The TAL's August 1 deadline for getting a long extension thus came and went; the August 15 deadline for submission remained. Now Hamoudi was forced to call (August 6)[63] for a Leadership Council to take over the negotiations, and for this M. Barzani joined the other leaders already in Baghdad. Negotiations moved to the Kitchen on August 8. Three days later, on August 11, one of the key participants, Abdul Aziz al-Hakim, the leader of SCIRI, in front of a large demonstration in Najaf announced the fundamental demand for a southern Shi'ite region of nine provinces. When the August 15 deadline for submitting a draft to the assembly was not met, Sheikh Hamoudi asked the National Assembly to grant a week's extension by constitutional amendment; this was granted. By this time, the commission was simply a drafting organ for the Kitchen, from which the Sunni representatives were more or less completely excluded. There were two illegal extensions on August 22 and on August 25; on August 25, the Sunnis were called in only to be told of the results, which they had to take or leave. They then formally suspended their participation in the commission and were left to appeal to the United States, the United Nations, and the Arab League, of course in vain. No Sunni group or even major Sunni politician previously in the IGC or the Transitional Government—not Adnan Pachachi, Vice President Yawer, and certainly not the leaders of the Iraqi Islamic Party (whom Galbraith calls proconstitutional)—supported the new draft. More surprisingly, the leaders of the majority of the National Assembly, the Shi'ite and Kurdish parties, who negotiated bilaterally and produced a draft without Sunni agreement, also did not feel confident enough to have that assembly (which they controlled) actually vote on their draft constitution, so they precipitously approved it by executive fiat. Acting entirely extralegally, they compromised both the consensual decision rule previously agreed upon with the Sunnis and the prescription of the TAL (arts. 60, 61a) on which the process up to that point depended.[64] Thus they violated the TAL through executive fiat rather than through the vote of the freely elected assembly, though of course the executive, having a majority in that assembly, could count on not being challenged by the legislative majority. Technically, they carried out a scarcely disguised coup against the TAL and the National Assembly.[65] All this was done, as we will see, in the name of a mediocre document full of holes and inferior to the TAL itself, leaving some of the most fundamental constitutional questions for later majorities or qualified majorities to decide.

No one disagrees that Sunni exclusion took place, though remarkably some in the Kurdish camp still refer to the constitution-making process as negotiating a "tripartite peace treaty." Some of the excluders argue that the fault alone lay with the excluded. "The Sunni Arabs objected to practically everything that was proposed to them, frustrating the Shi'ites and the Kurds to the point that they stopped negotiating with them."[66] According to this train of thought, the sole objective of the Sunni representatives was to run out the clock, given the misguided American insistence on rigid deadlines. If no draft could be submitted by August 15, then according to the TAL (art. 61g) new elections would have to be held, and the Sunni parties that were able to force it could redeem their earlier mistake in calling for a boycott and achieve greater representation in the National Assembly.[67] To counter this strategy, the Sunni representatives had to be excluded, and short extensions of the drafting period had to be sought after all. This argument fails if one were really serious about achieving a peace treaty, not to speak of a working constitution that presupposed a working state, which itself presupposed pacification. One does not make peace with one's friends, only with one's adversaries. It was already understood that such a process would take time. A constitutional amendment on August 15 could have been secured for the six-month period originally foreseen by the TAL, giving genuine negotiations a chance, if that was what was desired. Moreover, the only reason the Sunnis had to seek greater representation in a constituent assembly by a roundabout way, if they really did, was because they were not taken seriously in a process that was supposed to be consensual.

In any case, the whole set of self-serving explanations seems spurious in light of one fundamental fact: Hakim's bombshell announcement. Nothing in the process was more spectacular and decisive than this August 11 demand by the leader of SCIRI for a region of nine southern Shi'ite provinces, when the Kitchen, presumably still containing members from each group, had just begun to meet to iron out the remaining issues left over from the Constitutional Commission.[68] If implemented, the SCIRI proposal would lead to the creation of a powerful region containing all the ports, 70 to 80 percent of the current oil, and half the population of Iraq, and where Iran would have a decisive influence. If Iraq stayed together in such a "federation" of three very unequal regions, the southern region would dominate it both because of its size and resources and because the Shi'ites would also control, through their majority, the central government. It would be the Prussia of the new Iraq. And if the formation of the region demanded by Hakim led to Iraq's breakup, a high likelihood since the Kurds were not about to accept Shi'ite dominance on a new basis,[69] Iran, which always argued for Iraq's unity, could easily deflect responsibility to the Americans, who indeed had destroyed the Iraqi state, among other things, by encouraging Kurdish separatism in the first place. From the Sunni point of view, a three-region "federalism," or "confederacy" if the Kurdistan model was adopted, would mean an impoverished, resource-poor Sunni region without any influence in the government of Iraq itself. Self-government and autonomy would appear rather insignificant tradeoffs given the probable losses of revenues from the two oil-rich regions.

Little remembered now are two facts connected to this announcement, facts that demonstrate that Hakim's demand was by no means consensual within the Shi'ite community itself. One was the immediate opposition to the idea by Prime Minister Jaffari. The other much more important fact was a series of "round-robin" meetings just before Hakim's speech between the Grand Ayatollah Sistani, Moqtadah al-Sadr, and Hakim. Given Sadr's attitude before and after, and Sistani's before and Jaffari's after, it is not impossible to deduce that the two were trying to convince the leader of SCIRI not to throw his idea of a nine-province megaregion into the constitutional negotiations or at least to stay with the less destructive three-province version of the TAL. Whatever the case, and some say that Sistani by not speaking revealed his tacit acceptance,[70] Hakim went ahead, with significant popular support. The consequences for the Sunni negotiators had to be devastating. It is generally conceded now that they had come to accept, however reluctantly, the idea of a Kurdish federacy, as it was then constituted, with the possible addition of Kirkuk as the next-to-last straw, perhaps. A Shi'ite region similarly constituted, a superregion in size and power, was beyond the limits of the possible and even imaginable for them. The Hakim demand, advanced in the most radical manner possible, brought home reality in the hardest possible way.

It may be the case, though I doubt it, that Hakim was not making a new demand constitutionally speaking, because the draft as it stood at that particular moment (it is not available to me) already contained, on Kurdish insistence, the possibility of multiprovince regions.[71] That fact, if it were true, would change little. It is generally agreed that the demand "shook up the negotiations."[72] Second, even if the abstract option had been in a draft, now the possible meaning and effects of that text were made crystal clear. Most importantly, the text was still the object of negotiation. So far among the Shi'a, political centralism was the prevailing emphasis; after all, they were expected to dominate the central government, which in a democratic

Iraq could not form without them. Even in the Kitchen, Prime Minister Jaffari should have counterbalanced Hakim, and the Kurds were expected to be neutral if the Shi'ites themselves were divided on the issue of how the rest of Iraq was to be organized. So in principle even (asymmetrical) territorial federalism and a fairly strong central state were not out of reach for Sunni negotiators, if the new concessions to the Kurds were limited to Kirkuk. With Hakim having gone to the street and having for the moment neutralized Sadr and Sistani, the worst possible option was suddenly very much more likely. If a strategy of seeking new elections emerged, this could have happened because of the new and radical Shi'ite demand. In any case, if in light of this new situation a Shi'ite-Kurdish constitutional bargain was to be consolidated, this required the exclusion of the Sunni from real negotiations. To the extent that their resistance delayed the process, short extensions had to be admitted after all. If these could be used to detach one Sunni actor from the inevitable front of rejection, so much the better. But even such a result was not mandatory from the point of view of the Shi'ite and Kurdish leaders dominating the process. Hence the paucity of concessions they offered to the Sunnis, until they began to worry about the referendum.

The efforts to detach at least one Sunni party would have occurred at the insistence of U.S. Ambassador Khalilzad. Sunni inclusion was his mission, responsibility, and probably personal project as well. Once again, as with the Kurds previously, we have to ask how the representatives of the earth's one and only superpower could have been so weak. In defense of Khalilzad, one must say that he was presented with contradictory tasks and had to play contradictory roles. He was to engineer Sunni inclusion and had to insist on the rigid deadlines of the TAL, which were now American benchmarks for reasons having nothing to do with Iraq. He had to be present to accomplish anything, but his presence was a huge embarrassment to the Iraqis, who this time wanted to avoid even the appearance of constitutional imposition. What his ubiquitous presence achieved in the end was the worst of both worlds from the point of view of the United States: the appearance of imposition without the reality. The only threat he really had was U.S. withdrawal, but the U.S. government apparently wanted to stay in Iraq. He had no legal authority to order anyone to do anything. Ultimately he could only persuade, but the United States was deemed too self-interested for the words of its ambassador to be taken at face value. Moreover, his success would depend on Iraqis meeting expected "benchmarks" in a timely manner, and this absurd idea made Khalilzad prisoner of the only forces that could produce that result, even if only on an entirely formal level: the Shi'ite and Kurdish parties that dominated all of the venues of constitution making. Only where they disagreed, as on religious issues, did Khalilzad have a chance, and apparently he blew even that chance at constructive intervention. When he chose to go up against the coalition openly, as in the case of amending the TAL on August 15, he suffered an embarrassing defeat,[73] all the more unnecessary because the extra week thus granted to the drafters was in line with his attempt to get at least one Sunni party to agree to a revised constitutional draft.

Let me emphasize that Hakim's demand and the ability of the Kurdish and Shi'ite negotiators to wreck consensual negotiations was a function of the continued occupation, which unlike the constitution-making process was not tied to any schedules or deadlines, arbitrary or otherwise. Evidently, embittering the Sunnis led to the continuation of the insurrection and the possibility of open civil war. As long as the Americans remain to deal with the military consequences, the internal reasons for the Shi'ites seeking a *modus vivendi* are greatly vitiated. Had the Americans made any threats concerning their stay in Iraq or established any timetables for leaving, the results might have been different. Of course, wishful thinking may play a role here as well, because the Shi'ites cannot really predict what the Americans will do in the face of an insurrection exacerbated by the constitutional disaster they are now causing. At the same time, the Sunnis, who may also be guilty of wishful thinking, may not think that the Americans can stay forever in the face of continued losses, and therefore they may figure they have no reason to accept second-class status within the current quadrangular configuration of forces—a configuration predicated on a U.S. presence. The situation leads to imposition on the one side and bargaining by means of the insurrection on the other side, which weakens moderate and constructive forces on all sides.

Focusing on Khalilzad and the Americans may make it appear that only they constituted an external factor that mattered. Such could not have been the case. Few have noticed how strongly Iran supported the new constitutional draft.[74] In fact, Iran's attitude may have counted for more in the outcome than did the vector sum of the Shi'ite attitudes. To the extent that the United States so publicly identified itself with a consensual solution for the constitution-making process, it was much too easy to bring that process down through the acts of a proxy introducing a new demand that made consensus impossible. The temptation to greatly embarrass the Americans was there, and it is hard to believe that Teheran did not take advantage of the opportunity, especially because a policy was available that presented them with a very favorable opportunity of extending their influence in Iraq without having to take any responsibility for the chaotic consequences of pursuing that goal. Undoubtedly, from Iran's point of view, Hakim's new demand would not only wreak havoc with American plans for a consensual solution of constitution making but had its own independent rationale of helping to sustain a political crisis where the Sunni insurrection would tie down the Americans for years and force them to accept the consolidation of Shi'ite power.[75]

In any case, once Hakim's demand for the creation of a Shi'ite superregion was introduced, all attempts to save the process were doomed, including President Bush's pointless and embarrassing phone call to the SCIRI leader on August 25. First, resisting Kurdish demands to weaken the central state and extend their regional structure to the whole of Iraq had to depend on Shi'ite resistance and their defense of the unity of Iraq, as the main beneficiaries of that unity. When Shi'ite leaders themselves championed regionalism in a more radical version, the Sunni were left alone.[76] It is not the case that either Kurdish or Shi'ite demands were in themselves irresistible. Galbraith argues that M. Barzani (whose key advisor he was) dominated the process of making the final constitution. And it is true: the Kurds kept everything the TAL gave them, made new gains with respect to a further weakening of the jurisdiction of the federal government and the ultimate disposition of Kirkuk as well, and even managed to gain a kind of mediating position with respect to some issues such as the question of Islam and the state. Most of this was prefigured by the TAL, as the default position guarded by its amendment and ratification rules. The Kurds could not lose anything in the process, and if one wanted their consent on anything new, concessions had to be offered to them. Nevertheless, a more united Arab position against them could have held them to a position more or less in the TAL, one that the Sunnis could now live with. If the Kurds played their cards right, it was because they helped to delegitimate the role of the Sunni delegates and kept their coalition with the Shi'ites intact. This way, a new constitutional bargain between Kurds and Shi'ites could be cemented entirely at the expense of the Sunnis.[77] This alliance in turn made Hakim's radical proposal also impossible to resist. The proposal perhaps surprised the Kurds, though they were not in principle opposed to it.[78] With respect to the issue of "federalism" there now was a Shi'ite-Kurdish bargain, which, similar to the American-Kurdish bargain earlier, was difficult to change, but this time the bargain was one no Sunni party could possibly accept.

That the Shi'ite demands were not entirely irresistible is shown by the fate of another contentious issue. The dominant clerics were also demanding a much stronger constitutional statement on behalf of the role of Islam in civil and family law than the combination of provisions in the TAL provided for. The effort of getting them to compromise was somewhat more successful in this area, where the Americans, Kurds, and secular deputies could concentrate their pressure, however inconsistently. A similar coalition was not available in the area of "federalism." Here the timing of Hakim's bombshell, so late in the game and supported by a Kurdish-Shi'ite deal, meant that there was no time to work on a complex compromise formula that could allow all sides to provide input and save face. Here, the American acceleration of the process reaped its bitter fruit. They insisted on the artificial deadlines, but others learned to use them better than they.

The New, Supposedly Permanent Constitution

In the end of the official or legal process, between August 15 and August 22, only a small unilateral concession was granted to the Sunni in the domain of "federalism," and it was not enough to gain the support of even the Iraqi Islamic Party. The draft (art. 114) as it stood on August 15 allowed the creation of new regions of any size both from provinces and old regions simply through the request of one-third of the provincial legislature or one-tenth of the voters and the approval of the majority in a provincial referendum. In case of failure, two-thirds of the provincial legislature or one-fourth of the voters would have to request a repeat of the referendum—how soon it was not said. On August 22, the implicit reference to size was gone, but the constitutional right of any province to form regions of undetermined size remained. While the request for forming a region was the same as before, what approval entailed was no longer clearly specified. A new article 115 (in the current version, art. 117)[79] stated that the "Council of Representatives shall pass a law that fixes the executive procedures relating to establishing regions by simple majority in a period that does not exceed six months from the date of the first session." Since this law would be passed by simple majority, the mechanism of region formation it clearly had in mind would most likely also operate by simple majority or by majorities in referenda or assemblies. It would be possible, of course, that the majorities involved would indeed operate on any or even a combination of three levels: the provincial electorate, the provincial council, and the National Assembly. At the same time, since forming a region was still defined as a right of provinces (art. 116; current version: art. 118), a future Supreme Court may declare any law interfering with that right unconstitutional. In any case, the crucial point was that everything that might have been objectionable in the August 15 version to the Sunni leaders could be reestablished by simple majority. There might be one rub: as a law, the new legislation dealing with establishing regions might be open to vetoes—in the transitional period the Kurds were able to insist on the veto of any of the three members of the presidential council (art. 135; current text: art. 137, 5th clause). But the same article explicitly exempts laws concerning the establishment of regions from the possibility of a veto.

Thus, the unilateral concessions that went into the August 22 draft were entirely unacceptable to the Sunnis, who assumed that very likely the Kurds and the religious Shi'a together and possibly the latter alone would have at least a majority in the next National Assembly, and even if they, the militant Sunnis, controlled one member of the presidential council, the relevant veto would not apply to the law on region formation (which is how it turned out with respect to Vice President al-Hashimi in 2006). The bottom line of the Sunni delegates was that it would have to be two-thirds, that is, the constitution-amending majority, that would have to work out the rules governing federalism. Since it was possible that a Shi'ite-Kurdish coalition would get two-thirds of the seats in the next parliament, even this solution carried an element of risk, admittedly for both sides, in the debate. But this solution was decisively rejected.

At issue was both the question of region formation and the kind of powers regions would have. Any cursory look at the TAL and the draft of the permanent constitution approved on August 28 (or in the current version) will reveal that it is simply not true that "the list of exclusive federal powers is much shorter" in the latter.[80] In fact, the list was now almost the same length, if differently organized and numbered, with the addition of control over external water supplies entering the country and the right to take a census of the population and the subtraction of control over natural resources and telecommunications (TAL art. 25 versus Constitution art. 109;

current version: art. 113). It is also disputed whether or not the power of taxation is accorded to the federal government; according to some experts, control over fiscal policy in the Arabic formulation contains that power.[81] It is outside this particular regulation that new gains for the Kurds must be sought. First, the right of organizing self-defense and internal security is now explicitly accorded to the region (art. 118, 5th clause; current version: art. 120, 5th clause). This undermines the monopoly in defense and security provided to the federal government by articles 108 and 109. Similarly, the right to have offices for regions in embassies abroad (118, 4th clause) undermines the monopoly in foreign affairs. The right of nullifying federal laws except in the case of exclusive powers remains from the TAL (art. 118, 2nd clause), but now a new provision is added that makes regional law trump federal law in the case of a conflict (art. 112) of whether it is a question of either unenumerated powers of the federal government or concurrent powers. Thus while the Federal Supreme Court can still adjudicate conflicts between the center and the regions (art. 91, 5th clause), it can lawfully side with the center only in the case of its few exclusive, enumerated powers. Nathan Brown is right that with these provisions Iraq can "lurch in a confederal direction, especially if a Federal Supreme Court emerges as a powerful body even mildly friendly to the regions."[82] What I do not see is how such a lurch could be stopped by a court otherwise disposed, because it is not given what the Germans call *Kompetenz-Kompetenz*, the competence to decide questions of competence regarding these questions, in the case of conflicts.

The big issue, of course, was that the management of natural resources—the oil—no longer appears under the exclusive powers of the federal government as in the TAL (art. 25e) but separately, in a very confusing and unclear formulation (arts. 109–110; current version: arts. 110–111). Evidently there was no real compromise here either. The Kurds and Shi'a were to gain important rights when compared to the TAL. The issue was, of course, that even regional federalism could have been made more acceptable if the two oil-rich regions had made clear and precise provisions to fully share their wealth with the third. Given the lack of trust in the country, the desideratum could be guaranteed only by central government control, which the TAL still provided among the exclusive powers of the federal government (art. 25e). It is true that the new constitution (art. 109; current version: art. 110) stated that "oil and gas are the property of all the Iraqi people," but it adds "in all the regions and the provinces." The actual dispensation comes in the next article. The federal government was to administer "current fields," but in cooperation with the regions, on condition that the distribution be fair, and with a quota defined to make up for past wrongs (that is, for the benefit of Shi'ite and Kurdish provinces). Thus even current fields would not be fully under central control, and even that only under legally contestable conditions. There were, however, future fields to be explored, in terms of the brand-new concept of "current," and about these potentially much more important resources we get no clear regulation. In line with the premise that powers not defined as exclusive or shared powers of the federal government belong to the regions or to provinces (art. 112; current version: art. 113), one possible conclusion to draw is that future fields would be under regional administration. Galbraith certainly draws this conclusion but hopes to avoid it by pretending that all regions are likely to have future oil resources.[83] Officials of oil companies, who may know better, expect nothing but contested jurisdictions, chaos, and disorganization deeply undermining the financial capacities of the Iraqi state for a long time to come.[84]

As opposed to all matters having to do with the issue of federalism, where the Shi'ite and Kurdish forces apparently made a deal to support each other no matter what, compromise was possible where the two forces did not fully agree and where opposition to the majority view was not represented by the Sunnis. Thus the solution of the issue of the role of the Shari'a in the constitutional setup had *apparently* a far different structure, demonstrating what type of compromise was needed, formally speaking, in order to include the Sunnis on the question of federalism. What happened here, in contrast to the debate on federalism, was that the Kurds were in principle opposed to the positions of the Shi'ite clerics on the role of Islam in the state and on the question of the personal status law. Had Ambassador Khalilzad sided with the Kurds, most likely the positions of the TAL could have been reaffirmed. This he did not do, and in particular he supported the key Shi'ite position that no role for Islam in the state could be guaranteed unless there were Shari'a experts as well as secular judges on the Supreme Federal Court (art. 89–91; new version: 91–93), the body that was now to unite the earlier planned two bodies of a Supreme Court and a Constitutional Court (defined as vaguely as it was in the TAL, which left more room, however, for another highest court of appeals, the Federal Court of Cassations).[85] Khalilzad may have done this to meet deadlines in the face of Shi'ite recalcitrance or because he was hoping for tradeoffs to the benefit of the Sunnis. He got only the first. But when the Kurds went public with secular grievances, Khalilzad too had to moderate his support for the Shi'ite position. In the end, the Kurds were satisfied to go along with Khalilzad because they too wanted to rush, now that they had gotten their way on federalism and Kirkuk,[86] and as a prize they received the all-important concession of stripping the Federal Supreme Court of the power to review the constitutionality of regional laws.[87] Whether or not their negative view on constitutional adjudication was reinforced by *Bush v. Gore*, as Galbraith rather absurdly suggests, I leave for others to determine.[88] I would rather think that anyone building a confederal enclave would resist extending the jurisdiction of a federal court for structural reasons well explored already by John C. Calhoun, that old enemy of federal judicial review.

The outcome was relatively complex, reflecting a compromise weighted in the direction of the majority's position, but still a compromise. The constitutional draft once again made Islam as well as democracy and the rights of the constitution standards that all legislation would have to adhere to (arts. 2a, 2b, 2c). As before, these standards were likely to be contradictory, and conflicts would have to be resolved by the constitutional court, the Federal Supreme Court. Here lay the innovation sought by the Shi'a clerics, who understood that the declarations of the TAL remained merely symbolic without proper enforcement. That court, most dangerously from the secular point of view, was to contain both judges and experts in Shari'a jurisprudence (art. 90; current version: art. 91). The number of judges and the form of appointment, however, would be determined by the next National Assembly (similarly to the executive rules for region formation), but by a two-thirds majority! In this area, therefore, the way was open to a future consensual solution of the deferred issue (or to a hopeless stalemate), showing quite clearly that in the area of "federalism" (where a simple majority would decide), deferral was intended only as a smokescreen for the same nonconsensual solution on which agreement today is not possible.

The place of Islam in the state is not a function of the compromise concerning the court alone. Secular Iraqis, especially women, have been especially concerned about the repeated attempts of Shi'ite clerics to change the personal status law of 1959, according to which marriage, divorce, and inheritance law are legislated by the state and are uniformly administered by secular courts. The constitutional draft (art. 39; current version: art. 41) establishes the "freedom" of Iraqis to choose their status "according to their own religion, sect, belief and choice" and leaves the organization of these choices to an ordinary parliamentary law. Thus the majority will be free, as

Nathan Brown shows, to give as much or as little weight to a secular alternative and a uniform administration as it chooses, or to establish religious predominance over all cases where even one litigant or interested party may so desire.[89] The mechanism here, as in the case of federalism, defers the decision in favor of later majoritarian imposition rather than operating in a constitutional, consensual process.

Let us put the two major proposals concerning the relationship of Islam and law together. The Supreme Federal Court can only be formed by a wide compromise. The personal status law, which could be judged unconstitutional by such a court, can be established by simple majority. But a court may not be able to form at all unless the Shi'ites get the number and type of Shari'a experts they want, and that their mode of appointment is acceptable to them. In either case (with a friendly court or with no court at all), a status law could be enacted by a simple majority that does not have to worry about constitutional review. No wonder that advocates of women's rights and secularism are very upset about the end result of the process and about the betrayal of their cause by the American ambassador, who wound up accepting and even praising the relevant parts of the draft. They should have nevertheless noticed that in the first parliamentary session, each of the three members of the Presidency Council would have veto rights over parliamentary legislation (art. 135, 5th clause, A; current version: art. 137, 5th clause, A). Thus the election of one secular member could interfere with, but only for a single parliamentary period, the establishment of a status law that definitively decides the issue in favor of religious jurisdictions in this area.

There are finally issues having to do with the structure of government, issues we have heard little about in the press but that are of great importance. Here the Shi'ite majority and the Kurdish minority once again did not have the same interests, and probably the divergence again facilitated compromise solutions. The TAL, as I have argued, sought to reconcile an ultimately confederal bargain about the state with a centralistic version of parliamentarianism, by using consociational structures rooted mainly in the three-person presidency rather than by a bicameralism characteristic of a federal state. From the Shi'ite point of view, such a double defense of Kurdish positions had to seem illogical: if one has established a quasi-independent confederacy, why should the same force maintain veto rights over the government of the rest of the country? To the Kurds, the desire for this double defense was based not on logic but experience. It was clear that if they could not control the federal state, they did not mind incapacitating it, a position obviously inimical to the majority. A move in a more federal direction in the earliest constitutional drafts (acceptable to only literal nationalists among the Kurds) would have been based on the combination of a new, second, federal parliamentary chamber and the replacement of the consociational presidency council by a single, more ceremonial president who *had to* offer the prime ministership to the largest parliamentary bloc. The new draft, probably because of the inability of its framers to agree on a federal formula, solves these questions by somehow combining all these competing alternatives into a single package. There would be a second parliamentary chamber, a Council of the Union, including representatives of regions *and* provinces not in regions. But the definition of its rules of formation and powers (!) are left to the lower chamber, the Council of Deputies (Representatives) voting by two-thirds majority—and not the current Council of Deputies, but the one elected in the next elections (arts. 63 and 134; current version: arts. 64 and 136). An important consequence of this very unusual delay was the restoration for a single parliamentary period of the three-person, consociational Presidential Council of the TAL, elected on a single slate by a two-thirds majority, this time with a veto for each of the members, obviously as a replacement for the role of a federal chamber in national legislation (art. 135; current version: art. 137). These vetoes, as I have already said, do not exist in the case of region formation but apply to the new law governing personal status, the two-thirds law governing the composition of the Supreme Court, and indeed to constitutional amendments requiring presidential assent.

The amending structure of the new constitution, though rigid enough, is in fact more flexible than that of the TAL. Initiatives for amendments can come from the president and cabinet together or from one-fifth of the lower chamber, the Council of Representatives, which is the only parliamentary chamber given a right of participation in constitutional revision. Where in the case of the TAL no amendment could be made at all that would abridge rights, here (art. 123, current version: art. 125, 2nd clause) the basic principles of chapter 1 and the rights and freedoms of chapter 2 are unamendable only for the first two parliamentary cycles.[90] Subsequently, they can be amended according to the general rule that applies to most of the constitution: namely, two-thirds of the members of parliament, agreement of the president, plus majority support in a referendum. In the first parliamentary period, this means that the presidential council, one way or the other (by either the amendment rule or the ordinary rule of legislation as now revised), has the option of a consociational veto for each of its members. Finally, and given what is at issue today most importantly, no amendment is allowed that would lessen the powers of regions without the consent of their legislature and population in a referendum, unless one of the very few exclusive powers of the federal government is at issue (4th clause). This means that since the constitution already recognizes the powers of the Kurdistan Region (art. 114; current version: art. 116), no constitutional amendment can touch them.[91] But interestingly enough, powers given by simple majority to new regions in the first session also would become by this clause amendment proof. If Iraq begins to break up according to the dispensation of the current draft, for example, a duly elected parliament would be powerless to legislate any countermeasures, regardless of the majority supporting them. If the state structure of the new constitution did not work, only a revolutionary overthrow could remedy the situation.

The Illegal Road to Another Interim Constitution?

After the refusal to *legally* extend the process of constitution making as permitted by the TAL, the process was nevertheless extended in a manner that was most astonishing and in significant part illegal. In my view, the August 15 amendment that provided for one week's extension was legal, although even this view has been contested. But the formal date of August 22, by which the draft should have been concluded and approved, came and went. Two illegal extensions were decided upon on August 22 and August 25. The constitutional text, though never voted on, was pronounced final on August 28, only it was not. A new text was brought to the National Assembly on September 13.[92] These illegal extensions and the absurd claim supposedly based on the TAL (art. 60) that the National Assembly "writes" but does not "vote" on the constitution ("The National Assembly shall write a draft of the permanent constitution of Iraq") would raise very serious questions in almost any situation concerning the meaning and legitimacy of the constitution being written. But Iraq is not at all an ordinary context for constitution making, and here illegality was an irrelevant detail almost no one cared about (at the time, on the Web, Nathan Brown, Juan Cole, and I were the exceptions).[93] Admittedly, it was much more important to register the fact that the thing could not be completed because, whatever the deadlines,

Sunni inclusion or even the inclusion of one Sunni party could simply not be given up, both in light of the ongoing pressure of the American Embassy and for rational considerations, which very likely helped to reopen the question. Despite the original calculation of the two-thirds figure for each of the three provinces needed to block ratification, it occurred to the makers of the constitution that perhaps if the Sunni decided to participate and if their rejection were truly unanimous, the Shi'ite-Kurdish constitution might actually fail in three provinces.

Had such fears been there all along and been really serious, I believe that the whole negotiation process would have turned out quite differently. After all, it was the Kurdistan veto that made the Shi'ites make their deal with the Kurds within the TAL, a document they considered humiliating because of that veto, among other things. Would the Kurds have kept all they had in the TAL and have gained some new concessions without the veto? Their own advocates hardly think so. There was no comparable fear of a Sunni veto; if there had been, the Kurds would not have dared challenge the Sunnis as openly as they did. It was only in the end, when their own actions completely antagonized the Sunni community, bringing together radical and more moderate elements who were equally badly treated, that the Shi'ite and Kurdish parties lost a little of their confidence that the ratification rule was only a Kurdish veto after all. I doubt that they really thought a Sunni veto would work, but they wanted to make absolutely sure that it would not. Or, very possibly, what they feared was that they might have to engage in the fixing of the results of the referendum in the eyes of the international press. Thus their attitude changed with respect to the American effort to engineer more Sunni inclusion.

Negotiations concerning changes continued, and several changes were indeed made before the referendum of October 15, one on central control of water resources and another on having two deputy prime ministers. The most dramatic change came on October 12, three days before the referendum. Finally, a concession that appeared to be a genuine compromise was offered to the Sunni parties and was accepted by one of them, the Iraqi Islamic Party. In a highly revealing manner, the compromise came right after the failure of an attempt to guarantee the referendum results through open manipulation of the TAL text. We were told that originally it was the Independent Electoral Commission of Iraq that decided, absurdly and certainly against the most obvious intentions of the drafters and the plain meaning of the text itself, that the two-thirds of the voters of three provinces that would have to vote against the new constitution in order to reject it would have to be two-thirds of the *eligible* rather than the *actual* voters. In this case, two-thirds could be mustered perhaps in one province.[94] But when UN officials had some serious qualms about allowing this ruling to stand,[95] the National Assembly proceeded to vote by simple majority on October 2 that it must indeed be two-thirds of eligible voters in each of three provinces voting against the constitution if the text is to be rejected.[96] If the Shi'ites and Kurds wanted to do this, they should have legally attempted to amend the TAL by three-fourths of the votes, preferably when still under the veil of ignorance, and when the Kurds had reasons to preserve the veto they had long fought for. What the governing parties attempted to do instead, under the guise of mere interpretation of the TAL, was to interpret "voters" in the same sentence once as actual (when it had to do with approval by majority) and the second time as eligible (when it had to do with rejection by two-thirds of each of three provinces). Most embarrassingly, under open UN and this time fortunately tacit U.S. pressure, the very same National Assembly was forced, two days later, to withdraw the measure and return to *actual* rather than *eligible* voters, in the case of *both* majority approval and three-province rejection of the draft.[97]

The solution may have raised the possibility of rejection anew. The compromise package offered to the Iraqi Islamic Party could have made a crucial difference in at least one Sunni-majority province, Nineveh, where the vote would be closer; we will never know for sure. In the actual event, 97 percent of the voters of Anbar, 82 percent of Salahddeen, but only 55 percent of Nineveh voted against the draft. Whatever the reasons, the constitutional referendum failed by two-thirds in only two Sunni provinces, and thus a document rejected by the immense majority of the Sunni community was ratified. But was the compromise offer a really serious one?

In its most positive interpretation, the October 12 deal once again reduced the constitution just passed to a provisional one and made the newly elected National Assembly yet another constitutional assembly given the time extension foolishly denied to its predecessor. What was done, technically speaking, seems, to be sure, more modest. The text of the draft that was subsequently voted on in the referendum was amended by a new article, 141 (which the voters never saw),[98] stating (my italics):

> *First:* The parliament shall form, *at the start of its work*, a committee from its members, representative of the main components of the Iraqi society.

The task of the committee is to present a report to the parliament, *in not more than four months*, including a recommendation of the necessary amendments that could be made to the constitution. The committee is dissolved after a decision about its suggestions is taken.

Second: The amendments suggested by the committee shall be presented, in one bulk, to the parliament to be voted on, and it is considered to be passed by the approval of the absolute majority of the members of the parliament.

Third: The articles amended by the parliament according to what came in provision (second) of this Article shall be put to the people for a referendum, not more than two months after the passing of the amendments in the parliament.

Fourth: The referendum on the amended articles is successful, by the approval of the majority of voters, and if not refused by two thirds of the voters in three governorates or more.

Fifth: *The effect of Article (125) (related to amending the constitution) of this constitution is stopped*, and its effect starts again after the amendments in this article are decided on.[99]

Since the three-tiered and in all respects very difficult amendment rule of the new constitution was thereby suspended, everything could be changed for the four-month period, and the road was in principle indeed open to a historic compromise among the main groupings. The rights of regions could be altered, even without their consent. The most basic rights could be altered without waiting for a third parliamentary session. The new rule was more difficult only than the third, easiest amendment route of the constitution that dealt, by default, with mostly matters of the federal government and its branches. However, all this was true only in principle. Whether there was *substantive* hope for the Sunnis to alter a solid Shi'ite-Kurdish agreement on the major contentious issues was another matter. At the same time, the road was to be made *formally* very difficult by the restoration of the old three-province veto by two-thirds of the *actual* voters of each (see the fourth clause, above). As in the case of the TAL, that veto protected most of all those who would benefit from the current constitutional draft, since a rejection of a package of amendments would not return Iraq to a condition without a constitution, or even to the TAL itself, but to the new arrangements approved on October 15. The constitution itself was the new default position! Thus the same text could be viewed as provisional and permanent at the same time, depending on how one judged the likelihood of it being actually transformed. The supposed compromise maintained the dramatic inequality of the Sunni Arabs with respect to the other two main groups, because if in principle the Sunnis too could use the three-province veto (forgetting the experience of Nineveh), it would be useless to them given a situation where the fallback position was a constitution they entirely rejected. They were, in effect, delivered to the good will of their partners (assuming it existed), with the remote possibility that with allies they could hold government formation itself hostage to a prior constitutional deal.

Why the Iraqi Islamic Party accepted such a deal is difficult to comprehend. A few days before the referendum, they could play the card of delivering some Sunni votes, and in return this was the best deal they could get. Perhaps it was not much of a card and therefore not much of a deal. If they were bluffing and could not deliver any voters, which is possible in light of the results, the deal was then probably a concession worth having. But in return they lent the whole process more legitimacy and allowed the branding of their much more realistic partners as hardline rejectionists, which some of them undoubtedly were. If, however, they had the votes to defeat the referendum, the deal was a very poor one. New elections and new constitutional negotiations would have been preferable for the whole Sunni community and would have earned more credit with the insurrectionists, credit that could later have been cashed in on behalf of perhaps a slightly better political formula. Finally, it may very well be the case that they wanted to be in the new government at any cost and were waiting for sufficiently plausible cover, which the October 12 agreement finally gave them. Support for the referendum was then their ticket into a government of "national unity."

Whether or not there was realistic hope to renegotiate the constitution, even the slightest chance of it depended on Sunni electoral performance. As part of the overtures toward moderate Sunnis, the (Transitional) National Assembly did in fact change the electoral rule, but by adopting a compromise formula. Of the 275 seats, 230 would be elected on non-turnout-dependent provincial lists and only forty-five on a turnout-dependent national compensational list.[100] Facing in small part the same danger as before, and hoping perhaps after all to be able to renegotiate the constitution possibly on the basis of a role in a governmental coalition, Sunni parties and most armed groups of the insurrection now urged participation in the parliamentary elections of December 15. The apportionment of seats by the Independent Electoral Commission on the basis of ration cards caused some consternation; Sunnis felt that their districts received too few seats, but they nevertheless worked for a strong performance. Their initial hope was that with possible allies such as Allawi's secular list (now called the Iraqi National List), they could have one-third of the seats in the National Assembly, and with that they could hold the election of the Presidency Council hostage to a constitutional deal, and along with it government formation, because there was no way that the candidate of the largest parliamentary group could be nominated as prime minister other than by that council. This was not to be. While the combined vote of the two Sunni lists, the Iraqi Accord Front dominated by the Iraqi Islamic Party and the Iraqi National Dialogue front led by al-Mutlaq, received over 19 percent and thus more or less an accurate demographic proportion of the vote, the Allawi list lost dramatically with respect to its earlier performance. There was no blackmail potential for the opponents of the constitution unless the Sadrists, now in the UIA, were to join them, and they were certainly unwilling, at that time at least, to break with the Shi'ite alliance supported by Sistani on behalf of the friends of the insurrection. Of course, the support of Kurdish parties for a constitutional deal would have been an adequate substitute, since without them it would be difficult for the Shi'ites to form a government if Allawi and the Sunnis too were in opposition. But the Shi'ite-Kurdish alliance was strong, and most likely there already was a new Barzani-Hakim deal over Kirkuk, in line with the new constitution, and the Kurds were about to get what the Jaffari government so far had denied them in exchange for support on the other major issues, namely a referendum over the fate of the city and possibly the province—a referendum that would allow them to take control of both.[101]

Thus no pressure could be exerted on the level of government formation for a new constitutional deal. The Iraqi Accord Front was welcome to join a government of national unity and even propose one member of the Presidency Council as a reward for its earlier support, but it had few bargaining chips left outside of the public-relations aspects of having some well-known Sunni leaders aboard (Adnan al-Dulaimi was now with the Iraqi Accord Front). With respect to the continuing insurrection, it probably had fewer ties with it now than did other Sunni parties and groups. In any case, the insurrection was no bargaining chip at all as long as the Americans were willing to fight it on behalf of the new Shi'ite-Kurdish alliance. That is also probably how Iran preferred it, looming in the background, waiting for the inevitable day when it would replace the Americans as the defender of the Shi'ite cause.

The victors together were much weaker than in the previous parliament and did not quite have the two-thirds necessary to name a Presidency Council, pass the laws that required two-thirds of the National Assembly, or amend the constitution (when this would be allowed in the ordinary way during this parliamentary session). They needed one other partner at least, and there was a lot of pressure to build a national unity government including Allawi and the Iraqi Accord Front. That would happen, not under Jaffari,

TABLE 4
Summary of the December 15, 2005, Iraqi Council of Representatives election results

ALLIANCES AND PARTIES	VOTES	%	SEATS	GAIN/LOSS
United Iraqi Alliance	5,021,137	41.2	128	–12
Democratic Patriotic Alliance of Kurdistan	2,642,172	21.7	53	+22
Iraqi Accord Front	1,840,216	15.1	44	+44
Iraqi National List	977,325	8.0	25	–15
Iraqi National Dialogue Front	499,963	4.1	11	+11
Kurdistan Islamic Union	157,688	1.3	5	+5
The Upholders of the Message (Al-Risaliyun)	145,028	1.2	2	+2
Reconciliation and Liberation Bloc	129,847	1.1	3	+2
Turkmen Front	87,993	0.7	1	–2
Rafidain List	47,263	0.4	1	0
Mithal al-Alusi List	32,245	0.3	1	+1
Yazidi Movement for Reform	21,908	0.2	1	+1
Total (turnout 79.6%)	12,396,631		275	

Source: Wikipedia.

the first nominee of the UIA, but rather Nuri al-Maliki, another Da'wa leader also supported by the Sadrists.

Here I am not concerned with the disastrous record of this "Government of National Unity," inaugurated May 20, 2006, four and a half months after the general elections. The Constitutional Committee agreed upon in the compromise of October 12, "representative of the main components of the Iraqi society," should have been formed by then, but it was not. Nor was it formed by this government, which noisily announced a national reconciliation program. It was only when the Council of Representatives (for the moment the only chamber of the National Assembly) wished to take up the issue of region formation under the constitution (art. 115), which certainly should not have been done before the four-month period for extraordinary amendments was over, that Tariq al-Hashimi of the Iraqi National Accord, now a vice president of Iraq, was able to gain as one of two concessions that the Constitutional Committee would now also begin to meet. The other concession was that whatever law was passed on region formation, it would be suspended for eighteen months.[102] However, another law was passed, with Sunnis and many Sadrists boycotting, providing that once (as provided by the constitution) one-third of a provincial council or one-tenth of the citizens of a province called for the establishment of a region, this could now be done by the majority of a simple referendum of the province's inhabitants. This law in effect reestablished the constitutional regulation of August 15 that was struck out on August 22 to please the Sunnis, but this time it was reestablished by a simple majority vote that would not have to be ratified as constitutional text. Once a region was thus formed, the result would be constitutional-amendment proof, because the rights of regions would be involved. Of course, the law could still be negated somehow by the results of the deliberations of the Constitutional Committee. But how realistic—and even how legal—would that be?

As to legality, the October 12 amendment to the constitution stated: "at the start of its [the council of representatives'] work" and "no more than four months." That work could have started on March 19, 2006, when (then interim) President Talabani convened it; on April 22, when a speaker was elected; or on May 20, when the government took office. Or perhaps one should count the four months only from the time when the committee was set up, presumably in October or November. This means that the deadline for submitting a package of amendments has long past (the deadline being, under the most generous interpretation, May 2007).

Any amendments submitted now could easily be challenged as irrelevant and illegal.

Regarding political viability, even before the test of the three-province veto, amendments would have to be passed by the very same majority (138 votes exactly) that more or less passed the federalism law last October. Why would they do so? There are only two factors (or their combination) that could help achieve the historic compromise that would lead to a renewal of the constituent process and significant, consensual constitutional amendments. The first would be a possible split in the Shi'ite camp itself, as indicated by the earlier opposition of the Sadrists and the Jaffari government to the Hakim plan of nine-province regionalism, as well as recent proposals by people as different as Sadr himself (who now controls a significant bloc of deputies) and Kanan Makiya to table the "federalism" question for a lengthy period.[103] In effect, these proposals all mean a return to the TAL's formula of an asymmetric structure with a confederal status for Kurdistan, leaving the exact nature of the organization of the rest of Iraq undetermined, but with the eventual possibility of elements of provincial federalism as well as the formation of smaller, weaker regions. So far, all such proposals have been swamped by the strength of SCIRI, with the probable backing of Iran. Their slight chance of success has become therefore dependent on what the Americans choose to do.

By "what the Americans choose to do" I don't mean the strength of their visible pressure, which may actually be counterproductive. If it is true that they want a significant force to stay indefinitely in Iraq, the Americans have little leverage to impose a really fair bargain, however much they talk about benchmarks and inclusion. The Shi'ites need not fear a Sunni insurrection as long as it is more or less neutralized by a superpower, nor need the Shi'ites take the Sunni political wing seriously. The amazing thing is that at least Secretary of State Rice and Ambassador Khalilzad, if not the Pentagon as well, in the end probably came to understand that they were guarding Iran's prize and that many of the Sunnis they were shooting at were their geopolitical allies. But there is nothing they can do about this as long as they also want to stay in Iraq, because in that case the Sunnis regard them as their main enemy, while the Shi'ites, though they hate the occupiers too, are willing to treat them as allies, however unlikely such an alliance between the United States and close friends of Iran may be. Undoubtedly, leaving suddenly would indeed produce the chaos that would make the already very real failure of the U.S. government visible to all who now choose to pretend otherwise. Though they may have come to this conclusion belatedly, the Democrats in Congress are absolutely right: what the United States could and should do if it wishes to salvage something from the whole lamentable operation is to produce a timetable for withdrawal to pressure the Shi'ites to take their own promise to renegotiate the constitution seriously. In addition, the United States should use a regional agreement supported by an international, Security Council–authorized coalition to make sure that Iran does not take up the slack as they progressively withdraw. But will anyone listen to them after the fiasco that the adventure in Iraq has become?

Conclusion

Writing this on February 7, 2008, almost nine months after finishing the sixth and final chapter, very little has changed with respect to Iraq's constitutional conundrum. Finally, although many months too late and therefore technically in violation of the 2005 constitution, a Constitutional Review Committee was created. And if it ever submits amendments to the National Assembly, that too will be too late, in terms of the initial six-month deadline tied to initial government formation, which occurred in early 2006! Since no one cares about these legal niceties, it is much more important to point out that the likelihood of passing amendments acceptable to the Sunni parties in parliament is very small; the passing of such amendments by the National Assembly, which has already passed a law on regions in October 2006 incompatible with them, is even smaller; and ratification, given the possibility of a veto by three provinces, has almost no chance at all.[1] The constitution remains a source of fundamental and nearly irreconcilable division across Iraq's large ethnoreligious political groupings. None of this has stopped the White House from rating progress on the "benchmark" of constitutional amendments as "satisfactory" nor prevented President Bush from repeatedly touting the new Iraqi constitution as one of the great achievements of the war and occupation. Nor has the U.S. Senate[2] been stopped from enacting a nonbinding resolution to the effect that Iraqis should adopt exactly the system that the benchmark of a new constitutional agreement was designed to somehow alter: the decentralized, partitioned "federation" of three entities on the model of Kurdistan, allowed but not required by the 2005 constitution, as the U.S. Senate seems to think.[3]

There has now been some learning on the American side. Toward the end of my last chapter, I wrote: "The amazing thing is that at least Secretary of State Rice and Ambassador Khalilzad, if not the Pentagon as well, in the end probably came to understand that they were guarding Iran's prize and that many of the Sunnis they were shooting at were their geopolitical allies. But there is nothing they can do about this as long as they also want to stay in Iraq. . . . " I was only wrong in writing the last phrase. General Petraeus and Ambassador L. Crocker have shown that they could do something, namely accept the overtures of the tribally based Sunni fundamentalist forces, who eventually grouped under the name of the Anbar Salvation (or Awakening) Council (Sahawa al Anbar), to join the Americans to fight Al Qaeda in Mesopotamia. These forces (who have undoubtedly killed numerous Americans) are also allied against the friends of Iran, and are thus enemies of the government that supposedly rules in Baghdad. It was this move, probably much more than the military surge, which has led to a perhaps temporary decline in the level of violence in Iraq in the second half of 2007. But the costs are also potentially very great. The United States has now helped to arm yet another militia that cannot be absorbed by an Iraqi government but is itself impotent to become that government or even the main force behind it. Its relation to older Sunni forces (the Iraqi Islamic Party, Sunni Endowment, Association of Muslim Scholars, etc.) being unclear, it is not even strong enough to fully control the Sunni-majority provinces.

This takes me back to the issue of constitutional learning. Using the older deals and amendments to the 2005 constitution are surely not going to help in reconciling the three main groups or bring the new Sunni extraparliamentary actor into the process. As late as February 2008, even a new de-Baathification law and a law dealing with oil resources have not been fully achieved. A deal on federalism is much more remote. Thus a new renegotiation of the procedures to deal with the problems would be required, especially because of the appearance of this powerful Sunni actor, which has more American support than any before. But once again, the actors should have learned not to approach that matter in the same old way, which led to disaster—to do so, according to Einstein, is the sure sign of insanity. For the American actors, "sanity" would mean that finally they understand that compelling the Iraqis without a timetable for leaving is impossible. Whether that lesson has been learned will now depend on the American electorate. The two Democratic candidates still standing have more or less the right approach even if so far they have paid little attention to what should happen in Iraq when we leave; the one Republican has the wrong approach. He wants to stay indefinitely, whatever happens in the political process. He thinks of Iraq as a war zone, and he would have the power to keep it one, indefinitely, if we let him.

As to the Iraqis, the lesson they need to learn is that in a strongly divided but culturally and socially interpenetrating country (whether Iraq or Israel) with differential resources, three or more sides heavily armed, and international allies, the desire to either impose a regime or to cleanly separate will lead to perpetual conflict. Only a historic compromise of all the major forces and the real sharing of power on many levels can lead to the way out. Whether this lesson has been learned in Iraq (or Israel) is doubtful.

I now come to what I myself have learned from this study—I dare to hope I learned quite a lot. What I did *not* learn about Iraq can also be discerned from the preceding chapters, and undoubtedly, because of my linguistic and geographical limitations, there is much under this heading for even sympathetic critics to find. I feel more secure regarding some conclusions I came to in the areas of methodology and theory. As to methodology, I learned something about the advantages and limits of an interpretive use of comparative methods. With respect to theory, I have now come to understand much better the superiority of the "postsovereign paradigm" of constitution making, on both the normative and functional levels.

I came to the topic of the book as a comparativist and a theorist, and indeed I had no other justification (intense political concern was only a motivation) for writing on Iraq but some previous work in these two areas. As a comparativist, I faced the problem that any historian could have predicted for almost any comparison, namely that no dictatorship was ended nor any constitution made in a manner like Iraq's. Undeterred, in my first chapter I focused on a Germany/Japan comparison as a form of immanent critique of the conception of the occupiers themselves, who believed, with Charles Krauthammer, that these old cases proved that anywhere where the United States cared enough and put in sufficient resources it could impose a political order of its choice. Right away, however, here a causal form of comparative analysis tends to break down, because the now almost universally admitted insufficiency of U.S. troop involvement meant that arguably from the beginning the United States did not care enough after all (even if it should have or could have). I register this problem, but since my concern is constitution making, I note two other major differences (along with many other historical givens). The first has to do with the problem of imposition versus autonomy. In Germany, the American occupiers sponsored an almost entirely autonomous form of constitution making, while in Japan, where they imposed a constitution, they disguised their imposition behind the legality of the inherited system. In contrast to these, in Iraq they imposed and did not hide that state of affairs. The second difference had to do with the related problem of stateness. In Japan, the occupiers maintained the inherited state, whereas in Germany, where such a state was destroyed through the war itself, they allowed the rapid, bottom-up reconstruction of autonomous provincial "statehood." Assume then that the occupying forces were insufficient in strength in Iraq. Could following either German or Japanese state- and constitution-making patterns (state destruction and an autonomous process *or* state continuity and an imposed process) have worked? I believe that we will never know, and this is the point where my analysis has to avoid all strong causal claims. The advantage of the interpretive, rather than causal, method that I use is that I am still able to say something of significance, namely that if the level of force did not itself doom the whole enterprise, not following either the German or Japanese pattern was in any case disastrous, even fatal, unless some other method was developed that could compensate for the missing autonomy (Germany) or legal continuity (Japan).

That is where the constitution-making method, the two-stage "post-sovereign" constitution making that was actually used, comes in. In principle, it could have had virtues that made up for much that was lacking in comparison to the German and Japanese models. At the same time, here the framework of comparison becomes very tenuous, because none of the previous examples of this constitution-making method—Spain, various central European states, and South Africa—involved external constitutional imposition of any kind. Similarly, regarding the issue of insufficient force, one could argue that this difference alone would have led to failure in the Iraqi case. Again, we will never know, because the method itself was adopted in a deviant manner, leading to pathologies. Some of these could be traced back to the factor of external imposition, but I believe that some were strongly contingent. My interpretive method focuses on what was contingent without being able to make strong causal claims for these factors.

I do not underemphasize the deterministic dimension. If the United States could be compared to the foreign sponsor of some of the state parties in central Europe in the late 1990s, nevertheless its role in pushing for a radical transition was unique. In its own (though never in Iraqi or international) eyes, this role gave it legitimacy and a moral mission that has no parallel in any relevant country, with respect to the agency that held the major means of violence during the transition. The deformations and pathologies that followed from this role were more like those the Soviet Union was guilty of when setting up its client states in the late 1940s (entirely legitimate, but only in its own eyes) than the timid role this imperial state played in the 1980s and 1990s. Again, we cannot know if this factor in itself doomed the process, but it is certainly plausible that it did.

But at the same time there was also contingency. The U.S. authorities were free, however they interpreted their own mission, to include all Iraqi forces in political bargaining, or at least many more political forces than they did, and to avoid making a fundamental state deal, subsequently almost etched in stone, with the Kurds alone. Elsewhere, from Hungary to South Africa, broad inclusion of political forces was the key to even partial legitimacy of the inevitably nondemocratic first stage of the process, and learning from these cases would have meant insisting on broad and deep inclusion. If the built-in differences of imposition and the external role did not lead to failure in itself, then the failure of inclusion certainly did. And it was not counterbalanced by subsequent belated attempts that I treat under the failure of sequencing, again in comparison with all the other cases.

Could other deviations from the pattern followed in other countries compensate for the negative effects of imposition and exclusion? There is only one such major deviation, the role of referenda, and its consequences were in many respects rather negative. No other country using the two-stage method felt obliged to give "the people" another channel beyond that of the voice of elected representatives. To me, a final ratificatory referendum may be a fallback into sovereign constitution making, and it was adopted in Iraq only because it was already contained *both* in the Bonapartist proposals of the Americans and the radical populist demands of the Grand Ayatollah Sistani, the two plans that had to be reconciled in the model adopted. More specifically, it was then used to hamstring the elected National Assembly, by tying it to the default position of the Transitional Administrative

Law, which would be enforced by the possibility of three Kurdish provinces easily mustering the necessary two-thirds vote to veto a final constitution. Adding to the legitimacy problems of the authorization and negotiation of the TAL, such a restriction of the freely elected assembly meant, among other things, a violation of the UN-mediated compromise with Sistani. In the end, the National Assembly was reduced to less than even a rubber stamp, and the process returned to a kind of collective Bonapartism, in which the Kurdish and Shi'ite party leaders used the referendum to confirm their joint political diktat to the population. Certainly, with respect to the excluded, even the momentary passing hope that the three Sunni provinces could perhaps vote down the constitution did not compensate for their earlier exclusion.

Many lessons are implicit in these comparisons, but it is worthwhile to highlight them, especially within the context of the "rescue operation" I discussed in my preface. Given the multiple causes for failure just indicated, it is difficult to sort out the weight of each, and it is possible that some interpreters will blame in small or large part the constitution-making method itself, which I expressly want to avoid doing. My critics could take two different and opposite approaches. The first would deny that the method of constitution making matters at all and would claim (to the extent that admitting that this problem area is relevant at all) that it was the result (i.e., the constitution that was written) that doomed the prospects of a solution to Iraq's problems. One interpretation of this argument is that pure imposition would have been fine as long as it produced the right constitutional result. I certainly agree that the TAL's combination of confederal/federal/centralistic and consociational formulas was incoherent, and the solutions of the not fully completed final constitution were even worse. But I would deny that this was independent of the method of constitution making adopted; indeed, most of the untenable results followed from exclusionary bargaining and private dealings with the Kurds. The learning mechanisms I analyzed in terms of amendment and ratification rules were even more directly the results of the special Kurdish role in the process. A different and less deformed process would have produced different results.

Pure American imposition could have avoided all these substantive difficulties, but only at the cost of vastly exacerbating the already grave legitimacy problems. Here the burden of proof is on those who maintain the very implausible position that even the gravest legitimacy problems connected to constitution making do not matter as long as the result is good. Of course, if imposition were successfully hidden behind an apparently Iraqi process, then we would have had a better chance of acceptance. But then the constitution-making paradigm devolves into the Japanese example—but with the total destruction of old state institutions and the failure to form a provisional government, there were no Iraqi forms behind which to hide the imposition. What if they had not destroyed the Iraqi state? Forgetting the other vast differences with Japan, for the model to work, a plausible program would have required the immediate creation of an Iraqi government, relying on a more or less professionally intact ministry of justice, all controllable by the Americans. None of this was very likely given the divisions of Iraqi society and the different relationships of its groups to the invaders.

The second line of criticism would insist that the sovereign constitution-making method, a single-stage one such as that proposed by Sistani's camp, could have produced more legitimate results and without the incoherence of the two Iraqi constitutions. There is little doubt that a higher degree of coherence would have been achieved, but only at the expense of legitimacy. Elections for the constituent assembly would then have been won, as they were later won, by a unified Shi'ite list of some kind. Despite some efforts, Sistani never managed to become the leader of a united Iraqi nationalist challenge to the occupation, perhaps because he expected the Americans to guarantee free elections against antidemocratic forces that, initially at least, were too strong. Whatever the reason, his side (assuming away its own internal divisions) would then have been in the position to impose a constitution on something like one-half of the Iraqi population, perhaps more if we also count secular Shi'ites. While one cannot exclude some compromises even in that situation, such a constitution would have been that of the bare majority and unrestricted by any prior rule or agreement. In such a situation, without prior constraining rules, a victorious party usually has difficulty controlling its own radical elements. If a constitution favoring two of the three major groups produced havoc, another favoring only one of the three would have probably fared worse—unless the whole effort turned against the occupation, and of that there was very little sign. And even in that last case, a civil war with the Kurds would have been impossible to avoid.

Thus, a method born out of a compromise between external imposition and internal populism would probably have been the right one, if practiced in the right way. There are strong theoretical reasons for this being the case, and paradoxically two missing elements of the Iraqi formula, "legitimacy" and "stateness," have helped me understand why much better.

For some time I have stressed that where there is no democracy one cannot begin democratically.[4] I have also tended to add that there are nevertheless legitimate and illegitimate beginnings, and I have treated legal continuity, revolutionary legitimacy, pluralistic inclusion, and other principles such as consensus and publicity from the point of view of an initial nondemocratic legitimacy.

This is relevant to populist democratic constitution making. Its overwhelming superiority is supposed to be because in this model the sovereign people, and no one but the sovereign people, gives itself a constitution. This position is based on unacceptable political mythology, incoherent originalism, and what has been called the metaphysics of presence.[5] Both historical analysis and logical considerations reveal that the *legal* identity of the sovereign people, one capable of action only *within* representation, is determined by *prior* electoral and procedural rules that must be given to the "people" by elites who thereby constitute them as a people capable of action.[6] Hans Kelsen already argued that "the people—from whom the constitution claims its origin—comes to legal existence first through the constitution."[7] This idea, as I see it, contains two: (1) some kind of nonpopular beginning of popular constitutions and (2) the legal, representative character of the people within constitutions. Regarding both, one needs to distinguish the "we" that speaks words like "we, the people" and the "we" in whose name these words are spoken.[8] The first "we" that speaks (the "actor") is not the "people" (one cannot begin democracy under nondemocracy democratically), and the second "we" (the "author") never acts. The first "we" claims that it is a "representative" of the people and therefore has a right to act in its name.[9] How can this act of representation—or equally substitution and arguably usurpation, given its element of arbitrariness—by a self-designated agent be made legitimate? Advocates of the classical democratic method of constitution making (who have often criticized liberal constitutionalists in terms of their result rather than process orientation) in the end answer in terms of the result: to the extent the constitution actually contributes, performatively, to the creation of its supposed author, the unified people.[10] Leaving aside the irrelevance of that ideal to a divided society like Iraq—or even to the peaceful European Union—the formula resembles that of Joseph Weiler's biblical "We will do, and hearken" (that is, impose a covenant first and understand the divine dispensation later), which was applied to a more appropriate model of European pluralistic culture of constitutional tolerance. Here too the initial process was redeemed by the result, and asking for its initially democratic credentials is equivalent to asking an unfree people to participate in the creation of freedom, forever privileging that unfree subject as the constitution's author.[11] Thus Weiler goes so far as to make heteronomy not only inevitable but a virtue as well.

Nothing like a biblical dispensation from on high occurred in Europe, but Iraq shows the consequences of thinking along lines like Weiler's. But the model of actor-author, somewhat relativized and further differentiated, very much helps to explain the power of the new model of constitution making. Here that model becomes reflexive, differentiating its components and indicating that a legitimate version has organizational requirements. What in the single-stage model is a single set of utterances made by one speaker(s) in the name of another subject that never speaks becomes two utterances, with two acting subjects, in two distinct stages, with increasing but never complete legitimacy. Unlike the speaker of the classical populist model, the speaker of neither stage here is able to fully identify itself with the popular sovereign. And yet their legitimacy can be greater. This is so fundamentally because of the changed character of the very beginning of the process. While the arbitrariness is still there in the first stage, it does not lead to an arbitrary and potentially self-serving imposition of initial rules. What can only be to an extent arbitrary is the choice of negotiating partners and decision rules, but sociological, historical, and moral criteria of inclusion and fairness exist for these, even if an old legal order has been disrupted. Inclusion may never be perfect, but as we have seen in Iraq one can do much better or much worse, at the very least. If the first stage is accomplished fairly, what was simply an actor in the classical populist model is now bifurcated into a subject of action (with its now receding arbitrary element) and authorized agent (authorized by all or most of the political organizations of the country). The speaker(s) who write an interim constitution speak at the same time directly in the name of political organizations, and they establish a process by which a democratically authorized set of speaker(s) can be elected. Still, it is the decision makers of the first stage that constitute the people as a legal entity capable of action. Broadly understood, they are representatives not only of political groups but of the population understood in terms of politically articulated segments. Evidently, they also constitute, performatively, the population in terms of these segments, by their action if not always by the rules they generate. They thus refer to the people in two possible senses, and this can lead to problems (for example, the freezing of consociationalism or power sharing) later on. Much depends on the extent to which they are genuinely superseded by the second set of speakers, both as authors who can legitimate an unchanged interim constitution and as actors creating a new one.

The speakers in the second stage are also representatives, this time of the citizens understood in terms of universal suffrage (who in turn are themselves only representatives, since not all citizens can or do vote, and the electorate represents the nonvoters as well). Their legitimacy can be higher than that of a classical constituent assembly, because the manner in which they were chosen was less arbitrary and more inclusive. Yet in the two-stage process, the rulemakers of the first stage, who structure the process as a whole, have no interest in mythologizing the second set of speakers as *identical* to the people and especially as direct embodiments of a constituent power outside of law. Nevertheless, in the second stage the representatives have the democratic authority to speak in the name of the people or the citizens.[12] Because they are neither identical to the people nor seen as such, their power can, should be, and always is to an extent limited. But one must be very careful with these limitations. This is so because the constitutional actors in the second stage are authorized, unlike those in the first, from a democratic point of view, or, if that begs the question, from a universalist and egalitarian one. What has become crystal clear in Iraq is that since the role of the first stage is to limit the *more* democratic one, the legitimacy of both stages is extremely important. Thus it is by no means irrelevant how one initiates that first stage. The element of heteronomy, if it is logically inevitable, must be as reduced and confined as possible. And the missing democratic legitimation, while it cannot be fully replaced, must be compensated for. Understanding the nonidentity of the actors—even of the democratic stage—with the people allows the first stage to partially define and limit them. But understanding the greater deficiency of the first stage requires that the second stage not be neutralized through either impossible learning mechanisms or executive usurpation. These are the lessons from the pathological case of Iraq, lessons that could not be clearly seen where the processes worked more or less properly.

Finally, state destruction and the failure of state (not nation!) rebuilding play extremely important roles in this book. There is no need to again rehearse the "no state, no constitution" thesis here. But I would like to again stress the priority of state building and rebuilding to constitution making and even make this argument entirely general. What I have in mind is the empirical regularity (though not entirely universal) that even in revolutions surviving institutions, organs, associations, and so on from the inherited state play important roles in constitution making even where the strict legal continuity of the state has been disrupted (in domestic if not international law).[13] This phenomenon has to do with the necessity of political integration for political agency, which goes far beyond what Arendt recognized in the case of America, namely the role of small, inherited republics in the making of the big republic. Some *pouvoir constitué* is always part of the *constituant*,[14] except perhaps, very tenuously, in the ideal limiting case of what Carré de Malberg and Kelsen called the "first" constitution.[15] All previous constitutions contribute to the making of the following ones. Thus we can have a juridical theory also of revolutions, something that Carré de Malberg and Kelsen thought unlikely (though the latter came up with it in his rather implausible theory of international law).[16] In terms of the model of actor and author, as several contemporary analysts now recognize, in some respects these two agents or agencies must be seen not only as two parts of the *constituant* but also as *constitué*: the actor by the old state and the author (who is both an actor and an author) by the new regime. But that constitution by the old order means the survival of some organ or agency as part of the state structure, organizational, political, or symbolic.[17]

And this is not only because of the impossibility of beginning *ex nihilo* in revolutions and the need to rely on some inherited structures, institutions, organizational patterns, or groups to integrate society. The role of continuity is obviously even greater under reform, regime change, and transformations from above, the types discussed in chapter 1 along with revolution. In any significant large-scale transformation, the specter of revolution plays a major a role, and, whatever their historical reality, revolutions can in principle and in our imagination challenge the state structure and the regime. Great structural reforms are undertaken to preempt revolutions, and, likewise, negotiations of political power with important oppositional forces are undertaken to work out the parameters of regime change. In the case of the latter, both the structure of the regime and political power over the state is likely to change. All the participants need guarantees: the opposition must be confident that the existing power will not use state resources against them during the process, and the governmental forces need assurance that new incumbents will not later use the state in a repressive way. Agreement concerning constitutional rules is not enough; it is even more important that state structures be so organized that forces of violence, material resources, and population groups be so distributed and governed as to protect all negotiating partners from worst-case scenarios. Where the repressive role of the state (its administrative and military organs) with respect to some population groups plays a major role in the demise of an old regime, renegotiating the state structure so that it cannot happen again under new management is of prime importance. But to some extent, relevant questions such as the disposition of the militias of political organizations must be dealt with in all negotiations. It also follows that all those capable of materially affecting the relevant questions through the actual or potential use of violence of their own become the most important members of these negotiations, and their exclusion tends to make state bargaining at the very least difficult if not generally futile.

Once again we should be able to see a central advantage of the two-stage process of constitution making. From the point of view of the state-regime distinction, the great lesson of Iraq is that the first stage is necessarily the locus of the state bargain and the second stage can shift more in the direction of regime construction. Of course, the distinction is analytical only, and both types of issues are generally dealt with in both stages, with the added proviso that the first stage must contain both state and regime rules for the transitional period. But logically at least, the part of the first stage that should be negotiated among the main political actors controlling, or capable of controlling, the means of violence is the one that has some claims of being enshrined against the democratic will of the electorate as represented in a constituent assembly. In political life, the ethics of responsibility requires that we do not try to treat as equal those who cannot be in fact reduced to equality. However, making the distinction between state structure and regime should help in reducing the number of areas where this undemocratic element is given some of its due. Since this was not done in Iraq, in addition to the confederal state structures conceded to the Kurds, they were also granted consociational regime structures, which led to an entirely unjust arrangement from the point of view of Arab Iraqis, who can rightly say, "they have separated off their quasi-state where we have no say, but they are in a position to deadlock our political and constitutional development."

Again, it will never happen anywhere that the first stage, even if dedicated to peacemaking, can be entirely kept away from constitutional or regime-building areas. But from the point of view of the new model as understood through the lens of Iraq, we can understand the centrality of state making in other first stages. In South Africa, for example, the interim constitution involved making important deals regarding the military forces of both sides and about the inherited administration, police powers, and federal arrangements. Not all issues regarding the state structure were enshrined in the thirty-four principles, but when they were, as in the case of federalism, the Constitutional Court wound up using its extraordinary powers even against the new dispensation of the freely elected constitutional assembly. In unitary states with more homogenous societies, I would grant that state rebuilding is very implicit, at best during the first stage of negotiations. But even in Hungary, for example, there was a contentious issue, which had to be resolved, regarding the Communist Party's militia. More importantly, consensus about all state-related issues guarantees the continuity of the transition, which can then concentrate on regime change exclusively.

I realize now (especially after a friendly suggestion by Nehal Bhuta) that I have been concerned with state continuity even before Iraq, under the heading of legal continuity.[18] Not being a follower of Kelsen, who has influenced me in a number of ways, I do not consider the two to be the same. But I have always argued that legal continuity from authoritarian to rule-of-law states has a fictional aspect. Amendment rules, for example, which were never the real rules of system change, are suddenly used for real, masking actual ruptures. If there is state continuity, then legal discontinuity, even acts of illegality (as in America in 1787, where the individual states supplied what was continuous), may be of relatively little consequence for constitutional stability. But without state continuity, legal continuity is impossible. It may be therefore true that the deeper continuity that really mattered in a Japan or a Hungary or a South Africa was state continuity, and it is another lesson of Iraq that without state continuity the stabilization of a democratic revolution or transition becomes extremely difficult. In the end, we may only have the German case to indicate that such a thing is possible, but that was under extraordinary and perhaps unrepeatable circumstances. The theoretical problem of Iraq was whether the two-stage, postsovereign method of constitution making could initiate a second major instance of democratic transformation in the context of state collapse. The challenge should never have been there to take up: first, because Iraq should not have been invaded, and second, because its state should not have been destroyed. Given that this challenge was taken up, we will never know whether the results could have been positive, because of the remarkable misjudgments and policy failures this book has documented.

Notes

Preface

1. See, however, my op-eds and interviews at http://www.nepalnews.com (September 29, 2006; February 26, 2007; and July 7, 2007). I visited Nepal to consult and lecture in September 2006.

1. The Externally Imposed Revolution and Its Destruction of the Iraqi State

1. But see the fairly precise recent formulation by Carl Conetta, "More Troops for Iraq? Time to Just Say No," *Project of Defense Alternatives Briefing Memo* 39 (January 9, 2007): "What the Bush administration sought to do, at the point of a gun, is thoroughly reinvent Iraq—its public institutions, legal system, security structures, economy, and political order. This is a revolution as profound as any, but foreign in origin, design, and implementation." Below, I will distinguish between two types of revolution: revolutionary regime change and revolutionary state destruction. In these terms, there may be a difference between the revolution the Bush administration sought to have and the one it wound up having.
2. A. Arato, "The Occupation of Iraq and the Difficult Transition From Dictatorship," *Constellations* 10, no. 3 (2003); on the concept of revolution, see chapters

1 and 3 of my *Civil Society, Constitution, and Legitimacy* (Lanham, Md.: Rowman and Littlefield, 2003). The legal part of my argument in chapter 3 is superseded by J. Kis, "Between Reform and Revolution: Three Hypotheses About the Nature of Regime Change," *Constellations* 1, no. 3 (January 1995); and J. Kis, "Between Reform and Revolution," *East European Politics and Society* (Spring 1998). I will rely on his version of the argument below.

3. Other authors' use of the term is sporadic, unsystematic, and sometimes misleading. See, e.g., P. Galbraith, *The End of Iraq* (New York: Simon and Schuster, 2006), 119, where he speaks of the completion of the revolution in Iraq by the American destruction of the Baath party, the army, and the security services. These moves amounted to state destruction, which, however, is neither necessary to a revolution (regime change is sufficient) nor does it complete a revolution (only the institutionalization of a new regime can). Some authors of radical leftist backgrounds also sense the revolution problem here: G. Packer, *The Assassin's Gate: America in Iraq* (New York: Farrar, Straus and Giroux, 2005), 57, has Christopher Hitchens speak of a "revolution from above" in an early discussion where the "above" meant the Americans. Also see P. Cockburn, *The Occupation* (London: Verso, 2006), 70–71, who on the whole operates within a classical "imperialism" paradigm that I consider partial rather than wrong. Cockburn's imperialist intervention is a failure just as much as my externally imposed revolution is (see 220–222). On this issue of imperialism, I have more to say below. With respect to Iraq, on my side of the political divide, only Nehal Bhuta seems to have given the *concept* of revolution systematic consideration, even if he does not focus on the term. See his outstanding "A New Bonapartism," in A. Bartholomew, *Empire's Law* (London: Pluto, 2005). Despite the title, the epigram introducing the essay refers to a French revolutionary attempt to introduce republican government in Italy by force in 1792. Carl Schmitt's category of sovereign dictatorship, which Bhuta uses to characterize what he calls transformative occupation, indicates the internal relationship between revolutionary populist and Bonapartist forms of constitution making. In Iraq's revolution, as I will show in chapter 3, populist and Bonapartist forms were to compete. But as we have recently seen in Venezuela (1999), the two can be complementary as well.
4. Some authors argue that "success" is part of the term, but they mean only successful conquest of power. See C. Tilly, *From Mobilization to Revolution* (Reading, Mass.: Addison-Wesley, 1978). In this context, I tend to go with H. Arendt, who makes "constitution" part of her definition of revolution, but usually (if not consistently) only as an aim, not as an accomplishment. See her *On Revolution* (New York, 1963), 35. Otherwise she would have to deprive "permanent revolutions," including the French process, the very title of revolution.

5. C. Schmitt, *Die Diktatur*, 4th ed. (Berlin: Duncker u. Humblot, 1928 [1923]); and C. Schmitt, *Verfassungslehre* (Berlin: Duncker u. Humblot, 1928); as well as Arendt, *On Revolution*.
6. Or, to play it safe, the imposed part of the country's revolutionary process defined by the current period of the continuing American occupation. What I do not and cannot exclude is that during this now seemingly permanent revolutionary process an actor or set of actors emerges that will in the end, in spite of it all, establish a stable regime of some type.
7. J. Dobbins et al., *America's Role in Nation Building from Germany to Iraq* (Rand, 2003); and N. Feldman, *What We Owe Iraq: War and the Ethics of Nation Building* (Princeton, N.J.: Princeton University Press, 2004).
8. B. Anderson, *Imagined Communities*, new ed. (London: Verso, 2006 [originally published in 1983]). At this point, I find only the definition of nationalism in this famous book fully tenable and its disregard of the problem of state building its most serious fault. I find no single volume on nations and nationalism fully satisfying, but together with Anderson's, books by J. Breuilly, E. Hobsbawm, E. Gellner, and R. Brubaker (and many others) cover the field very quite impressively. Reading any of them seriously would stop one from confusing state and nation building, of course.
9. Habermas's constitutional patriotism is not the equivalent of nationalism, nor are the people of a constitutional regime the stand-in for the nation where the "imagined community" extends beyond the jurisdiction of the constitution. Today, a German "nation" of citizens and the object of constitutional patriotism have come much closer, but this was not the achievement of any external nation building.
10. See K. Shoichi, *The Birth of Japan's Post-War Constitution* (Boulder, Colo.: Westview, 1997); J. Dower, *Embracing Defeat: Japan in the Wake of World War II* (New York: Norton, 1999); and P. Merkl, *The Origin of the West German Republic* (New York: Oxford University Press, 1963).
11. The literature is now enormous, so I will stick to a few classics and semiclassics: O. Hintze, *The Historical Essays of Otto Hintze* (New York: Oxford University Press, 1975); N. Elias, *The Civilizing Process II* (New York: Pantheon, 1982); G. Poggi, *The Development of the Modern State* (Stanford, Calif.: Stanford University Press, 1978); C. Tilly, *The Formation of National States in Western Europe* (Princeton, N.J.: Princeton University Press, 1975), especially the very fine essay by S. Finer as well as Tilly's comprehensive introduction; T. Skocpol, *States and Social Revolutions* (Cambridge: Cambridge University Press, 1979); and P. B. Evans, D. Rueschmeyer, and T. Skocpol, *Bringing the State Back In* (Cambridge: Cambridge University Press, 1985). For a careful distinction between state and nation building, see J. Linz and A. Stepan, *Problems of Democratic*

Transition and Consolidation (Baltimore, Md.: The Johns Hopkins University Press, 1996), chap. 2. For a particularly interesting essay on the relationship of state and national identity, see B. Kimmerling, *The Invention and Decline of Israeliness: State, Society, and the Military* (Berkeley: University of California Press, 2001), chap. 2.

12. N. Podhoretz, "World War IV: How It Started, What It Means, and Why We Have to Win," in G. Rosen, *The Right War: The Conservative Debate on Iraq* (Cambridge: Cambridge University Press, 2005), 123, 135ff. C. Krauthammer, who prefers the term democratic realism for his own position, sticks to nation building ("In Defense of Democratic Realism," in *The Right War*, 197–198) but does not seem to explain why.
13. And the volume he edited: see P. Chattarjee, ed., *Nation-Building: Beyond Afghanistan and Iraq* (Baltimore, Md.: The Johns Hopkins University Press, 2006), 3–4.
14. F. Fukuyama, "Guidelines for Future Nation-Builders," in *Nation-Building: Beyond Afghanistan and Iraq*, 232. In this essay, minimal state reconstruction and building of new institutions are two steps of the process described as "nation building." What was previously an ambiguity between state and democratic government thus becomes two stages. The model is inapplicable to Iraq, as he himself sees.
15. J. Dobbins, "Learning the Lessons of Iraq," in *Nation-Building: Beyond Afghanistan and Iraq*, 220.
16. Ibid., 218.
17. M. Pei, S. Amin, and S. Garz indeed define nation building by *regime change*. "Building Nations," in *Nation-Building: Beyond Afghanistan and Iraq*, 64–65. They go on to add the criteria of deployment of a large number of American troops and the use of U.S. personnel in political administration. It is not clear, however, whether these are understood as part of the overarching concept, or, more likely, only of the smaller set of cases they wish to study, which involve both U.S. intervention and regime change.
18. Ultimately, it is I. Kant in "Perpetual Peace": see the section "First Definitive Article of Perpetual Peace," in *Perpetual Peace and Other Essays* (Indianapolis, Ind.: Hackett, 1983), 112–113. In the face of the objection focusing on the history of earlier republics, see B. Constant, "The Spirit of Conquest and Usurpation," chaps. 1–4, 6; and B. Constant, "The Liberty of the Ancients Compared with That of the Moderns," in B. Fontana, ed., *Political Writings* (Cambridge: Cambridge University Press, 1988). Otto Hintze has helped us see the difference between wars between representative forms of government within the same civilization and wars representative governments may likely fight against other civilizations and forms of government, wars that are likely to be understood

as crusades and thus will not be under the Kantian limitation. See "The Preconditions of Representative Government in the Context of World History," in F. Gilbert, ed., *The Historical Essays of Otto Hintze* (New York: Oxford, 1975). Finally and most brilliantly, A. de Tocqueville in volume 2 of *Democracy in America* (London: Penguin, 2003), chaps. 22–23, 26, developed the most differentiated perspective. While of all nations democracies have "the greatest attachment to peace," of all armies democratic ones are the "most keen upon war" (753). Further, "there are two things which will always be difficult for a democratic nation to do: beginning and ending a war" (755). Among a plurality of interconnected democratic nations "that equally dread war and long for peace . . . wars become less frequent but spread over a larger area once they break out" (768). And, while officers and noncommissioned officers are a force for war, ordinary soldiers are a force for peace as long as the nation itself "is enlightened and energetic" (761).

19. "Perpetual Peace," 1st section, article 5: "No nation [*Staat*] shall forcibly interfere with the constitution and government of another" (109, but see also 116–118, 124–125).
20. I define the terms below.
21. Linz and Stepan, *Problems of Democratic Transition and Consolidation*, 57.
22. P. Cockburn rightly points to the importance of this state of affairs in that government but not society was defeated in the American war. See *The Occupation*, 55. While Dobbins et al. note the total defeat of Germany and Japan (4, 25, 28), in the comparative conclusion they draw a dangerous equivalence between "defeat" and "liberation" of populations: "defeated or liberated populations are often more docile, co-operative and malleable than usually anticipated" (195). It is this mindset that quickly turns liberation into oppressive occupation. On this see below.
23. Linz and Stepan note military defeat in the case of Greece and Argentina in *Problems of Democratic Transition and Consolidation*, 131, 191–192, but they only compare these cases to each other in considering the remaining role of the internal military in the transition (weak in Greece, much stronger in Argentina) and not to completely defeated countries and the role of external militaries that do play a role in their typology. Thus the confusion of choice of transition type and type of preexisting dictatorship I have in mind cannot even come up in their analysis. It may be a more general problem than I can explore here. Or is it that successful transitions never involve such a confusion? In G. O'Donnell and P. Schmitter's *Transitions from Authoritarian Rule: Tentative Conclusions About Uncertain Democracies* (Baltimore, Md.: The Johns Hopkins University Press), 18, Greece and Argentina are not even counted as externally caused transitions because the military government actions in Cyprus and the

Falklands/Malvinas were according to them already the results of internal "tottering" and "stalemate."

24. I don't want to get into the legalistic argument here of whether the 2003 war was arguably a continuation of the 1991 conflict and relevant UN Security Council authorizations (nos. 678, 687) and permitted by UN SC Res. 1441. See N. Bhuta, "A Global State of Exception? The United States and World Order," *Constellations* 10, no. 3 (2003); and M. Byers, "Agreeing to Disagree: Security Council Resolution 1441 and Intentional Ambiguity," *KeepMedia Online*, for two different and interesting views. I am still convinced by Bhuta concerning the illegality of the actions of the United States and the United Kingdom in 2003 and think that the very real duality Byers discovers is between the rule of law and imperial law. See also "British Attorney General's Advice to [PM] Blair on the Legality of the Iraq War," March 7, 2003 Global Policy Forum—UN Security Council.
25. A comparison of America's post–World War II role in different countries would support this assumption, with the level of intervention into internal processes in Germany, Japan, Italy, and France (in that order) being correlated with the degree of previous authoritarianism (positively) and internal political organization of new forces (negatively). But again, this is an argument merely from history. America was different then than now. Even after World War II, significant measures were taken to weaken communist forces among the oppositions in the defeated or liberated countries, and this could reach the level of intervention and imposed solution, as in the Greek civil war. Of course, Linz and Stepan may answer that the typology refers to successful transitions only. So it may mean that only cases where there is a poor fit between regime type and transition strategy will fail as transitions to democracy. But will they also fail as transitions from dictatorship? Transitions to where? That is the question in Iraq.
26. Below I will discuss the transition plans of the U.S. administration, which indicate both of these mistakes and how they were combined in the competition concerning transition scenarios.
27. Kis first used the concept of "regime change" (in the Hungarian manner) for coordinated transition, and so did I, but I now prefer to keep "regime" as the class concept for all four transformations. In the second version of his thesis, he saw the space between reform and revolution more as a continuum, with three ideal types, two involving round tables, two involving legal continuity, but only one, the most general and stable version, the negotiated transition proper, involving both. See articles by Kis cited above, which were developed as critical reflections on and expansion of Hans Kelsen's legal concept of revolution (*General Theory of State and Law* [Cambridge, Mass.: Harvard, 1945], 117ff.)

and which I have also used in my *Civil Society, Constitution, and Legitimacy,* 89–91. While I consider the argument of Kis to supersede mine, I expand his scheme by identifying continuity of legitimacy *cum* legal rupture as *autogolpe,* i.e., coup or revolution carried out by a legitimate authority in place.

28. See Kelsen, *General Theory of State and Law.*
29. Aside from Kelsen, see H. L. A. Hart, *Concept of Law* (Oxford: Oxford University Press, 1961).
30. R. Dahl, *Polyarchy* (New Haven, Conn.: Yale University Press, 1971).
31. C. Tilly, *From Mobilization to Revolution* (Reading, Mass.: Addison & Wesley, 1978), 190–193. Tilly himself cannot keep war and revolution entirely apart and speaks of an uncertain area between them, in particular regarding cases that for me resemble the political situation in Iraq.
32. N. Bhuta, "A New Bonapartism."
33. I have come to understand the distinction between the two revolutionary scenarios, annexation and constitutional imposition, on the basis of Julian Arato's 2007 Columbia University B.A. thesis "L'exportation de la Liberté," which discusses French attempts to apply both in Belgium in 1792–1793.
34. See chapter 4 of Linz and Stepan, *Problems of Democratic Transition and Consolidation.* In O'Donnell and Schmitter's *Transitions from Authoritarian Rule,* "where the *via revolutionaria* is taken the prospects for political democracy are drastically reduced" (11).
35. Skocpol, *States and Modern Revolutions,* provides both historical comparisons and logical arguments in a more Tocquevillian tradition, which complement my treatment here.
36. Arendt, *On Revolution.*
37. C. J. Friedrich, *Constitutional Government and Democracy* (New York: Blaisdell, 1968), chap. 8, is right to emphasize that empirically one can only speak of a constituent group and should not confuse the ideological claims made on behalf of the universality of the constituent power, usually "the people," with sociological realities. This duality between claim and reality makes the classical category of the constituent power unstable. For two extended sets of case studies, see E. Morgan, *Inventing the People* (New York: Norton, 1988); and K. Baker, *Inventing the French Revolution* (Cambridge: Cambridge University Press, 1990).
38. Even Hitler's "legal revolution" was based on the exploitation of the opportunities of a presidential dictatorship, provided for by Article 48 of the Weimar Republic and the ability of the president to dissolve the Reichstag. The combination was not intended by the constitution makers.
39. A. Arato, "Good Bye to Dictatorships?" *Social Research* 67, no. 4 (2000); C. Schmitt, *Die Diktatur.*

40. Quoted by S. Chesterman, "Occupation as Liberation: International Humanitarian Law and Regime Change," *Ethics and International Affairs* 18, no. 3 (2004).
41. R. R. Palmer, *Age of Democratic Revolutions* (Princeton, N.J.: Princeton University Press, 1959); and Julian Arato, "L'exportation de la Liberté."
42. V. A. Belaunde, *Bolivar and the Political Thought of the Spanish-American Revolution* (New York: Octagon, 1967); B. Loveman, *The Constitution of Tyranny* (Pittsburgh, Penn.: University of Pittsburgh Press, 1993), chaps. 5–6.
43. See Krauthammer, "In Defense of Democratic Realism," 198; J. Kurth, "Iraq: Losing the American Way," in G. Rosen, ed., *The Right War* (Cambridge: Cambridge University Press, 2005), 42–43, who rightly insists on the crucial case of South Vietnam; and especially Pei, Amin, and Garz, "Building Nations," who come up with two successful cases (Germany and Japan), two in my view dubiously successful ones (Panama and Grenada), two unfinished ones (Afghanistan and Iraq), and eleven outright failures out of seventeen, or charitably, three successes (including Grenada) out of fifteen completed ones. But the whole sample is distorted in relation to Iraq by the irrelevance of the German and Japanese cases, implied by these authors (see 78) and admitted more or less by James Dobbins in the same volume. See "Learning the Lessons of Iraq," 225ff. Finally, S. Kinzer's *Overthrow: America's Century of Regime Change from Hawaii to Iraq* (New York: Times Books, 2006), examines only interventions where the United States is the aggressor (an important classificatory move) and as aiming at goals other than their stated claims (impose ideology, increase power, gain control of resources). He judges them to be mostly unsuccessful from the point of view of achieving greater security for American interests (1–6). For the record, three of his cases (the annexed Hawaii, the colonized Philippines, and tiny Grenada) may be counted as democratic "successes" by the most charitable neoconservative standard, seven as failures. The last number is inflated by the lamentable fact that the goal for some of the regime-change operations (e.g., Chile in 1973) was the overthrow of democracy in the first place.
44. A. Arato, "The Occupation of Iraq and the Difficult Transition from Dictatorship," and A. Arato, "Empire's Democracy," in A. Bartholomew, *Empire's Law* (London: Pluto, 2006).
45. As in my previous work (*Civil Society, Constitution, and Legitimacy*), I use the term primarily in the sociological sense established by Max Weber, according to which legitimacy depends on the *belief* of relevant populations of the validity or rightness of rulers to rule. While following Habermas (*Legitimation Crisis* [Boston: Beacon Press, 1975]), I do not consider this sociological sense to be entirely independent of the normative sense of the rightness or validity itself;

I think nevertheless that the empirical meaning is certainly not reducible to the normative one, and the normative one, as Habermas later realized, is a complex result of historically situated ("ethical") and universal ("moral") criteria. I do not, as the followers of Kelsen and other lawyers do, make the fatal mistake of identifying legality and legitimacy. In this I follow Weber, Schmitt, and Habermas.

46. Arendt, *On Revolution*, 29–35, 141–142.
47. Schmitt, *Verfassungslehre*.
48. This dialectic is studied by Cockburn, *The Occupation*.
49. Galbraith, *The End of Iraq*, 122; Dexter Filkins, "Where Plan A Left Ahmad Chalabi," *New York Times*, November 5, 2006; Dobbins, "Learning the Lessons of Iraq," 224; Packer, *The Assassin's Gate*, 195.
50. To begin with, there is some confusion here. Occupation is legally a matter of fact, not of declarations and recognitions, and it was already so indicated by an earlier UNSC resolution, 1471. The only thing recognized by the United States, the United Kingdom, and resolution 1483 was a status of belligerent occupation, which in fact puts restrictions on the occupying power rather than establishing powers for them in comparison to other forms of occupation, e.g., one based on *debellatio* (see below).
51. My own views here were strongly influenced by my students. During a masters seminar in Cape Town, South Africa, in January 2006, African students strongly challenged my Arendt-influenced view that whatever else, the overthrow of a dictatorship like Saddam's was "liberation." They would not even be moved by my personal testimony, coming from the Hungary of 1945, that an external force can be immediately a liberator to some and an occupier to others, a view I still consider correct. More recently, Frederick Miles, a New School graduate student and U.S. Army member, has raised the question of whether we can speak of externally steered revolution and liberation where there is not a significant internal force such as the Northern Alliance in Afghanistan, which was able to become almost immediately the subject of the revolutionary process upon liberation. This would of course have implications for the assessment of a process in which there was such a potential subject but it was not allowed to play the dominant role. All these considerations led me to the following analysis of the problems of the category of liberation.
52. And in turn, as I have just realized, these two meanings can be linked to the so-called liberty of the ancients and the moderns, both of course highly relevant to the modern world. See Constant, "The Liberty of the Ancients Compared with That of the Moderns." Though a partisan of the liberty of the moderns, Constant rejected external liberators, mostly because of the consequences for the country doing the liberating.

53. Nor even the immediate replacement of a colonial ruler by an indigenous dictator, even if nationalists might disagree. Historically, this scenario tends to follow a previous liberation and the failure of revolution.
54. This later took the form of looking for an Iraqi Karzai, since a new MacArthur (rule by an American general) would be unacceptable. See B. Woodward, *State of Denial* (New York: Simon & Schuster, 2006), 131.
55. See Y. Nakash, *The Shia Revival*, 2nd ed. (Princeton, N.J.: Princeton University Press, 2003), xx; A. Cordesmans and A. Hashim, *Iraq* (Boulder, Colo.: Westview, 1997), 352–354.
56. Lenin saw this problem very clearly in 1905, even if in 1908 his calculations did not actually work out when he occupied the seats of provisional governmental power. See "Two Tactics of Social Democracy in the Democratic Revolution" [1905], in *Selected Works* (Moscow: Progress, 1970), 468–471.
57. The idea that the Iraqi Leadership Council was representative even though it did not include the Sunni Arabs because they supported the old order, and that it was "chosen by the most democratic means available," i.e., by an exile conference in London, are both preposterous. Galbraith, *The End of Iraq*, 124. A group does not become representative when it excludes a very significant part of the population, whatever its views, and "most democratic available" is meaningless in the Iraqi context of the time, as all the choices were entirely undemocratic.
58. D. Phillips, *Losing Iraq: Inside the Postwar Reconstruction Fiasco* (Boulder, Colo.: Westview, 2005), chaps. 8, 9, 12; Packer, *The Assassin's Gate*, 80, 90; Cockburn, *The Occupation*, 26–32; Galbraith, *The End of Iraq*, 116–117; R. Chandrasekaran, *Imperial Life in the Emerald City* (New York: Knopf, 2006), 51–53; Ricks, *Fiasco: The American Military Adventure in Iraq* (New York: Penguin, 2006), 104–105, 154; Woodward, *State of Denial*, 145, 175–178; M. Danner, "Iraq: The War of the Imagination," *New York Review of Books*, December 21, 2006; and especially Bremer, *My Year in Iraq* (New York: Simon & Schuster, 2006), 42–44.
59. Woodward, *State of Denial*, 145 (based on the views of Secretary Powell); and Chandrasekaran, *Imperial Life in the Emerald City*, 51–52, for a more detailed elaboration.
60. Galbraith, *The End of Iraq*, 117, is incisive on this point, though I do not agree that a clean decision for either a rapid turnover to exiles or for a long occupation would have likely worked. The decision for contradictory alternatives continued even under Bremer, where a structure was set up for a long occupation but then dismantled relatively soon, and when an American administrator with dictatorial powers was instituted, but so was the structure originally intended to be the provisional government, in an advisory capacity.

61. See A. Arato, "Sistani v. Bush: Constitutional Politics in Iraq," *Constellations* 11, no. 2 (2004): 175, where I speak of American military dictatorship behind the façade of the IGC. For my definition of dictatorship, formulated in 2000, see "Good Bye to Dictatorships?" *Social Research* (Winter 2000): 934–935. According to Cockburn, *The Occupation*, 69, speaking of Bremer: "Flying into Baghdad on May 12, he became dictator of Iraq as soon as he landed." Cf. Bremer, *My Year in Iraq*, 12–13, where he speaks of formally being given full authority "with all executive, legislative and judicial functions" in Iraq. For Brahimi's remark, see Terence Neilan, "UN Envoy Urges Iraqis to Give New Leaders a Chance," *New York Times*, June 2, 2004. "Mr. Brahimi struck a mildly surprising note when, in answer to a reporter's question, he referred to the American occupation administrator, L. Paul Bremer III, as 'the dictator of Iraq.' 'He has the money,' he said. 'He has the signature. Nothing happens without his agreement in this country.' "
62. Woodward, *State of Denial*, 111, 130–131, 145, 158.
63. Bremer, *My Year in Iraq*, 36–37; Ricks, *Fiasco*, 267–268; Cockburn, *The Occupation*, 147–148; Woodward, *State of Denial*, 249, 252.
64. Woodward, *State of Denial*, 197; Cockburn, *The Occupation*, 67–69; and Chandrasekaran, *Imperial Life in the Emerald City*, is best on the style of the CPA's form of rule.
65. T. Dodge, *Inventing Iraq* (New York: Columbia University Press, 2003), chaps. 1–2.
66. See Bremer, *My Year in Iraq*, who does not understand that under the mandate, at least under the impact of the 1920 revolt, the English actually had a more democratic scenario in mind than his seven-point program!
67. N. Feldman, *What We Owe Iraq*, chap. 2, is right in that the application of the law of belligerent occupation implied a kind of trusteeship, in my view largely a conservative one, but he goes wholly astray when he tries to generate a model of "nation building" involving a long-term, developmental trusteeship that could live up to high ethical standards, e.g., putting Iraqi interests ahead of American ones. The reasons why trusteeships of the mandate type are universally rejected today is on the realistic assumption that occupying countries will look to their own interests first. His own book shows that this is what has happened in Iraq. It is implausible to treat all the disastrous decisions of the U.S. occupiers he recounts as mere mistakes or errors and not to see the pattern, namely badly or ideologically interpreted self-interest, behind it all.
68. Cockburn, *The Occupation*, 108.
69. Ibid., 72, 107–108, 112–114.
70. Bhuta, "A New Bonapartism?"; Schmitt, *Die Diktatur*; Arato, "Good-Bye to Dictatorships?"

71. Cockburn, *The Occupation*, 13–14, 32, 69, 107. For the early British attempt to apply direct rule see Dodge, *Inventing Iraq*, 7ff.
72. Bremer, *My Year in Iraq*, 170–171, 205, 209; Woodward, *State of Denial*.
73. Bremer, "Iraq's Path to Sovereignty," *Washington Post*, September 8, 2007; Bremer, *My Year in Iraq*, 163–164; Chandrasekaran, *Imperial Life in the Emerald City*, 78.
74. Bremer himself is very skeptical whether a formal transference of sovereignty actually ends an occupation regime, at least in the eyes of those still occupied by an "occupying army," whatever it is called. See Bremer, *My Year in Iraq*, 205: This was a point of rare agreement between him and the always more perceptive General Abizaid.
75. See the "Agreement on Political Process" (November 15), point 2, which foresaw a bilateral status-of-forces agreement by March 2004. Admittedly, such an agreement has been impossible to negotiate. While the positive political effects of such a move would be obvious, the U.S. government has never chosen to renounce the intention of having future military bases in Iraq.
76. Documented by G. Fox, "The Occupation of Iraq," *Georgetown Journal of International Law* (April 2005); Bhuta, "New Bonapartism"; and my "Sistani v. Bush" and "Interim Imposition," *Ethics and International Affairs* 18, no. 3 (2004)
77. Juan Cole's *Informed Comment* was the best of the latter. I was a frequent contributor in 2004 and 2005. See http://www.juancole.com.
78. Bhuta, "A New Bonapartism?"
79. Constant, "Usurpation," 95–97; See also R. Michels, "Bonapartist Ideology," in *Political Parties* (New York: The Free Press, 1962); P. Rosanvallon, *Le démocratie inachevée* (Paris: Gallimard, 2000), chapter 5.
80. This seems to be even the view of even Chandrasekaran (*Imperial Life in the Emerald City*, 290), with whom I agree concerning what could have been done instead of creating the CPA, namely establishing an internationally led inclusive process. Perhaps the question of the CPA should be separated from that of belligerent occupation, as it would have temporarily existed if that alternative or almost any other were followed, at least temporarily.
81. Chesterman, "Occupation as Liberation," *Ethics and International Affairs* 18, no. 3 (2004), rightly notes that occupation is a fact according to the Hague and Geneva Conventions and does not depend on the occupying power's recognition or intentions. The recognition, however, should have implied the recognition of the restrictions as well. As Fox, "The Occupation of Iraq," documents in detail, it certainly did not in many areas. On this see below, regarding state destruction in this chapter and constitution making in chapter 3.
82. Inviting the IGC to submit in cooperation with the CPA, and, circumstances permitting, with the special representative of the Secretary-General, "a time

table and a programme for the drafting of a new constitution of Iraq and for the holding of democratic elections under that constitution" (par. 7), resolution 1511 thus sided with Bremer against Sistani, just before the CPA was forced to compromise with the Grand Ayatollah. At the time of this resolution (October 2003), there was no special representative of the Secretary-General in Iraq, nor were there plans to send one!

83. On the latter see J. Benomar, "Constitution-Making After Conflict: Lessons for Iraq," *Journal of Democracy* 15, no. 2 (2004).

84. Dodge, *Inventing Iraq*, 17–18; Cockburn, *The Occupation*, 68–69; and Chandrasekaran, *Imperial Life in the Emerald City*.

85. Bremer, who made the contrary decision, makes pretty strong arguments here (*My Year in Iraq*, 42–44, 49), and, while he finds little support among the more important commentators on his other two major decisions regarding the dissolution of the army and de-Baathification, here he finds significant agreement. See, e.g., Packer, *The Assassin's Gate*, 64; Chandrasekaran, *Imperial Life in the Emerald City*, 77–78. Galbraith, *The Occupation*, 117, represents a contrary view, but I am assuming that as always he is in part speaking for the Kurdish leaders among the group. Some Iraqis, including Kurds, felt that the failure to form an Iraq interim government early was an Iraqi failure first and foremost. See M. Gordon and B. Trainor, *Cobra II: The Inside Story of the Invasion and Occupation of Iraq* (New York: Pantheon, 2006), 470.

86. Galbraith, *The End of Iraq*, 116, 123–124. He thinks, almost alone, that Sunni nonrepresentation or electoral boycott is a relatively small matter from the point of view of representativeness. Where Galbraith is right is that Bremer's handpicked additions to the IGC were not later electorally successful, though even here he neglects the Iraqi Islamic Party, which was to become the core of the Iraqi National Accord. But his whole argument disguises the crucial point that by pushing the original ILC as the core of an interim government, Galbraith agrees about excluding the politically organized Sunni, who were to receive about 20 percent of the votes in December 2005 elections, and that even Bremer did slightly better in this respect by including, eventually, the religious Sunni Iraqi Islamic Party. Cockburn, *The Occupation*, 148–149, seems to agree on interpreting the electoral results, if not on Sunni exclusion. But without a detailed consideration, he only speaks of getting "the most votes" in the two 2005 elections, which does not take into account the advantages of incumbency.

87. Note finally the double standard used by Galbraith. He argues for the representative nature of officials that were appointed by the Americans initially, but he denies the same to Sunni officials appointed between the two elections to redress the ethnic balance, although they too were to perform

roughly according to the numbers of their inclusion (i.e., 20 percent) (*The End of Iraq*, 194). The point was made much more insistently in his article "The Last Chance for Iraq," *New York Review of Books* 52, no. 15 (2005). It is true that the Iraqi Islamic Party was part of the IGC. But it was not part of the ILC formed in London. It also boycotted the first elections. Thus its members too had to be appointed to the Constitutional Committee, or rather Commission, afterward, for Sunni inclusion. It is also true that the Iraqi National Accord, an all-Sunni Islamic formation this party sponsored (but which included much more radical elements, such as Adnan al-Dulaimi) outperformed the neo-Baathists four to one (*The End of Iraq*, 195), but on the other hand it is the latter's perspective that Sunnis followed overwhelmingly in the constitutional referendum. The electoral post hoc arguments for the exclusion of Arab nationalists are political and spurious.

88. As Jay Garner saw from the beginning. See Woodward, *State of Denial*, 133, 135. See also Arato, "The Occupation of Iraq and the Difficult Transition from Dictatorship," 416; and Cockburn, *The Occupation*, 108; as well as Chandrasekaran, *Imperial Life in the Emerald City*, 290. It is simply preposterous, not to say self-serving, to argue that an international authority of ad hoc composition would have the same problems with putting self-interest before Iraqi interests as an American occupier representing a generation-old project in the Gulf (Feldman, *What We Owe Iraq*, 90). The interests of such an international body would not even be formed in advance, and its multilateral structure would lead to a process of decision making that would have to take a larger variety of perspectives into consideration. Moreover, in case of internal conflicts, decision making would more likely be structured by public-regarding arguments. Of course, a condominium of states could be as self-interested as a single state. But the structure of an international governing authority and its choice of leadership could avoid such a condominium rather easily. The problem with an international body is effectivity or the impasse of decision making, not legitimacy and deliberative process.

89. L. Diamond, *Squandered Victory: The American Occupation and the Bungled Effort to Bring Democracy to Iraq* (New York: Holt, 2005), 116, 207–208, 310–311; Gordon and Trainor, *Cobra II*, 440–449. Elections organized by Marine commanders were cancelled in Najaf by the CPA because the "wrong guy" was about to win. Gordon and Trainor, *Cobra II*, 493; see also Cockburn, *The Occupation*, 132 (Mosul), 182 (elections). Feldman more or less provides the ideological justification for canceling elections that would have the wrong result: see *What We Owe Iraq*, 98, 114. Marines on the ground, according to Gordon and Trainor, did not have much sympathy for such arguments.

90. Bremer, *My Year in Iraq*, 277 (Sunni inclusion), 325 (Sadrist inclusion).

91. According to UN SC Res. 1511, the "sovereignty of Iraq resided in the State of Iraq," and the IGC and its ministers "embodied" this sovereignty (point 4). Temporarily, however, that sovereignty was exercised, under an admittedly not very clear authorization, by the CPA (point 1). That, in any case, was where the sovereign power lay, whatever the UN Security Council meant to affirm. Thus, on June 28 what was to be transferred to the interim government was the exercise of sovereign powers. To be sure, this transfer was in large part fictional.
92. According to Cockburn, the problem with generation of national leaders was the ethnicization of Iraqi politics, for which he does not primarily blame the Americans. See *The Occupation*, 93ff., 150–151.
93. L. Brahimi, "Comments," at Security Council 4952nd Meeting, April 27, 2004 (*UN News Center*). See Bremer, *My Year in Iraq*, 358ff., who tends to put the blame for crossing Brahimi on the IGC but belies this through his rhetoric. Cockburn, *The Occupation*, 157ff. According to Chandrasekaran, *Imperial Life in the Emerald City*, 244–245, "Brahimi felt used. The Americans did not want his advice. Just his imprimatur." I did my best to advise the UN team how to avoid this outcome in an American election year, but to no avail. They should have focused on legitimate inclusive procedures, not on persons. The idea of the round table (206) was my suggestion. I agree that a great opportunity was lost for all.
94. The Avalon Project at Yale Law School, *Laws of War: Laws and Customs of War on Land (Hague II)*, July 29, 1899 (Washington, D.C.: Government Printing Office, 1968).
95. Fox, "The Occupation of Iraq."
96. Who turns the phrase "unless absolutely prevented" into a general permission to go against the letter and the spirit of the whole regulation. Statement of John Yoo: "Iraqi Reconstruction and the Law of Occupation: Hearing on Constitutionalism, Human Rights, and the Rule of Law in Iraq Before the Subcomm. On the Constitution, Subcomm. On the Judiciary," 108th Congress (2003).
97. J. Cohen, "The Role of International Law in Post-Conflict Constitution Making: Toward a Jus Post-Bellum for Interim Occupations," forthcoming in *New York Law School Law Review*; Chesterman, "Occupation as Liberation: International Humanitarian Law and Regime Change."
98. Bhuta, "A New Bonapartism?"
99. A. Arato, "Empire's Democracy," in A. Bartholomew, ed., *Empire's Law* (London: Pluto, 2006), 225–226.
100. H. Kelsen, "The Legal Status of Germany According to the Declaration of Berlin," *The American Journal of International Law* 39, no. 3 (1945): 518–526.
101. See the preamble, which refers to the constituent power of the German people. The military commanders had no objection to this phrase, one that should have been meaningless to Kelsen, given the doctrine of *debellatio*.

102. Cohen, "The Role of International Law in Post-Conflict Constitution Making"; Chesterman, "Occupation as Liberation"; both citing E. Benvenisti, *The International Law of Occupation* (Princeton, N.J.: Princeton University Press, 1993), 92–96. *Debellatio* is a factual matter, Benvenisti argues, and unconditional surrender alone does not establish it. A state has to be totally defeated in war, its allies must cease fighting, and its national institutions should have disintegrated for there to be *debellatio*. Thus it is inexplicable why he then accepts the application of the doctrine to Japan as well as Germany. Shoichi's extremely careful work *The Birth of Japan's Post War Constitution* shows the repeated application of The Hague 43 to Japan by American as well as international representatives even as the process of imposed constitution making took place, which is the fact Benvenisti focuses on to indicate the absence of belligerent occupation. Actually, there *was* belligerent occupation, whose rules were violated by the United States, a rather different matter.
103. Chesterman, "Occupation as Liberation," 54.
104. See Bhuta, "A Global State of Exception"; and Byers, "Agreeing to Disagree."
105. Anne-Marie Slaughter, "Good Reasons for Going Around the UN," *New York Times*, March 18, 2003. Her argument was in my view normative-theoretically fallacious, since even given the open and processual nature of international law, the outrightly illegal cannot be simply dubbed legitimate unless a deontological principle of legitimacy such as international public opinion or the moral majority (the nine members of the Security Council) supported an action that was stopped by a veto or veto threat alone, as in the Kosovo case she cites. Moreover, that which is illegal but legitimate should be able to become a principle of a new and better legality, and it is hard to see how the actions of the United States vis-à-vis the Security Council and the UN Charter could yield that. According to Slaughter, if weapons of mass destruction were found and/or the Iraqi people welcomed the Americans and their allies, and if the United States turned "immediately back to the UN" for after-the-fact approval and to help rebuild Iraq, and the United Nations agreed, the invasion would have become legitimate. It is hard to think that she was speaking as a lawyer and not as a sociologist, to whom legitimacy is only belief in a claim of validation or justification. Even then, her first two conditions have not been satisfied: WMDs have not been found, and the Iraqis on the whole did not welcome the invaders. As far as the most "important" point is concerned, the United States has indeed gone back to the United Nations for approval and for help in rebuilding Iraq. For legitimacy in the sociological sense, it is hard to believe that a Security Council resolution giving the Americans a free hand in the political sphere, which they in any case have, could have ever made much difference. Undoubtedly the occupation was legalized in terms of international law. But

this act did not retroactively legalize the war nor make either the war or the occupation sociologically legitimate in Iraq itself. I wonder what she thinks about this sorry business today.

106. Kelsen does not distinguish between state and government, in his argument for *debellatio* in Germany, where both were destroyed. In Iraq, the key decisions (CPA orders 1 and 2) were made on May 16 and May 23, whereas UN SC Res. 1483 is dated May 22; thus, arguably, the state as a legal entity was not yet destroyed. But Kelsen would rightly say that its sovereignty nevertheless was gone and that no entity remained to which that sovereignty could be retransferred. Thus *debellatio* rightly understood refers to the governmental center of sovereignty, whose survival the old Hague regulation presupposes.
107. Bhuta, "A New Bonapartism?"
108. See Benvenisti, *The International Law of Occupation*, xi, who interprets 1483 in this spirit, one that moreover quite contradicts his own convincing claim that the same resolution strongly affirms the transference of the sovereignty focused on by the law of occupation from government to people. To accept the constituent role of the occupying authority means the confiscation of the most important dimension of popular sovereignty, a point that could not have escaped some of the country representatives that signed on to 1483, even if it did Benvenisti. Thus Jean Cohen's interpretation, which I follow here, is obviously sounder, even admitting that the ambiguity is one of the cases stressed by Byers (regarding 1441), when the Security Council deliberately decided something with two possible interpretations. However, that is no reason why we should go with the theoretically inconsistent and normatively less acceptable interpretation.
109. Chesterman, "Occupation or Liberation," 61, refers to 1483 as an "uncomfortable compromise that straddled" the divide between permission and prohibition (Hague) of regime change. That is certainly true. But I, following Cohen, believe an equally important divide was straddled between regime change carried out by the occupation authority and by autonomous Iraqi actors (Geneva).
110. Cohen, "The Role of International Law."
111. Today, a great external power certainly cannot take on the mantle of the disinterested foreign lawgiver, a figure that has in any case been universally abandoned since the modern democratic revolutions.
112. See my "Forms of Constitution Making and Democratic Theory" in *Civil Society, Constitution, and Legitimacy*, where I outline a set of procedural principles (consensus, plurality, publicity, fiction of legality, and empirical veil of ignorance) that allow the attribution of democratic legitimacy.
113. See, e.g., Bremer, *My Year in Iraq*.
114. Arato, "Sistani v. Bush," and "Interim Imposition."

115. See chapters 3 and 4, below.
116. All this is noted by Cockburn, *The Occupation*, 220–222, without really trying to explain why such a hopeless imperialist strategy was in fact adopted and pursued even when obviously failing. The only thing he observes, partially correctly, is that the priorities of the American presidency were ultimately domestic. With this move, contradicting the imperialism thesis, he deciphers the second of several components that went into the process of making the key decisions.
117. "Don't Attack Saddam," *Wall Street Journal*, August 15, 2002.
118. Even in the nineteenth century, some of the most powerful arguments for imperialism used the doctrine of popular sovereignty. See N. Dirks, *The Scandal of Empire* (Cambridge, Mass.: Harvard, 2006), esp. the chapter on sovereignty.
119. "What does the United States really want?" Iraqis asked Cockburn and each other this at the London Metropole conference of 2002. Sometime in 2004, Jamal Benomar (Brahimi's chief of staff) told me: "I spent days in a presidential palace in the Green Zone, with Ron Blackwill [National Security Advisor Rice's special representative], with Bremer and the others; I ate with them, had tea with them, talked with them all the time. I have no idea what they want." The answer can only be that they wanted many things, often incompatible, things that in this particular administration, with a strong-willed but cognitively weak chief and without a policy process, were never reconciled. First and foremost, they wanted that president reelected, and that was Brahimi's opening, one that he missed.
120. For an especially careful and differentiated treatment, see E. Nell and W. Semmler, "Economics of Oil," *Constellations* 10, no. 3 (2003).
121. Woodward, *State of Denial*, 408–409. Note the confusion between al Qaeda and Saddam—or was it one? Perhaps Kissinger believed in Nixon's crazy-man doctrine as the most effective deterrent: if you attack me, I am capable of doing anything to anyone.
122. The idea is that if there is a one-percent chance of a state using or allowing nonstate actors to do us grave harm, we should attack it first. The idea is absurd, because a one-percent chance would have landed us in war simultaneously with several countries, with Iraq certainly not being the first. Pakistan, a known proliferator that cannot control a large part of its territory—thus a failed state—would have been the most likely target. Attacking Iraq but not Pakistan does not deter other such states; it makes them go nuclear.
123. See D. Suskind, *The One Percent Doctrine* (New York: Simon & Schuster, 2006); and U. Preuss, "The Iraq War: Critical Reflections From Old Europe," *Constellations* 10, no. 3 (2003).
124. "Don't Attack Saddam," *Wall Street Journal*, August 15, 2002.
125. Phytian, *Arming Iraq*.

126. Podhoretz, *World War IV*, 155–156.
127. Documented by Woodward in astonishing detail.
128. W. Gibbs, "Scowcroft Urges a Wider Role for the UN in Post War Iraq," *New York Times*, April 9, 2003.
129. I have made this argument first in "The Occupation of Iraq and the Difficult Transition from Dictatorship." Of the commentators, only Cockburn, *The Occupation*, sees the issue clearly (68–69, 149), though of course everyone is aware of it. Few have noticed, however, that in light of the electoral rule eventually chosen, one that required no census at all, only birth certificates or other proof of citizenship at voting, the reasons for delaying elections were phony. An electoral law could have been passed at any time. The only issue was public security, which the delay of elections was likely to worsen.
130. A. Przeworski, *Democracy and Market* (Cambridge: Cambridge University Press, 1991), 10ff., 40ff.
131. Arato, "Empire's Democracy."
132. Bhuta, "A New Bonapartism?"
133. Dobbins, "Learning the Lessons of Iraq," 227–228; See Bremer, *My Year in Iraq*, 17, 19, 37–38.
134. C. J. Friedrich, "Military Government and Democratization," in C. J. Friedrich et al., *American Experiences in Military Government in World War II* (New York: Rinehart, 1948), 11–15.
135. P. Merkl, *The Origin of the West German Republic* (New York: Oxford University Press, 1963), 20.
136. See especially K. Takayanagi, "Some Reminiscences of Japan's Commission of the Constitution," in D. F. Henderson, ed., *The Constitution of Japan, Its First Twenty Years, 1947–1967* (Seattle: University of Washington Press, 1968). Takayanagi, an important participant with a "collaborative theory," nevertheless writes: "All legislation for the democratization of Japan during the occupation was guided and supervised by the SCAP [Supreme Commander for the Allied Powers]. No legislation was enacted by the 'free will of the Japanese' in the sense that the enactment was accomplished 'without any outside interference' " (77). Other interpreters believe the level of compulsion used was much more drastic, and few apparently share Takayanagi's judgment that the new constitution was "a rather moderate revision of the Meiji constitution on democratic lines." Even a cursory reading of the two texts, as well as Takayanagi's own comparison, refutes this claim. Koseki Shoichi's argument (in *The Birth of Japan's Post War Constitution*, surely the leading single volume on the subject) against pure imposition is much more sophisticated. Koseki stresses not so much the formal process, which was legally continuous and based on inherited Japanese rules, but rather the very important constitutional discussions

that occurred in society and among intellectuals and that (1) went into the work of the American drafters and (2) guaranteed that the results would be favorably received by most of Japanese society. However, in my view even this strong argument, more social-historical than legal, does not deflect from the imposed character of the fundamental process. The Americans could have allowed the autonomous forces from which they learned to have their own autonomous process, but they certainly did not. They acted in their place and they created a compromise among Japanese forces and interests entirely according to their own wishes.

137. On this see W. G. Beasley, *The Rise of Modern Japan* (New York, 1990), 177ff.; and Karel van Wolferen, *The Enigma of Japanese Power* (New York: St. Martin's, 1989), 39–41.

138. J. Maki, "The Japanese Constitutional Style," in Henderson, ed., *The Constitution of Japan*, 8–10; Takayanagi, "Some Reminiscences of Japan's Commission of the Constitution," 79; and A. Bouterse et al., "American Military Government Experience in Japan," in Friedrich et al., *American Experiences of Military Government*, 350–351. On such fictions, see Arato, *Civil Society, Constitution, and Legitimacy*, 143–145, 174–175.

139. These points are mostly adopted from "The Occupation of Iraq and the Difficult Transition from Dictatorship"; see also Kurth, "Iraq: Losing the American Way"; G. Rosen, ed., *The Right War* (Cambridge: Cambridge University Press, 2005); and Arato, "Empire's Democracy," in *Empire's Law*.

140. I do not regard (in this comparison especially) the government under the old monarchy as a constitutional government, though it indeed had a constitution from 1924 to 1958 that for short periods may have given that appearance. See N. Brown, *Constitution in a Non-Constitutional World* (Albany, N.Y.: SUNY Press, 2002).

141. According to Benjamin Constant, "the French revolution saw the invention of a pretext for war previously unknown, that of freeing peoples from the yoke of their governments which were supposed to be illegitimate and tyrannical . . . the worst of all conquests is the hypocritical one." In *The Spirit of Conquest and Usurpation and Their Relation to European Civilization* [1813/1814], in B. Fontana, ed., *Political Writings* (Cambridge: Cambridge University Press, 1988), 65. In the same passages, Constant vividly unmasks the lies used to justify preemptive wars.

142. H. Otake, "Two Contrasting Constitutions in the Postwar World: The Making of the Japanese and the West German Constitutions," in Y. Higuchi, *Five Decades of Constitutionalism in Japanese Society* (Tokyo: University of Tokyo Press, 2001).

143. To their credit, Garner and some of the U.S. commanding officers grasped the importance of both of these factors, but they were overruled by Bremer.

144. Dobbins, *America's Role in Nation-Building from Germany to Iraq* (Rand, 2003).

145. Bremer, *My Year in Iraq*, 9–10; Woodward, *State of Denial*, 190, notes that Bremer never followed up. Also see Gordon and Trainor, *Cobra II*, 477–478, who note that Bremer's understanding of the Rand report was superficial. They also point to the conscious rejection of the Bosnia/Kosovo model by the Bush administration and especially Rumsfeld (Fukuyama, "Beyond Nation-Building," 464, 477, 495), because it would encourage dependency of the host country on American nation building.
146. Dobbins, "Learning the Lessons of Iraq," 225.
147. Krauthammer, in *The Right War*, 198.
148. Dobbins, "Learning the Lessons of Iraq," 198–225.
149. Ibid., 198.
150. J. Kurth, "Iraq: Losing the American Way," in *The Right War*.
151. See two great books on this: H. Batatu, *The Old Social Classes and the Revolutionary Movement in Iraq* (Saqi Books, 2004); and Y. Nakash, *The Shi'is of Iraq*, 2nd ed. (Princeton, N.J.: Princeton University Press, 2004).
152. We have no complete study yet of the disorganization of life in Iraq, but Chandrasekaran and Cockburn make a good start.
153. Bremer, *My Year in Iraq*, 115.
154. Given state destruction, the German occupation, with its democratic process organized from below, relied on a very large occupation force, one that was between those of Bosnia and Kosovo, and over four times larger than Japan (Dobbins, *America's Role*, 197). But given the presence of the Soviet army, it is difficult to assess the meaning of this number.
155. M. Weber, *Economy and Society* (Berkeley: University of California Press, 1978), 1:55–56.
156. G. Jellinek, *Allgemeine Staatslehre*, 3rd ed. (Berlin: Springer, 1920); R. Carre de Malberg, *Contribution à la theorie générale de l'etat* [1920] (Paris: Dalloz, 2004), 1:2–7.
157. O. Duhamel, *Droit constitutionnel* (Paris: du Seuil, 2000), 2:17.
158. Legitimacy is absent from the definitions of Tilly and his colleagues. C. Tilly, ed., *The Formation of National States in Western Europe* (Princeton, N.J.: Princeton University Press, 1975), 70.
159. Weber, *Economy and Society*, 1:56; more radically, Kelsen, *General Theory of State and Law*, 181–192.
160. Giddens following Durkheim: A. Giddens, *The Nation-State and Violence* (Berkeley: University of California Press, 1985), 17.
161. I was reminded of the importance of this dimension by B. Kimmelring in his very fine book *The Invention and Decline of Israeliness* (Berkeley: University of California Press, 2003), chap. 2. By his lights, I neglect the rather strong sense of "collective identity" that he insists on when speaking about a state. Such a collective identity, which may have existed in Israel before 1967 or 1973, steps across

the line to a national identity of a particular type. I would go easy with making it part of the definition of the state. What could be called social integration of the state also enters my conception on the Weberian level of legitimacy and with the minimum idea of belonging inherent in the idea of the state's people in the French definitions, which is unfortunately often called "nation" in France. Following Kimmerling, I add state rituals and symbols, which he rightly shows are communicated through a variety of socializing systems. But I keep the idea of national identity or even constitutional patriotism separate from state identity in a more minimal sense. In any case, only the latter was a general phenomenon in Iraq and only it has a slim possibility of being currently reconstructed.

162. G. Poggi, *The Development of the Modern State*, 1, makes the first choice; Giddens, *The Nation-State and Violence*, makes the second.
163. J. P. Nettl, "The State as a Conceptual Variable," *World Politics* (July 1968): 559–592. It is not, however, useful to treat state and government as somehow inversely proportional in importance. What supposed statelessness in the context of strong governments indicates is generally just a different type of state. See S. Skowronek, *Building the New American State* (Cambridge: Cambridge University Press, 1982).
164. Kelsen, *General Theory of State and Law*, 228.
165. N. Luhmann, "Ends, Domination, and System," in *The Differentiation of Society* (New York: Columbia, 1982).
166. O'Donnell and Schmitter's definition of regime is more complex and has somewhat wider implications in drawing in empirical patterns of social life, but it amounts to the same perspective. My stress is on the "institutionalization" part of their definition. *Transitions from Authoritarian Rule*, 73.
167. D. Grimm, "The Constitution in the Process of Denationalization," *Constellations* 12, no. 4 (2005): 447.
168. Kelsen, *General Theory of State and Law*, 124ff.; Hart, *The Concept of Law*, chapter 5.
169. Kelsen, *General Theory of State and Law*.
170. Grimm, "The Constitution," 448; Kelsen too was getting at this problem with his important distinction between constitution in the formal and in the material senses. But in the terms of his pure theory of law, both constitutions are normative-legal. While following Grimm, I wish to indicate the structural importance of a third domain, an empirical one, which may be entirely unknown to the actors until political science uncovers it.
171. All three types are located in table 1, which focuses on types of regime change alone. Here what I am indicating is that a modality of change involving legality/illegality can be on the level of government, regime, or state. Thus in effect I am multiplying my four- or eight-part scheme by three.

172. Cf. Lenin, *State and Revolution* (1917), which contains the distinction I have in mind: "all previous revolutions perfected the state machine, whereas [in the proletarian revolution] it must be broken, smashed." In Lenin, *Collected Works*, 2:306, with "How Should We Organize the Workers' and Peasants' Inspection?" (1923). After years of Soviet power and civil war, he writes, "our state apparatus is to a considerable extent a survival of the past and has undergone hardly a serious change. It has only been slightly touched up on the surface, but in all other respects it is a relic of our old state machine" (3:771). His solution in 1923 involved adding new members with a different class background rather than extensive purges, to control rather than to replace the old, expert officials. Already in 1917, the idea of smashing the state machine could be made consistent with the idea of dictatorship only because he thought of an "undivided power backed by the armed force of the entire people," i.e., an alternative state that did not exist (2:304).
173. See Skocpol, *The State and Modern Revolutions*, 182, 190 (France), 209–211, 216–217 (Russia).
174. Schmitt, *Verfassungslehre*, 93–94, 99.
175. Weber, *Economy and Society*, vol. 2. Thus his views were the obverse of the Lenin of *State and Revolution*, for whom the revolutions of the past were state strengthening, as opposed to the future state-destroying one.
176. Skocpol, *The State and Modern Revolutions*.
177. Schmitt, *Verfassungslehre*, 92.
178. A. Esmein, *Eléments de droit constitutionnel français et comparé* [1914] (Paris: Panthéon-Assas, 2003), 583–586; Carré de Malberg, *Contribution à la theorie générale de l'etat*, 1:49, 1:65–66, 2:500–501. B. Ackerman documents such a role for established institutions in the revolutionary or radical reformist making of the U.S. Constitution in *We the People II* (Cambridge, Mass.: Harvard University Press, 1998). I have done so myself in "Constitution and Continuity in the East European Transitions," in *Constellations* (following Arendt's argument for constituted constituent powers in America, in *On Revolution*), distinguishing between legal and institutional continuity. My article is now in my *Civil Society, Constitution, and Legitimacy*.
179. Tilly, *From Mobilization to Revolution*, 198–199.
180. R. Bensel, *Yankee Leviathan: The Origins of Central State Authority in America, 1859–1877* (Cambridge: Cambridge University Press, 1990).
181. Feldman, *What We Owe Iraq*, 1; Packer, *The Assassin's Gate*, 197–198; Bremer, *My Year in Iraq*, 17, 19, 36–37, 42; Dobbins, *America's Role*, 225.
182. Those who warned were Garner, the CIA resident in Baghdad, and a variety of generals. See Ricks, *Fiasco*, 159–161; Gordon and Trainor, *Cobra II*, 483–485; and Chandrasekaran, *Imperial Life in the Emerald City*, 70–72.

183. Bremer, *My Year in Iraq*, 9–10. See Gordon and Trainor, *Cobra II*, 485, on this double error.
184. Cockburn, *The Occupation*, 221, rightly introduces some much needed skepticism in this regard, but even he cannot deny that too small a force made many of the problems he discusses much, much worse.
185. Galbraith, *The End of Iraq*, 118.
186. On the decision and the blame, see Bremer, *My Year in Iraq*, 39–42, 45, 54–57; Woodward, *State of Denial*, 193–198, 200, 209, 219–220. On the options before: Gordon and Trainor, *Cobra II*, 476, 480–485 (and on the combined effect with not having enough U.S. troops); Packer, *The Assassin's Gate*, 194–195.
187. Bremer's surprise that Abizaid had "always" opposed CPA order 2 could not have been genuine: *My Year in Iraq*, 223–224. If McKiernan and Abizaid were consulted, it is hard to believe they did not express their private disagreement. According to Gordon and Trainor, *Cobra II*, 483–484, they considered the decision "an abrupt and unwelcome departure from their previous planning," as they should have, given how many soldiers they were going to lose because of it. On the other hand, the Joint Chiefs and the secretary of state were not consulted at all. The charge that U.S. soldiers were directly put at deadly risk was made by General Petraeus to Walter Slocombe, the architect of CPA order 2.
188. Such inclusive stress is present in Rumsfeld's directive for establishing a brand new force that would be "a model of ethnic cooperation." Such an idea was illusory, given a prior campaign against the Sunni military, who, having been made enemies, could not be included in the new ethnic mix. On the other hand, organized militias became almost impossible to keep out.
189. Bremer, *My Year in Iraq*, 55–56; Galbraith, *The End of Iraq*, 120–122.
190. The only cost Bremer was to take into account, only to dismiss it in an amazingly facile manner, was "administrative inconvenience" or "inefficiency." See Bremer, *My Year in Iraq*, 40, 45.
191. For the text, see Gordon and Trainor, *Cobra II*, 586.
192. Chandrasekaran, *Imperial Life in the Emerald City*, 76–77; Cockburn, *The Occupation*, 72.
193. Ricks, *Fiasco*, 191.
194. Forman, "Striking Out in Baghdad," 204.
195. The symbolic injury was multiplied in the eyes of Iraqi nationalists when, on Kurdish insistence, the old, pre-Baathist flag of Iraq was replaced. Cockburn, *The Occupation*, 145–146. It is noteworthy that the Kurds do not fly any Iraqi flag, old or new, in Kurdistan.
196. See Batatu, *The Old Social Classes and the Revolutionary Movement in Iraq*, 26, passim; Dodge, *Inventing Iraq*, 137ff., for the historical importance and signifi-

cance in Iraq of having a military in the face of a potentially colonial or semicolonial situation. For current interpretations in context of the dissolution of the army, see Packer, *The Assassin's Gate*, 195; Ricks, *Fiasco*, 163; Chandrasekaran, *Imperial Life in the Emerald City*, 76; and Cockburn, *The Occupation*, 72.

197. A. Cordesman and A. Hashim, *Iraq: Sanctions and Beyond* (Boulder, Colo.: Westview, 1997), 38–39.

198. Chandrasekaran, *Imperial Life in the Emerald City*, 69–73.

199. Ibid., 71–73; and Forman, "Striking Out in Baghdad," 205.

200. Cockburn, *The Occupation*, 71.

201. Packer, *The Assassin's Gate*, 193.

202. Ibid., 191, and see the interesting, detailed article by J. L. Anderson, "Letter From Iraq," *New Yorker* (November 15, 2004).

203. R. Chandrasekaran, "On Iraq, U.S. Turns to One-Time Dissenters," *Washington Post* (January 14, 2007).

204. Compare Woodward, *State of Denial*, 195, to Ricks, *Fiasco*, 162.

205. Ricks, *Fiasco*, 163–164; Chandrasekaran, *Imperial Life in the Emerald City*, 69ff.

206. Packer, *The Assassin's Gate*, 192.

207. Gordon and Trainor, *Cobra II*, 476.

208. Bremer, *My Year in Iraq*, 44.

209. Galbraith, *The End of Iraq*, 122–123.

210. I cannot here treat the very important area of privatization or its failure, which in conjunction with de-Baathification led to a disorganization of the state-owned sector. The legal arguments against are presented by G. Fox, "The Occupation of Iraq." The actual failed experiment is best described by Chandrasekaran, *Imperial Life in the Emerald City*, chaps. 6, 12. The consequences of these "experiments" for unemployment do not show up in the statistics on de-Baathification, although they are related.

211. Before Saddam's two wars, much more than that. See P. Marr, *The Modern History of Iraq* (Boulder, Colo.: Westview, 2004), 163–164; Chandrasekaran, *Imperial Life in the Emerald City*, 111.

212. According to the Iraq Study Group Report, Sunni neighborhoods in Baghdad received (in late 2006) two hours of electricity a day and no garbage collection at all. See 20ff. for a general breakdown of formerly state services.

213. Galbraith, *The End of Iraq*, 92–93; Cockburn, *The Occupation*, 44–48.

214. Marr, *The Modern History of Iraq*, 162–168; Chandrasekaran, *Imperial Life in the Emerald City*, 110–111.

215. According to the Iraqi Study Group Report.

216. Fox, "The Occupation of Iraq"; Chandrasekaran, *Imperial Life in the Emerald City*, 117–118.

217. Chandrasekaran, *Imperial Life in the Emerald City*, 111–119, 225–226.
218. Chandrasekaran, "On Iraq, U.S. Turns to One Time Dissidents."
219. Carre de Malberg, *Contribution à la theorie générale de l'etat*, 1:65–66.
220. See most recently Grimm, "The Constitution in the Process of Denationalization," *Constellations* 12, no. 4 (2005).
221. See A. V. Dicey, *The Law of the Constitution*, part 1, chap. 3, concerning the formation of federal states as the basis of the U.S. example, and Schmitt, *Verfassungslehre*, esp. the chapter on the "Bund."
222. See Fox, "The Occupation of Iraq," essay in note 17. He is very persuasive on this point.
223. Best documented by G. Fox, "The Occupation of Iraq," *Georgetown Journal of International Law* (April 2005).

2. Postsovereign Constitution Making: The New Paradigm (and Iraq)

1. A. Arato, "The Occupation of Iraq and the Difficult Transition from Dictatorship," *Constellations* 10, no. 1 (2003): 415ff, where I argue for the grafting of a "negotiated or coordinated transition onto the externally imposed revolutionary model." I was very skeptical that this could or would be done under a U.S. rather than an international authority. It was this article that led to my short and not very successful informal role as an advisor to the relevant UN personnel.
2. I documented this in "Sistani v. Bush: Constitutional Politics in Iraq," *Constellations* 11, no. 2 (2004). When it happened, after the making of the agreement of November 15, I mistakenly thought I personally had something to do with the adoption of the new model. This was because at a time when everyone, including Noah Feldman (then an advisor to the CPA on constitutional matters), was speaking and writing about various purely imposed and Bonapartist models, I told Feldman (in October 2003, after his NYU lecture) that an interim constitution could solve the conflict with Sistani. I still remember him saying that Sistani would never accept it, and this in the end did turn out to be right, even if it was not inevitable. But in any case I now think that the formula emerged from the conflict itself, and there are some not entirely clear pieces of evidence coming from journalists that the formula of an interim constitution had been previously discussed, though first rejected by Bremer. I will discuss this below.
3. I exaggerate, because the Shi'ite clerics of the IGC in the end signed the TAL, while Sistani, who was not at the table himself, rejected it. But it was his pressure that achieved the constitution-making format, and thus his rejection was

symbolically of central importance. The Shi'ite double move of rejecting and accepting the TAL was also not entirely unprecedented in this type of constitution making. All this I will try to show in chapter 4 below.

4. See my *Civil Society, Constitution, and Legitimacy* (Lanham, Md.: Rowman & Littlefield, 2000), chaps. 1, 5, and 7; "Constitutional Learning," *Theoria* (April 2005); and "Post Sovereign Constitution Making and Democratic Legitimacy" in a forthcoming (German) volume of essays in honor of Ulrich Preuss, who was first to theorize this new paradigm. See his book *Constitutional Revolution* (Atlantic Highlands, N.J.: Humanities Press, 1995 [originally published in 1990]) and "The Roundtable Talks in the German Democratic Republic," in J. Elster, ed., *The Roundtable Talks and the Breakdown of Communism* (Chicago: University of Chicago Press, 1996).
5. For the most dramatic study, see part 1 of E. Morgan, *Inventing the People* (New York: Norton, 1988).
6. In French type I, the assembly is sovereign and there is no ratification. In French type II, the assembly is still treated as sovereign, but there is a test of this sovereignty in a popular referendum. One may say that the people have two bodies in this second version. It is generally assumed that "We the people" in the American formula refers to the ratifying instance(s), though a possible interpretation of this model would be that *sovereignty* refers to no instance or organ of representation but acts through all of them. In the former case, the American model would be the obverse of French type I; in the second case, it would anticipate my postsovereign model.
7. Elster even comes to the conclusion that only one round table, that of the German Democratic Republic, discussed the substance of the constitution, a conclusion in dramatic variance with his own subsections on bargaining over the presidency and parliament, i.e., eminently constitutional matters. See his introduction to *The Roundtable Talks and the Breakdown of Communism*. Moreover, he is outright wrong with respect to Hungary, somehow misled by the unclear and inaccurate treatment in his edited volume by Andras Sajo ("Roundtable Talks in Hungary," 92–93), which suggests that only a degraded set of transitory measures, delegitimated by the referendum of November 1989, came out of the Hungarian round table. For a set of contrary views, see A. Bozóki, ed., *The Roundtable Talks of 1989: The Genesis of Hungarian Democracy* (Budapest: CEU Press, 1992); and A. Bozóki, G. Halmai, and Cs. Tordai, in A. Bozóki et al., eds., *A rendszerváltás forgatókönyve* (Budapest: Magvető and Uj Mandátum Presses, 1999 and 2000), vol. 7, *Alkotmányos forradalom. Tanulmányok.*
8. A. Arato and Z. Miklosi, "Constitution Making and Transitional Politics in Hungary," forthcoming in the U.S. Institute of Peace collective volume on constitution making.

9. Andrea Bonime-Blanc, *Spain's Transition to Democracy: The Politics of Constitution Making* (Boulder, Colo.: Westview, 1987).
10. W. Osiatynski, "The Roundtable Talks in Poland," in Elster, ed., *The Roundtable Talks and the Breakdown of Communism*, 57.
11. M. Calda, "The Roundtable Talks in Czechoslovakia," in Elster, ed., *The Roundtable Talks and the Breakdown of Communism.*
12. R. Kolarova and D. Dimitrov, "The Roundtable Talks in Bulgaria," in Elster, ed., *The Roundtable Talks and the Breakdown of Communism*; and R. Peeva, "The Bulgarian Roundtable Negotiations from a Comparative Point of View" in Hungarian (an English translation is available from author), in A. Bozóki et al., eds., *A rendszerváltás forgatókönyve*, vol. 7, *Alkotmányos forradalom. Tanulmányok.* Elster (4–5) well understands the specificities of the Czechoslovak, Bulgarian, and GDR round tables, even if he misunderstands the nature of the Hungarian one.
13. Arato, *Civil Society, Constitution, and Legitimacy*, chap. 6; and Arato and Miklosi, "Constitution Making and Transitional Politics in Hungary."
14. For Kelsen's famous distinction and definitions, see his *General Theory of State and Law* (Cambridge, Mass.: Harvard University Press: 1945), 124ff., 258ff. For Hart's refinement of a part of the argument, though with a very British neglect (here at least) of the problem of the formal, documentary constitution, see *The Concept of Law* (Oxford: Oxford University Press), chap. 5.
15. In Hungary and South Africa, massive amendments produced a new, interim constitution.
16. In Kelsen's material sense; see his *General Theory of State and Law*, 124ff., 258ff.
17. The American model anticipates this naturally, because during the process of constitution drafting all other powers are left intact, in their originally constitutionalist framework. But constitutional transformations of constitutional republics are rare, and it is not certain that the model is even practicable in transitions from dictatorships.
18. C. Schmitt, *Die Diktatur* (Berlin: Duncker & Humblot, 1922), chap. 4; *Verfassungslehre* (Berlin: Duncker & Humblot, 1928), 59–60.
19. Kelsen, *General Theory of State and Law*, 124.
20. As Kelsen would say, the interim constitution would then be one also in the formal sense.
21. See Liberation Government, Ordonnance no. 45–1836, August 17, 1945; available online at http://mjp.univ-perp.fr/france/co1944–5.htm; and Provisionary Government of the Republic, Loi consitutionnelle, November 2, 1945; available online at http://mjp.univ-perp.fr/france/co1945.htm.
22. Elected at the same vote as the referendum, in the case of a negative answer to the first question of the referendum, the assembly would have been an ordinary legislative body under the Third Republic.

23. The case is interesting, because it is demonstrable that de Gaulle deliberately fought for the second question and the positive response to it that yielded an eight-article interim constitution in order to inhibit the emergence of a sovereign revolutionary "convention government" having the plenitude of all powers even for a limited amount of time. It was innovative because here the interim constitution had been independently authorized by the same source as the new assembly, the popular vote. See M. Troper, F. Hamon, and G. Burdeau, *Droit constitutionnel* 25, 2nd ed. (Paris: LGDJ, 1997), 368–374; O. Duhamel, *Droit constitutionnel* (Paris: Seuil, 2000), 2:140–141; J. Godechot, ed., *Les constitutions de la France depuis 1789* (Paris: Flammarion, 1995), especially quoting de Gaulle's press conference with its three options, 358–359; and O. Beaud, *La puissance de l'état* (Paris: PUF, 1994), 272–276.
24. This was first noticed as far as I know by Beaud in *La puissance de l'état*, 269–272, but I think he sees more continuity between preconstituent decisions previously and this new instrument than I would.
25. As opposed to these examples, interim constitutions in the Middle East often signified illegitimate attempts to make supposedly temporary authoritarian and/or paper constitutions permanent or semipermanent through subterfuge, the last glaring example being the Iraqi interim constitution of 1970, which lasted, formally speaking though without much meaning, for thirty-four years, until the Americans overthrew Saddam. See N. J. Brown, *Constitutions in a Nonconstitutional World: Arab Basic Laws and the Prospects for Accountable Government* (Albany, N.Y.: SUNY Press, 2001), 70 (Syria), 79 (Egypt), 86–87 (Iraq). I am grateful to this author for this important, careful, and serious work, which I have greatly relied on.
26. This was formulated by the early writings of Sieyès and developed with some inconsistencies through the first two French constitutional assemblies of 1789–1791, 1792–1795, and most clearly that of 1848.
27. See Schmitt, *Die Diktatur* and *Verfassungslehre.*
28. Legal continuity did not exist in the case of France, because the overthrow of the Vichy government was "revolutionary" in the legal sense, and even the return to the Third Republic ("no" on the first referendum question) would have implied a revolutionary restoration.
29. Neither is inevitable in coordinated transitions: democratically inclined incumbents, as in Spain, can enact fully competitive interim rules; informal agreements may substitute for round tables as in Slovenia; and internal as well as external pressure can be used to enforce favorable legislation allowing democratic elections, as in the German Democratic Republic, where the round table designed a permanent constitution that was never enacted.
30. Arato and Miklosi, "Constitution Making and Transitional Politics in Hungary."

31. Kelsen, *General Theory of State and Law*, 124. With this idea, despite the aims of the pure theory of law, he came close to affirming the normative idea of "constitutionalism." Of course, the arbitrary changing of norms could itself be the *Grundnorm* of a material constitution, e.g., the *Fuehrerprinzip*.
32. If these arrangements are to work, they cannot be exposed to a generally flexible amendment rule. "Sunset" provisions are able to limit the longevity of mutual guarantees that are desirable only in the initial phase of the transition. During the operation of the interim constitution, actors in a divided society can learn to interact politically and to seek guarantees that are more compatible with majority rule and the freedom of the constitutional legislature, as in South Africa, where constitutionalism replaced consociationalism.
33. However, this is not a unique example. The enshrining of much prior legislation as two-thirds laws by the Hungarian interim constitution of 1989 was greatly mitigated in the constitutional pact of 1990, which reduced the number of such laws to a minimum. This can be chalked up either to the virtues of the two-stage process or to the amendability of the interim constitution, depending on how we interpret the 1990 pact.
34. Such an amendment process, however, should not contract the forms of legitimacy authorizing the interim constitution itself, as happened in Hungary when the old, not freely elected parliament reneged on some of the round-table agreements. See Arato and Miklosi, "Constitution Making and Transitional Politics in Hungary."
35. Indeed, the one great danger of interim constitutions even in nonauthoritarian settings is that they work too well and make themselves permanent not through the free choice of a democratic assembly but by dramatically interfering with that choice. "Rien ne dure que le provisoire!" it was said soon after the making of the emphatically provisional *Grundgesetz*, which is still, fifty-five years later, Germany's valid constitution. Even when there is no interference with the freedom of a future assembly, as in Hungary, the absence of any provisions (rules, incentives, disincentives) for making the permanent constitution can lead to the interim becoming permanent. See Arato, "Refurbishing the Legitimacy of the New Regime: Constitution-Making Endgame in Hungary and Poland," in *Civil Society, Constitution, and Legitimacy*, 199–228; and Arato and Miklosi, "Constitution Making and Transitional Politics in Hungary." Beyond its own amendment rule and sunset provisions, it is therefore extremely important for the interim constitution to regulate in a plausible way the timeframe and the procedures for making the permanent constitution.
36. C. Murray, "Participating in the Design," and C. Rickard, "Contested Citizenship in South Africa," in P. Andrews and S. Ellman, eds., *The Post-Apartheid Constitutions* (Athens: Ohio University Press, 2001).

37. The making of the Fifth Republic was a boundary case here, because the amendment rule of the Fourth Republic was first used to amend itself (a very questionable *révision de la révision*, after a formally similar move at the beginning of the Vichy Regime) before the new rule was used to inaugurate the Fifth.
38. Preuss, *Constitutional Revolution*, last chapter.
39. It is true that there was one important anticipation of the interim constitution within a classical democratic model, namely of the French type II utilized in 1945–1946, when a referendum was asked to approve a very short set of regulations (*La loi constitutionnelle du 2 Novembre 1945*), a *préconstitution* (or *la petite constitution*) that would minimally bind the constituent assembly and the provisional government to be elected during the same voting procedures. But neither the limited contents nor the extent of the limits on the constituent assembly make this important forerunner an actual example of the new model. The importance of a referendum authorizing the *préconstitution*, which in turn established another referendum to control the work of the assembly, suggests treating this case as a deviant or transitional one of sovereign constitution making. In contrast, the new model does not involve referenda, except in the deviant or pathological case of Iraq.
40. Linz and Stepan, *Problems of Democratic Transition and Consolidation*, chap. 6; and A. Bonime-Blanc, *Spain's Transition to Democracy*, represent alternative views, with the latter stressing informal consultation and dialogue leading to the Law of Reform.
41. Second version of his article, "Between Reform and Revolution" [B], in *East European Politics and Societies.*
42. For a systematic analysis, see Kis, "Between Reform and Revolution" [B], 347ff. Kis, however, shows that though both unelected, the legitimation resources of the Hungarian opposition and of Polish Solidarity were quite different. Also see L. Lengyel, "A kerekasztal hősei," 213; Halmai, "Az 1949es alkotmány jogállamositása," in A. Bozóki, ed., *A rendszerváltás forgatókönyve*. For the GDR, see Preuss, "The Roundtable of the GDR," 106–107. Studies of the South African transition, however, do not indicate that the main actors were overly concerned with the problem of legitimacy.
43. This could take the form of confirming a difficult amendment rule, which they use to amend the inherited constitution, a rule that would have been the easiest to change during the round table. At times this meant a permissive rule, as in Hungary, and at times the very opposite, as in Czechoslovakia.
44. For discussion, see A. Arato, "Forms of Constitution Making and Theories of Democracy," in *Civil Society, Constitution, and Legitimacy*, 229–256. For one such answer, see the now famous train of argument in Joseph Weiler's *Constitution of Europe* (Cambridge: Cambridge University Press, 1999), "Introduction:

'We will do, and hearken . . .'" which is admittedly much more sophisticated than arguments made for imposition elsewhere.

45. Jon Elster, "Constitutional Bootstrapping in Philadelphia and Paris," in Michael Rosenfeld, ed., *Constitutionalism, Identity, Difference, and Legitimacy: Theoretical Perspectives* (Durham, N.C.: Duke University Press, 1994), 102; and J. Elster, "Arguing and Bargaining in the Federal Convention and the Assemblée Constituante," in R. Malnes and A. Underdal, eds., *Rationality and Institutions* (Oslo: Universitetsforlaget, 1992).
46. In contrast to Elster, who was examining single-stage processes when coining the distinction, I treat electoral legitimacy at the beginning of the second stage as "midstream," while for him this would be "upstream" with respect to the central process. In countries with interim constitutions, at least recently, the forging of that constitution represents the beginning of the stream. As does Elster, I leave downstream legitimacy to final enactment and/or ratification processes, but I do not discuss this here, since it is irrelevant to interim constitutions in general.
47. D. Atkinson and S. Friedman, *Small Miracle* (Johannesburg, 1994); Andrews and Ellman, eds., *The Post-Apartheid Constitutions*; H. Ebrahim, *Soul of a Nation* (Oxford: Oxford University Press, 1998).
48. Ebrahim, *Soul of a Nation.*
49. Elster, "Arguing and Bargaining." I agree that the demand for publicity at all stages would be counterproductive, dangerous, and even impossible, yet it would stress the importance of public discussion at some key junctures.
50. In my view, this way of proceeding is actually a first step in building a genuine rule of law. See Arato, "Constitution and Continuity in the East European Transitions," in *Civil Society, Constitution, and Legitimacy*, 167–198.
51. In some Latin American countries (and it seems possibly in South Africa), the usage is being established to call such an assembly constitutional, rather than constituent, exercising a *pouvoir constituant derivée* rather than *originaire.* I rely on Renata Segura's excellent 2007 New School for Social Research dissertation on constitution making in Colombia and Ecuador for this point. This idea corresponds to an older notion of R. Carré de Malberg, according to which the amendment rule rather than revolutionary rupture should be the key to the concept of the *pouvoir constituant.*
52. This problem is now becoming serious in Nepal, where the elections to the Constitutional Assembly have been delayed, at the cost of an increasing legitimacy crisis.
53. Ebrahim, *Soul of a Nation*, 180.
54. Nor should some other historical parallels mislead us. It is true that the South African interim constitution's provision for electing a two-chambered legisla-

ture that would meet under one roof as the constitutional assembly was anticipated by the French Third Republic. But under that system, it was the amendment rule that involved this provision, while the national assembly that made the original constitutional laws of 1875 was unicameral, entirely unbound, and could not have formed a senate if it so desired. The South African constitutional assembly thus represented the new model with respect to all our older historical predecessors.

55. Sieyes, "What is the Third Estate?" in *Political Writings* (Indianapolis, Ind.: Hackett, 2003), 139.
56. R. Carré de Malberg, *Contribution à la theorie générale de l'etat* (Paris: Dalloz, 2004 [1920]), vol. 2, chap. 4, sect. 1–2; M. Hauriou, *Précis de droit constituionnel* (Paris: Recueil Sirey, 1923), 280–292.
57. Arato and Miklosi, "Constitution Making and Transitional Politics in Hungary."
58. An appointed legislature always creates problems because there is little justification for picking one set of representatives rather than another. In Nepal, a serious mistake was perhaps made when the elected legislature of 1999 restored in 2006 was not simply expanded with Maoist representatives. Instead, an entirely new interim legislature was appointed by party agreement. The exclusions involved were subsequently very difficult to defend.
59. G. Austin, *The Indian Constitution: The Cornerstone of a Nation* (Oxford: Oxford University Press, 1966).
60. C. Schmitt, *Verfassungslehre*; Beaud, *La puissance de l'état*, 359–371; Klein, *Theorie et pratique du pouvoir constituant* (Paris: PUF, 1996).
61. Calda, "The Roundtable in Czechoslovakia."
62. However, in Czechoslovakia a large number of co-opted members were added to the inherited Communist legislature, while in Nepal the new co-opted legislature contained many of the MPs carried over from the lower chamber reconstituted earlier. This may be a fundamental difference rather than a marginal one, as I first was tempted to believe.
63. Kis, "Between Reform and Revolution," [B] 317ff.
64. Arato and Miklosi, "Constitution Making and Transitional Politics in Hungary."
65. G. Austin, *Working a Democratic Constitution: A History of the Indian Experience* (Oxford: Oxford University Press, 1999), parts 2 and 3 (chap. 15).
66. Articles by Murray and Rickard in Andrews and Ellman, eds., *The Post-Apartheid Constitutions.*
67. In Germany, too, only amendments can be declared unconstitutional, although who knows what might have happened if the promise of a constitution upon unification had been taken up.
68. See Ebrahim, *Soul of a Nation*, and the articles by Murray and Rickard in Andrews and Ellman, eds., *The Post-Apartheid Constitutions.*

69. As to the intention, it is clear that the veto in question, invented by the Kurds, was intended as a Kurdish one. As to the result, while there was a desperate attempt in October 2005 to apply it as a Sunni veto, the two-thirds threshold could not be reached in the third of the required governorates. This is undoubtedly why a two-thirds threshold was used in the first place. A simple majority in each of three provinces would have had the same result for the Kurds but would have clearly involved a Sunni veto as well. See Article 61C of the Transitional Administrative Law.
70. That difference, based on demography and political control of the governorates, was blurred by the rule that was adopted (approved as long as two-thirds of the voters of any three governorates do not vote against), and in that sense the referendum came to serve the asymmetric and exclusionary model that I will detail below.
71. A. Arato, "Interim Imposition," *Ethics and International Affairs* 18, no. 3 (2004); and chapters 3 and 4 below.
72. See chapter 5, on the illegalities in the making of the final constitution.
73. See my "Constitutional Learning" in *Theoria.*
74. Atkinson and Friedman, *Small Miracle*; Andrews and Ellman, eds., *The Post-Apartheid Constitutions*; Ebrahim, *Soul of a Nation.*
75. There is a great deal of work available on the South African case: Atkinson and Friedman, *Small Miracle*; Ebrahim, *Soul of a Nation*; Andrews and Ellman, eds., *The Post-Apartheid Constitutions*; and M. Faure and J-E. Lane, *South Africa: Designing New Political Institutions* (London: Sage, 1996) is only a portion of what is available.
76. Kis, "Between Reform and Revolution" [B].
77. I myself have been a witness to repeated attempts by Adam Michnik and János Kis to learn about the Spanish transition in the late 1980s, as well as an extended visit by South African Constitutional Court members to Hungary in 1994 to learn about the jurisprudence of a very strong court in a democratic transition.
78. See Roberto Unger's elegant solution to an analogous problem, the origin of liberal institutions as a second-best outcome, in his *Law and Modern Society.*
79. See A. Przeworski, *Democracy and Market* (Cambridge: Cambridge University Press, 1990), whose analysis has influenced me in the present context, although I put much more emphasis on ideas and perceptions than he does.
80. For Spain, see Bonime-Blanc, *Spain's Transition to Democracy*; for Hungary, see Arato and Miklosi, "Constitution Making and Transitional Politics in Hungary"; for South Africa, see Ebrahim, *Soul of a Nation.*
81. See the great book by R. Barros, *Constitutionalism and Dictatorship: Pinochet, the Junta, and the 1980 Constitution* (Cambridge: Cambridge University Press, 2002).

82. Przeworski, *Democracy and Market*; Arato, *Civil Society, Constitution, and Legitimacy*, chap. 1.
83. This was true even in the case of the Soviet Union, which managed to retain its influence in democratic Finland for a very long time. But it is much more true for a democratic imperial power.
84. Bremer, *My Year in Iraq* (New York: Simon & Schuster, 2006), 213–214.
85. Suarez still used the argument, according to Linz and Stepan, that he had no one to negotiate with since only elections could produce a partner. This argument is completely fallacious, because it presupposes that he has legitimacy, which he did not, only the legality of the old regime. That marginal advantage certainly should not have led to preferring the imposition of rules of the game over negotiating them. Linz and Stepan, *Problems of Democratic Transition and Consolidation*, 94.
86. As we have seen in the previous chapter, and as others have amply documented, there was no unity in Washington. But the negotiations were farmed out to Bremer, and even when his initial plans were abandoned, this was done by pressuring him to come up with a new one and not by having independent agents bargain with the Iraqis.
87. When I first tried out the idea of an interim constitution on Noah Feldman, then still an expert advisor of the CPA, after his late October 2003 lecture at NYU School of Law, he was still advocating, as in a slightly earlier *New York Times* op-ed (September 24, 2003), that the IGC as it was then constituted should and could produce a final constitution that would be approved in a referendum without provoking Sistani's opposition. Subsequently, during a Columbia debate in the spring of 2004, he informed me that the idea of the interim constitution was earlier discussed among advisors to the CPA. This is now confirmed at least by Chandrasekaran, in *Imperial Life in the Emerald City* (New York: Knopf, 2006). There is no trace of the idea of "interim constitution" in Diamond's reconstruction until the November 15 Agreement. See *Squandered Victory: The American Occupation and the Bungled Effort to Bring Democracy to Iraq* (New York: Holt, 2005), 41–51, esp. 47, with Bremer's seven-step plan, 14, and 51. In Woodward, *State of Denial* (New York: Simon & Schuster, 2006), 264, the interim constitution appears only in a memo of November 4. Previously, all models presupposed the making of a permanent constitution by some kind of co-opted body or assembly and free elections only afterward. In the most aggressive version, it was frankly advocated that the United States could and should impose a new constitution on Iraq. See John Yoo's Senate testimony of 2003 on this subject, "Iraqi Reconstruction and the Law of Occupation." The crude errors of this conception in interpreting that law do not change the fact that it was hegemonic for a period where it counted. See Jean Cohen's article in this issue.

88. Some traces, like my proposals for a round table submitted through Jamal Benomar, curiously surface in some of the histories (Diamond, *Squandered Victory*, 253; Chandrasekaran, *Imperial Life in the Emerald City*, 207) like the hat of Clementis on Gottwald's head, once described by Milan Kundera. I feel lucky that they did not adopt something under this name, which I imported from central Europe, because a round table would have accomplished little as a mere mechanism of government selection. As for the interim constitution, the Americans were never going to allow its renegotiation at a new forum.
89. Kis, "Between Reform and Revolution" [B].
90. Arato, "The Occupation of Iraq."
91. There are two different matters and two senses of legitimacy here. As to population segments such as the Kurds, at issue is sociological legitimacy, in the sense of acceptance of American rule as valid or justified. International legitimacy, however, was provided in the strict legal sense by UN SC Res. 1483, which authorized the occupation regime. Of course old regimes in the model were internationally recognized, but that recognition was not a new one that would lend prestige, and in all the relevant cases they were also under strong international pressure to change.

3. Sistani Versus Bremer: The Emergence of the Two-Stage Model in Iraq

1. http://www.sistani.org/monasebat/messages/qanon-ara.htm. The translation is by my student Nida Alahmad. A different translation by Juan Cole refers to a constitutional "convention" instead of an "assembly," but he tells me that this choice was made only with regard to the American reader. The Alahmad translation indicates the deliberate choice of a European-type constituent body rather than a mere council.
2. Even if they were centrally important to some American ideological tendencies, that certainly did not dominate the CPA, as one can see from Bremer's memoirs. See N. Feldman, "Imposed Constitutionalism," *Connecticut Law Review* 37. Obviously, the issue of religion *was* important to the CPA, and on some points even here there was imposition. But in general it was understood that the United States would be playing with fire to no important national purpose if it tried to separate state and Islam in Iraq. Imposition need not be total to be imposition.
3. Or a liberal trumping of autonomy or participation in the name of equality or universal rights or whatever. On this position, one he eventually rejects, see Feldman, "Imposed Constitutionalism."

4. Bremer, *My Year in Iraq* (New York: Simon & Schuster, 2006), 213–214.
5. Chandrasekaran, *Imperial Life in the Emerald City* (New York: Knopf, 2006), 186.
6. Trudy Rubin mentions the cases of India, Germany, and Japan only to eliminate the relevance of all three. "Can U.S. Afford to Be Imperial?" in *Willful Blindness* (Philadelphia: The Philadelphia Enquirer, 2004). But India and Germany were even more irrelevant than Japan, the former because of its very long colonial timeframe, the latter because its political process was autonomous.
7. Bremer, *My Year in Iraq.*
8. Ibid., 94; and Woodward, *State of Denial* (New York: Simon & Schuster, 2006), 263. As to his famous role model: "[MacArthur] said that he had issued no orders or directives, and that he had limited himself merely to suggestions. . . . He stated that it was his belief, that it was his conviction, that a constitution, no matter how good, no matter how well written, forced upon the Japanese by bayonet would last just as long as bayonets were present, and he was certain that the moment force was withdrawn and the Japanese were left to their own devices they would get rid of that constitution." Recorded on January 29, 1946, by Nelson T. Johnson, Sec. Gen. of the Far East Commission. Cited by Koseki Shoichi in *The Birth of Japan's Postwar Constitution* (Boulder, Colo.: Westview, 1997), 75–76.
9. See J. Benomar, "Constitution-Making After Conflict: Lessons for Iraq," *Journal of Democracy* 15, no. 2 (2004): 92.
10. See Feldman, *What We Owe Iraq: War and the Ethics of Nation Building* (Princeton, N.J.: Princeton University Press, 2004), 40, with a different, supposedly official translation of the fatwa of Sistani on 140.
11. "We'll just get someone to write another fatwa," they believed, as Chandrasekaran was told later by a Bremer senior aide. Chandrasekaran, *Imperial Life in the Emerald City*, 80.
12. Chandrasekaran, *Imperial Life in the Emerald City*, 79, 163. I pay no attention to his switching to the American term "constitutional convention," when the British used "constituent assembly," and he himself still intended a "selected group," i.e., a conference, if these words have any meaning.
13. Marr, *The Modern History of Iraq* (Boulder, Colo.: Westview, 2004), 27–28, 31–32. There was a famous Shi'ite boycott of these elections, with very negative consequences for the sect and its clerical leaders, one that Sistani must have recalled as well. See Nakash, *The Shi'is of Iraq*, 2nd ed. (Princeton, N.J.: Princeton University Press, 2004), 79–84.
14. In fact, the sequence from Sistani's fatwa to Bremer's seven-point program is the same as the sequence from the process of making the 1793 constitution through a freely elected assembly that involved a popular referendum to the first Napoleonic plebiscite.

15. Statement of John Yoo: "Iraqi Reconstruction and the Law of Occupation: Hearing on Constitutionalism, Human Rights and the Rule of Law in Iraq before the Subcomm. On the Constitution, Subcomm. On the Judiciary," 108th Congress (2003).
16. Apparently, at least initially UN Special Representative Sergio de Mello told the Ayatollah Sistani that elections in Iraq could be held relatively quickly, and he only reversed himself under pressure from Bremer. See Bremer, *My Year in Iraq*, 94–95.
17. This is especially true because in Iraq there would not have been, American style, a separate legislative assembly. After 1780 in Massachusetts and 1787 in the rest of the country, we associate this double differentiation with the American model.
18. Arato, "Sistani v. Bush: Constitutional Politics in Iraq," *Constellations* 11, no. 2 (2004); V. Nasr, *The Shia Revival* (New York: Norton, 2006), 94–95; Feldman, *What We Owe Iraq*, 40. It is a little disingenuous to imply that Feldman himself would have advocated nothing but this ("any competent international lawyer") in light of his publicly arguing for the Bremer scenario: N. Feldman, "Democracy, Closer Every Day," *New York Times*, September 24, 2004. This was after the fatwa, not before! Anyway, why "international" rather than "constitutional" lawyer? Feldman himself is an expert in Islamic law but has also studied constitutional jurisprudence.
19. Nasr, *The Shia Revival*, 172–173.
20. S. Arjomand, *The Turban for the Crown* (New York: Oxford, 1988), refers to the body by the undoubtedly correct term, "National Consultative Assembly." In its selection process, it involved delegation by privileged orders of the realm along with ordinary elections. However, traditionally it seems that the term "constituent assembly" has become established for this body: Nakash, *The Shi'is of Iraq*, speaks of a Constituent National Assembly for 1906, whereas for Arjomand only the body elected in 1925, convoked by the Majles, which established the Pahlavi dynasty was *the* Constituent Assembly. However, under the authoritarian leadership of a military officer, that process is not one that the Shi'a look back on with interest.
21. Y. Nakash, *Reaching for Power: The Shi'a in the Modern Arab World* (Princeton, N.J.: Princeton University Press, 2006), 8–9.
22. Nakash, *The Shi'is of Iraq*, 79ff. Bremer was to taunt Shi'ite leaders with this experience, according to his recollections. Bremer, *My Year in Iraq*, 202.
23. For these reasons too it makes little sense to argue as does Feldman that the view articulated by Sistani concerning elected constitutional assemblies simply expressed the common sense of international lawyers. The point was not that an elected constitutional assembly was to have the main role, but under what conditions it was to have that role.

24. It is simply incorrect to say that he has won every battle with the American CPA, as does Galbraith, in *The End of Iraq* (New York: Simon and Schuster, 2006), 137. It is specifically false that Bremer accepted the idea of an elected constituent assembly by the summer of 2003. But Sistani lost the fight concerning the TAL being written by the CPA and the IGC without any ratification by an elected assembly. He certainly did not get his choice on the leadership of the interim executive either. However, it is certainly true that he won the ideological battle, the battle about democratic legitimacy, and that on the whole he made the CPA look weak.
25. UN officials were exempted from the ban and thus it is not so that the ban on meeting Americans was a general one due to political quietism. Galbraith, *The End of Iraq*, 37.
26. R. Chandrasekaran, "How Cleric Trumped U.S. Plan for Iraq," *Washington Post Foreign Service*, November 26, 2003; Nasr, *The Shia Revival*, 175.
27. Nakash, *Reaching for Power*, 9–10.
28. Bremer, *My Year in Iraq*, 100–102.
29. See ibid., 93–99; Sergio de Mello's only success according to Jamal Benomar, who was then with him in Baghdad, was to add the Communists. De Mello's greatest failure was to fail to get representation for Arab nationalists (personal interview with Benomar). Bremer's story on the Communists is slightly different (*My Year in Iraq*, 95), but it could have been de Mello working through the British.
30. Chandrasekaran, *Imperial Life in the Emerald City*, 196.
31. J. Benomar, "Iraq's Constitution Making Process: A Framework Proposal." According to Bremer, finding Sunni leaders was difficult because "Saddam had either co-opted or killed most of them" (*My Year in Iraq*, 189) or because they were trying to shoot their way into power (277). Both arguments were incredibly spurious. If they were co-opted, they could be co-opted again. But many of the Ba'athists were in fact long excluded by Saddam. If they were (some of them) now shooting, this is what all the other participants of the IGC had done previously as well.
32. Chandrasekaran, *Imperial Life in the Emerald City*, 196.
33. Ibid., 129.
34. Ibid., 187.
35. Bremer, *My Year in Iraq*, 97–98.
36. Bremer, *My Year in Iraq*, 164; Chandrasekaran, *Imperial Life in the Emerald City*, 187.
37. Bremer, *My Year in Iraq*, 211. The claim seems to be true at least for the Kurdish chair, Fuad Masoum. See T. Rubin, "Democratizing Iraq Will Get the Troops Home," in *Willful Blindness*.

38. Chandrasekaran, *Imperial Life in the Emerald City*, 187–188.
39. Bremer, *My Year in Iraq*, 190.
40. Chandrasekaran, *Imperial Life in the Emerald City*, 192–193. Bremer himself seems to represent the initiative to abandon the earlier plan as having come from him to counter Pentagon plans and to deal with Sistani. But he notes some impatience in Washington. *My Year in Iraq*, 188–189.
41. According to Chandrasekaran, *Imperial Life in the Emerald City*, 197, these plans were first formulated in the middle of October 2003, when Bremer rejected them. In Woodward's presentation (*State of Denial*, 264), the new plan involving an interim constitution first appears however only in a November 4 memo.
42. Bremer, *My Year in Iraq*, 212, 215.
43. Ibid., 213.
44. This is an exact reproduction of the agreement, in its original formatting, as it was first posted on the CPA's Web site (http://www.cpa-iraq.org/audio/20031115_Nov-15-GC-CPA-Final_Agreement-post.htm). Subsequently it was replaced by an altered version, using at the very least a different terminology (http://www.iraqcoalition.org/government/AgreementNov15.pdf). Note that the formula for federal arrangements has apparently shifted between the two versions (probably because of Kurdish protests).
45. Bremer, *My Year in Iraq*, 216, 214.
46. Bremer, *My Year in Iraq*, 218, 228–229; Woodward, *State of Denial*, 264. Note, however, that it is clear from Bremer's report (229) that the version Sistani approved involved direct elections for a transitional legislature, a version dropped immediately after his approval. Also, we cannot tell how clearly he was informed that the fundamental law or the TAL would be drawn up by the IGC under the CPA, or how constitutional it would be in nature. These were the two points he was to address in his next fatwa of November 26, denouncing the agreement.
47. Bremer, *My Year in Iraq*, 215–216, 217–218, 225; Chandrasekaran, *Imperial Life in the Emerald City*, 198–199.
48. Bremer, *My Year in Iraq*, 218, 229–230.
49. Chandrasekaran, *Imperial Life in the Emerald City*, 199–200.
50. See again Bremer, *My Year in Iraq*, 225, for its silence on this score.
51. Ibid., 229. In Washington, only R. Blackwill had doubts about the caucuses, and he was overruled. Chandrasekaran, *Imperial Life in the Emerald City*, 200. That part of the session apparently appealed to Bremer, and it was probably then that he became attached to the caucuses.
52. Chandrasekaran, *Imperial Life in the Emerald City*, 200–201; Bremer, *My Year in Iraq*, 229–231.

53. All frankly documented by Bremer, *My Year in Iraq*, 230–231, amazingly enough.
54. Ibid., 214.
55. http://www.juancole.com.
56. See the UN report "The Political Transition in Iraq: Report of the Fact-Finding Mission" (February 6–13, 2004), 5; J. Benomar, "Constitution-Making After Conflict: Lessons for Iraq," 93. Benomar is obviously also the author of the report.
57. For the version deemed appropriate to the conditions of mid-January and that refers to the TAL, see http://www.iraqcoalition.org/government/AgreementNov15.pdf.
58. For the purposes of this chapter only, I refer to a January draft of this interim constitution called "Law of Administering the Iraqi State for the Transitional Period" (hereafter, "January Draft"). The original was published in Arabic in the Kuwaiti daily *al-Qabas*. The translation is by Nathan J. Brown, who supplies intelligent commentary as well.
59. The TAL was to get no amendment rule until the election of the constitutional assembly, a very strict one that was used just once, at the very end of the constitutional assembly.
60. The "January Draft" repeats this formulation but adds: "This security agreement shall be presented to the Transitional National Assembly for approval in the month of June 2004."
61. "The Political Transition in Iraq: Report of the Fact-Finding Mission," 6.
62. According to the November 15 Agreement, the Fundamental Law would have been entirely unamendable, a peculiarity critically observed in the UN fact-finding report. See ibid., 5.
63. "January Draft," Article 2. Along with Nathan Brown, I find this provision odd, and not only in terms of Iraqi history. It was probably motivated by the desire to avoid constitutional tinkering by the transitional legislature. But the consequence could easily have been the rejection of the interim set up as a whole if it ceased to function or if the transitional assembly wished to assert its supposed sovereignty.
64. Note that in press reports the issue of who was to give Iraq its permanent constitution was continually confused. If the transitional assembly claimed a right to do so, few in America would have noticed the act of usurpation—unless they were ready to take Sistani's word for it.
65. See A. Arato, "Forms of Constitution Making and Democratic Theory," in *Civil Society, Constitution, and Legitimacy* (Lanham, Md.: Rowman & Littlefield, 2000).
66. The January Draft or at least the literal Brown translation speaks only of a "constitutional *conference*" producing the permanent constitution (Article 42).

This implies a further devaluation of the freely elected body. I keep asking: did they really believe that Sistani and his advisors would not notice what they were doing?

67. "Sovereign," that is, if we forget about the continued and nonaccountable possession of the most significant means of violence by the American military forces. I was not the only person reading the November 15 Agreement this way. See the UN Report, "The Political Transition in Iraq: Report of the Fact-Finding Mission," 6, 16. And if Benomar read it this way, there is a strong likelihood that Sistani too read it this way. I admit that the TAL could have made the terms of the two legislatures consecutive rather than partially simultaneous, had the Transitional National Assembly actually been set up. From Sistani's point of view, it was better not to have the unelected assembly at all.
68. "The Political Transition in Iraq: Report of the Fact-Finding Mission," 6, par. 19.
69. The three dates signify three periods of dual power or at least legitimacy: the Soviets and the provisional government in 1917; the constituent assembly and the Bolshevik government in 1918; and parliament and the presidency, each in charge of a constitution-making effort, in 1993. In each case, armed force decided the issue.
70. See Ackerman, *We the People II* (Cambridge, Mass.: Harvard University Press, 1998), for the debate even there.
71. Ultimately that is what counts. Thoughtful observers (Jamal Benomar, Juan Cole) point to divisions among the clerics and the presence of many secular Shi'ites, which could make the assumptions of the electoral strength of Sistani's faction illusory. Personally, I bet on Shi'a unity in the founding election at least, reinforced by Sistani's success in taking on the national mantle in opposing American imposition.
72. Reul Marc Gerecht, "The Sabotage of Democracy," *New York Times*, November 14, 2003.
73. "The Political Transition in Iraq: Report of the Fact-Finding Mission," 5.
74. I have analyzed this paradox in detail in "Interim Imposition," *Ethics and International Affairs* 18, no. 3 (2004), and I will do so again here.
75. Galbraith, *The End of Iraq*, 138. Actually, the term interim constitution came first, and it was disguised first by "fundamental law" and then by "transitional administrative law." The option that could have perhaps avoided the trouble was never even considered. Contrary to Galbraith, I think the TAL's intent was to preempt constitutional assembly more on Kurdish than "on American terms," as its ratification provision *made in Erbil* indicates. This was an originally unintended consequence, however, and I will discuss it in the next chapter.
76. See Arato, "Forms of Constitution Making and Democratic Theory."

77. A democratic outcome in a predemocratic setting generally involves most actors opting for a solution that may only be their second-best preference. This is possible only if the negotiating framework and implied sanctions for failure make the first-best outcome, usually a nondemocratic or purely majoritarian democratic one, impossible. When a party attains a majority in a majoritarian assembly, it no longer has to accept the second-best outcome. I thank Julian Arato for reminding me of this notion in the present context.
78. Evidently some political parties or groupings would use their participation in any comprehensive process to try to bring it down and make an agreement impossible. The theoretical rule for admission ought to be acceptance of a pluralistic, constitutional democracy as the second-best solution. Practically, this demand is difficult to test. One way of doing so may be to insist that participating groups, hopefully coalitions if there are not too many members, publish their full political platforms in advance.
79. See Benomar, "Constitution-Making After Conflict: Lessons for Iraq," 92.
80. "The Political Transition in Iraq: Report of the Fact-Finding Mission," 6.
81. The "January Draft" alters these arrangements in only one crucial respect: the cumbersome three-stage process is reduced to something closer to a two-stage one. The organizing committee in each province would still pick the province's representatives, proportionally allocated, from notables, by a vote of eleven out of fifteen (Articles 21 and 22). There is still something resembling a notable assembly, namely the Governorate Selection Caucus in each province, now called electoral assemblies (Article 27). But now there is no implication of the caucuses deliberating and *nominating*, as in the slightly more democratic formula of the November 15 Agreement, which spoke of "a transparent, participatory, democratic process of caucuses" (heading 3). Astonishingly, the response to Sistani's democratic demands was to make the proposals even less democratic!
82. The exclusion is more specific in the "January Draft." Aside from having to be over thirty years old and holding a degree, candidates to the Transitional Assembly cannot have belonged "to the dissolved Ba'ath Party or be affiliated with the agencies of repression or have contributed to the oppression of citizens" (Article 23). Enforcement and appeals are placed squarely in the hands of each organizing committee "in cooperation with the CPA." The procedure is clearly meant to exclude all those already excluded from the process, including members of the new Arab Nationalist Parties and the Sunni council, who may have previously been in the Ba'ath. The now irrelevant idea of monitoring by courts and UN agencies, which may have been relevant for more autonomous caucuses, is added but qualified by the nonsensical phrase "if feasible."

83. Article 32 of the "January Draft" explicitly postulates the end of both the CPA and the IGC with the formation of the Transitional Executive based in the Transitional Legislature.
84. See articles and census design in the *New York Times*, December 3 and 4, 2003.
85. Bremer, *My Year in Iraq*, 242.
86. Chandrasekaran, *Imperial Life in the Emerald City*, puts a more liberal cast on all this: "popularly elected Iraqis might not produce a document that endorsed a separation of mosque and state, provided equal rights for women, or enshrined any of the other elements sought by the White House." This too was playing a role, out of authentic or public-relations considerations. In either case, the argument was deeply undemocratic, quite obviously. For a thorough critique of someone sympathetic to the argument, see Feldman, "Imposed Constitutionalism." I buy less than he the idea that such considerations were always authentically represented.
87. See A. Przeworski, *Democracy and the Market* (Cambridge: Cambridge University Press, 1991).
88. See remarks by Lakhdar Brahimi in Carol Giacomo, "U.N. Envoy Warns Against Premature Polls in Iraq," Reuters, January 27, 2004: "elections are a very divisive process. They create tensions. They create competition. And in a country not stable enough to take that . . . one has to be certain it will not do more harm than good."
89. Benomar, "Iraq's Constitution Making Process": "Elections for constituent assemblies often legitimize the domination of the process by electoral victors. The winners consider their electoral victory a mandate for exerting decisive influence over the constitution and eschew negotiations with other actors on constitutional principles. The longevity and legitimacy of constitutions is thereby compromised, because they do not represent a societal consensus over the future of the state . . . premature elections for any type of representative body must be avoided."
90. Delays in the implementation of the November 15 timetable inevitably meant delaying the agreement on security. Commander of the American forces General Abizaid no longer expected such an agreement by July 1 (actually, the deadline for this part of the timetable was supposed to be the end of March 2004). According to the general, until there is an agreement, the U.S. military's role would continue "as an evolution of the current track that we're on." *New York Times*, January 30, 2004.
91. Chandrasekaran, *Imperial Life in the Emerald City*, 204–205.
92. Bremer, *My Year in Iraq*, 239–240.
93. Ibid., 214, 213.

94. This was widely recognized among the more cynical members of the IGC: The sarcastic remarks of al-Rubiae of the Dawa party, now close to Sistani, clearly point to the newfound opportunity: "Some Iraqis perceive the process as being too rushed to fit the American presidential elections. We don't mind helping our partners. We understand their requirements. And we will consider helping them." Ahmed Chalabi was even more blunt, openly saying that the scenario envisaged by the November 15 Agreement was tailor-made for Bush's reelection. "The whole thing was set up so President Bush could come to the airport in October for a ceremony congratulating the new Iraqi government. When you work backwards from that, you understand the dates the Americans were insisting on." Joel Brinkley and Ian Fisher, "U.S. Plan in Iraq to Shift Control Hits Major Snag," *New York Times*, November 27, 2003.
95. For an early view of UN staff concerning the process in Iraq, see Diamond, *Squandered Victory: The American Occupation and the Bungled Effort to Bring Democracy to Iraq* (New York: Holt, 2005), chap. 3. He is right to concentrate on Benomar, who was not only the constitutional expert of the several UN missions to Iraq but also a top advisor first to de Mello and then to Brahimi. He was L. Brahimi's chief of staff on the missions to Iraq.
96. This was at first pointed out also by Diamond, *Squandered Victory*, 62, who claims that in a memo to Secretary Rice he had included both the desiderata of making the creation of the TAL more participatory and that of giving the UN mission a role in it. These were the considerations stressed in my conversations with Benomar, the future chief of staff of the Brahimi mission. Strangely, Diamond forgets these requirements when he describes the actual making of the TAL, in which he participated. The basic issue was that many fundamental issues had already been negotiated by the time the Brahimi mission even showed up in Iraq.
97. Indeed, during the first meeting with Sistani, Brahimi apparently discussed the final compromise formula without even raising the question of the making of the TAL. See Diamond, *Squandered Victory*, 137–138. The omission was to make the compromise break down in the end.
98. See Benomar, "Constitution-Making After Conflict: Lessons for Iraq," 92–93. Benomar's short critique of these instruments is still one of the best.
99. Ibid., 93.
100. Ibid., 92.
101. "The Political Transition in Iraq: Report of the Fact-Finding Mission," 7, par. 21; Chandrasekaran, *Imperial Life in the Emerald City*, 206.
102. "The Political Transition in Iraq: Report of the Fact-Finding Mission," par. 23–24.

103. Ibid., par. 26–28.
104. Chandrasekaran, *Imperial Life in the Emerald City*, 207; Diamond, *Squandered Victory*, 253–254.
105. Chandrasekaran, *Imperial Life in the Emerald City*, 207.
106. Benomar, "Constitution-Making After Conflict: Lessons for Iraq," 93.
107. Paine, "Of Constitutions," in *The Rights of Man*.
108. Some people insist on misunderstanding me all the same. See, e.g., the last chapter of *Civil Society, Constitution, and Legitimacy*, "Constitutional Learning," and "Sistani v. Bush."
109. Schmitt, *Die Diktatur* (Berlin: Duncker & Humblot, 1922), chap. 4; Schmitt, *Verfassungslehre* (Berlin: Duncker & Humblot, 1928), 59.
110. Arato, "Good-Bye to Dictatorships?"
111. Evidently, his theory was democratic populist. But he also stood on the ground of the interest of the majority and was not thinking in terms of formulas of reconciliation and substantive compromise.

4. Imposition and Bargaining in the Making of the Interim Constitution

1. The title of this chapter freely adapts a couplet used by Jon Elster, "Arguing and Bargaining in Two Constituent Assemblies," *University of Pennsylvania Journal of Constitutional Law* 2 (2000): 345. See also Paul Magnette, "La convention européenne: argumenter et négocier dans une assemblée constituante multinationale," *Revue Française de Science Politique* 54, no. 1 (2004/2).
2. A. Arato, "Interim Imposition," *Ethics and International Affairs* 18, no. 3 (2004); see the discussion "Imposed Constitutionalism," with N. Feldman's lead article in *University of Connecticut Law Review* 37. To be sure, "imposed constitutional*ism*" is merely wishful thinking. There is no constitutionalism either in a more or a less demanding sense in Iraq. But there is now the second constitution in place. The first was ultimately, and in many of its details, imposed, and it was the highly constricting framework within which the second was made. See P. Dann and Z. Al-Ali, "The Internationalized *Pouvoir Constitutant*—Constitution-Making Under External Influence in Iraq, Sudan, and East Timor," *Max Planck Yearbook of United Nations Law* 10 (2006).
3. M. Weber, *Economy and Society* (Berkeley: University of California Press, 1978), 1:50–51, where Weber explicitly discusses constitutional order in the sociological sense.
4. J. Habermas, *Between Facts and Norms* (Cambridge, Mass.: The MIT Press, 1996), 165–168. I stay close to Habermas in stressing the need for both persua-

sion and compromise, and his notion of unfair bargaining comes close to the notion of imposition here, but I prefer to distinguish the two ideas even more clearly. For my purposes, there is no need to distinguish ethical and moral bases of coming to an agreement.

5. But for a rare attempt outside those venues, see K. Makiya, "A Model for Post-Saddam Iraq," *Journal of Democracy* 14, no. 3 (July 2003).
6. J. Rawls, *Political Liberalism* (New York: Columbia University Press, 1993); Habermas, *Between Facts and Norms.*
7. Bremer, *My Year in Iraq* (New York: Simon & Schuster, 2006), 269, 293; Crisis Group, "Iraq's Transition: On a Knife Edge" (April 27, 2004). It is certainly wrong to say that this body "drafted the TAL in January–March 2004," especially given the Crisis Group's own description: "it functions by open invitation and virtually everyone turns up: a majority of the members of the IGC or their designated representatives."
8. It is available in Professor Nathan Brown's translation, along with his short commentary, at http://www.geocities.com/nathanbrown1/taldraftjan2004.html; L. Diamond, *Squandered Victory: The American Occupation and the Bungled Effort to Bring Democracy to Iraq* (New York: Holt, 2005), 140ff.; D. Phillips, *Losing Iraq: Inside the Postwar Reconstruction Fiasco* (Boulder, Colo.: Westview, 2005), 185.
9. See Crisis Group, "Iraq's Kurds," 3.
10. Bremer, *My Year in Iraq*, 292.
11. Crisis Group, "Iraq's Transition: On a Knife Edge."
12. I am not entirely convinced concerning Sistani's overly great interest in religious issues playing a major role in constitutions, but all the sources indicate (usually on the basis of mere assumptions) that he was. We have no fatwa that concentrates on this problem.
13. "The TAL was mostly written by U.S. Government Lawyers and political appointees." P. Galbraith, *The End of Iraq* (New York: Simon and Schuster, 2006), 139; "The TAL was largely the responsibility of two of Bremer's assistants (dubbed 'the west wingers'), one an extremely capable but relatively junior Foreign Service officer and the other a young political appointee from the Pentagon's stable of neoconservative nation-builders. Imbued with grand ideas such as remaking the Iraqi judiciary with a U.S.-style Supreme Court, they apparently neglected to consult an international lawyer." P. Galbraith, "Iraq: The Bungled Transition," *New York Review of Books*, August 25, 2004. Actually, Roman Martinez, the neoconservative, was opposed to setting up a U.S.-style Supreme Court.
14. Phillips, *Losing Iraq*; Diamond, *Squandered Victory*, 142–144.
15. Nevertheless, they should be distinguished, because one was an Iraqi committee and the other basically an American one, as it is clear from the description

of Ali A. Allawi, even though he and his nomenclature unfortunately do not clearly differentiate between the two entities. See A. Allawi, *The Occupation of Iraq: Winning the War, Losing the Peace* (New Haven, Conn.: Yale University Press, 2007). I have not had a chance to consult this important book, the first by an Iraqi on the occupation, before completing the penultimate draft of this chapter. But I found his work important enough to go back and indicate some places where he confirms my departures from previous interpreters, as well as a few points where he and I disagree. Admittedly, he is an insider and knows much more about the politics and culture of Iraq than I do. But he is not a constitutional or electoral expert, and he occasionally does not properly evaluate institutional choices in these areas. More importantly, he is a partisan, if a muted one, of a moderate religious Shi'ite perspective, and this colors some of his interpretations in a particular way, as I will try to indicate. This is not to say that he is uncritical of the religious Shi'ites. Far from it.

16. R. Chandrasekaran, *Imperial Life in the Emerald City* (New York: Knopf, 2006), 241, supports this description.
17. Nor an international one, according to Galbraith, *The End of Iraq*, but Chandrasekaran says S. Chalabi was an international lawyer (*Imperial Life in the Emerald City*, 241).
18. Diamond himself is a specialist in institutionalist design, but as I know from experience, the relevance of that knowledge does not make up for a lack of legal skills. As to Istrabadi's knowledge of comparative constitutionalism, his experience seems to be restricted to memories of the making of Iraq's first constitution and law-school knowledge of the problems of the Philadelphia Convention. Many of his comparative views are thus bizarre, though I do not exclude that as a working lawyer in the process he could not and did not have excellent ideas. We have Diamond's testimony that he did. For his published views, see F. Istrabadi, "Reviving Constitutionalism in Iraq: Key Provisions of the Transitional Administrative Law," in *New York Law School Law Review* 50 (2005–2006), where, for example, he defends the extremely difficult amendment rule of the TAL by saying that all constitutions have difficult amendment rules (300). Meanwhile, he omits a serious discussion altogether of the ratification rule or of the strange system of presidential veto in the document. Perhaps this product is unrepresentative because he was ambassador to the United Nations at the time, defending provisions that he may not have initially supported.
19. Chandrasekaran, *Imperial Life in the Emerald City*, 244ff.
20. Chandrasekaran admits that what he calls the Istrabadi-Chalabi draft did not address several of the most contentious issues among Iraqis, which is right, leaving them to be hashed out among council members, which is quite wrong

regarding "the status of the Kurdistan Region," as his subsequent presentation in fact shows. Ibid., 242–243.

21. This interpretation is now fully confirmed by Allawi, *The Occupation of Iraq*, 221–222, who relies on interviews with S. Chalabi.
22. Ibid., 243; Diamond, *Squandered Victory*, 141, 163.
23. Bremer, *My Year in Iraq*, 269. Without knowing these lines or his memoirs, I analyzed the making of the TAL in just these two tracks, state making and regime creation, in my forthcoming article "From Interim to 'Permanent' Constitution in Iraq." See also S. Choudhry, who speaks about constitutive and normal constitutional politics to highlight the same contrast: "Old Imperial Dilemmas and the New Nation-Building: Constitutive Constitutional Politics in Multinational Polities," *Connecticut Law Review* 37 (2005): 938.
24. Diamond, *Squandered Victory*, 162; Galbraith, *The End of Iraq*, 167. Allawi, *The Occupation of Iraq*, 221, states that Bremer himself went to Kurdistan three times.
25. Bremer, *My Year in Iraq*, 296ff.
26. Diamond, *Squandered Victory*, 171, 172; Allawi's judgment on the Shi'a House's role in the making of the TAL is devastating. According to him they produced no drafts and were uninvolved in part by their own choice until February. But they kept assuring Sistani they had everything under control. Allawi, *The Occupation of Iraq*, 221–222. According to his reliable views, Sistani considered the Shi'a caucus to have bungled the process of managing the TAL (223). Indirectly, Allawi seems to blame Adel Abdul Mahdi, the leader and organizer of the Shi'a House (205) who seems to have persuaded his colleagues not to present their own draft of an interim constitution (221). He does not say, as he did later, that Mahdi represented already a pro-Kurdish opinion among the Shi'a.
27. Galbraith, *The End of Iraq*, 163, writes quite persuasively why the leader should not directly participate in negotiations. The leader has a strong tendency to say "yea" while a good negotiator should enjoy saying "no." In one context, this was an implied criticism of Talabani and Barzani. But it also applies to Bremer, who was a very poor negotiator, being either totally inflexible or prone to giving in to the other side in an unexpected and uncoerced manner.
28. Phillips, *Losing Iraq*, 187.
29. Diamond, *Squandered Victory*, 78, 162.
30. While I often disagree with the choices and conclusions of the latter, I am of course highly impressed by their professional talents and the depth of their political commitments. Aside from Galbraith's already cited works, see B. O'Leary et al., *The Future of Kurdistan in Iraq* (Philadelphia: University of Pennsylvania Press, 2005). I note that Galbraith learned his negotiating skills with Richard Holbrook in the Bosnian conflict (not that Dayton was such a

success—quite on the contrary), and O'Leary was highly expert in consociational forms of government and gathered around himself several specialists in comparative federalism.

31. This is clearly what happened, with the Governance Team at first being kept in the dark with respect to the Kurdish-American bargain and then expected simply to codify its results. Allawi, *The Occupation of Iraq*, 221–222.
32. Galbraith, *The End of Iraq*, 160–161. Cf. Zebari's speech in Crisis Group, "Iraq's Constitutional Challenge," November, 13, 2003, revealing still an attitude that searches for devolution and autonomy.
33. "Iraqi Kurdish Claim for Federalism. A Kurdish-Arab Partnership," originally in Arabic in Al-Ta'akhi, December 21, 2003. Available in English from http://www.KurdistanObserver.com.
34. Bremer, *My Year in Iraq*, 269; Diamond, *Squandered Victory*, 161.
35. Of course, Pachachi must have hoped both that representatives of the world's one superpower could have bent to their will a landlocked, dependent people of five million with many enemies and that American interests in Iraq and the region required that this happen. He was entirely right, and we still must explain the astonishing weakness of the CPA vis-à-vis the Kurds, regardless of the sophisticated experts and clever strategy of the latter. Given Sistani's challenge, the Sunni insurgency, the declining support for the occupation among Arabs, and the unfeasibility and unpopularity of military action even as a threat (since the Kurds could publicize such a threat), there was little the United States could immediately do to force the Kurds to quickly abandon basic positions. So, for example, when orders came from Washington that the Kurds had to give up their Kurdistan Regional Government, they could refuse and use the opportunity to renegotiate an earlier package they may have mistakenly agreed to. All the same, continuing to negotiate in the selfsame situation was a losing proposition for the CPA. They should have called the negotiations off and called the Kurds' bluff: try to secede. We are going ahead with reorganizing Iraq with or without you.
36. Crisis Group, "Toward a Historic Compromise?" 3; Bremer, *My Year in Iraq*, 271.
37. On this point I learned much from my son Julian Arato, who has completed a history BA thesis on the French adventure in Belgium in 1792–1793, under the title "L'exportation de la liberté." As his argument shows, the most fundamental point around which Belgian "statists" and "democrats" could not agree were the institutions of constitutional compromise that would negotiate a constitution. The available answers "estates general" or "national convention" already presupposed the substantive answers of constitutions that fundamentally divided the sides. This issue, substituting Kurds and Arabs or binationalists and civic nationalists for the Belgian sides, is even prior I think to Chaudhry's

fundamental and related inquiry about amendment rules. The answer must be, in the words of a Crisis Group paper, a negotiation format evolving "from full deliberations of Iraqi actors" and one that cannot be imposed by the Kurds, the Arabs, or the Americans. "Iraq's Constitutional Challenge," 13. But what if just such a deliberation were treated as an imposition by the Kurds? While not entirely untrue, that suggestion should have been rejected, nevertheless. It would have been legitimate imposition.

38. Diamond, *Squandered Victory*, 138, is clearly wrong regarding the Kurds.
39. Crisis Group, "Toward a Historic Compromise?" 1–2. O'Leary and K. Salih are in error when they suggest that only the original Arabic text of the November 15 Agreement contained the passages Talabani's critics later objected to ("The Denial, Resurrection, and Affirmation of Kurdistan," in *The Future of Kurdistan*, 30–31). The original English had the same passages (see chapter 3 above), and O'Leary and Salih are misled by the CPA's subsequently publishing a summary version on its Web site.
40. Crisis Group, "Iraq's Constitutional Challenge," November 13, 2003, 15ff.
41. But see Diamond, *Squandered Victory*, 173 and elsewhere, supporting the case for Sunni weakness and exclusion.
42. As William Patterson asked in Philadelphia: "If a proportional representation were right, why do we not so vote here?" In J. Madison, *Notes of the Debates of the Federal Convention* (New York: Norton, 1987), 123.
43. There is an echo of this in Diamond, *Squandered Victory*, 60–61, though he is dealing with an international-law issue, namely the illegality of an occupying power transforming the internal territorial state structure during an occupation.
44. To be sure, this was only after the agreement on amendment and ratification rules for the TAL, which were not yet crafted at the time of the Brahimi-Sistani agreement on the elections. But in retrospect, UN officials realized that the whole TAL process "prejudices the final outcome and created a process that alienated Sistani and undermined Brahimi's role." ICG interview with a high UN official in April 2004. See "Iraq's Transition: On a Knife Edge," 26.
45. Galbraith, *The End of Iraq*, 161 and elsewhere.
46. Most recently: "Iraq's Barzani Interviewed on Kurdish Affairs, Iranian Role, Ties with Israel," *BBC Monitoring International Reports*, April 8, 2007; Crisis Group, "Iraq's Constitutional Challenge," 12–15; Crisis Group, "Iraq's Kurds: Toward a Historic Compromise?" 20; and Galbraith, *The End of Iraq*. Galbraith is a liberal, but he reproduces the nationalist history and invariably agitates in the direction of independence. This could very well be the mainline Kurdish position among politicians and intellectuals rather than the more liberal and more integrationist (vis-à-vis Iraq) version represented by O'Leary. Compare the titles of their books. One speaks of the "end of Iraq," the other of "the future of Kurdistan in

Iraq." The difference is not due only to their differing publication dates. During this period, it is tough to identify KDP and PUK positions around ethnic and liberal nationalist attitudes, though it is easy to say that the important independent Mahmoud Othman is more liberal and more friendly to being in Iraq than Mahmoud Barzani (KDP). Jalal Talabani (PUK), the current president of Iraq, may be somewhere between these poles. He was the one to reassure Turkey after Barzani's recent provocation. I think, however, the divisions cut across the parties, and sometimes (or often) the same person can oscillate between them.

47. This supposedly answers Gellner's criticism of the general ethnic nationalist claim, according to which it cannot be claimed that the world's roughly eight thousand languages should all have a state. "The Kurds are an ethnicity and a very large one . . . so if anyone deserves a state they do, on justice-based grounds" (Galbraith, *The End of Iraq*, 148). But the point is that no ethnicities including the ones that already have states deserve them on justice-based grounds according to the general argument: "any two of them could share a just state . . . suitably organized, like the German, French and Italian Swiss e.g. do. France, Germany and Italy are not more just than Switzerland." A. Stepan takes the trouble to answer another of Gellner's arguments according to which two nationalisms in the state are impossible by proposing his (and Linz's) concept of a state-nation, where a citizen could have multiple identities and allegiances, e.g., Spanish and Catalan. "Modern Multi-National Democracies: Transcending the Gellnerian Oxymoron," in *Arguing Comparative Politics* (Oxford: Oxford University Press, 2001). We might say that O'Leary follows Stepan, while Galbraith is Gellnerian.
48. Barzani, "Iraqi Kurdish Claim for Federalism: A Kurdish-Arab Partnership."
49. A Canadian model has been pushed for Kurdistan by people who are not ethnic nationalists of any kind. See John McGarry, "Canadian Lessons for Iraq," in *The Future of Kurdistan in Iraq*. This is rather surprising given (1) the highly unusual spatial (political-geographical) environment of Canada, (2) the very different history of the origins and development of the Canadian state in an actual and ongoing process of federation (Iraq was born through forcible imperialist amalgamation and was always centralized), and (3) the very serious constitutional problems with the Canadian federation precisely since it has become asymmetrical, which are manageable most likely because of conditions 1 and 2. The last issue has just been highlighted in a highly interesting unpublished paper by S. Choudhry, "Does the World Need More Canada? The Politics of the Canadian Model in Constitutional Politics and Political Theory." In my view, India would have been a better model for Iraq, though its high level of centralism would have been admittedly unrealistic for Kurdistan. A decentralized version of India, then.

50. O'Leary, "Power Sharing, Pluralist Federation, and Federacy," in *The Future of Kurdistan in Iraq*, 52–59.
51. Makiya, "A Model for Post-Saddam Iraq"; Wimmer, "Democracy and Ethno-Religious Conflict in Iraq," paper presented at the Center on Democracy, Development, and the Rule of Law, Stanford University, May 5, 2003; and Pachachi and Istrabadi according to Diamond, but not in the article the published on the TAL, where he avoided the subject. See Diamond, *Squandered Victory*, 167–168.
52. Makiya, "A Model for Post-Saddam Iraq."
53. See both Wimmer, "Democracy and Ethno-Religious Conflict in Iraq"; and Makiya, "A Model for Post-Saddam Iraq."
54. Wimmer, "Democracy and Ethno-Religious Conflict in Iraq." This last position came close to the starting position of the American negotiators of the CPA. See O'Leary, "Power Sharing, Pluralist Federation, and Federacy," 63ff.; O'Leary and Salih, "The Denial, Resurrection, and Affirmation of Kurdistan," 32–34.
55. Stepan, "Modern Multi-National Democracies," 195–197; "Toward a New Comparative Politics of Federalism, (Multi)nationalism and Democracy: Beyond Rikerian Federalism," 359–360; and "Toward Consolidated Democracies," 309, all in *Arguing Comparative Politics.*
56. Logically, on the basis of historical examples such as India and Spain, the position should accept ethnically and linguistically defined units, greater decentralization, and possibly asymmetry as well, perhaps more readily if introduced gradually. The problem in Iraq was that all these features were introduced from the outset.
57. Advocated by Istrabadi according to Diamond, *Squandered Victory*, 168.
58. O'Leary and Salih, "The Denial, Resurrection, and Affirmation of Kurdistan"; and O'Leary, "Power Sharing, Pluralist Federation, and Federacy," both in *The Future of Kurdistan in Iraq*, xvii–xviii, 33–36.
59. The difference has to do with the weight one wishes to concede to an Iraqi identity. Where that weight is zero, one retreats to the ethnic nationalist position. Where it is equal for both Arab and Kurd, one has a symmetric version of Linz and Stepan's state-nation. Where the weight of Iraqi is greater, one has the postnationalist position. Finally, where the weight of Arab and Kurd tends to zero, one has the civic nationalist position.
60. O'Leary and Saleh, "The Denial, Resurrection, and Affirmation of Kurdistan," xvii.
61. O'Leary, "Power Sharing, Pluralist Federation, and Federacy," 34.
62. Crisis Group, "Iraq and the Kurds: The Brewing Battle of Kirkuk," July 18, 2006; "Iraq and the Kurds: Resolving the Kirkuk Crisis," April 19, 2007.

63. O'Leary et al., "Negotiating a Federation in Iraq," in *The Future of Kurdistan in Iraq*, does not seem very insistent on consociationalism for the future, if it can get a rightly constituted senate-type chamber.
64. But he is also more willing than the ethnic nationalist to trade for more territorial independence in return for surrendering some consociational guarantees. O'Leary et al., "Negotiating a Federation in Iraq," in *The Future of Kurdistan in Iraq*, 125. The real point may be that this position considers the two types of guarantees as functionally equivalent and interchangeable and not as logically requiring one another as O'Leary himself first implied in "Power Sharing, Pluralist Federation, and Federacy," 52.
65. O'Leary, "Power Sharing, Pluralist Federation, and Federacy," 57–58. Here the contrast with Galbraith is impressive, with the latter conjuring up *Bush v. Gore* to support his position! Galbraith, *The End of Iraq*, 139, 200. Galbraith does not seem to realize the importance of constitutional courts in many recent democratic transitions, especially the successful ones, nor does he see that despite the name "Iraq," a civil-law country got a constitutional court—not the highest court of appeal in the ordinary federal system of courts.
66. T. Ali, *Bush in Babylon* (London: Verso, 2003), chap. 4. He quotes Pachachi, before the elder statesman's entry into the IGC, as a typical Iraqi nationalist, expressing strong reservations about joining a U.S.-dominated advisory council of any kind, on 41.
67. Crisis Group, "Toward a Historic Compromise," 17; Diamond, *Squandered Victory*, 128.
68. Ali, *Bush in Babylon*.
69. Diamond, *Squandered Victory*, 29; Istrabadi, "Reviving Constitutionalism in Iraq," 292.
70. Diamond, *Squandered Victory*, 142. I met him in New York at a UNDP meeting in May 2006, when he was forced, in full public-relations mode, to defend indefensible things, such as the process of the making of the final constitution.
71. Chandrasekaran, *Imperial Life in the Emerald City*, 242.
72. Crisis Group, "Toward a Historic Compromise?" 2.
73. Ibid., 1–2.
74. Diamond, *Squandered Victory*, 162.
75. Crisis Group, "Toward a Historic Compromise?" 2.
76. "Iraqi Kurdish Claim for Federalism. A Kurdish-Arab Partnership."
77. Crisis Group, "Toward a Historic Compromise?" 3.
78. Ibid.; Diamond, *Squandered Victory*, 161. This is where it makes immediate sense that it was the chairman Pachachi's suggestion that Bremer go to Erbil. But two things were wrong with this: "one" representative going for the plurality of Iraq, and the American CPA being that representative.

79. Crisis Group, "Toward a Historic Compromise?" 4.
80. Diamond, *Squandered Victory*, 140.
81. See Brown's translation at http://www.geocities.com/nathanbrown1/taldraft jan2004.html. O'Leary refers to a publication in Asharq-al Aqsat (February 14, 2004) that seems to have been untranslated, and he calls even this only a prior and not yet definitive version of the Pachachi draft. Prof. Brown too admits that the text he translated was later changed, and the text O'Leary comments on seems to be slightly different from the one I have. But ultimately the differences on the relevant issues do not seem to be earth shattering.
82. Crisis Group, "Toward a Historic Compromise?" 4.
83. O'Leary, "Power Sharing, Pluralist Federation, and Federacy," in *The Future of Kurdistan in Iraq*, 59ff.
84. Ibid., 60.
85. Crisis Group, "Toward a Historic Compromise?" 3; Phillips, *Losing Iraq*, 188–189.
86. Bremer, *My Year in Iraq*, 271.
87. According to the Crisis Group's information ("Iraq's Kurds: Toward a Historic Compromise," 3), an agreement for a status quo plus, namely the Kurdistan Region in return for deferring the Kirkuk question to other than some demographic adjustments, was already reached at this meeting. This seems to be incorrect in terms of both Bremer's and Diamond's separate recollections. The Crisis Group also misses the reversal that occurred with Washington's temporary decision to eliminate the Kurdistan Region from the TAL.
88. Diamond, *Squandered Victory*, 162.
89. Chandrasekaran says (*Imperial Life in the Emerald City*, 242–243) that he became convinced the Kurds would never embrace an interim constitution without a Kurdistan Region and a regional government. Thus he decided to go against his bosses in Washington on this matter, constituting (he follows Diamond here) his "finest hour." In my mind this is when he, as a supposed representative of the world's last superpower, buckled, eventually dragging his bosses, who were right for once, with him. When this happened exactly I am not sure.
90. Galbraith, *The End of Iraq*, 163.
91. Ibid.
92. Chandrasekaran, *Imperial Life in the Emerald City*, 243.
93. Galbraith, *The End of Iraq*, 166–167.
94. O'Leary, "Power Sharing, Pluralist Federation, and Federacy," 58–59; Crisis Group, "Toward a Historic Compromise?" 4.
95. O'Leary is much more anxious to hide the American role and stress compromise with the Arabs, apparently, which is a function of his greater commitment to stay-

ing within some kind of Iraqi federation. But the American role is clearly revealed on the CPA side by Bremer and Diamond, supporting Galbraith's version.

96. For the full text: O'Leary et al., *The Future of Kurdistan in Iraq*, appendix 1: "Kurdistan's Constitutional Proposal"; and Galbraith, *The End of Iraq*, appendix 1.
97. Galbraith, *The End of Iraq*, 166–167; O'Leary's five-point summary is not always accurate, and point 5 especially is misleading in light of the veto that went into the TAL
98. Galbraith, *The End of Iraq*, 167–168.
99. Diamond, *Squandered Victory*, 166–167.
100. Interestingly, this pattern would continue for the permanent constitution too, where initially (for one parliamentary session) at least both regional powers and consociational participation would grow together. But now consociationalism was to have a sunset clause, and the plan was to shift to a second parliamentary chamber. It is another question whether that will be possible, since the constitution makers put off all the difficult questions concerning powers and type of representation.
101. First presented on February 13, the document was put on the KRG Web site only on February 20. R. Chandrasekaran, "Kurds Reject Key Parts of Proposed Iraq Constitution," *Washington Post*, February 21, 2004.
102. Bremer, *My Year in Iraq*, 295; Diamond, *Squandered Victory*, 167ff.
103. "Confederations" would also have the right of unilateral secession that the Kurds did not seek, at least until the Vienna Convention on Treaties of 1968. After that treaty, the term "confederation" or "treaty organization" very closely expresses what the Kurds wanted for "Iraq."
104. Diamond, *Squandered Victory*, 173; O'Leary et al., "Negotiating a Federation in Iraq," 125.
105. Chandrasekaran, "Kurds Reject Key Parts of Iraq's Proposed Constitution," *Washington Post*, February 21, 2004.
106. Bremer, *My Year in Iraq*, 295.
107. Diamond, *Squandered Victory*, 168; TAL art. 53c.
108. This important point I added after reading Allawi, who stresses that the diagnosis is actually Sistani's! See *The Occupation of Iraq*, 221–223. To be sure, he would not consider the debate about the role of Islam in the state a distraction (though he pays only relatively minor attention to it) and may deny that Sistani's interest at this time was not at all focused on this issue. The fatwas, however, support my position. If Sistani thought of democracy as instrumental (209–210), and Allawi is in a better position to know that than I am, then it is the instrument he wanted to use rather than the IGC for establishing the kind of Islamic state he wanted.
109. Feldman, "Imposed Constitutionalism," 877–879: It has been shown that the case he imagines to be unidirectional, Japan, was highly interactive before

and after the making of the draft by the Government Section. See K. Shoichi, *The Birth of Japan's Post War Constitution* (Boulder, Colo.: Westview, 1997). The correct formula for Iraq is: some parts were imposed after bargaining with the Kurds alone, other, less important parts were not, and as I show below, the whole was also imposed.

110. "Iraq's Hidden War," *Newsweek*, March 7, 2005.
111. "The Civil Opposition In Iraq": http://www.ww3report.com/iraq1.html.
112. See statement of January 14, 2004.
113. See letter of January 23, 2004.
114. Yochi J. Dreazen, "Long Way From Indiana," *Wall Street Journal*, April 12, 2004.
115. CPA Order 96, 4 (3).
116. Bremer, *My Year in Iraq*, 295.
117. Ibid., 293; Diamond, *Squandered Victory*, 172.
118. Bremer, *My Year in Iraq*, 293. There is little evidence outside of Bremer's claims that it was the Ayatollah Sistani who was driving the symbolic demands about Islam and thus distracting the assembly. Even Bremer indicates that he was softening on the role of Islam and tended to always focus on his political demands (e.g., 294). Sistani never showed the slightest interest in the ability of Shi'ite provinces to form regions, and late in the game, during the making of the permanent constitution, he seemed to oppose this idea when it emanated from SCIRI.
119. Diamond, *Squandered Victory*, 171–172.
120. It may have been the Drafting Committee that managed to take this provision out of the draft of the TAL, at the urging of the weak secular postnationalist or Iraqi nationalists, and thus it was easy to restore.
121. Feldman, "Imposed Constitutionalism," 878–879.
122. Bremer, *My Year in Iraq*, 295–296; Diamond, *Squandered Victory*, 172.
123. Bremer, *My Year in Iraq*, 299.
124. The idea that in this form the religious Shi'ites did not object to the provision, as claimed by Galbraith, *The End of Iraq*, 144, makes little sense, since it also diminishes the freely elected assembly. Moreover, it is unsupported anywhere else. There is no evidence the provision was ever discussed. It is another matter that after the actual ratification rule for the permanent constitution was enacted some Shi'ites might have preferred the original Kurdish proposal. But even here I see little evidence to support that.
125. Bremer, *My Year in Iraq*, 296.
126. Galbraith, *The End of Iraq*, 140. It seems absurd to claim, moreover, that the Kurds were silenced during the IGC discussions. On the principles of negotiations, see O'Leary et al., "Negotiating a Federation in Iraq," 118.
127. Bremer, *My Year in Iraq*, 296.

128. According to Bremer, the "they" were the Kurds (*My Year in Iraq*, 297). According to Galbraith, Bremer and (Talabani's deputy) Barham Salih (PUK) together cooked it up (*The End of Iraq*, 144). According to Diamond, it was Rowsch Shaways (KDP), Barzani's deputy. Apparently, there is an inner Kurdish feud concerning the authorship of this admittedly brilliant idea, fateful for the course of everything that followed.
129. Advocates of the Kurds, perhaps a little embarrassed about the fact, tend to disagree. See O'Leary's two inconsistent statements in "Power Sharing, Pluralist Federation, and Federacy," 77, and in O'Leary et al., "Negotiating a Federation in Iraq," 122–123, the first of which is the public-relations line, while the second involves more careful analysis and comes to the same conclusion I do. The issue was not only that the Kurdistan Region had three provinces, since there were three Sunni-majority provinces as well. Still, Galbraith is wrong to claim that this was therefore a Kurdish and Sunni veto both, because of two small details: the default position in case of a veto and the number two-thirds. As to the default position, if the constitution was vetoed, the TAL favored the Kurds but not the Sunni. Thus the Sunni had little to gain from a veto except to go from worse to bad. The two-thirds figure is even more revealing. Had the provision allowed a majority of voters in three provinces to reject a constitution, that would have been a Sunni-Kurdish veto clearly. But requiring a two-thirds qualified majority had a different effect. That figure was easy to achieve in the Kurdish provinces, as O'Leary says, but very difficult in the third of the Sunni-majority provinces, Nineveh, for two key reasons: this province had a large Kurdish minority and a significant chunk of it was administered de facto and under the TAL by the Kurdistan Regional Government. Thus Kurds controlled part of the referendum in Nineveh. Galbraith's idea that the Shi'ites objected to the veto clause only because Sunni Arabs also could veto the constitution is unexplained, wrong, and lacks support in any Shi'ite statement. Sistani's argument, restated by Galbraith (*The End of Iraq*, 144–145), based on what the cleric took to be a subversion of the concession of an elected assembly, was quite sufficient for Shi'ites to oppose the provision.
130. Galbraith, *The End of Iraq*, 144.
131. This is has been my oft-repeated argument and the thrust of O'Leary's analysis as well, e.g., Arato, "Interim Imposition" and "Empire's Democracy"; and O'Leary et al., "Negotiating a Federation in Iraq," 120–123.
132. Bremer, *My Year in Iraq*, 298–301.
133. I don't know what the reason is for this discrepancy. But the two stories complement one another regarding the issue at hand, the introduction of the ratification rule to the IGC. Indeed, Diamond has deduced, before the appearance of the Bremer memoirs, that the "brilliant tactical maneuver" was

"planned long in advance" (*Squandered Victory*, 174). How long in advance can be surmised differently according to whom one has in mind as the planner of the strategy of getting this provision adopted, Bremer or the Kurds, and whose scenario, Bremer's or Diamond's, one accepts. If we assume the Kurds and Diamond's scenario, the strategy would have been planned very long before. If Bremer came up with the final tactic of how to impose the thing, then it would have been just before the plenary of the IGC, especially given his shorter timeframe. Even then, the ratification rule had to be thought out well in advance. Incidentally, the default rule, namely falling back into the TAL in case of failure of ratification (61e), was probably a lawyer's device already in the TAL before the new ratification rule was put in, but it gained new importance only with this latter rule, which would make such failures much more likely.

134. Diamond, *Squandered Victory*, 173. Diamond's account was available when Bremer published *My Year in Iraq*. Diamond is a nonperson in Bremer's account: his book is not referenced, and there is not one single word about the different chronology he presents. This reminds me of old Stalinist practice.
135. Diamond, *Squandered Victory*, 173–174.
136. I owe this to a personal communication from Mr. Haider Hamoudi, who was an expert legal advisor to the IGC during this period.
137. Allawi, *The Occupation of Iraq*, 223 and n. 120 on 477. Elsewhere (412) he identifies Mahdi as an advocate of a pro-Kurdish position within the Shi'ites.
138. See, e.g., O'Leary, "Power Sharing, Pluralist Federation, and Federacy," 63ff. O'Leary and Salih, "The Denial, Resurrection, and Affirmation of Kurdistan," 32–34.
139. P. Cockburn, *The Occupation* (London: Verso, 2006), stresses this all-important factor.
140. See "Sistani v. Bush" and chap. 3, above, as well as Diamond, *Squandered Victory*, 160–161.
141. See Istrabadi, "Reviving Constitutionalism in Iraq."
142. Ghazi Yawar, a Sunni, later the transitional president, called it a "dangerous land grab," but only when it was still a Kurdish proposal, on February 20, 2004. See Chandrasekaran, *Imperial Life in the Emerald City*.
143. Thus it is excessive modesty on the part of Galbraith to claim that the TAL was written by the CPA's lawyers, since the KRG's advisors are obviously responsible for whole chunks of it!
144. Galbraith is shockingly open on this point (*The End of Iraq*, 135–136, 168), sometimes forgetting that the Kurdish "national" interest may not be the American one. The dismantling of all militias and the keeping of all prior agreements may have been exactly such matters.

145. This has been traditional advice since the British, who, since Lord Curzon's performance of the Lausanne Congress, have followed it themselves. No one ever wants territory in Iraq for the oil. See P. Sluglett's fine book *Britain in Iraq: Contriving King and Country*, 2nd ed. (New York: Columbia University Press, 2007), 53, 71ff., esp. 73.
146. Crisis Group, "Iraq's Kurds: Toward a Historic Compromise," 18; O'Leary et al., "Negotiating a Federation in Iraq," 129.
147. Galbraith, *The End of Iraq*, 167–168.
148. Crisis Group, "Iraq's Kurds: Toward a Historic Compromise?" The researcher (or at least one of them) for this article seems to have been Sophia Wanche, who has also written for the openly pro-Kurdish O'Leary volume. I mention this because there is simply no major discussion available today that would reconstruct the constitutional negotiations from an Arab or Iraqi nationalist or a postnationalist point of view. I think the Crisis Group should have been more careful with the selection of a team to take up issues that were so divisive on these lines.
149. O'Leary, "Power Sharing, Pluralist Federation, and Federacy," 60.
150. These acts Galbraith justifies, as we will see below, by the thesis of the supposed abrogation of the TAL.
151. O'Leary, "Power Sharing, Pluralist Federation, and Federacy," 60.
152. Ibid., 51.
153. Stepan, "Modern Multi-National Democracies," 191.
154. Ibid., 79.
155. Traditionally, the right of secession would have been included among the distinctions of confederations from federations, but after the Vienna Convention on the Law of Treaties (January 27, 1969; 1980 entry into force), members of treaty organizations (e.g., the European Union) do not have the right of unilateral abrogation or secession unless the treaty provides for it explicitly. Granted, it would be possible to define a confederation as a treaty organization with the right of unilateral abrogation written in, though one wonders how many such treaties would be agreed to (United Nations, treaty series, 2005, Part V., art. 54–57).
156. O'Leary, "Power Sharing, Pluralist Federation, and Federacy," 68–69.
157. Ibid., 52–60.
158. Ibid., 56–57.
159. O'Leary et al., "Negotiating a Federation in Iraq," 125.
160. Diamond, *Squandered Victory*, 167–168.
161. Sometimes sources simply should not be believed, like Adel Abdel-Mahdi of SCIRI: "The TAL was a turning point. It's when Bremer stopped acting like a dictator." Chandrasekaran, *Imperial Life in the Emerald City*, 244. That is un-

believable in light of Mahdi's refusal to sign and the whole subsequent Shi'ite response to the TAL. But it is consistent with the depiction that Mahdi was for a long time an ally of the Kurds within the Shi'a House.

162. Arato, "Interim Imposition," and chap. 2, above.
163. This division of roles is not absolute. The governmental and especially state structure adopted for the interim may represent facts that will be very difficult to change for the final constitution. The amendment rule of the interim constitution, on the other hand, may contribute to the fluidity or rigidity of the interim arrangements themselves.
164. O'Leary et al., "Negotiating a Federation in Iraq," 119–123, where they treat the second and third rules. I have discussed all three (amendment, ratification, and the failsafe rule) in "Interim Imposition"; "Empire's Democracy," 232; and in "From Interim to 'Permanent' Constitution in Iraq." O'Leary et al.'s analysis of the default rule (my failsafe rule), while fully convergent, is more detailed than mine.
165. Arato, "Interim Imposition." Niklas Luhmann in his legal sociology spoke of normative learning: how not to learn in the face of the first disappointment. This dimension is especially important for constitutions if one is to have the two-track structure of constitutionalism rightly stressed by Bruce Ackerman. Nevertheless, under a new constitution there must also be the opportunity to correct obvious deficiencies unanticipated by the framers, as in the case of the U.S. election of the president and vice president on a single ballot, which was corrected by the Twelfth Amendment of 1804. In this sense, an interim constitution properly constructed extends the two-track structure to constitution making itself, by providing for normal rather than extraordinary alteration for a period of time. See Arato, "Constitutional Learning," *Theoria* 106 (April 2005), where I draw on the competing perspectives of Holmes and Ackerman.
166. Istrabadi, "Reviving Constitutionalism in Iraq," 300.
167. Since the makers of the interim constitution (and their American advisers) forgot (or deliberately omitted) the elementary requirement to enshrine the amendment rule if they wished to make anything else unchangeable, everything in the TAL can be changed after free elections legally, using a two-step procedure. The same mistake was made by the authors of Article V of the U.S. constitution, but at that time no one knew whether self-referring rules could be valid or not. See the famous article of H. L. A. Hart, "Self-Referring Laws," in *Essays in Jurisprudence and Philosophy* (Oxford: Oxford University Press, 1983); and Peter Suber, *The Paradox of Self-Amendment* (New York: Peter Lang, 1990). Since the making of the *Grundgesetz*, which has enshrined its amendment rule protecting unchangeable provisions, similar in fact to many such sections of

the TAL, textbook knowledge of amendment rules would require following the German example.

168. I am inferring simple majority, since nothing else is stated. If it is interpreted as a law, the presidential council would have veto power over the draft submitted to the people, which could mean, as I will discuss below, either veto by one or only all three members. But it could be a special law where referenda replace the executive, which is not mentioned by the very poorly drafted text in this context.

169. Nathan Brown, whom I greatly respect, disagrees with my claim that the rejection of the new constitution and the preservation of the TAL could occur an indefinite number of times, because, according to him, the TAL does not allow the extension of the time limit of the interim period by amendment (art. 3a). But the indefinite number of failed ratifications and preservation of the TAL requires no amendment, only following the plain text of the TAL (art. 61e), which does not limit in any way the number of times this can occur.

170. As I said, O'Leary's term "default" is more exact than my "failsafe," but I reject his term "federal" for the ratification rule, which could be called with a little more justification a confederal rule that even John C. Calhoun would have preferred to Article V, which gave quite sufficient protection to the slave interests (three out of eighteen in Iraq versus four out of thirteen in the United States could veto amendments, and four out of thirteen could veto ratification, according to Article VII, which was still a treaty rule). Formally, O'Leary's point is that the numbers do not matter, because a confederation (like the United States in 1781) requires unanimity. Here one Kurdish state could not, like Rhode Island, veto. Thus formally he is right: it is not a treaty or a confederal rule. But in substance, one Kurdish province was exactly the same as three. To the Kurds, this was in effect, or functionally, a ratification rule of a treaty, just as the Kurdistan Chapter's rule would have been. The only difference was that the new rule gave the Kurds even more negotiating power. Substantively less than a confederal rule, formally more than one!

171. The fact that at the last minute the National Assembly (in July or August 2005) sought to change the rule from a two-thirds majority of those voting to a two-thirds majority of those registered also supports my contention that the regulation was crafted by demographics. Suddenly it was realized that passion on the Sunni side might in Nineveh counteract demographics. However, the last-minute change had to be rescinded, and demographics or local Kurdish control over parts of Nineveh triumphed. See my "From Interim to 'Permanent' Constitution in Iraq" and chap. 5, below.

172. O'Leary, "Power Sharing, Pluralist Federation, and Federacy," 80, is very open about this. In fact, the Kurdish governorates were regarded by the Kurdish side

as Trojan horses of the integrationists or territorial federalists. See O'Leary and Salih, "The Denial, Resurrection, and Affirmation of Kurdistan," 33.

173. If the Kurds, as Galbraith claims, sent Bremer Article VII of the U.S. Constitution and this is what helped him change his mind on the Kurdistan veto (i.e., art. 61c of the TAL), then Bremer did not understand (1) the difference between 9/13 and 15/18 needed to ratify and 4/13 and 3/18 able to block and (2) the difference between blocking ratification for Kurdistan (Kurdistan Chapter) and for Iraq as a whole (TAL art. 61c). Galbraith, "Kurdistan in a Federal Iraq," in *The Future of Kurdistan in Iraq*, 275.
174. O'Leary et al., "Negotiating a Federation in Iraq."
175. Arato, "Interim Imposition."
176. A point that the more sophisticated O'Leary fully appreciates, while Galbraith downplays it.
177. A. V. Dicey, *Introduction to the Study of the Law of the Constitution*, 8th ed. (London: Macmillan, 1915), 78–81; Hart, *Concept of Law* (Oxford: Oxford University Press, 1961), chap. 4.
178. M. Troper, "L'Europe politique et le concept de souveraineté," which provides a fourth dimension of sovereignty, imputation to a collective subject, next to Carré de Malberg's three: negative state sovereignty as the power that has no internal equals or external superiors, sovereignty in the sense of specific powers, and the organ exercising the latter. See also Kelsen, *General Theory of State and Law* (Cambridge, Mass.: Harvard, 1945), 261.
179. S. Choudhry, "Old Imperial Dilemmas and the New Nation Building," 939, 941ff.; "Does the World Need More Canada?" 25ff.
180. That would have meant five governorates needed for a veto; in effect, two minorities could veto the constitution of the majority but one could not.
181. Arato, "Sistani v. Bush," "Interim Imposition," "Empire's Democracy"; Diamond, *Squandered Victory*, esp. 240; Galbraith, *The End of Iraq*, 140ff.; O'Leary et al., "Negotiating a Federation in Iraq," 117–118. But see Chandrasekaran, *Imperial Life in the Emerald City*, 243–244. To be fair, almost all these authors consider the TAL in one respect or another to have been an important achievement. To me it was mostly a failure.
182. Arato, "Sistani v. Bush," 175ff.; Arato, "Interim Imposition," 35–40.
183. See Diamond, *Squandered Victory*, chap. 7: "Sales Effort."
184. Galbraith, *The End of Iraq*, 140, stresses the absence of "public comment and input," not realizing why that would have been impossible and what that would have meant for the Kurds; O'Leary et al., "Negotiating a Federation in Iraq," 117–118, speak of "negotiated and agreed without any pretence of transparency, serious public education, or extensive public education." Same question to them. Moreover, did the permanent constitution and its making involve any

of these things? They predicted it would, but when it did not they missed the opportunity to say so (119).

185. Diamond, *Squandered Victory*, 175.
186. Admitted by O'Leary and also inconsistently even by Galbraith.
187. This reminded me of the probably uncoordinated strategy of the Hungarian opposition, whose moderates signed the round-table agreements in October 1989, with the radicals not signing but without exercising their veto power. Subsequently, they proceeded to change the agreement through a popular referendum, and both sides of the opposition wound up winning: the radicals their constitutional objectives and the moderates the first free elections.
188. That in my view was up to the CPA until the transfer of sovereignty (versus Diamond, *Squandered Victory*, 177, who writes that there was no mechanism for this. After all, the annex was subsequently added on the same bases, though without the revisions sought by the Shi'ites).
189. Diamond is right to notice the majoritarian consequences of the claim, but he is wrong to say that accordingly the TAL does not take effect until it is approved by the national assembly's majority. Sistani does not claim that the provisional government until the elections cannot be bound by the TAL, under which it would be set up. Only free elections rupture the continuum between the TAL's rules and a political body's rights.
190. Bremer, *My Year in Iraq*, 311.
191. About which Bremer is deafeningly silent, but see Diamond, *Squandered Victory*, 248–249.
192. The future National Assembly will be shackled by many restrictions that will prevent it from undertaking what it sees as congruent with the interests of the Iraqi people. A nonelected council (the Interim Governing Council), in coordination with the occupying authority, foisted upon the future National Assembly a "strange" law to administer the country during the transitional phase. It also dictated—and this is most dangerous—specific principles, rules, and mechanisms with regard to the writing of the permanent constitution and organizing a referendum. Crisis Group, "Iraq's Transition: On the Knife's Edge," 25. The rest is paraphrased: "the elections on which Sistani spent so much energy will lose a great deal of their meaning and will be of little use and the three member Presidency council enshrines sectarianism . . . thus auguring a possible partitioning of the country." While the Crisis Group leaves this out, it seems that Sistani also made the point that Iraqi government thus constructed would be able to decide very little, inviting interference by the occupier. He warned in his letter that he would boycott a coming visit to Baghdad by Brahimi, refusing to "take part in any meetings or consultation" conducted by him or his emissaries unless the United Nations offered guarantees that it

would not endorse the interim constitution. John F. Burns, "The Struggle for Iraq: Shiite Ayatollah Is Warning U.N. Against Endorsing Charter Sponsored by U.S.," *New York Times*, March 23, 2004.

193. Thus there is no evidence that this is the issue that is moving him, as P. Galbraith claims: "Iraq: The Bungled Transition," *New York Review of Books*, September 23, 2004.

194. Diamond, *Squandered Victory*, 254, explicitly admits this but forgets his own role in the relevant moves. See also Crisis Group, "Iraq's Transition: On the Knife's Edge," 26.

195. Terence Neilan, "U.N. Envoy Urges Iraqis to Give New Leaders a Chance," *New York Times*, June 2, 2004: "Mr. Brahimi struck a mildly surprising note when, in answer to a reporter's question, he referred to the American occupation administrator, L. Paul Bremer III, as 'the dictator of Iraq.' 'He has the money,' he said. 'He has the signature. Nothing happens without his agreement in this country.' "

196. Brahimi speaking: "I welcome the clarification made recently by Ambassador Bremer who, among other things, stressed that 'the Interim Government will not have the power to do anything which cannot be undone by the elected government which takes power early next year.' The fact is that the TAL is exactly what it says it is, i.e., a transitional administrative law for the transition period. It is not a permanent Constitution. Indeed, it is not a constitution at all. The Transitional Law (or any other law adopted in the present circumstances) cannot tie the hands of the National Assembly which will be elected in January 2005 and which will have the sovereign responsibility of freely drafting Iraq's permanent constitution." Security Council 4952nd Meeting, April 27, 2004 (UN News Center). I cannot tell if Brahimi deliberately or inadvertently confused "interim government" in Bremer's formulation with "Transitional Administrative Law" in his own. As to their ability to bind, the two were not the same. An interim executive obviously cannot bind a constitutional assembly. An interim constitution, as in South Africa, could, at least in principle. The fact that he refused to call it a constitution did not change much in the case of a document that definitely tried to regulate the state structure, the whole governmental process, and the constitution-making process under the National Assembly. To avoid purely majoritarian implications, Brahimi again quoted Bremer: "Iraqi unity requires a constitution that all of Iraq's communities can support. It is a fundamental principle of democracy that the constitution should provide for majority rule but also protect minority rights."

197. *Informed Comment*, Juan Cole's Web site. My emphasis.

198. Phillips, *Losing Iraq*, 10, 208, speaks of the Bush administration's decision to abrogate the TAL, which is sheer fiction, I think.

199. Under IVth Hague Convention (art. 43) 1907 (affirmed by Fourth Geneva Convention, arts. 54–56, 64).
200. Galbraith, *The End of Iraq.*
201. Galbraith, "Iraq: The Bungled Transition"; the later book by Galbraith, *The End of Iraq,* is less clear about what it wants to say (141, 146), probably for obvious reasons: the TAL was not abrogated and it served the Kurds very well in its somewhat doubtful status.
202. Galbraith, "Vistas of Exits from Baghdad," in *The Future of Kurdistan in Iraq,* 295–296.
203. Ibid.
204. Galbraith, *The End of Iraq,* 168.
205. The argument confuses morality and legality. See Kelsen on unconstitutional law in *General Theory of State and Law,* 155–157, where he shows that laws must be regarded as valid if legislated by a proper organ until they are declared unconstitutional, again by a proper organ. In relationship to the issue at hand, the Iraqi Federal Supreme Court could not be this second type of organ, because it is set up by the very law it is supposed to declare invalid, the TAL. However, Galbraith's challenge is international, based on international law, so it would have to be an international court or some other instance that would have to invalidate the TAL according to his reasoning. For political organs to do so in Iraq would require revolutionary acts, or coupes d'etat, or simply illegal resistance to parts of the law. All the latter may be legitimate, but they are not legal.
206. As I have argued in "Empire's Democracy," a literal reading of the Hague 1907 requirement would be nonsensical in a case where a dictatorship like Saddam's is overthrown, whether in a legal or illegal war. One cannot simply preserve the laws and practices of a dictatorship. The spirit of the law is another matter. Now, my argument is supported by Jean Cohen (cited in chap. 1), who goes beyond it by distinguishing between the Hague stress on governmental sovereignty and the Geneva stress on popular sovereignty. The spirit of these regulations would now entail enabling measures by the occupying power for popular sovereignty to become effective. This was not what was done by the American occupiers, and even UN SC Res. 1483 and 1516 facilitated the objectives very unclearly and inconsistently.
207. D. Filkins, "Iraqi Leader Says He'll Respect Kurd Desire for Autonomy, at Least for Now," *New York Times,* June 10, 2004. Both sides saw the issue quite clearly, but the Kurdish side seemed to have accepted Allawi's affirmation of the TAL and feared only what the freely elected assembly might do. That they would break with the TAL was always a possibility, certainly not reduced by the way article 61c was imposed. See also the follow-up article by S. R. Weisman, "The

Constitution: Kurds Find U.S. Alliance Is Built on Shifting Sands," *New York Times*, June 11, 2004, where charges later made by Galbraith and O'Leary are made by Kurdish politicians but where the spokesman for the U.S. State Department downplays the significance of 1546 not mentioning the TAL. Interestingly, the same article mentions statements by Diamond and Feldman that were at variance with other positions they have taken. Diamond here speaks of a Kurdish overreach, of which there is no sign in his thorough book, while Feldman points out that the United States seems to be afraid of Sistani. At a conference a few weeks before (at the Carnegie Institute in New York City), he claimed that it was Sistani who overreached himself with his appeals to the United Nations.

208. Galbraith, "Iraq: The Bungled Transition"; "Vistas of Exits from Baghdad," 296.

209. Order of Safeguarding National Security, July 6, 2004, whose article 11 declares that the TAL cannot be abrogated "in whole or part," while other articles, to be sure, suspend TAL protections in many areas. Also, article 12 declares: "No article in this order can be used to delay elections according to the timetable specified in the Transitional Administrative Law." The order was declared under the authority of the TAL (the provisions of section 2 of the TAL annex) as indeed countless other orders of the Allawi government. See http://www.washingtonpost.com/wp-dyn/articles/A33496–2004Jul7.html and http://www.nahrain.com/d/news/04/07/07/nhr0707b.html. I do not believe that a constitution could be directly enacted as an executive "order with the force of law."

210. Galbraith, *The End of Iraq*, 141, which of course contradicts O'Leary's claims concerning article 61, which has become according to him "legally inoperative." Galbraith, "Vistas of Exits from Baghdad," 296.

211. D. Filkins, "Iraqi Leader Says He'll Respect Kurd Desire for Autonomy, at Least for Now," *New York Times*, June 10, 2004.

5. The Making of the "Permanent" Constitution

1. T. Marshall and L. Roug, "A Central Pillar of Iraq Policy Crumbling," *Los Angeles Times*, October 9, 2005.
2. Crisis Group, "Unmaking Iraq: A Constitutional Process Gone Awry," September 26, 2005.
3. Galbraith, *The End of Iraq* (New York: Simon and Schuster, 2006), 170, 203–204.
4. Most surprisingly perhaps, Sieyès, in "What Is the Third Estate?" in *Political Writings* and "Préliminaire de la Constitution" (1789), in R. Zapieri, ed., *Ecrits Politiques* (Paris: Gordon & Breach, 1985). The contrast was already available

in the U.S. state constitutions, well known in France, which were all made by freely elected assemblies such as those of Pennsylvania and Massachusetts, though even here Jefferson, in *Notes on Virginia*, objected in the case of Virginia that the relevant "convention" was not elected for that specific purpose.

5. Of course, the way a particular case adheres to the norm still varies. It is still possible for the freely elected assembly to be either one specially elected for the purpose or an ordinary parliament that merely uses the existing amendment rule for a stealth round of constitution making, as in Hungary in 1990. The latter represents a boundary case still within the model, but only marginally so.
6. The popular participation and public openness some interpreters have missed in some of the first stages of the new paradigm in different countries could in fact come in either stage. There is no reason why the elite participants of the first stage could not organize extensive public communications around the process, or even consultations with relevant popular groups outside the process. When they do not do so, as in Iraq's first stage, there is little reason to predict such a development in the second stage. O'Leary et al. did in "Negotiating a Federation in Iraq," in *The Future of Kurdistan in Iraq* (Philadelphia: University of Pennsylvania Press, 2005), 119ff. The American role in the first stage, which could not be made public, makes for a potential difference, which here took the assumption that the second stage would be free of such interference. But there were other looming reasons why the second stage would not be more public or participatory.
7. Even in Hungary, the amendments of 1990, which left much of the supposedly interim constitution in place when the pacting parties had a chance to replace it, helped legitimate the whole package.
8. As Ali Allawi, ex-minister under the interim and transitional governments, writes in an important new book, Sistani's prestige was at this time at an all-time high because of his successful attempt to defuse a confrontation in Najaf between the Ayad Allawi interim government and Moqtadah al Sadr: A. Allawi, *The Occupation of Iraq: Winning the War, Losing the Peace* (New Haven, Conn.: Yale University Press, 2007), chap. 18. I have been able to fully consult and refer to this important book only in the rewriting of this chapter, but I have used it occasionally to check more speculative hunches and projections I made earlier. Those earlier references were noted.
9. A. Allawi is thus wrong when he ascribes the rule to the CPA's initiative, though it is quite possible that they argued for it in the manner he suggests. Ibid., 335.
10. Ibid.
11. However, in December 2005, territorial lists were used and the number of parties receiving seats was exactly the same during both elections, namely twelve.

12. The rule chosen, with a cutoff at 5 percent, could have been used to produce both a legislative and a constitutional assembly, and a census could have been still avoided.
13. This is why I argued for the latter; see A. Arato, "Sistani v. Bush: Constitutional Politics in Iraq," *Constellations* 11, no. 2 (2004): 181; it is a point still curiously missed by Allawi, even though the problem was remedied, consciously, for the second elections, as he notes (*The Occupation of Iraq*, 440). It is on points like this that he reveals an implicitly partisan and polemical attitude.
14. Though it may not happen if the insurrection chose to encourage it, as it did, interestingly enough, in December 2005.
15. Diamond's short analysis (*Squandered Victory: The American Occupation and the Bungled Effort to Bring Democracy to Iraq* [New York: Holt, 2005]) fully corresponds to mine: cf. Arato in *Informed Comment* (http://www.juancole.com). Allawi says that Diamond was against a multidistrict rule at the time because of his desire to limit the number of seats attained by big Islamic parties. See Allawi, *The Occupation of Iraq*, 485 n. 1).
16. M. Ghazi, "Forty-Seven Bodies Boycott Iraqi Elections," *World Crisis News Web: The Daily Crisis News*, November 18, 2004. Of the forty-seven, only the AMS (the Association of Muslim Scholars) was truly important, but they were followed eventually by all important Sunni organizations.
17. Allawi, *The Occupation of Iraq*, 346.
18. M. Howard, "Main Sunni Party Pulls out of Iraqi Election," *New York Times*, December 28, 2004.
19. It is much less plausible to argue that the Sunni boycott came about because they anticipated that more than two-thirds of the seats would be in the hands of the Shi'ite and Kurdish parties that would then be able to dictate the terms of Iraqi politics, including the constitutional settlement (Allawi, *The Occupation of Iraq*, 390). The claim is unconvincing first because it was impossible to clearly foresee the electoral results; in particular, Allawi's Iraqi List was expected to do much better. Second, even as far as the actual results go, the over two-thirds received by the UIA and the Kurds in both votes and seats was attained only because of the boycott. In the second elections, with Allawi performing even more poorly but with the Sunnis participating, the combined vote of the two lists slipped to 63 percent, and only the less proportional electoral rule brought it to slightly under 66 percent.
20. I agree with Ali Allawi that in the end the results of the boycott were disastrous, but that was only because the co-opted Sunni participants in the constitution-drafting process were in the end not treated seriously by the electoral winners. I think this was neither predetermined nor wise. There is no reason to assume that they would have treated a minority in parliament any better.

Allawi's idea that the Sunnis, instead of boycotting, should have voted for the Iraqi List of Iyad Allawi (*The Occupation of Iraq*, 390) is right on the substance but very unlikely politically and symbolically, since the prime minister was so obviously the candidate of the American occupiers.

21. Ibid., 390–391.
22. Crisis Group, "Iraq: Don't Rush the Constitution," 1, refers to the text of a governance agreement ("Foundations and Principles Agreed by the UIA and the KLC Concerning the Operation of the Interim Government") between the UIA and the Kurdistan Coalition List on April 13, 2005, that expressly confirmed the TAL.
23. The agreement could be interpreted as a defeat of Sistani, who had long campaigned against the straightjacket of the TAL. Formally it was not, however, since now a freely elected assembly would be confirming the TAL under the governmental agreement. (Actually, this never happened.) And it would not be a defeat materially if the Kurds were ready to concede all that Sistani hoped to achieve through democratic power. All the same, the agreement expressed a power shift from Sistani to the pro-Kurdish wing of the UIA, one that may have already been involved in allowing article 61c of the TAL to pass when it was first introduced, an event Sistani regarded as Shi'ite bungling.
24. They could be described as "court Sunnis" by their external opponents. Allawi, *The Occupation of Iraq*, 399.
25. Galbraith, *The End of Iraq*, 193ff., maintains that Khalilzad merely inherited decisions for Sunni inclusions made before his arrival by Secretary Rice (who made a key visit to Baghdad in May) and others, which "complicated his task." Whatever was his task then? Galbraith just said so: the negotiation of a tripartite peace treaty. Without the Sunni? Ali Allawi, though he gets the date of Khalilzad's arrival (June 21 instead of "May") wrong, seems to be more on target when he identifies the whole project with Khalilzad's mission and writes: "It was the prime mandate of Khalilzad to increase the participation of Sunni Arabs in the political process, and in particular in the constitutional talks." *The Occupation of Iraq*, 399, 397–398. Galbraith, however, had direct personal contact with Khalilzad, especially during the all-important negotiations in the so-called Leadership Council. He may be reflecting on the ambassador's relatively easy abandonment of the Sunni positions in this process, projecting this outcome backward, or discovering that Khalilzad himself, personally, was never in favor of too much "inclusion" in the first place.
26. Ibid., 398–399.
27. The issue was again whether Iraq was one of the relatively rare situations where the logically prior act (or stages) of state making could be accomplished at the same time as (the stages of) constitution making. Consciously or not, that was the double task facing the makers of the TAL.

28. Evidently I do not buy the purely formal claim that Iraqi sovereignty was restored in June 2004 and the occupation ended at that time. Sovereignty should be linked with control over military forces, and legality with minimum effectivity. The Iraqi government has no effective control over its military forces, and especially over the MNF (Multi National Force) that in effect still occupies Iraq, with the constrained permission of its government.
29. And not only in the sense of the generation of legitimacy.
30. I argued for this in my first article on Iraq: "The Occupation of Iraq and the Difficult Transition from Dictatorship," *Constellations* 10, no. 3 (2003).
31. Interestingly, it is supporters of the Kurds who often speak of the constitutional settlement as a peace treaty, forgetting General Y. Rabin's warning that peace is to be made with enemies like the Sunni and not friends like the Shi'a. See K. Soltan, "Think of It as a Treaty," October 23, 2005, on the Web site of the KRG: http://web.krg.org/articles/article_detail.asp?LangNr=12&RubricNr=&ArticleNr=6955&LNNr=28&RNNr=70, which references me, and alas, a year and a half later, I still stand by my position: the constitution is disastrous, and the peace treaty he is speaking about, one that excludes the side with which one was fighting, is ridiculous. Where is Soltan's "suspended civil war" engineered by this constitution? What is "an incomplete peace treaty"? Which part of the treaty is complete? The Shi'ite-Kurdish part, the sides that were not fighting? See also Galbraith's *The End of Iraq*, where he speaks of the constitution-making process as the negotiations of a tripartite peace treaty (193), which given what he says (203) about the making of an exclusively Shi'ite-Kurd rather than national compact should be described as a failure! J. Morrow, also a supporter of the Kurds, expresses a more cogent position on the same subject. While he too speaks of the project of constitution making as a peace treaty, he at least admits failure in this regard. J. Morrow, "Iraq's Constitutional Process II: An Opportunity Lost," *USIP Special Report*, November 2005.
32. And I disagree with Allawi when he argues that the Sunnis could organize themselves as a plausible, representative caucus in the IGC. *The Occupation of Iraq*, 222. It is another matter that the Iraqi nationalist position was intellectually represented there. The point is contradicted by Diamond, *Squandered Victory*. The main point in any case is organizational presence and representation, and here only the Iraqi Islamic Party counted. But their role in the making of the TAL seems negligible.
33. Allawi, *The Occupation of Iraq*, 405.
34. The Crisis Group indicates both sources: "Iraq: Don't Rush the Constitution," June 8, 2005, 8ff.; and "Unmaking Iraq," 3; Allawi, *The Occupation of Iraq*, 406–408. Galbraith blames only the Americans but says the Kurds and the

Shi'ites were the beneficiaries: *The End of Iraq*, 195; Morrow, "Iraq's Constitutional Process II," 8–11.

35. Crisis Group, "Iraq: Don't Rush the Constitution," 3 and n. 19.
36. Allawi, *The Occupation of Iraq*, 395, on the Kurds.
37. I myself have made a proposal here, relatively early. See Juan Cole's Web site *Informed Comment*, "Arato Guest Editorial: The Iraqi Constitution," December 28, 2004 (http://www.juancole.com). I did not predict the electoral outcome very well, and the eventual solution is superior to mine in that light. The Crisis Group offered the most extensive discussion and suggestions, unfortunately somewhat confusing the very different issues of Sunni inclusion with civil society and other forms of participation. "Iraq: Don't Rush the Constitution," 2–5.
38. The most accurate summary is in Nathan J. Brown's report "The Iraqi Constitutional Process Plunges Ahead," *Carnegie Endowment for International Peace Policy Outlook* (July 2005). Brown does not mention the numbers. Now also see the Crisis Group, "Unmaking Iraq: A Constitutional Process Gone Awry," September 26, 2005.
39. Galbraith, *The End of Iraq*, 194, who was an expert participant on behalf of the Kurds makes this charge, but others, for example A. Allawi, who sympathizes with the Shi'ite side, conspicuously do not follow him.
40. Allawi, *The Occupation of Iraq*, 406; and Galbraith, *The End of Iraq*, who is especially vociferous and propagandistic on this whole question. All this is out of line for an expert for the Kurds, who seems to be wishing to pick his opponents' negotiating team in what he himself called a peace negotiation, a nonsensical position.
41. J. Morrow, "Iraq's Constitutional Process," 11. Morrow is now an advisor to the Kurdistan Regional Government and thus an unimpeachable source on this subject. I wonder why he did not share this particular piece of information with Peter Galbraith, with whom he runs a consultancy firm. His piece on the negotiation process is excellent, though I do not share his conclusion, which ultimately still reflects the KRG point of view.
42. Crisis Group, "Unmaking Iraq," 3. This report also argues that the Sunni representatives made an effort in good faith to participate, at considerable personal risk to themselves.
43. Galbraith challenges this view without mentioning the constitutional referenda where the Sunnis overwhelmingly voted against the constitution. He says that the rejectionist Mutlaq party, the Iraqi Front for National Dialogue, won just eleven seats, 20 percent of the Sunni vote, in December 2005, while the Iraqi Accord Front, which included the "proconstitutionalist" Iraqi Islamic Party, won 80 percent. This analysis is entirely spurious. The IIP was part of the Sunni delegation, was excluded from the Leadership Council phase, with-

drew from the process, and rejected the constitution as it stood on August 28, together with the al-Mutlaq group. To call them proconstitutionalist is absurd; they are for the renegotiation of the constitution. The Iraqi Accord Front also included more radical, anticonstitutionalist elements, e.g., Adnan al-Dulaimi of the Sunni Endowments. The real distinction between the two Sunni parties contesting the elections of December 2005 was religious versus secular, and, alas, the religious party (The Iraqi National Accord) did much better.

44. A. Przeworski, *Democracy and Market* (Cambridge: Cambridge University Press, 1991).

45. E.g., there have been surprising alliances and conversations among the most radical Shi'a, al-Sadr, and some radical Sunni forces, the Association of Islamic Scholars.

46. We still do not know who killed two of the initial Sunni members (Sheik Mijbil Issa, a full member, and one advisor): Crisis Group, "Unmaking Iraq," 3; Morrow, "Iraq's Constitutional Process," 9. Just before his murder, Sheik Issa complained to the Crisis Group about not being seriously included by the Constitutional Commission.

47. See Brown, "Iraq's Constitutional Process Plunges Ahead" (available online at http://www.carnegieendowment.org/files/PO19Brown.pdf) for the reasons and his criticisms, as well as Crisis Group, "Iraq: Don't Rush the Constitution."

48. In theory, the group included Talabani and Barzani, Hakim and Jaffari, and for the Sunni al-Mutlaq, al-Dulaimi, and Iraqi Islamic Party leaders including Tarek al-Hashimi (Allawi, *The Occupation of Iraq*, 413). In practice, the Kitchen was constituted by the first four. Morrow, "Iraq's Constitutional Process," 9. According to Allawi, they were joined by Peter Galbraith, and Ambassador Khalilzad was often present as well.

49. Morrow, "Iraq's Constitutional Process," 3.

50. "The National Assembly shall write a draft of the permanent constitution of Iraq. This Assembly shall carry out this responsibility in part by encouraging debate on the constitution through regular general public meetings in all parts of Iraq and through the media, and receiving proposals from the citizens of Iraq as it writes the constitution."

51. There was a constitutional outreach unit of the National Assembly, but it is hard to see what outreach could consist in unless the assembly itself was to have a long and relevant role in the process. Morrow, "Iraq's Constitutional Process." He makes a strong case for the expectations concerning popular constitution making, expectations I consider somewhat unrealistic under the circumstances regarding popular inputs into the process. In any case, he is right about the effect of the time constraint in this area.

52. This is where I disagree with Morrow, who seems to suggest that the only point of extending the timeframe would have been for the Sunni to learn to live with federalism as defined by the Kurdish-Shi'ite agreements.
53. They were to complain that too much had been agreed upon before their arrival, but in fact, with or without them, the Constitutional Commission was producing a product they could have lived with.
54. Text of the Draft Constitution, raised for discussion at the Constitution Drafting Committee: http://www.iraqfoundation.org/projects/constitution/arabicconstitution_unsept1505.doc.
55. See Kirk Semple, "Constitution Proposes Some Limits on Role of Clergy," *New York Times*, August 4, 2005.
56. "Executive Authority," arts. 1 and 2.
57. Chap. 6, arts. 1a and 1b.
58. Brown, "Iraq's Constitutional Process Plunges Ahead," 14. I regard electoral rules as part of the constitution in the material sense, but Iraq follows the usual pattern of having only some general constitutional statement of principles, along with a rule legislated by the parliamentary majority.
59. Crisis Group, "Unmaking Iraq," 3.
60. Ibid., 9.
61. In a news conference on August 16, 2005, Ambassador Khalilzad tried to pretend that the three-sided process was still working. See "Ambassador Khalilzad Comments on Progress Drafting Iraq's Constitution," U.S. Embassy, Baghdad.
62. Ibid., 10; The Crisis Group indicates that it was Sheik Hamoudi who refused the demands of other committee members such as Othman, but this probably was on the instruction of his chiefs. See "Unmaking Iraq," 4–5, n. 22. See also Allawi, *The Occupation of Iraq*, 407–408, who focuses on the considerations of the Shi'ite leadership. Galbraith claims that all Iraqi party leaders wanted the six-month extension (*The End of Iraq*, 195). It may be a question of when they were asked the relevant question and a possible difference between Shi'ite and Kurdish intentions as well. The American attitude, in any case, was unambiguous and decisive.
63. He made the call originally on July 26: See E. Knickmeyer and R. Wright, "Special Summit Set on Charter for Iraq," *Washington Post*, July 27, 2005. But he did not yet abandon his attempt to extend the process.
64. According to the TAL, the National Assembly "shall write a (the) draft of the permanent constitution of Iraq," but the National Assembly did not write anything, and could not, without voting. Only the Constitutional Committee wrote a text without the authority to submit it to the electorate.
65. Cole, in the *Informed Comment* Web site on August 23; Arato, "[Il]legality and [Il]legitimacy"; Brown in "Iraq's Constitutional Conundrum," 2, puts it like this: "the notion that the TAL's requirement for the Assembly to write a con-

stitution could be satisfied by handing the speaker an incomplete draft a few minutes before the deadline is beyond implausible."

66. Galbraith, *The End of Iraq*, 193–194.
67. Morrow, "Iraq's Constitutional Crisis," 11, does not identify with this claim of a "nuclear option" on the part of the Sunnis.
68. "Key Shiites Demand Autonomy in Southern Iraq as Deadline Nears," *Reuters*, August 11, 2005.
69. In retrospect, the Kurds should have opposed a structure making the creation of a Shi'ite megaregion possible, but this they found difficult to do on the constitutional level, because they wished to expand their own region to at least the Kirkuk governorate, and maybe more. It is possible, however, that the Kurds are informally pushing for a Shi'ite regionalism well short of Hakim's dreams.
70. Allawi, *The Occupation of Iraq*, 409.
71. Ibid., 410.
72. Galbraith, *The End of Iraq*, 197; this is implicitly inconsistent with the picture of Sunni recalcitrance, since apparently they had some reason to be disturbed and opposed to things as they were proceeding.
73. Questioned about but papered over in his news conference. See "Ambassador Khalilzad Comments."
74. "'Iran satisfied with Iraq charter': Teheran, Aug. 29 (UPI) — Iran expressed satisfaction Monday over the completion of Iraq's new draft constitution, despite Arab Sunnis' reservations on several articles of the charter. Foreign Ministry spokesman Hamid Asafi was quoted by the Iranian News Agency, IRNA, as saying, "Iran hopes the political process in Iraq will lead to a referendum on the constitution and the creation of a government as planned. . . . There is no doubt that establishing peace and security in Iraq will lead to economic prosperity and will serve the interests of all the Iraqi people."
75. The role of Iran behind the new SCIRI posture is supported by Morrow ("Iraq's Constitutional Process," 13), but without very specific evidence.
76. Admittedly, had they received more support from the Da'wa party of Prime Minister Jaffari or from Ayatollah Sistani, the combined pressure of the Kurds and SCIRI could have been resisted. But all signs of a Shi'ite split disappeared after a few days, with even the Sadrists putting up only feeble resistance against the idea of a southern megaregion. Again, one should suspect the hand of Iran in all this.
77. Galbraith, *The End of Iraq*, 198ff.
78. Morrow, "Iraq's Constitutional Process," 13.
79. There are a variety of texts of the constitution available and none is fully authenticated. I am using the generally accepted penultimate text used also by

Brown in his commentary alongside the current, amended text according to the compromise of October 13, 2005. The latter is almost never used, at least in its English version. The Iraqi Independent Electoral Commission's unofficial translation on its official Web site is closer to the first of these texts but is not entirely the same. Here the variation seems to be only very slight, involving the numbering of the paragraphs, though evidently something has been struck out as well. What is amazing is that there is no authenticated text including the revisions of October 13, 2005, what I call the current text. The Independent Electoral Commission provides a separate list of amendments: http://www.ieciraq.org/English/Frameset_english.htm and http://www.ieciraq.org/final%20cand/AmendstoConstengOct13[1].pdf.

80. Galbraith, *The End of Iraq*, 169.
81. Ibid., 169–170; and Morrow, "Iraq's Constitutional Process," 7, expressing the Kurdish position, versus Crisis Group, "Unmaking Iraq," 7, relying on Nathan Brown.
82. N. Brown, "The Final Draft of the Iraqi Constitution: Analysis and Commentary," Carnegie Endowment for International Peace Web site, http://www.CarnegieEndowment.org, p. 13.
83. P. Galbraith, "The Last Chance for Iraq," *New York Review of Books* 52, no. 15 (2005): 22. The Crisis Group disagrees with him but without providing an alternative argument: "Unmaking Iraq," 7.
84. M. Karouny and G. Ghantous, "Devolving Power in Iraq Threatens Oil Development," *Reuters*, September 8, 2005.
85. Brown, "The Final Draft of the Iraqi Constitution: Analysis and Commentary." Amazingly enough, neither constitution ever clarifies the relationship of the two highest courts of appeals, and thus both represent an eclectic mixture of American-type supreme and European (Kelsen)-type constitutional courts.
86. Gone was Jaffari's attempt to slow down the Kurdish drive to take over the city and the province. The regulations of the TAL survive, but it was agreed that a referendum would be held by December 31, 2007, in art. 136 (current version: art. 139): Galbraith, *The End of Iraq*, 201–202.
87. Galbraith, *The End of Iraq*, 199–200. He is sustained by the relevant absence in the text. The Constitution, old version, art. 91 (fifth point) mentions court jurisdiction regarding conflicts between federal government and regions; the current version leaves out regions and has only provinces in its place: art. 92 (fourth point). I cannot tell if that is the function of two different translations or a further erosion to the benefit of Kurdistan's autonomy.
88. Ibid., 200.
89. Brown, "The Final Draft of the Iraqi Constitution: Analysis and Commentary."

90. This provision was put in the place of the early draft's idea of a revision in two parliamentary cycles, which would bring up the possibility of amendments by one cycle but would have protected basic rights better in the long term, since the new regulation does not then require that two parliaments in general approve amendments of certain articles.
91. It is this provision that enshrines a confederal state once it is formed, as opposed to the amendment rule of the early draft, which allowed ordinary constitutional amendments to change the whole regional structure.
92. Crisis Group, "Unmaking Iraq," 2.
93. But later also Morrow ("Iraq's Constitutional Process," 15), who is hardly a mere apologist for the Kurds and who also registers in general the remarkable uninvolvement of the National Assembly in a constitution it was supposed to write.
94. Galbraith, "Iraq's Last Chance," 22. This author-participant is in a good position to know that the ruling is wrong, but rather scandalously does not say so.
95. See Juan Cole's *Informed Comment* and M. Karouny, "Sunni Arabs Seek UN Guarantees on Iraq Referendum," *Reuters*, September 13, 2005.
96. R. F. Worth, "Election Move Seems to Ensure Iraqis' Charter," *New York Times*, October 4, 2005. "'I think it's a double standard, and it's unfair,' said Mahmoud Othman, a Kurdish assembly member who, like many other lawmakers, said he had not been present during the vote and only learned of it afterward. 'When it's in your favor, you say 'voters.' When it's not in your favor you say 'eligible voters.'"
97. R. F. Worth and S. Tavernise, "Iraqi Lawmakers Reverse Rule Change," *New York Times*, October 5, 2005.
98. Here I am focusing on the amendment that has to do with new procedures of constitution making. In addition, the following compromise formulations were offered to Sunni Arabs: (1) a mention of the constitution guaranteeing the unity of Iraq (added to art. 1), (2) a mention of Iraq being a founding member of the Arab League (added to art. 3), (3) use of both Kurdish and Arabic in Kurdistan (added to art. 4), and (4) past membership in the Ba'ath is not a criminal offense and de-Baathification will be monitored and reviewed by a parliamentary committee (added to art. 131). See the Web site of the Independent Electoral Commission: http://www.ieciraq.org/.
99. The language of the translation of the IEC is different: http://www.ieciraq.org.
100. http://www.ieciraq.org/final%20cand/ELECTORAL%20LAW%20FINAL%20gazetted.pdf.
101. S. Tavernise, "U.N. Rejects Sunni Demand for New Vote in Iraq," *New York Times*, December 28, 2005. The vote for the constitution was 63 percent "yes" in Kirkuk province. Honest or not, that percentage can be probably duplicated in a referendum concerning the political fate of the province.

102. Q. Abdul-Zara, "Iraqi Parliament Passes Federalism Law Over Sunni Objections," *AP*, October 11, 2006; "Sunni Accuse Shiites of Dirty Tricks in Passing Controversial Federalism Law," *International Herald Tribune*, October 12, 2006.
103. See "Pact of Honor," as reported on by Gilbert Achkar in *Informed Comment*, December 9; as well as Kanan Makiya's recent op-ed in the *New York Times* ("Present at the Disintegration," December 11, 2005).

Conclusion

1. For once I almost completely agree with Peter Galbraith's assessment in his newest article, "Iraq: The Way to Go," *New York Review of Books*, August 16, 2007. I say "almost," because Galbraith cannot stop himself from justifying the violation of the promise made to the Sunnis by saying, absurdly, that they themselves did not live up to their part of the bargain when the electorates of three provinces massively voted against the constitution but in Nineveh short of the necessary two-thirds needed to block ratification. The bargain, however, was not made by the voters, who are not a single agent capable of adhering to a bargain, but by the Iraqi Islamic Party, and they strongly recommended a "yes" vote. Probably this move had some influence on the outcome, possibly securing the failure of the "no" in Nineveh after all. We will never know. Interestingly, the text the voters voted on did not even contain the revisions and the promises made to the IIP.
2. I do not exclude learning on the part of some senators, of course. See the full text of Barack Obama's excellent interview with the *New York Times*, November 2, 2007.
3. [Note written on September 30, 2007] Urging the American administration "to actively support a political settlement in Iraq based on the final provisions of the Constitution of Iraq," constitutionally, this Biden-Brownback resolution should have been a nonevent in Iraq. If it were an act of Congress, it would be akin to H. L. A. Hart's famous legislation of Moscow traffic rules by the parliament in Westminster. Things are a little different in the given situation. Politically, the resolution is extremely damaging for its initiators, since it produces nothing but resistance from most Iraqi forces. That may be a good thing if Sistani, for example, chooses to actively oppose the so-called federalist option promoted by the Kurds and what used to be SCIRI (Now ISCI, or the Islamic Supreme Council of Iraq). No one even notices anymore that such neoimperial resolutions violate international law, though they certainly do, most obviously.
4. A. Arato, *Civil Society, Constitution, and Legitimacy* (Lanham, Md.: Rowman and Littlefield, 2003), 230–231, and the rest of chap. 7; also see my "Constitutional Learning" in *Theoria*.

5. Hans Lindahl, "Sovereignty and Representation in the European Union," in M. Loughlin and N. Walker, eds., *Sovereignty in Transition* (Oxford: Hart, 2003).
6. It is important to admit that in a political community, any legal identity cannot exhaust the symbolic meaning of the people. A given legal identity can be challenged in the name of other competing legal identities in the name of the same "people." But that "people" is a symbolic identity whose place, following Claude Lefort, is legally and politically an empty one. Claims to fully embody it are always usurpations, as Carré de Malberg already argued in his defense of *national* and critique of *organ* sovereignty. I would distinguish political meanings of the people from legal ones, only to leave open the possibility of alternative institutional options, some of which are not yet realized. The legal meaning of the people need not be understood very narrowly in terms of the legislature and the electorate, and it can encompass any number of pluralistic forms in civil and political society. The political meaning is available to take up the rest of the forms. As Kelsen realized, the political people are likely to be more minoritarian than the legal people. But only the symbolic meaning, which may encompass future generations too, is fully universal. Note that outside the symbolic meaning of the people, the other meanings may be redundant and contradictory.
7. H. Kelsen, *General Theory of State and Law* (Cambridge, Mass.: Harvard, 1945), 261. This problem has been since thematized by a variety of diverse thinkers from Derrida to Weiler. See the very detailed and serious treatment by my friend János Kis, "Népszuverenitás [Popular Sovereignty]," *Fundamentum* 2 (2006); and the critique of the metaphysics of presence by Lindahl, "Sovereignty and Representation in the European Union." Kelsen himself admittedly added that in a political if not a juristic sense a people can be seen as the source of the constitution, but then they would certainly be only a minute part of the whole people.
8. Bert van Roermund, "Sovereignty: Unpopular and Popular," in *Sovereignty in Transition*, 47ff. Roermund uses the Hobbesian actor/author distinction in this context, which works less well for the specifically cited American case, where the Constitutional Convention *technically* treated itself as a recommender of mere language (as Rousseau's legislator) and the ratifying conventions as both (en)actors/authors of the famous phrase. In light of the fact that the Federal Convention constituted the rules under which the rest of the process was to proceed and the relatively narrow freedom of the state conventions to approve or disapprove but not to amend, something like the same distinction can be upheld also in this case. The new postsovereign method breaks with the model by making it reflexive, as I will show. Only it establishes the actorship of the authors in both stages.

9. This is done in the classical European version by freely elected constituent assemblies, occluding their inevitably arbitrary beginnings. The American convention of the 1787 type does not claim representative status, but in effect the ratifying conventions do. The drafting convention thus plays the role of the instance that makes the electoral rule (in effect, it did that by choosing state conventions), and the arbitrariness here had to do with its extralegal actions.
10. This is so even in the cited reflections of Kis, Roermund, and Lindahl, all of which are brilliant, but none of them offer a challenge to the first claims of being authorized, which evidently can be arbitrary or legitimate to very different degrees, even if arbitrariness can never be eliminated and legitimacy at that stage cannot be complete. I rely upon all of them, but based on the positive experience of the successful cases and the negative experience of Iraq, I am hopefully able to take one or two additional steps.
11. J. H. H. Weiler, *The Constitution of Europe* (Cambridge: Cambridge University Press, 1999), chap. 1.
12. Kis, "Népszuverenitás [Popular Sovereignty]."
13. A. Esmein, *Elements de droit constitutionnel français et comparé* [1914] (Paris: Panthéon-Assas, 2003), 583–586; Carré de Malberg, *Contribution à la Theorie générale de l'Etat* [1920] (Paris: Dalloz, 2004), 1:49, 1:65–66; 2:500–501.
14. A. Arato, "Dilemmas Arising from the Power to Create Constitutions in Eastern Europe," in M. Rosenfeld, ed., *Constitutionalism, Identity, Difference, and Legitimacy* (Durham, N.C.: Duke University Press, 1994), 178–186. Revised as chapter 4 of Arato, *Civil Society, Constitution, and Legitimacy*. This problem of the relativization of the *constituant* and *constitué* distinctions now greatly occupies authors such as Lindahl, "Sovereignty and Representation in the European Union," 105ff., who start out with Foucault's description of the supposed contradiction of sovereignty both under law and *legibus solutus*. See the contributions of N. Walker and B. V. Roermund to *Sovereignty in Transition*, 19, 34–35, 38ff. It remains unclear how any of their solutions solve Foucault's paradox, if it is one.
15. Even there, Maurice Hauriou probably rightly insisted on the constitutive rule of custom, which precedes all state formation and should not therefore be identified with the origins of law. See *Precis de droit constitututionnel*, 2nd ed. (Paris: Sirey, 1929), chap. 3.
16. That reduces revolution (contrary to the point of view of the domestic system, of course) to a kind of constitutional amendment under international law. See Kelsen, *General Theory of State and Law*, 219–220, 368ff.
17. I must admit that as a general proposition, state continuity seems to be a symbolic matter above all. Organizationally, territory, people, or the administrative apparatus could all play the relevant role, but with respect to each it is possible

that there is significant discontinuity, yet the "state" survives, and not only as a center of international-law obligations that serves the interests of other states. This survival is symbolic and discursive, and tentatively I think it would require the continuity of either territory or at least population as well. Possibly an intact military-administrative structure could play this role with some of the people and territory only.

18. In chapter 5 of my *Civil Society, Constitution, and Legitimacy*, "Constitution and Continuity in the East European Transitions," I argued (170–173) that Arendt's thesis of continuity in the midst of change, which she discerned even in the American revolution, can be differentiated along her two axes of power and law. While she rightly maintained that in America it was the power axis (intact small republics) that were relied on, I argued that in central Europe it was the law axis that was the locus of continuity. Either (constituted bodies or constitutive rules) avoid the constituent power being in the state of nature. I now think both aspects express a more fundamental state continuity.

Index

Abd-al-Rahman, Sami, 142
Abizaid, John, 45, 288n. 187, 308n. 90
Afghanistan, 273n. 51
"Agreement on Political Process," 276n. 75
Allawi, Ali, 212, 311n. 15, 332n. 8
Allawi, Ayad, 21, 24, 48, 196; Iraqi List party of, 208, 211, 245, 246, 333n. 19; legality of, 200; TAL confirmation by, 201–2
Al Qaeda, 31, 252
amendment rule, 149; Articles of Confederation and, 80, 81; Carré de Malberg on, 296n. 51; as consociational limit, 187; of *Grundgesetz*, 325n. 167; in interim constitution, 86, 325n. 163; neutrality of, 192; of permanent constitution, 224–25, 239–40; of South Africa, 186; for TAL, 185–88, 191, 224, 239–40, 305n. 59, 312n. 18, 325n. 167, 326n. 169; of Transitional National Assembly, 242–43
amendments: CPA power of, 186–87; deadline for, 247–48; in France, 79–80; of Fundamental Law, 117, 130, 305n. 62; in Hungary, 332n. 5, 332n. 7; to IGC constitution, 116–17; of interim constitution, 69, 117, 185–86; Istrabadi on, 185–86; legality of, 247–48; minority ratification power of, 70; by Presidency Council, 186, 187, 188; on regional formation, 240, 247
American-Kurdish bargain, 135–36, 163, 170–75
Anbar Salvation Council, 252
annexation, 7
Arabization, 161
Arabs: ethnic nationalism of, 152; identity positions of, 154; nationalism of, 152–53, 307n. 82
Arato, Julian, 314n. 37
Arendt, Hannah, 8; on legitimacy, 10; on revolution, 11, 12, 42, 266n. 4; on state continuity, 345n. 18
Argentina, 5, 6, 119, 269n. 23
Aristotle, 39, 40
Articles of Confederation, 80, 81
Asafi, Hamid, 339n. 74

Assemblée Constituante, 1789, 79, 206
Association of Muslim Scholars, 108, 210, 333n. 16
authoritarians, 90

Baghdad, 289n. 212
Barzani, Massoud, 143, 156, 161, 315n. 46; Bush letter of, 197–98; on Leadership Council, 227, 232; TAL amendment by, 172
"Basic Structure Doctrine," 85
Belgium, 271n. 33, 314n. 37
Benomar, Jamal, 129–30, 145, 282n. 119, 309n. 95
Benvenisti, E., 280n. 102
Bhuta, Nehal, 7, 266n. 3
Bill of Rights, 71
black turbans, 143, 154, 196
Blackwill, Robert, 109, 130, 142
Bonapartism, 18, 32, 255, 256
borders, 34
Bosnia, 36, 37, 44
Brahimi, L., x, 285n. 145; on Bremer, 15, 196, 275n. 61, 329n. 195; Chandrasekaran on, 279n. 93; on elections, 129; interim government power of, 24; al-Sistani and, 145, 195–96, 197; on TAL, 329n. 196; transitional executive plans of, 130
Bremer, L. Paul, 14, 23, 47, 313n. 27; A. Chalabi and, 48; dictatorship of, 15, 196, 275n. 61, 329n. 195; on Drafting Committee, 157, 160; on elections, 104, 128; at Erbil, 157; on ethnic federalism, 164; exclusion by, 122; on fatwa, 109; Garner and, 45; IGC creation by, 107; on Iraqi constitution making, 101, 102–3; on Iraqi democracy, 76, 276n. 74; Kurdish negotiation with, 141–42, 164, 170–73; on occupation forces, 44; protests against, 46; ratification and, 120, 327n. 173; resolution 137 opposition by, 167; seven-point program of, 17, 102, 103, 109, 275n. 66, 301n. 14; Shi'a House negotiation with, 169; al-Sistani opposition by, 105, 109, 125, 128; on Sunnis, 303n. 31
Brown, Nathan, 235, 237–38, 326n. 169
Brownback, Sam, 166
Bulgaria: Grand National Assembly in, 79; representation in, 78; round table, 63, 73
Bush, George H. W., 30
Bush, George W.: Barzani and Talabani letter to, 197–98; Bremer's authority from, 15; A. al-Hakim call of, 232; Iraq goals of, 265n. 1; on Iraqi constitution, 251
Bush v. Gore, 237

Calhoun, John C., 237, 326n. 170
Canada, 159, 316n. 49
Carpenter, Scott, 140
Carré de Malberg, Raymond, 53, 327n. 178, 343n. 6; on amendment rule, 296n. 51; on state, 53
caucus, 123, 130, 133–34, 304n. 51, 307n. 81. *See also* Governorate Selection Caucus
centralism, 153
Chalabi, Ahmed, 14, 15, 22; Bremer and, 48; de-Baathification program of, 23, 46, 48; on November 15 Agreement, 309n. 94
Chalabi, Salem, 140
Chandrasekaran, Rajiv, 47, 109, 127–28; on Brahimi, 279n. 93; on KRG removal, 161–62; on Kurdistan, 319n. 89; on TAL work, 141
Cheney, Dick, 59
Chile, 90
China, 41
Choudhry, Sujit, 191, 192
civic postnationalism, 148–50, 154
clientelism, 123
coalition forces, 54
Coalition Provisional Authority (CPA), 14, 99, 276n. 80; amendment power of, 186–87; army dissolution by, 46; authority of, 116; democracy creation by, 32; as dictatorship, 126; duration of, 17–18, 199; IGC and, 20–21, 22–23; interim constitution making of, 95–96, 121; interim constitution power of, 87, 101; mistakes of, 44; in November 15 Agreement, 111; order 1, 47–48; order 2, 46, 288n. 187; sovereignty of, 116; state

destruction by, 45; TAL sovereignty transfer from, 117; territorial control of, 51
Cockburn, Patrick, 17, 28, 269n. 22, 283n. 129
Cohen, Jean, 25, 281n. 108, 330n. 206
Collected Works (Lenin), 287n. 172
colonialism, 28
Conetta, Carl, 265n. 1
confederation, 180, 320n. 103, 324n. 155; Kurdistan as, 248; O'Leary on, 179, 326n. 170. *See also* Articles of Confederation
Confederation Congress, 119
consociationalism: amendment rule and, 187; constitutionalism and, 223, 294n. 32; in constitution making, 70, 86; Istrabadi's objection to, 141; for Kurdistan, 181, 224, 262; O'Leary on, 318n. 63; al-Sistani on, 204; in South Africa, 70; sunset clause for, 320n. 100; in TAL, 86–87, 181, 203–4, 238
Constant, Benjamin, 273n. 52, 284n. 141
constituent assembly: constitutional legislature and, 77; elections for, 78, 308n. 89; in Latin America, 296n. 51; in one-stage process, 126; representation in, 78; rules for, 79; terminology of, 72
Constituent Assembly, of Iraq, 102, 105, 302n. 20
constitution, 102; Arendt on, 10; Bush on, 251; choice of, 74; continuity of, 53; definition of, 39–40; enforcement of, 55; of France, 69, 72–73; interim, 62; Japanese, 33; Kirkuk vote on, 341n. 101; minimal, 42; revolutionary, 41–42, 53; unconstitutional, 85; of U.S., 71, 191, 291n. 6, 325n. 165, 325n. 167. *See also* préconstitution
constitution, interim: amendment of, 69, 117, 185–86; amendment rule in, 86, 325n. 163; constitutional assembly and, 66; of CPA, 87, 95–96, 101; democratic deficit in, 74–75; enforceability of, 71; in Hungary, 62, 63, 65, 67, 68, 71, 88, 294n. 33, 294n. 34, 294n. 35; IGC work on, 99–100, 110, 144; in Iraq, 63, 293n. 25, 299n. 87; learning advantage of, 69–70; legitimacy of, 75, 120, 121; for negotiated transition, 67–68, 92; in Nepal, 63; nonsovereign constitutional assembly and, 66; from November 15 Agreement, 120; permanent constitution and, 70–71, 185, 294n. 35, 325n. 165; protection of, 68–69; ratification of, 120, 121, 171, 172; as regime change, 64–65; al-Sistani's rejection of, 60; in South Africa, 63, 65, 71, 263, 296n. 54; in Spain, 65. *See also* Transitional Administrative Law
constitution, permanent: amendment rule of, 224–25, 239–40; electoral rule of, 225, 338n. 58; federalism in, 233, 234–35, 248; interim constitution and, 70–71, 185, 294n. 35, 325n. 165; ratification power in, 234; regional formation in, 233–34; TAL making of, 188–89, 204–6; Transitional National Assembly making of, 188–89, 337n. 50, 337n. 51, 338n. 64, 338n. 65
constitutional assembly: under Constitutional Court, 85; nonsovereign, 60, 65, 66; as parliament, 133; with préconstitution, 67–68
Constitutional Commission, 216, 217, 338n. 53; deadlock of, 219–20; electoral rule of, 225; Morrow on, 226; Sunni inclusion in, 221–23; timetable of, 219–20
Constitutional Committee, of IGC, 87, 216, 247
constitutional convention, 117; nonsovereign, 132–33; in November 15 Agreement, 118–19; rules for, 188; in two-stage process, 126, 132; U.S., 343n. 8
Constitutional Court, of Hungary, 84, 85
Constitutional Court, of South Africa, 84, 85, 86, 263
constitutional courts, 68, 71, 298n. 77; Galbraith on, 318n. 65; of Iraq, 168
constitutionalism: consociationalism and, 223, 294n. 32; in constitution making, 65–66, 68, 69, 72, 74–75; imposed, 100–101, 301n. 8, 310n. 2; Kelsen and, 294n. 31; two-track structure of, 325n. 165

constitutional law, 64, 330n. 205
constitutional patriotism, 267n. 9
Constitutional Preparatory Committee, 103; al-Sistani receptiveness of, 107; U.S. opposition of, 109
Constitutional Review Committee, 251
constitution making, 52; autonomous, 19, 254, 301n. 6; consociationalism in, 70, 86; constitutionalism in, 65–66, 68, 69, 72, 74–75; by CPA, 95–96, 121; in Czechoslovakia, 81, 91; delegate elections for, 206; democratic, 258–59; dictatorship during, 66–67; drafting process in, 71–72; in France, 64, 72, 79, 291n. 6, 295n. 39; future guidelines for, xi–xii; in Germany, 254, 301n. 6; Grimm on, 53, 286n. 170; by IGC, 54, 110, 116–17; imposed, 28, 44, 100–103, 131; inherited legislature in, 261; insurrection and, 56, 213, 214–16, 245; interim, 95–96, 121; internationalization of, xi; Iran on, 231–32, 246; in Iraq, viii, 101, 102–3, 131, 231–32, 246; in Japan, 35, 44, 254, 257, 320n. 109; in Latin America, viii; legitimacy of, 54, 259; liberation and, 27; minority protection in, 70; new paradigm of, 61–62, 89; norms of, x–xi; occupation with, 19, 103; one-stage, 115, 126; as peace treaty, 335n. 31; people's role in, 72; in Poland, 63; postsovereign, vii–viii, 60, 72; rule of change in, 191–92; rules in, 79; in South Africa, vii–viii, 60; sovereign, vii, 64, 257; in Spain, 63, 73; state and, 53, 56–57; state building and, 334n. 27; state destruction and, 56; TAL, 188–89, 204–6; top-down, 89, 131; by Transitional National Assembly, 188–89, 337n. 50, 337n. 51, 338n. 64, 338n. 65; in transitional polity, 94; two constitutions in, 62, 114; two-stage, 60, 64, 69, 71–72, 77, 79, 93–97, 99, 114–15, 121, 125–26, 132, 206–7, 254, 259–60, 263; of U.S., 53–54, 62, 71, 73
coups d'états, 40
CPA. *See* Coalition Provisional Authority
Crocker, L., 252
Czechoslovakia: appointed legislature in, 80, 83; constitution making in, 81, 91; round table of, 62–63

Da'wa, 21
de-Baathification, 23, 46–48, 307n. 82; economic consequences of, 51, 289n. 210
debellatio, 25, 26; Benvenisti on, 280n. 102; Kelsen on, 33, 279n. 101, 281n. 106
Declaration of Friendly Relations, 1970, 25
default rule, 189, 191
de Gaulle, Charles, 14, 293n. 23
de Mello, Sergio, 23, 107, 302n. 16, 303n. 29
democracy: Bremer on, 76, 276n. 74; constitution making with, 258–59; CPA-created, 32; electoral beginning to, 121, 131; through force, vii; interim constitution and, 74–75; Iraqi, 76, 276n. 74; Lefort on, 72; legitimacy of, 27, 122, 127; of neoconservatives, 30; in Nepal, viii, 61, 92; new, 27, 72–73, 75, 78, 100; realism of, 37; regime change of, 30; through revolution, 9; round tables and, 75; as second-best solution, 307n. 77, 307n. 78; in TAL, 169; theory of, 27, 78; U.S. creation of, 30–31, 270n. 25; wars of, 268n. 18
democratic interventions, viii
Democratic Patriotic Alliance of Kurdistan, 207, 208, 246
democratization: allies from, 30, 35; external, 32; of Germany, 9, 32–36, 44; internal, 33; in Iraq, ix, 2, 9–10, 29, 33, 34–36; of Japan, 9, 32–36, 44, 283n. 136; neoconservatives on, 36
de-Nazification, 48
Diamond, Larry, x, 140, 141; background of, 312n. 18; on Kurdistan, 142, 143; on Pachachi draft, 157; on parliamentary government, 182; on TAL public-relations, 193
dictatorship, viii; Bonapartist, 18, 32; of Bremer, 15, 196, 275n. 61, 329n. 195; during constitution making, 66–67; CPA as, 126; defeat of, 4–5; elections with, 67, 206–7; as hostility initiator, 5;

in Iraq, 34; in Mexico, 90; revolutionary, 8; Schmitt on, 8, 64, 131, 266n. 3; in South Korea, 37; sovereign, 65, 131, 266n. 3, 330n. 206; top-down reform in, 93; tutelary, 16
"Dissolution of Entities," 46
Djilas, Milovan, 8–9
Dobbins, James, 3–4, 32
Drafting Committee, of IGC, 139, 140, 141; Bremer on, 157, 160; on federalism, 163; Iraq liberals on, 149; Kurds on, 156–57
Drafting Committee, Pachachi, 139, 140, 155
al-Dulaimi, Adnan, 217
Duverger, Maurice, 81

elections, 77–78; Brahimi on, 129; delegate, 206; of delegates, 206; dictatorship with, 67, 206–7; early, 206–7; human rights and, 126; in Iraq, 103–4, 113, 207–10, 308n. 88; in Iraqi Council of Representatives, 246; legality of, 104; legitimacy of, 120–21; in Najaf, 278n. 89; from November 15 Agreement, 117, 124; postponement of, 125; from round tables, 74, 104; al-Sistani and, 115, 119, 120, 127, 129, 130, 207, 302n. 16
electoral rule, 283n. 129
Elster, Jon, 75, 77, 137
Erbil, 142, 143, 145, 157
ethnic federalism, 182–84; Bremer's consent to, 164; Istrabadi's objection to, 141; protection of, 181; U.S. opposition to, 156, 159, 160
ethnicization, 50, 279n. 92
ethnic nationalism: of Arabs, 152; in Iraq, 152–53, 154–55, 181–84; of Kurdistan, 146–48, 151, 154–55, 181–84

Fallujah, attacks on, 210
fatwa: Bremer on, 109; first, 102, 104; second, 127, 304n. 46
federacy, 149; within federation, 180; of Kurdistan, 179, 180, 194, 203, 229
federalism, 128; fiscal, 148; IGC Drafting Committee on, 163; in India, 149; in Iraq, 148, 149, 158–59, 180–84, 223, 228–29; Kurdistan as, 223; in permanent constitution, 233, 234–35, 248; Shi'ite-Kurdish bargain on, 233, 234, 236, 338n. 52; for Shi'ites, 164, 165; Sunni inclusion in, 236; in TAL, 157–59, 163. *See also* ethnic federalism
Federal Supreme Court, 235, 236, 237, 330n. 205
federation: enforcement of, 152; federacy within, 180; U.S. Senate resolution on, 251–52, 342n. 3
Feith, Douglas, 47
Feldman, Noah, x, 2; on army dissolution, 16; on nation building, 3, 275n. 67; on Shi'ite Islamists, 168
Fifth French Republic, 65, 66, 71, 206, 295n. 37
Finland, 299n. 83
formal action theory, 39
four-actor model, 109
Fourth French Republic, 65, 66, 295n. 37
France: amendment in, 79–80; constitution making in, 64, 72, 79, 291n. 6, 295n. 39; constitution of, 69, 72–73; legal continuity in, 293n. 28; liberation of, 81–82; Liberation Government of, 84; revolution of, 9, 41, 284n. 141; type I constitution making in, 72, 79, 291n. 6; type II constitution making in, 72, 79, 291n. 6, 295n. 39. *See also* Fifth French Republic; Fourth French Republic; Third Republic National Assembly
Friedrich, Carl J., 33
Fukuyama, Francis, 3, 268n. 14
Fundamental Law, 110–11, 116; amendment of, 117, 130, 305n. 62; expiration of, 119; freedoms in, 126; legitimacy of, 130–31. *See also* Transitional Administrative Law

Galbraith, Peter, 21, 120; background of, 313n. 30; on Barzani, 232; on constitutional courts, 318n. 65; on federal courts, 237; international-law argument of, 200; on Kurdistan, 143, 161, 170, 171, 178, 199; nationalism of, 315n. 46; on negotiations, 313n. 27; on control ofregional oil, 236;

Galbraith, Peter (*continued*)
on Sunni exclusion, 277n. 86, 277n. 87, 342n. 1; on TAL, 311n. 13
Garner, Jay, 14–15, 22; Bremer and, 45; de-Baathification program of, 48
Geneva Convention, 20, 24, 25, 26
genocide, 150
Germany: autonomous constitution making in, 254, 301n. 6; democratization of, 9, 32–36, 44; Feldman on, 2; Fukuyama on, 3; Hungarian occupation by, 13; legal revolution in, 271n. 38; occupation force in, 285n. 154; occupation legislation in, 25; religion in, 34; round table of, 63, 291n. 7, 293n. 29. *See also Grundgesetz*
"Good Reasons for Going Around the UN" (Slaughter), 280n. 105
Governance Team, 140, 141, 314n. 31
government: definition of, 39; interim, 11, 13–14, 15, 20–24, 64, 65, 68, 198, 277n. 86, 329n. 196; parliamentary, 182; rule-of-law, 34; state and, 286n. 163; unity, 60, 245–47
Government of National Unity, 247
Governorate Selection Caucus, 112, 123, 307n. 81
Greece, 5, 6, 269n. 23
Greenstock, Jeremy, 142
Grimm, Dieter, 40, 53, 286n. 170
Grundgesetz, 25, 35, 71, 206, 294n. 35; amendment rule of, 325n. 167

Habermas, Jürgen, 267n. 9, 272n. 45
Hague, 43, 280n. 102
Hague Convention, 1907, 7, 20; on occupation legislation, 24, 26, 200
al-Hakim, Abdul, 114, 127–28, 227; Bush call to, 232; Shi'ite regional power demand of, 228, 229, 232
al-Hakim, Muhammad Baqir, 14
Hamoudi, Sheik H., 226, 227, 338n. 62
al-Hashimi, Tariq, 247
Hauriou, Maurice, 344n. 15
heteronomy, 260
Hintze, Otto, 268n. 18
Hitler, Adolph, 271n. 38
Hughes, Pat, 45
human rights: elections and, 126; in Iraq, 126–27; resolution 137 and, 167–68
Hungary, 263; amendments in, 332n. 5, 332n. 7; Constitutional Court in, 84, 85; interim constitution in, 62, 63, 65, 67, 68, 71, 88, 294n. 33, 294n. 34, 294n. 35; occupation of, 13; political opposition in, 74, 328n. 187; round table in, 291n. 7, 294n. 34, 328n. 187
Hussein, Saddam, 30, 46, 303n. 31

identity: of Arabs, 154; constitutional, 192; of Iraq, 150, 154, *154*, 165, 192, 220–21, 285n. 161, 317n. 59; of Israel, 285n. 161; legal, 343n. 6
IGC. *See* Interim Governing Council
IIP. *See* Iraqi Islamic Party
ILC. *See* Iraqi Leadership Council
imperialism, 28–29, 32, 266n. 3, 282n. 116, 282n. 118
inclusiveness, 76
Independent Electoral Commission of Iraq, 241–42, 245
India, 300n. 6; federalism in, 149; government structure in, 80, 316n. 49; mixed electoral rule in, 209; nation building in, 3
Indian National Congress, 3
infrastructure, 50
insurrection: constitution making and, 56, 213, 214–16, 245; occupation and, 213, 214
Interim Governing Council (IGC), 20; caucus role of, 123; Constitutional Committee of, 87, 216, 247; constitution making by, 54, 110, 116–17; CPA and, 20–21, 22–23; dependency of, 140; Drafting Committee of, 139, 140, 141, 149, 156–57, 160, 163; empowerment of, 27–28; ethnic quotas in, 214; IIP in, 277n. 87; interim constitution work of, 99–100, 110, 144; Kurdish leaders on, 156; November 15 Agreement and, 114; ratification in, 322n. 133; representation in, 107–8; resolution 137 repeal by, 167–68; sovereignty of, 110, 116; staffing of, 22–23; Sunni exclusion from, 144; TAL role of, 140

interim government, 11, 65, 68; Brahimi's power with, 24; in Iraq, 13–14, 15, 20–24, 198, 277n. 86; revolution with, 64; TAL and, 329n. 196
internationalization: of constitution making, xi; of Iraq occupation, 22, 278n. 88; legality of, ix, 87; by UN, x
Iran: Constitutional Revolution of, 104; influence of, 339n. 76; on Iraqi constitution making, 231–32, 246
Iraq: appointed legislature in, 80; army dissolution in, 16, 19, 38, 45–46, 51, 175; autonomy of, 18, 19, 180; binationalism in, 144–48; British in, 16, 131; Bush's goals in, 265n. 1; caucuses of, 123; census in, 124; centralism in, 153; Constituent Assembly of, 102, 105, 302n. 20; constitutional court of, 168; constitution making by, viii, 101, 102–3, 231–32, 246; constitution of, 251; de-Baathification in, 23, 46–48, 51, 289n. 210, 307n. 82; democracy in, 76, 276n. 74; democratization in, ix, 2, 9–10, 29, 33, 34–36; dictatorship in, 34; dual power in, 119; elections in, 103–4, 113, 207–10, 308n. 88; electoral rule in, 208–10; ethnic nationalism in, 152–53, 154–55, 181–84; federalism in, 148, 149, 158–59, 180–84, 223, 228–29; Federal Supreme Court of, 235, 236, 237, 330n. 205; flag of, 288n. 195; human rights in, 126–27; identity of, 150, 154, *154*, 165, 192, 220–21, 285n. 161, 317n. 59; interim constitution in, 63, 293n. 25, 299n. 87; interim government of, 13–14, 15, 20–24, 198, 277n. 86; interim legislature in, 82; internal uprisings in, 14; Iran and, 231–32, 246; Islamization, 173; liberals in, 149; local elections in, 22; Ministry of Planning, 124; nationalism in, 23–24, 37, 45, 153, 154, 165; nation building in, 2, 3; negotiation in, 49, 220–21; occupation costs in, 36, 37; occupation of, 22, 278n. 88; oil in, 142, 144, 162, 165, 178, 324n. 145; parliamentary elections in, 21; parliamentary government in, 182, 221, 238; permanent constitution for, 112, 185, 220–21, 305n. 64, 339n. 79; proportional representation in, 208–9; religious conflict in, 49–50; round tables and, 76, 87, 220–21; sovereignty of, 26, 112, 198, 279n. 91, 281n. 106, 281n. 108, 335n. 28; state building in, 212; Sunni power in, 14; teachers in, 47; territorial structure of, 145–47; top-down constitution making in, 131; top-down reform in, 92–93; two constitutions in, 60, 114; unity government in, 245–47; violence decentralization in, 49, 209–10; as voluntary union, 192; women's rights in, 167–68
Iraq, U.S. in: compromises of, 95; democratization from, 9–10; election opposition by, 124; exclusion by, 255; imperialism of, 28–29, 32; imposition of, 100, 256–57; internationalization with, 22, 278n. 88; legitimacy of, 13, 94, 95–97, 280n. 105; November 15 Agreement and, 126; political exclusion in, 96; removal of, 230–31; as revolution, 1; Shi'ite fear by, 124–25; threats of, 135, 136; withdrawal of, 248–49, 253; WMD justification for, 31
Iraqi Accord Front, 245, 246, 336n. 43
Iraqi Communist party, 167
Iraqi Council of Representatives, 246, 247
Iraqi Front for National Dialogue, 336n. 43
Iraqi Islamic Party (IIP), 108, 210, 245, 246; in IGC, 277n. 87; as proconstitutionalist, 336n. 43; ratification compromise of, 241, 242, 244, 342n. 1
Iraqi Leadership Council (ILC), 21, 220; representativeness of, 274n. 57; Sunni exclusion from, 226
Iraqi List, 208, 211, 245, 246, 333n. 19
Iraqi National Dialogue, 245, 246
Iraqis, The, 208
Iraqi Stabilization Group, 109–10
Iraqi State Law, 115
"Iraq's Path to Sovereignty," 102
Iraq Study Group Report, 289n. 212
Islam, 166–69, 171, 300n. 2; in permanent constitution, 237; al-Sistani and, 169, 311n. 12, 320n. 108, 321n. 118; in TAL, 166–67, 168–69, 171

Islamists, 143; Shi'ite, 168–69
Islamization, 173
Israel, 148, 150–51, 285n. 161
Issa, Mijbil, 337n. 46
Istrabadi, Feisal, 140, 141, 155, 176; on amendments, 185–86; on ethnic federalism, 141; on ethnic power sharing, 182

Jaffari, Ibrahim, 114, 229, 230
January Draft, 305n. 60, 305n. 66, 307n. 81, 307n. 82
Japan: constitution making in, 35, 44, 254, 257, 320n. 109; democratization of, 9, 32–36, 44, 283n. 136; Feldman on, 2; Fukuyama on, 3; imposed constitutionalism in, 101, 301n. 8; Meiji constitution of, 33
Jefferson, Thomas, 331n. 4

KCL. *See* Kurdistan Coalition List
Kelsen, Hans, 25, 26, 258; constitutionalism and, 294n. 31; constitution definition by, 63, 68, 116, 286n. 170; on continuity, 263; on *debellatio*, 33, 279n. 101, 281n. 106; on juridical theory of revolution, 261; on legitimacy, 5–6; on people, 343n. 6, 343n. 7
Khalilzad, Z., 48, 212–13, 216, 226; authority of, 230–31; Shi'ite support of, 236–37; Sunni inclusion by, 334n. 25
Kimmelring, B., 285n. 161
Kinzer, S., 272n. 43
Kirkuk, 142, 144, 156, 319n. 87; Arabization of, 162; constitution vote of, 341n. 101; Kurdish rule in, 151, 158, 178; in TAL, 159, 177, 232
Kis, János: on legal continuity, 82–83; on legitimacy, 5–6, 295n. 42; on regime change, 270n. 27; on round tables, 73
Kissinger, Henry, 29, 282n. 121
Kitchen, 220, 337n. 48; Sunni exclusion from, 226, 227
Kosecki Shoichi, 283n. 136
Kosovo, 36, 37, 44, 280n. 105
Krauthammer, Charles, 37, 253
KRG. *See* Kurdistan Regional Government
Kurdistan, 45, 144, 339n. 69; autonomy of, 51, 56, 180, 191, 340n. 87; Bremer's negotiation with, 141–42, 164, 170–73; Bush letter regarding, 197–98; Canadian model for, 316n. 49; Chandrasekaran on, 319n. 89; as confederation, 248; consociationalism for, 181, 224, 262; ethnic nationalism of, 146–48, 151, 154–55, 181–84; federacy of, 179, 180, 194, 203, 229; as federalism, 223; Galbraith on, 143, 161, 170, 171, 178, 199; Iraq and, 143; liberal nationalism of, 150–52, 154, 155, 181–84; in permanent constitution, 235; Peshmerga in, 56, 161, 162, 178, 199, 204; proportional representation of, 223; ratification power of, 120, 121, 171, 172, 174, 189–90, 232, 238, 240, 241, 256, 298n. 69, 322n. 129; regional power of, 163, 240; Shi'ite deal with, 165–66; as state, 55; U.S. bargaining with, 135, 142–43, 163, 173–75, 179. *See also* Kirkuk
Kurdistan Chapter, 162, 177–78; Kirkuk ownership in, 178; Kurdish insistence on, 164, 170–71; ratification of, 190, 326n. 170
Kurdistan Coalition List (KCL), 207, 208
Kurdistan National Assembly, 156–57
Kurdistan Regional Government (KRG), 156, 159; in TAL, 161–62, 177, 179; U.S. opposition to, 173–74, 314n. 35
Kurth, James, 37
Kuwait, 30

language: Arabic, 159; Kurdish, 161
Latin America: constituent assembly in, 296n. 51; constitution making in, viii; revolutions in, 9; U.S. change promotion in, 6
Leadership Council, 227, 232
League of Nations, 16
Lefort, Claude, 72, 343n. 6
legal continuity: in France, 293n. 28; Kis on, 82–83; legitimacy with, 80–81; negotiation and, 83; préconstitution with, 81; in revolution, 83–84, 261; state continuity and, 263

legality, 6, 286n. 171; of Ayad Allawi, 200; of amendments, 247–48; of elections, 104; fictional, 81; international, 87; of Iraq occupation, 25–26; legitimacy and, 10, 83–84, 330n. 205; of November 15 Agreement, 116; revolutionary breaks in, 8; of round tables, 75, 77; of TAL, 87–88, 193, 200; from UN, 280n. 105
legislature, inherited, 80–81, 133, 261
legitimacy: Arendt on, 10; of constitution making, 54, 259; democratic, 27, 122, 127; dual, 306n. 67, 306n. 69; duration and, 18; early elections, 206–7; of elections, 120–21; electoral, 296n. 46; of Fundamental Law, 130–31; of indigenous revolutions, 10–11; of interim constitution, 75, 120, 121; Kelsen on, 5–6; Kis on, 5–6, 295n. 42; of Kosovo, 280n. 105; legal continuity with, 80–81; legality and, 10, 83–84, 330n. 205; of negotiated transition, 122; in Nepal, 296n. 52; of new democracy, 27; normative meaning of, 272n. 45; of November 15 Agreement, 116, 121–22; of occupation, 54–55, 83; pluralistic, 122; of revolution, 83–84; of round tables, 74; sociological, 300n. 91; of South Africa, 295n. 42; of state, 38; of TAL, 129, 193–94, 195–98, 199, 303n. 24, 313n. 26; upstream, 75, 296n. 46; of U.S. in Iraq, 13, 94, 95–97, 280n. 105
Lenin, Vladimir, 8, 40, 43, 274n. 56; on revolution, 287n. 172, 287n. 175
"L'exportation de la liberté" (J. Arato), 314n. 37
liberalization, 90
liberation, 10; constitution making and, 27; defeat and, 269n. 22; definition of, 12–13; of France, 81–82; ideology of, 17–19; occupation and, 11–13, 18–19, 27, 28, 37–38, 94, 273n. 51
Linz, Juan, 4–5, 9, 149
Luhmann, Niklas, 325n. 165

MacArthur, Douglas, 33, 101, 301n. 8
Madison, James, 72
Mahdi, Abdel, 114, 127–28, 313n. 26; ratification objection by, 172, 324n. 161
majority rules, 131–32
Makiya, K., 148, 150, 248
al-Maliki, Nuri, 247
Maoists, 92
Martinez, Roman, 140, 141, 142
Massachusetts Convention, 1780, 79, 302n. 17
McKiernan, David, 45
Meiji constitution, 33
Mexico, 90
Miles, Frederick, 273n. 51
minorities, 70
Mithal al-Alusi List, 246
MNF. *See* Multi National Force
"More Troops for Iraq? Time to Just Say No" (Conetta), 265n. 1
Morrow, Jonathan, 226, 336n. 41, 338n. 52
Multi National Force (MNF), 54, 335n. 28
al-Mutlah, Saleh, 217
My Year in Iraq (Bremer), 47

Najaf, 127–28
National Consultative Assembly, 302n. 20
National Ind. Cadres and Elites, 208
nationalism, 267n. 8; Arab, 152–53, 307n. 82; binationalism, 144–48; civic postnationalism, 148–50, 154; constitutional patriotism and, 267n. 9; ethnic, 316n. 47, 318n. 64; of Galbraith, 315n. 46; in Iraq, 23–24, 37, 45, 153, 154, 165; liberal, 150–52, 154, 155, 181–84, 192; republican, 148–50, 154; of Shi'ites, 154; of Sunnis, 155. *See also* ethnic nationalism
nation building, 1; Dobbins on, 3–4, 32; Feldman on, 3, 275n. 67; Fukuyama on, 3, 268n. 14; historically, 2–3; regime change and, 3, 4, 268n. 17; state building and, 3–4
"Nation Building and the Failure of Institutional Memory" (Fukuyama), 3
Nation-Building: Beyond Afghanistan and Iraq (Fukuyama), 268n. 14
negotiated transition, 293n. 29; balanced forces in, 89–90; of eastern central Europe, 6; interim constitution for, 67–

negotiated transition (*continued*)
68, 92; Kis on, 5; legitimacy of, 122; moderates in, 218–19; reform under, 90–91
negotiation: as balanced force replacement, 90; Galbraith on, 313n. 27; in Iraq, 49, 220–21; Kurdish, 141–42, 164, 170–73; legal continuity and, 83; Shi'a House, 169; Shi'ite, 168; for state building, 213; Sunni, 20, 341n. 98; in TAL, 143, 144, 168, 179; U.S. force in, 137
neoconservatives: democratic regime change of, 30; on democratization, 36; on regime change, 3; in United States, 1
Nepal, vii–viii; appointed legislature in, 80; democracy in, viii, 61, 92; interim constitution in, 63; interim legislature in, 82, 83; legality in, 84; legitimacy in, 296n. 52; representation in, 78
Nineveh, 242, 322n. 129, 326n. 171, 342n. 1
Nixon, Richard, 30
Northern Alliance, 273n. 51
Notes on Virginia (Jefferson), 331n. 4
November 15 Agreement, 110, 112; caucuses of, 123, 130, 133–34, 304n. 51, 307n. 81; constitutional convention in, 118–19; CPA in, 111; elections from, 117, 124; IGC and, 114; interim constitution from, 120; legality of, 116; legitimacy of, 116, 121–22; objections to, 315n. 39; SCIRI and, 127–28; security in, 126; al-Sistani and, 113–14, 115, 127–28; sovereignty transfer in, 126, 306n. 67; timeline of, 129, 133, 308n. 90, 309n. 94; as top-down model, 122–23; UN on, 129–30; U.S. in Iraq and, 126

occupation: alliances during, 248–49; belligerent, 20, 25, 273n. 50, 275n. 67, 280n. 102; constitution making with, 19, 103; costs of, 36, 37; duration of, 37–38; forces needed for, 38, 44–45, 52, 285n. 154; Geneva convention on, 24, 25, 26; Hague Convention on, 24, 26, 200; of Hungary, 13; insurrection and, 213, 214; internationalization of, 22, 278n. 88; law of, 25, 26; legality of, 25–26; legislation during, 24–25; legitimacy of, 54–55, 83; liberation and, 11–13, 18–19, 27, 28, 37–38, 94, 273n. 51; recognition of, 276n. 81; as regime change, 52; as revolution, 7; as state, 54–55; as state building, 52, 315n. 43; in UN Security Council Resolution 1483, 11–12, 20, 25, 26, 103, 199, 273n. 50
Occupation of Iraq, The: Winning the War (Ali Allawi), 312
oil, 51, 142, 144, 162, 165, 178, 324n. 145; regional control of, 235–36, 236
O'Leary, Brendan, 147, 151, 156, 159; background of, 313n. 30; on confederation, 179, 326n. 170; on consociationalism, 318n. 63; on federacy, 180; liberalism of, 315n. 46; on ratification, 189; on TAL, 199, 201
one percent, doctrine of, 30
On Revolution (Arendt), 8
Organization of Women's Freedom in Iraq (OWFI), 167
O'Sullivan, Meghan, 140, 142
Othman, Mahmoud, 151, 162, 315n. 46, 341n. 96
Overthrow: America's Century of Regime Change (Kinzer), 272n. 43
OWFI. *See* Organization of Women's Freedom in Iraq

Pachachi, Adnan, 113, 139, 143, 155; on ethnic power sharing, 182; KRG and, 314n. 35; as nationalist, 155, 318n. 66
Pachachi Draft, 157, 158, 159, 319n. 81
Pachachi Drafting Committee, 139, 140, 155
Pakistan, 282n. 122
parliamentary assembly, 74
peace treaty, 335n. 31
Pennsylvania Convention, 1776, 79, 80
Perelli, Carina, 208
personal status law, 166, 167, 237, 238
persuasion, 136, 137, 138, 139
Petraeus, David, 252
Philippines, 9
plurality, 75–76, 91
Poland: constitution making in, 63; political conflicts in, 74
police, 47

polyarchy, 6
Powell, Colin, 109, 114
PR. *See* proportional representation
préconstitution, 65, 66, 295n. 39; constitutional assembly with, 67–68; legal continuity with, 81
Presidency Council, 183, 184; amendment by, 186, 187, 188; legality of, 200; ratification rights of, 238, 239–40, 326n. 168; al-Sistani's reaction to, 194
Preuss, Ulrich, 61, 71, 74
privatization, 51–52, 289n. 210
proportional representation (PR), 78–79; single-district, 124; territorial, 124
protests: against Bremer, 46; of al-Sistani, 107, 118; by women, 167
Przeworski, Adam, 89, 94
publicity, 75, 296n. 49, 327n. 178; Elster on, 77; of TAL, 137–38, 193
public-regarding documents, 137–38

Al-Qaeda. See Al Qaeda

Rabin, Y., 335n. 31
Rafidain List, 246
Rand report, 36, 44, 285n. 143
ratification, 70, 86–87; Bremer and, 120, 327n. 173; in IGC, 322n. 133; IIP compromise on, 241, 242, 244, 342n. 1; of interim constitution, 120, 121, 171, 172; of Kurdistan Chapter, 190, 326n. 170; Mahdi's objection to, 172, 324n. 161; neutrality of, 192; Sunnis and, 189, 241, 242, 243–44, 298n. 69; in TAL, 120, 121, 171–74, 189–92, 232, 238, 240, 241–42, 255, 256, 298n. 69, 322n. 129; in Transitional National Assembly, 242, 326n. 171
realism: democratic, 37; Nixon doctrine, 30
rebellion, 1–2
Reconciliation and Liberation Bloc, 246
referenda, 86–87
reform: under dictatorships, 90–91; Kis on, 5; under negotiated transition, 90–91; top-down, 92–93
regime: definition of, 39, 40, 286n. 166; state structure and, 262
regime change, 1; democratic, 30; interim constitution as, 64–65; Kis on, 270n. 27; nation building and, 3, 4, 268n. 17; neoconservatives and, 3, 30; transition paths of, 7, 262; U.S. occupation as, 52
regional formation: amendments on, 240, 247; Iraqi Council of Representatives on, 247; in permanent constitution, 233–34; suspension of, 247; in TAL, 165–66, 176–77, 213–14; in Transitional National Assembly, 223
resolution 137, 167–68
revolution: Arendt on, 11, 12, 42, 266n. 4; civil war and, 42–43; classical, 6–7; constitution after, 41–42, 53; definition of, 40; democracy through, 9; executive power during, 8; externally imposed, 8–9, 96; of France, 9, 41, 284n. 141; in Germany, 271n. 38; indigenous, 9–11, 116; inherited legislature with, 261; interim government with, 64; internal logic of, 7–8; juridical theory of, 261; Kis on, 5; in Latin America, 9; legal continuity in, 83–84, 261; legality in, 8; legitimacy of, 10–11, 83–84; Lenin on, 287n. 172, 287n. 175; occupation as, 7; rebellion and, 1–2; state destruction through, 40–42, 266n. 3; state preservation through, 41, 42–44; Tilly on, 6–7; U.S., 8; war and, 7, 271n. 31
revolutionary radicalism, 52
Rice, Condoleezza, 109, 114, 162, 169, 171
round tables, 300n. 88; Bulgarian, 63, 73; Czechoslovakian, 62–63; democracy and, 75; elections from, 74, 104; German, 63, 291n. 7, 293n. 29; Hungarian, 291n. 7, 294n. 34, 328n. 187; inclusiveness of, 76; Iraq and, 76, 87, 220–21; legality of, 75, 77; legislature and, 80; legitimacy of, 74; new democracy and, 75; rules of, 77; South African, 76, 77
al-Rubaie, Mowaffak, 202
Rumsfeld, Donald, 288n. 188
Russia, 133

Sadrists, 21–22
al-Sadr, Moqtadah, 107, 218

Salih, Barham, 142, 151
Santorum, Rick, 166
Saudi Arabia, 30
Schmitt, Carl, 7, 136; on dictatorship, 8, 64, 131, 266n. 3; on revolutions, 41; *Verfassungslehre*, 53
SCIRI. *See* Supreme Council of the Islamic Revolution
Scowcroft, Brent, 31–32
secession, 43, 180, 184, 324n. 155
Segura, Renata, 296n. 51
Shahristani, Hussain, 105
Shari'a, 167, 236
Shi'a House, 141, 166, 169, 313n. 26
Shi'ite-Kurdish bargain, 165–66, 233, 234, 236, 241, 243, 338n. 52
Shi'ites, 37, 45, 93; bilateral negotiations of, 168; boycott by, 105, 301n. 13; election of, 207, 306n. 71; empowerment of, 31; exclusion of, 153; federalism for, 164, 165; Islamists, 168–69; Khalilzad's support of, 236–37; majority rule of, 105–6; megaregion of, 339n. 69, 339n. 76; as moderates, 108; nationalism of, 154; on occupation, 95; political empowerment of, 50, 59–60, 119; regional power demand of, 228, 229, 232; al-Sistani's moderation of, 108–9; TAL signing by, 194–95, 202–3, 290n. 3; U.S. fears of, 124–25
Siddiq, Irfan, 140
Sieyès, Emmanuel, 79, 293n. 26
al-Sistani, Ali Husaini, ix; Brahimi and, 145, 195–96, 197; Bremer and, 105, 109, 125, 128; on consociationalism, 204; defeats of, 106–7; elections and, 115, 119, 120, 127, 129, 130, 207, 302n. 16; exclusionary politics of, 105–6; first fatwa by, 102, 104; influences on, 104–5; interim constitution rejection by, 60; Islam and, 169, 311n. 12, 320n. 108, 321n. 118; leadership of, 59, 60, 257; November 15 Agreement and, 113–14, 115, 127–28; Presidency Council and, 194; protests of, 107, 118; referendum call by, 118; second fatwa by, 127, 304n. 46; Shi'ite moderation of, 108–9; TAL legitimacy challenge of, 193–94, 195–97, 198, 303n. 24, 313n. 26; U.S. challenge of, 21, 23–24, 95, 97
Slaughter, Anne-Marie, 280n. 105
Slovenia, 293n. 29
South Africa: amendment rule of, 186; consociationalism in, 70; Constitutional Court in, 84, 85, 86, 263; constitution making in, vii–viii, 60; interim constitution in, 63, 65, 71, 263, 296n. 54; legitimacy of, 295n. 42; political opposition in, 74, 91; proportional representation in, 78; round tables in, 76, 77; Thirty-four Constitutional Principles of, 68
South Korea, 9, 37
sovereign assembly, 131–32
sovereignty: Cohen on, 330n. 206; of CPA, 116; fourth dimension of, 327n. 178; IGC, 110, 116; of Iraq, 26, 112, 198, 279n. 91, 281n. 106, 281n. 108, 335n. 28; November 15 Agreement transfer of, 126, 306n. 67; of state, 212; TAL transfer of, 117; timeline for, 129
Soviet Union: client states of, 255; as enemy, 34, 35; Finland influence of, 299n. 83; Hungarian occupation by, 13. *See also* Russia
Spain, 89–90, 293n. 29; Andean possession of, 9; constitution making in, 63, 73; inherited legislature in, 80–81; interim constitution in, 65; Law of Reform in, 62; Suarez government in, 93, 299n. 85
Stalin, Joseph, 8–9
state: constitution making and, 53, 56–57; continuity of, 263, 344n. 17, 345n. 18; enforcement of, 55; government and, 286n. 163; Kurdistan as, 55; legitimacy of, 38; nation-, 149; occupation as, 54–55; preservation of, 41, 42–44; regime and, 262; social integration in, 39; sovereignty of, 212
state building: constitution making and, 334n. 27; in Iraq, 212; nation building and, 3–4; negotiation for, 213; by

occupation, 52, 315n. 43; of TAL, 176, 203, 204
state destruction, 49, 55; constitution making and, 56; by CPA, 45; four dimensions of, 50–52; through revolution, 40–42, 266n. 3
Stepan, Alfred, 4–5, 9, 149, 316n. 47
Suarez, Adolfo, 93, 299n. 85
Sunni Endowments, 210
Sunni National Dialogue Council, 216–17
Sunnis: boycott by, 210, 211–12, 333n. 19, 333n. 20; in Constitutional Commission, 221–23; exclusion of, 50, 108, 144, 155, 210, 211–12, 217–18, 226, 227, 243–44, 277n. 86, 277n. 87, 303n. 31, 342n. 1; in federalism, 236; inclusion of, 55, 217–18, 221–23, 236, 334n. 25; Iraq power of, 14; nationalism of, 155; negotiation with, 20, 341n. 98; ratification and, 189, 241, 242, 243–44, 298n. 69; TAL and, 214–16, 218; in Transitional National Assembly, 211–12; U.S. relationship with, 248
Supreme Council of the Islamic Revolution (SCIRI), 14, 21; November 15 Agreement and, 127–28; regional power demand of, 165, 228
Supreme Federal Court. *See* Federal Supreme Court
Suskind, David, 30

Takayanagi, K., 283n. 136
TAL. *See* Transitional Administrative Law
Talabani, Jalal, 114, 128, 142, 156, 161; Bush letter of, 197–98; Kurdish inclusion of, 143–44; politics of, 315n. 46
Third Republic National Assembly, 79, 80, 292n. 22, 296n. 54
Thirty-four Constitutional Principles, 68
Tilly, Charles, 6–7, 271n. 31
Tocqueville, A. de, 268n. 18
top-down reform: in dictatorship, 93; in Iraq, 92–93
Transitional Administrative Law (TAL), 63, 76; abrogation of, 201, 209, 227, 330n. 201, 331n. 209; Ayad Allawi confirmation of, 201–2; amendment rule of, 185–88, 191, 224, 239–40, 305n. 59, 312n. 18, 325n. 167, 326n. 169; amendment to, 172; as American-Kurdish bargain, 135–36, 163, 171–75, 179; Arabic language in, 159; bilateral negotiations in, 143, 144, 168, 179; Brahimi on, 329n. 196; consociationalism in, 86–87, 181, 203–4, 238; constitution making in, 188–89, 204–6; CPA sovereignty transfer to, 117; default rule of, 189; democracy in, 169; elections and, 328n. 189; exclusion in, 87; federalism in, 157–59, 163; Galbraith on, 311n. 13; IGC role with, 140; interim government and, 329n. 196; Islam in, 166–67, 168–69, 171; Kirkuk in, 159, 177, 232; KRG in, 161–62; Kurdish Chapter in, 177–78; Kurdish ratification in, 120, 121, 171–74, 189–92, 232, 240, 241–42, 255, 256, 298n. 69, 322n. 129; legality of, 87–88, 193, 200; legitimacy of, 129, 193–94, 195–98, 199, 303n. 24, 313n. 26; militia in, 178, 204; negotiation in, 143, 144, 168, 179; permanent constitution making from, 188–89, 204–6; Peshmerga in, 204; publicity about, 137–38, 193; ratification in, 86–87, 120, 121, 171–74, 174, 179, 183–84, 189–92, 232, 238, 240, 241–42, 255, 256, 298n. 69, 322n. 129; regional formation in, 165–66, 176–77, 213–14; representation in, 117; rules of change in, 192; Shi'ite signing of, 194–95, 202–3, 290n. 3; al-Sistani and, 193–94, 195–97, 198, 303n. 24, 313n. 26; state building of, 176, 203, 204; Sunnis and, 214–16, 218; timetable of, 215, 219, 226–27, 228, 230, 240–41; UN on, 129–30, 330n. 207; venues of, 139–41. *See also* Drafting Committee, of IGC
Transitional Executive, 117, 198
Transitional Legislature, 117, 118
Transitional National Assembly, 111–12, 182–83; amendment in, 186, 187; amendment rule of, 242–43; candidate requirements in, 307n. 82; electoral rule of, 244; majority control of, 234; permanent constitution

Transitional National Assembly (*continued*) making by, 188–89, 337n. 50, 337n. 51, 338n. 64, 338n. 65; public participation in, 220; ratification in, 242, 326n. 171; regional formation in, 223; restrictions of, 328n. 192; Sunnis in, 211–12
Turkey, 51
Turkmen Front, 208, 246
two-pillars policy, 30

UIA. *See* United Iraqi Alliance
al-Uloum, Mohammed Bahr, 109
United Iraqi Alliance (UIA), 207, 208; election win of, 211, 246
United Nations (UN): Declaration of Friendly Relations by, 25; election laws by, 124; internationalization by, x; Iraq intervention by, x; legality from, 280n. 105; on November 15 Agreement, 129–30; reputation of, 22; Security Council Resolution 1441, 270n. 24; Security Council Resolution 1471, 273n. 50; Security Council Resolution 1483, 11–12, 20, 25, 26, 103, 199, 273n. 50, 281n. 106, 281n. 108, 281n. 109, 300n. 91; Security Council Resolution 1511, 20, 28, 103, 116, 276n. 82, 279n. 91; Security Council Resolution 1546, 87, 198; on TAL, 129–30, 330n. 207
United States (U.S.): Civil War of, 42, 43; constitution of, 71, 79, 119, 191, 291n. 6, 302n. 17, 325n. 165, 325n. 167, 343n. 8, 344n. 9; constitution making of, 53–54, 62, 71, 73; democracies created by, 30–31, 270n. 25; elections in, 129, 173; errors by, xi, 94; ethnic federalism opposition of, 156, 159, 160; federation resolution by, 251–52, 342n. 3; KRG opposition of, 173–74; Latin American change promoted by, 6; neoconservatives in, 1; neutrality of, 49; occupations by, 2–3; opposition to, 94–95; revolution of, 8; as superpower, 36, 94
Upholders of the Message, the (al-Risaliyun), 246

Venezuela, 266n. 3
veto power. *See* ratification
Vienna Convention on Treaties, 320n. 103, 324n. 155

WAFDI. *See* Women's Alliance for a Democratic Iraq
war: civil, 42–43; defeat in, 4; of democracy, 268n. 18; Hintze on, 268n. 18; illegal, 25; preemptive, 201; revolution and, 7, 271n. 31
War on Terror, 31
Washington Post, 102
weapons of mass destruction (WMD), 31
Weber, Max, 136, 272n. 45
Weiler, Joseph, 258–59
What We Owe Iraq (Feldman), 2–3
Wilson, Arnold, 17
WMD. *See* weapons of mass destruction
Wolfowitz, Paul, 161–62
women, rights of, 167–68
Women's Alliance for a Democratic Iraq (WAFDI), 167

Yazidi Movement for Reform, 246
Yoo, John, 25, 103
Yugoslavia, 37

Zebari, Hoshyar, 151